CENTURY CITY

CENTURY CITY

Manchester City Football Club 1957/58

104 GOALS FOR - 100 AGAINST

The record of an historic season

DAVID WALLACE

King of the Kippax
25 Holdenbrook Close
Leigh, Lancs, WN7 2HL
Tel: 01942 515739
Email: dw001e8104@blueyonder.co.uk

A CIP catalogue record is available for this book from the British Library

ISBN: 978-0-9557056-0-1

Book Designed and Edited by Andy Searle

Printed and bound in Great Britain by Cromwell Press Ltd, Trowbridge, Wiltshire

CONTENTS

ACKNOWLEDGEMENTS

It was my intention to simply review the match programmes of the 57/58 season in order to reflect events, but on completion I realised that I needed to do much more research. Joe O'Neill and Wayne Garnett advised me to make use of archive material at Manchester Central Library, where they are both regular visitors, and I must particularly thank Wayne for his guidance and Joe for the proof reading. Thanks also to librarians (and Blues) Eddie and Helen for their assistance and further thanks to Joe and Dolores for their help and encouragement.

Describing the journey through this amazing season, I only expected to include brief match reports, but some of the writing I discovered was so graphic, in an age of little TV coverage, it just had to be included in full. Reports attributed to 'Special Correspondent', and particularly 'Old International' (who I am told was Don Davies, one of the reporters who died at Munich), and later Eric Todd, in *The Guardian*, are so rich in descriptive vocabulary they are a joy to read. *The Guardian* reports were generally written on the Monday following Saturday games, or the day after mid-week games. They were different from, and more reflective, than the 'blow by blow' accounts from the Saturday *'Pinks'* (usually by Eric Todd, unless otherwise stated) and 'Greens' (similarly by Eric Thornton). These latter reports I have generally condensed into one. In this respect I am totally indebted to the late Dennis Chapman, who went to great lengths to provide me with this information, obtained from newspapers from various parts of the country, wherever he happened to be living at the time.

I am also grateful to the staff at Aston Villa, the Burnley statistician and Burnley public library. Additional thanks to David Speed, the Hearts historian, Tommy Wright from Hibernians and Ian Cunningham from Portsmouth.

Certain gaps in the programme information have been filled by Chris Williams and Phil Noble. Missing Football Monthlys have been loaned by Ted Knott and Gary James, who has also been helpful, as always, with compiling statistics and most attendance figures have been taken from Gary's book *'Manchester City, The Complete Record'*. Gary and I have behaved like overgrown schoolboys on occasions in the 'City Social', sharing obscure facts and figures about the 57/58 season with exclamations of delight.

Ian Penney has given useful advice and his book *'Where Are They Now'* has provided a rich source of information. The City match programme feature, A to Z of post war City players from the 92/93 and 93/94 seasons, by the late John Maddocks, has also been invaluable and David Clayton, editor of the *Manchester City Magazine*, has given further assistance.

There will, no doubt, be mistakes and omissions in this book, which somehow seems inevitable where statistical information is included, for which I apologise in advance. I have been as thorough as possible, endlessly checking and double checking, then checking again. I guess that when this book is read it will raise all sorts of further memories and I regret that it could not somehow have been issued in draft, inviting further entries before the final edition was published.

During the course of writing this book I have had chats and meetings with Steve Fleet, Johnny Williamson (who had left the club before the 57/58 season, so is sadly not included), Ken Barnes, Paddy Fagan, Bert Lister, Ron Phoenix, Fred Eyre (who kindly agreed to write the foreword and has been a constant source of advice throughout), Roy Cheetham, Peter Horridge, and John Hartley Riley of The Former Players Association, and I thank them for their anecdotes and their hospitality. I have formed the impression, however, that they're all quite perplexed by my interest in a season from fifty years ago, and, more significantly, that anyone should be interested in buying and reading a book about it. Players had more humility in those days.

Memories have played tricks over the years, for both players and fans. Which players played in which games, who played where? I could have sworn that Dave Ewing came back first in his 'head cracking contest' with Nat Lofthouse in the November 1957 Bolton game, but the report says not. Some reports have different players down as twelfth man; similarly, contradictions occur regarding the players brought down in the box when penalties were given, but overall these were few and far between.

Great appreciation also to all the City fans who agreed to be interviewed, which I found to be most enjoyable, and I apologise to all my friends from *KOTK* especially, who were just too young to remember this particular season, which is sad, because they are generally far better writers than I am. Thanks to the advice of Howard Burr, from the Reddish branch of MCFC Supporters, I was able to meet up and reminisce with John Cleaver, my old school pal from forty odd years ago, which was particularly pleasant.

I would like to thank everyone who has encouraged me in this venture, fellow Blues like John Leigh, Roger Reade, Nigel Gregory, Chris Bailey and Ian Cheeseman, and I hope they are not disappointed with the outcome. It is a very different book from any I have seen before but, then again, it was a very different season and we are a very different club. I would like to make a dedication here to my dear friend Tony Grayson, who sadly died last year at the ridiculously early age of 54. Tony would have relished proof reading this book and would have told me if it was any good, or not.

It is usual to thank the kids for having a missing dad, but I've been lucky enough to be able to fit this 'labour of love' in between family events (I think). Nevertheless, it's a thank you to Marnie, Danny, Kaye and Alex, plus grandkids Heather, Joe and Ellie, who think I am quite mad.

And to the earliest inspiration of fans' style football writing - Joe Ashton, a fellow draughtsman (but different firm!), union member, and 'Owl', writing in the *Sheffield Star* in the early 70s. Joe later became Labour MP for Bassetlaw. And not forgetting Fred Eyre and his unique and ground-breaking book, *Kicked Into Touch*.

Thanks also go to Andy Searle for taking on more than he realised with this project, yet remaining good-humoured and enthusiastic throughout.

Last but not least, my thanks to the person responsible for the wonderful cartoons, caricatures and portraits and incredible support given for this piece of self indulgence, my good lady Suzanne, who really is the co-author of this work, for without her none of this would have been possible in any way, shape or form.

David Wallace, October 2007

FOREWORD

FOR MANCHESTER CITY supporters of a certain vintage the 1957/58 season means different things to different people.

After finishing two places above relegation the season before and the squad bolstered only by the signing of Roy Warhurst from Birmingham City, a feeling of pessimism could be felt in and around the streets surrounding Maine Road. That feeling was so strong that it spread along Lloyd Street, past Great Western Street, up Denmark Road and seeped into the classroom at Ducie Avenue, where I was finding it increasingly difficult to concentrate on my schoolwork, such was my concern at the prospect of facing England's finest without our inspirational captain Roy Paul, who had moved on to Worcester City.

As things turned out, our fears proved to be unfounded. Thanks mainly to sixty one goals from the striking trio of Barlow, McAdams and Hayes, plus the considerable contribution of eleven from Ken Barnes in midfield, Manchester City plundered an amazing one hundred and four goals that season. Unfortunately, but perhaps predictably, they also leaked in exactly one hundred at the other end!!

This hitherto unheard of statistic has provided football followers everywhere with a conundrum that has remained unanswered to this day: How on earth did they manage to score so many of those goals past the great Bert Trautmann?

Read on, you may find the answer.

Fred Eyre, Worsley,
September, 2007

INTRODUCTION

Why 1957/58?

Never has there been such a season for any club, before or since, as City both scored and conceded 100 goals, sporting a new formation for a short while, *The Marsden Plan*. Throw in the 5-1 cup loss at West Bromwich Albion and it becomes 105 for and against!

Leicester came close, scoring 91 and conceding 112, and Chelsea nearly made it in 60/61 with 98 for and 100 against, but this unique and dubious record will remain with City forever and should have provided an innocent 13 year old with an inkling of what was to come.

Nineteen fifty seven was the season when I decided to go to every home game and started to travel away to watch the Blues. A fascinating journey with particular interest in grounds, colours, programmes, players, songs and City's support, especially away from home.

I started to write notes for this book way back in 1958, for my own interest, and did in fact produce a couple of published articles on this particular season in the eighties. But life, love and career thwarted my writing ambitions, and only now, following my experiences editing the City fanzine *King of the Kippax*, have I decided to pick up where I left off so long ago.

57/58 was most probably overshadowed by the tragedy of the Munich Air Disaster and has therefore been overlooked somewhat from a City point of view.

However, having trawled through newspaper archives and old match programmes, particularly City's, which were packed full of information, comment and opinion about the Blues and soccer in general at the time, and after talking with fans and players to unearth some of their experiences in and around that era, I'm convinced that this is an oversight to be rectified. I believe, therefore, it is worth recording in more depth the events of that significant season.

We do, of course, live in a two club city and I make no apology for reflecting also on the events that unfolded 'over the road', which may intrigue or surprise you.

Most information is taken from newspapers and magazines of the day.

The season was also significant in many other respects. It was the year that the old Third divisions North and South were revamped to form the new third and fourth divisions.

Attendances were up by half a million; more goals were scored in the First and Second divisions than for twenty five years; all four home countries (England, N.Ireland, Scotland, Wales) reached the World Cup finals in Sweden, which Brazil won with their seventeen year old protégé Pele, establishing themselves as the major force in World football.

Real Madrid won the European Cup for the third consecutive season.

Wolves overtook United as the 'team of the fifties' and won the league, again; Bolton won the Cup, defeating United's patched up team after Munich.

City's Kippax stand was born and Maine Road hosted an F. A. Cup semi-final between Bolton and second division Blackburn in front of 74,800.

Every team had its characters, amongst them: Jack Kelsey, David Herd, Derek Tapscott at Arsenal; Villa's Gerry Hitchens, Peter McParland, Nigel Sims; Gilbert Merrick, Peter Murphy; Jeff Hall playing for Birmingham; Jimmy Armfield, Stan Matthews, Jackie Mudie at Blackpool; Eddie Hopkinson, Tommy Banks, Nat Lofthouse at Bolton; Burnley's Colin McDonald, Ray Pointer and Jimmy McIlroy; Reg Matthews, Jimmy Greaves and the Sillett brothers at Chelsea; Albert Dunlop, Dave Hickson, Derek Temple playing for Everton; Roy Wood, Jack Charlton, Wilbur Cush, Chris Crowe at Leeds; Arthur Rowley, Derek Hogg, Jack Froggatt at Leicester; Ron Baynham, Allan Brown, Syd Owen, Arthur Turner at Luton; our own Bert, Bill, Cliff, Roy, Ken, Dave, Colin, Joe,

Bobby, Paddy and Jack; Harry Gregg, Duncan Edwards, Eddie Colman, Tommy Taylor on United's books; Ronnie Simpson, Jimmy Scoular, George Eastham and Len White at Newcastle; Eddie Baily, Stuart Imlach, Bob McKinlay playing for Nottingham Forest; Norman Uprichard, Derek Dougan, Ray Crawford, Jimmy Dickinson at Portsmouth; Fred Else, Tom Finney, Tommy Docherty, Les Dagger for Preston; Bobby Smith, Tommy Harmer, Danny Blanchflower at Spurs; Sheffield Wednesday's Ron Springett, Albert Quixall, Alan Finney and the wonderfully named Redfern Froggatt; Johnny Bollands, Don Revie, Billy Bingham, Charlie Hurley at Sunderland; Maurice Setters, Don Howe, Bobby Robson, Derek Kevan, Ronnie Allen at W.B.A.; and Billy Wright, Peter Broadbent, Jimmy Murray, Eddie Clamp, Jimmy Mullen playing for Wolves.

Two second division teams reached the F.A.Cup semi-finals: Blackburn with Ronnie Clayton, Bryan Douglas, Peter Dobing, Ally McLeod and Fulham with Tony Macedo, Johnny Haynes, Bedford Jezzard, Jimmy Hill, Jim Langley.

They were all my heroes (apart from the you know who's!?) and I dedicate this book to them. Sure the '68 team was full of stars, but they were of a similar age to me, so it was more admiration than adulation. A bit like the rock scene. Fine when it was the American stars from far away, but when it became more local, where the girls who wouldn't even give you a goodnight kiss were swooning over some spotty youth from down your own street who just happened to be able to play three chords on a guitar, well that was just a tad different.

Almost every City match had some significance. Big wins at home to Chelsea 5-2, Spurs. 5-1, Everton 6-2, and away at Blackpool and Everton, both 5-2. Big defeats at Preston 6-1, W.B.A. 9-2, Spurs 5-1 and Leicester 8-4. Stirring comebacks v Luton at home to draw 2-2, and Blackpool to win 4-3, but losing to Wolves 4-3 after being 3-1 up with twenty minutes to go. Five friendlies were played. Only once did City fail to score, losing 4-0 at Birmingham, and we only kept four clean sheets. So what were the stories behind these games, who played well, who didn't, were we robbed, were we lucky?

Elsewhere there were big wins (or defeats!), including: Bolton 4-0 v United; Blackpool 7-0 v Sunderland; Burnley 7-3 v Leicester, and 6-0 v Sunderland; Chelsea 6-1 v Burnley and 7-4 v Portsmouth; Leicester 6-1 v Villa (and 8-4 v City); Luton 7-1 v Sunderland; Man. Utd 7-2 v Bolton; Forest 7-0 v Burnley; Preston 6-0 v Birmingham; Spurs 6-2 v Villa and 7-1 v Birmingham; West Brom 6-2 v Leicester (and 9-2 v City); Wolves 6-1 v Bolton; so it wasn't just City!!

Previously the Blues had notched the ton in 1927 (108) and 1928 (100), both in division two. Then in the Championship season of 1937 (107) (Later the 1st div title in 01/02 (108)) and conceded 100 in 1926 (but scoring 89) and then later 102 in the relegation season of 1963.

Why Blue?

I had little interest in football at my junior school, Moorside County in Swinton (Ryan Giggs was a pupil a bit later on), until the final year 1955, when football fever gripped me and my mates. I had no family influences. My dad was Northern Irish and supported Bolton, coming home from games slightly drunk and acting out to me what Nat (Lofthouse) had done that day: Leaping up in the air and banging his head on the glass lampshade to enact a header, with his shoe flying off as an imaginary thunderbolt shot was unleashed into the couch, then completing the theatrics by falling over. Otherwise he was quite intelligent, working in the offices at Houldsworth and Gibb's Mill, expert in shorthand (annoying when I found his diaries and they were written in s/h so I couldn't understand them!), reading George Bernard Shaw, Dickens, Hemingway, and taking *The Observer* on a Sunday, probably not a common choice amongst us council house tenants. He was also an enthusiastic cricketer, being a fast bowler and sometimes captain of Clifton Cricket Club.

My eldest brother Frank, ten years my senior, was a Blue but never took me to a game and I vaguely remember him telling me that "in this house you have to support City", though I don't think my Dad was listening. Only in the late sixties did we start attending games together on a regular basis. Second brother Don, eight years my senior, was a motorbike mad 'ted' and had no interest in 'the beautiful game'. I also had a sister Kathleen, four years older than me, who pursued far more refined interests. They would all pull my leg, saying, "If you set off walking today (Sunday) you'll be able to watch City at Arsenal on Saturday". Ridiculous, and I didn't find it at all amusing or helpful. They'd also pretend to pour hot tea down my neck, which they'd seen in a Three Stooges film. Only pretence, I know, but there was always the danger of a little accident! Who'd be the youngest son, eh?

In the football world all talk that year was of *'The Revie Plan'* - not 'The Babes', as City beat United three times: 3-2 at home, 5-0 away and 2-0 at home in the F.A.Cup, but I wasn't really aware of this. I was maturing into a goalkeeper, being hopeless outfield, so I was stuck in goal for the bomb site twenty-a-side games. I made one stupendous save, which I knew nothing about as my style was to march up and down from one set of coats acting as goalposts (which for some reason dogs used to find quite attractive) to the other. Once, whilst on the march in this manner, the local 'star' whacked in a shot which caught my knee in the ascendancy and the ball flew off down the 'pitch' apace, to everyone's amusement and delight.

Naturally Bert was my hero, as tales of his prowess were becoming legendary. At the time United only had Ray Wood and Bolton Ken Grieves, who was also an Australian cricketer for Lancashire in the summer. One day we were playing soccer on Deans Fields and a pal said, "hey, there's a lad over there in a City shirt". Until then I'd no idea what colours City played in. He was wearing this fantastic sky blue shirt, and I was hooked. I thought it was incredible. Anyone could play in red, but sky blue, well that was very special. It was the colour of the heavens on a bright summer's day, Wedgewood pottery and also of those inviting Californian swimming pools seen in the films. Coventry adopted it later, and many clubs use it today as their second strip. The wearer was called Eric, who in fact was a Bolton fan, though I've seen him at City many times over the years, but I've never owned up to him. He was a good footballer, best in Swinton (although Tony Morrin did make Stockport County and Wilf Tranter United), and I thought I might see him in an England shirt one day, but sadly he, like most of the others, didn't make it.

City lost the cup final 3-1 to Newcastle with ten men, with Jimmy Meadows going off injured after twenty minutes or so, which I watched on telly at the home of a friendly neighbour, Mr Andrews, who solemnly informed me that no team with ten men could win the cup (Forest did in '59 but they were two goals up, I think, when Roy Dwight went off with a broken leg, winning 2-1 v Luton). On the way to school on the Monday I came across my first incident of United fan jealousy and bitterness. Walking along with Tony, a red, I commented innocently, "Pity City lost on Saturday wasn't it?" "No, I'm glad," he countered, venomously spitting out the words. I was stunned.

Passing the eleven-plus, but aware that I was no academic, secondary education for me was Salford Technical High, in Leaf Square, where we were relocated after a brief period at 'Hanky Park' whilst waiting for Salford Grammar (Graham Nash, Alan Clarke, Michael Leigh, et al) to vacate the premises for their lush new green pastures in Buile Hill. We 'Swintonians' (Ged, Geoff, Pete and me) laughed at the Salford accents, then finished up with them! The Pendlebury lads from half a mile up the road spoke very broad Lanky - 'noooo yer doooon't dooooo that!' Everyone laughed at them. I don't remember any bullying at the school (only of the teachers), although there were plenty of fights, as you'd expect, with the Kelly twins being the worst, against each other! I remember it most for the humour, that special brand of Manchester/Salford insulting badinage epitomised by the local comedians of the day like Al Read. Once, I particularly recall, the headmaster, Mr. (Isaac) Quayle, insisting that "all boys must come to school tomorrow in their school caps", so the more rebellious pupils in the fourth and fifth years, who we younger lads looked up to, all turned up in their 'Ted' suits, the cool fashion of the day: Long jackets with velvet collars, tight trousers, 'brothel creeper' shoes, luminous green or orange socks and heavily greased 'southbank' hairdos complete with DA's, and the required school caps perched precariously on the backs of their heads. Not exactly 'Blackboard Jungle', but nevertheless, and not surprisingly, the school cap idea died an instant death. Other forms of dress were pale blue flecked sports coats, which when your red biro leaked in your top pocket, as mine did, looked like you'd been shot. Cavalry twill trousers purchased from 'Bargains Unlimited' on Broad Street (where I think Graham Gouldman from 10CC once worked) were pretty groovy too, and that's where we bought our jeans, which were just coming into fashion. Lunchtime playground soccer games were always in full flow and when the ball went over the wall it had to be retrieved from the Lancaster and Tonge engineering works, where the MD's son was actor Robert Powell, a red.

Season 55/56 I attended my first game with pals Ray and Col. Preston at home, October 15th, lost 2-0. We went out early, when it was only 1-0, so for years I couldn't accept the actual 2-0 result. My pals said: "Well City won't win the cup this year, Dave, we're off to watch Bolton and Nat, but expect you to carry on watching City with Bert." (which I did!). However, City doubled Bolton at Christmas and by the time of the sixth round cup tie v Everton they were both Blues again. Ray's Auntie lived near Maine Road and we would go round to her house after games, uninvited, and she would make us sandwiches and drinks. City went on to beat Spurs in the semi and the 'Iron Men of Birmingham' 3-1 in the Final, which we all watched on telly at Col's house.

I managed a dozen or so home games in 56/57, and in August '57 I was one of only two City fans in our class (2B) of around 30 lads (sadly co-educational high schools were still just over the horizon). My fellow Blue was John Cleaver, a more stoical individual who took the fortunes and failings of City better than I did, as I was a bit touchy and easily wound up (still am). The United kids called me 'City', which was meant to be insulting but which I found quite flattering.

By this time I'd made the school football team, and we played on Saturday mornings, which curtailed my City away support somewhat. We were dominant, winning every game in fact, playing at Littleton Road, Davy Lewis and Stott Lane, beating the likes of North Salford, Ordsall and especially Broughton Modern, our closest rivals. Why none of our team went on to play professional football I will never know. Galling when you think of Fred Eyre's contemporaries at Ducie and other Manchester schools - Neil Young, Waggy, and even the actor John Thaw (who was a Blue but changed to red after Munich). I never knew anyone famous at all until years later when my pal at Moorside Junior School, Krishna Banji, became Sir Ben Kingsley, the actor. As a child, the son of a local GP, he had lived on Pendlebury Road, as did City fan L. S. Lowry for a time. Neil Midgley from first Swinton cubs later became a qualified referee. This was our squad opposite, a great set of lads, from memory:

I've never seen any of them since leaving school in 1960. Johnny Ingham went on to play rugby for Salford, then emigrated. Bob Longworth became a professional golfer, Eddie Hindle I heard was George Best's bodyguard for a while, Teacher 'Avro' Ashton ("what are you selling today Gunning?" "Dummies, Sir!") traitorously left and went to teach at Salford Grammar. Unforgivable. 'Rudgie' trained as a dentist. John Cleaver wasn't eligible because he was too old, being born before the peculiar deadline of October, which is why half the team were from the year below. I later lost my place to 'Moggy' O'Neill, who was a foot taller than me, but he didn't even watch football, or model himself on anyone, like I did on Bert, so an early lesson to me of the unfairness of life. Most of us played in our successful rugby team too, playing in the finals at Salford's The Willows, an honour indeed.

Back Row: 'Budgie' Butterworth, Mr (Stalin lookalike?) Sumner, Jeff Gunning, Eddie Hindle, Me, Pete Spooner, Mr 'Avro' Ashton, Alan Jones 2, Bob Longworth, Front row: Nicholls, Robinson, Johnny Ingham, Alan Ryan, Ian Scott (whoa those revealing shorts!!), Rudge.

The Way It Was

Many fans, and players, over the age of 18, were doing National Service, in the R.A.F., Navy, or Army. It was generally accepted that if you were good at sport National Service was a breeze and gave you access to training facilities and playing experiences you might otherwise have been denied.

It was also quite normal at that time for shop floor workers to work Saturday mornings and travel direct to the match in their overalls.

Rationing, imposed during the war, was now relaxed. Televisions in black and white (colour was just a dream) were becoming more commonplace. ITV, with its adverts, was now an alternative to the BBC. Sports coverage was minimal, the odd live International match, the Cup Final, highlight of the season, *Sportsview* on a Wednesday night with Peter Dimmock (watched on a friendly neighbour's telly, if I was lucky, as TV was a long time coming to our house) and the *Pathe News* at the cinema. *Sports report* was essential listening on a Saturday night.

Rock 'n roll was well established as the antidote to some of the dreary stuff that preceded it - dreadful dirges (well they were to me) like, *The Lady Is a Tramp* and later *Mack the Knife,* which my big sister listened to and we were already sick of then - so it is a mystery to me that they continue to be sung ad nauseum on karaoke. There was some good stuff though by the likes of Frankie Laine, Johnny Ray and songs from the shows. Cinema seats were slashed and Teddy boys and girls danced in the aisles to *Rock Around The Clock*. Tory Politicians told us "You've never had it so good" and grown ups told us that schooldays were the best days of our lives (not for me!).

Rock and pop singers were beginning to challenge sport and film stars in the glamour stakes.

Paul Anka sang about *Diana*, Harry Belafonte *Mary's Boy Child*, Chuck Berry *Sweet Little Sixteen*. The Coasters were *Searchin'*, Perry Como was having *Magic Moments* and trying to *Catch a Falling Star*. The Crickets wondered if *That'll be the Day* and if it would be *Oh Boy*, then *Maybe Baby*. *All I Have to Do is Dream*, dreamed The Everley Bros and *I was a Big Man* sang The Four Preps, whilst Connie Francis lamented *Who's Sorry Now?*.

Michael Holliday told *The Story of My Life*, Buddy Holly *Rave*(d) *On* about *Peggy Sue*, Danny and the Juniors were *At The Hop*, Peggy Lee had the *Fever*, Jerry Lee Lewis *Great Balls of Fire* (ouch!) and there was *A Whole Lotta Shakin Goin On*.

Good Golly Miss Molly exclaimed Little Richard, Ricky Nelson was *A Poor Little Fool*, Elvis shook his pelvis to *Jailhouse Rock* and *Yes Tonight Josephine* crooned Johnny Ray, as Frankie Vaughan had *Kisses Sweeter than Wine*, but *Butterfly* was down to Andy Williams, *Reet Petite* Jackie Wilson, and Marvin Rainwater fancied *A Whole Lotta Woman*. Oh yes!

At the local cinemas in Swinton, my home town, The Ellesmere, The Essoldo and The Palace ('Bug hut'), we watched *Boy on a Dolphin* (Sophia Loren), *Quatermass 2*, *Woman of Rome*, *And God Created Woman* (Brigitte Bardot), *Doctor at Large*, *Campbell's Kingdom* (Dirk Bogarde), *Around the World in 80 Days*, *Bridge over the River Kwai* (Alec Guinness), and stars like James Dean and Rock Hudson. Films were shown, two a night, first and second houses. A feature first and last. With the B feature in the middle, and if you were clever you could stay and see the main film twice. They usually ran from Monday to Wednesday, films changed Thursday to Saturday and there was normally a horror pic or two on a Sunday (for the courting couples). I remember thinking it was marvellous that they could produce a new film in three days every week.

On TV we watched *Bilko*, *The Army Game*, *Double Your Money*, Saturday night variety shows included comedians like Arthur Askey, Dave King, Jimmy Wheeler, Tommy Trinder and Charlie Chester and we ended our weekends watching *Sunday Night at the London Palladium*. Then there was the *Black and White Minstrels show*, how well meant but horribly offensive was that? And *Muffin the Mule* would not pass the censor today, even without its 'Wally the Gog' character. That new species 'the teenager' was catered for with *Six-Five Special*, and we all empathised with Tony Hancock in *Hancock's Half Hour.*

On the radio it was *The Goon Show* (lost on me, but cult listening for my elder brother), *Educating Archie* (a ventriloquist on the radio!), the (awful) *Billy Cotton Bandshow*, *Have a Go* with Wilfred Pickles and *Two Way Family Favourites* on a Sunday, then *Sing Something Simple* in the evening. Meanwhile, in our bedrooms, tuning in on our transistor radios, we struggled to hear, through crackling interference, the latest pop music on *Radio Luxembourg*, interrupted by Horace Batchelor, remember him? Who could forget his *'K-E-Y-N-S-H-A-M'*?

On the street people would whistle and sing whilst heading for their destinations. Rob Hessian was the local street singer, who became the front man for *Herman's Hermits* but was devastated when he was later replaced by Peter Noone. There were characters like Nellie Click, who'd push a pram with coal in it, 'whistling' Winston Wood, 'Daft Cyril' and 'Eddie The Teddy' with the bright blonde hair. There were often fights outside Swinton Palais on Station Road after closing time.

We played football in the streets, often being admonished by and giving cheek to the neighbours, who then 'shopped' us to our mum or dad. I'd dribble a tennis ball in the gutter and along the pavement to hone my skills whilst running errands to the local shops, where I'd always be the last to get served no matter where I was in the queue.

You could buy a semi-detached house for £1500 and a decent car for £500. Skilled workers at 'Metro Vicks' were earning about £4 a week. Salford was 'over-spilling' to Little Hulton, and Manchester to Wythenshawe and Partington. We had May Queens and Whit Walks, rag 'n' bone men, 'bob-a-job' weeks, 'Wakes' weeks and day trips to the seaside with the British Legion in 'charabancs', or double-decker buses, and wore identification tags. There was also the cubs, scouts and guides with camps at Ringwood, Worsley, and North Wales, and every church had its Youth Club.

For me Christmases and New Years were celebrated at the homes of uncles and aunties, with lots of singing of Northern Irish songs. I was hauled up to stand on the table as a young boy to sing stuff like, *If you ever go across the sea to Ireland*, *When Irish Eyes Are Smiling* and *Now is the Hour* (Gracie Fields). These days I'd prefer to give my all to Oasis, AC/DC, Kaiser Chiefs or Bon Jovi!!

Holidays were spent in North Wales, or on the south coast. The annual choirboys trip, St Peter's Swinton, was to Southport and there would be day trips to Belle Vue and Blackpool. Night life wasn't of much interest to a thirteen year old. I was too young for the Palais, so it was the youth clubs, parks or street corners for us and playing football and rugby after school until dark, with a plastic 'Frido' ball which you had to keep well away from any rose bushes or it popped. I still refuse to have rose bushes in my garden. Afterwards the girls would come round, the plain ones could be categorised as 'nice to talk to', but that didn't fool anyone. As for me and girls, well I'm sure I wasn't the first to hear those immortal words, "I like you David, but not as much as Derek" (and he had acne, but worse, he was tougher than me!). However, I did meet that same girl a couple of years later and wondered what on earth I saw in her!

Honest.

Buildings in Salford and Manchester were usually black, due to years of smoke and smog (though Swinton Town Hall was, and still is, majestic), and it was amazing to later see monuments like the Cathedral cleaned up and pristine and realise that they hadn't actually been built out of black stone.

Footballers, without agents, were campaigning for a £20 per week maximum wage. Some had false teeth (lots of people had them all out by the time they were twenty five, whether they needed to or not - to save on dentist bills later!).

There were very few foreign or black players, but plenty of Irish, Welsh and Scots.

Johnny Haynes advertised Brylcreem, Don Revie Dextrasol, Jimmy Greaves Bovril. Players' hairstyles varied from side partings, centre partings, wavies, crew cuts, bop cuts, quiffs, flat straight backs, short back and sides, or Tony Curtis's, but United's 'Pancho' Pearson was probably the only 'teddy boy', with his 'southbank', D.A, and long sideboards. Bald players got merciless stick from the crowds, but waft-overs didn't really become fashionable until Bobby Charlton's and Ralph Coates' in the 60s.

There were plenty of Freds, Roys, Bills, and Alberts but still some exquisite names like Duncan, Bedford and Redfern, though Roy Shiner and Arthur Bottom were no-no's. Not many Leroys, Micahs, or Spencers. Wives were Elsies, Dorises, Jeans, Joans and Hildas, not many Samanthas, Penelopes, Tracys or Dawns. The Posh and Becks of the day were Billy Wright and Joy Beverley, but not quite on the same scale. Clubs with small gates, like Luton and Blackpool, could compete on the same basis with the big guns like City, United, Arsenal, Newcastle, Everton (though they had Pools millionaire John Moores) and Spurs, as one third of gate money went to the away team.

Rules - Goalies bounced the ball before kicking it out and could, and often were, shoulder charged. Professional fouls and tackles from behind were permitted. Players were not usually sent off for giving away penalties, nor were goalies for handling outside the box. Offside was still as confusing, referees and linesmen (not assistant referees) wore black, there were no red or yellow cards, pass backs to the goalie, who could then pick up the ball, were allowed, when the crowd would shout 'windy'. No substitutes were allowed as clubs could cheat by pretending a player was injured to make a tactical change. As if! Sportsmanship, and 'may the best team win' was the order of the day, but so were crunching tackles, and subsequent injuries could be career threatening. Goals were celebrated with a handshake or a pat on the head or back.

Boots were leather and had to be 'dubbined' to be broken in and studs could be lethal, but continental styles were emerging, endorsed by Tom Finney or Stan Matthews. The ball was brown leather with laces and gained weight during games. White ones were coming in and orange ones used in the snow. Shin pads were cumbersome. I had a pair with sponge on the back and when it rained they soaked it up and weighed a ton!

Chairmen and directors were old men of mysterious 'business' backgrounds, or butchers, bakers, candlestick makers, but not usually market stall traders or scrap metal merchants. They came later.

Police presences were minimal, and few stewards were seen.

Fans weren't searched, toilet rolls were thrown (I think), rattles whirled, the odd fight broke out, but there was no organised hooliganism. Outside the ground would be religious characters dressed in black wearing bowler hats and carrying placards with 'the end is nigh' painted on them. We'd queue for hours at big games to get in and paid cash at the turnstiles. Catering was risky and poor quality. Occasionally an unofficial mascot would be dropped over the wall by his mum and told to 'run round the pitch'. We'd suss where the M.E.N. 'face in the crowd' photographer would be (the side next to the main stand at the scoreboard end usually) and rush round hoping to get photographed and 'ringed' for five shillings. Fans were predominately male and dressed up in all sorts for Wembley, but generally blokes wore gabardine mackintoshes or duffel coats and trilby hats or flat caps. They often had shiny suits with pants that came up to their chests, held up by braces. There was also the odd 'Teddy boy' that you had to be wary of. If a game was boring the 'slow handclap' would break out. If it was good someone would shout 'Is everybody happeee?!'

Crowds would roar and amongst the City songs of the day, sung by the scoreboard 'rabble', those vociferous fans who stood behind the goal with their rattles, were:

1)

And when we yell we yell
And when we yell we yell
And when we yell we yell like hell
And this is what we yell
Who for why for
Who the hell are we for
C-I-T-Y City

2)
Bless 'em all
Bless 'em all
Bert Trautmann, Dave Ewing, Roy Paul
Bless Roy Little who blocks out the wing
Bless Ken Barnes the penalty king
And with Leivers and Sear so tall
And Johnstone the pride of them all
Come on the light blues
It's always the right blues
So cheer up me lads
Bless 'em all

3)
City's the team
The best team in the land
Playing at Maine Road
Always in command
We may lose a point or two
But never do despair
Cos you can't beat the boys in the old light blue
And they come from Manchester

4)
It's a long way to London Wembley
It's a long way to go
It's a long way to London Wembley
With the greatest team we know
Goodbye Piccadilly
Farewell Albert Square
It's a long, long way to London Wembley
But City are there

5)
2-4-6-8 who do we appreciate C-I-T-Y

Pitches were fine in August and September, quagmires in the winter, bone hard in the Spring, with little triangles of grass, just at the corner flags. There was an optional flag at the half way line, a yard back from the touchline. Early season form didn't always last when the heavy pitches came in the winter, when dainty teams would be "found out". In the cup games against lowly opposition, pitches could be a "great leveller", as City often found to their cost.

Goalposts were sort of oval, not often square (only at Hampden Park), and painted with diagonal stripes in far off countries (well, Hungary). Nets were held up by stanchions from which the ball would sometimes bounce back into play, which often continued without a goal being given! Pitch sizes in division one varied, from the smallest, Arsenal's at 110 x 71 yards, to the biggest, City's at 117 x 79 yards.

League placings, where points were identical, were determined on goal average (goals for divided by goals against) not goal difference. It was two points for a win and two up two down from the first and second divisions.

Games kicked off at 2.15 or 3pm on a Saturday and at various times on a Wednesday evening.

Programmes retained their fifties charm - Arsenal's, Chelsea's, City's and United's being the best, and City's probably the best value for money at 3d (you could buy four programmes for the present day 5p!).

Grounds - New stands and floodlights were springing up at grounds all over the country. Every ground was distinctive, Arsenal's being my favourite. The double-decker stands were impressive at places like Arsenal, Everton, Sunderland and Portsmouth, as were the huge Kops at Hillsborough, St Andrews, Villa Park and Molineux. Even the smaller grounds had their own charm, Bloomfield Road, Kenilworth Road. Some were wonderfully named, Deepdale, The Hawthorns, Molineux (which was un-pronounceable until identified by a radio commentator) and Highbury. Maine Road was one of the few grounds to have adverts along the stands, brightening the place up. Half time scoreboards were common, but some grounds had them on the perimeter walls. Sponsorship and 'corporates' were unheard of. Exiting the ground could be hazardous in the crush, but no-one gave it a second thought as we elbowed our way out of the exit gates, cheering when we were out.

Colours were traditional, reds, whites and blues, with City's sky blue, Blackpool's tangerine, Wolves' old gold and Leeds' blue and gold being the exceptions. Shirts were short or long sleeved with trim on the cuffs and with collars or V necks. Shorts, or knickers in some programmes, were longish, except for a few poseurs like Albert Quixall, who'd 'hitch' them up. Goalies wore green, or sometimes yellow or even black (if you were Lev Yashin) jerseys, and if the sun was in their eyes a flat cap. In this respect Bert went from looking like a film star such as Burt Lancaster to a total nerd like Norman Wisdom.

Line ups were 1-2-3-5 usually (City excepting!).

Internationals were generally played mid-week or on a Saturday when the top teams would lose their star players, all born and bred in their home country. They'd be photographed in their international caps looking slightly silly.

We travelled to games mainly by train, sometimes bus and coach, as the players often did. Not many people could afford a car. Many of us could cycle to home games, paying a few pence to leave them in someone's back yard near the ground. The City Supporters club had been formed in 1949 and was going strong, holding meetings and arranging travel to games. Long trips took all day - it was a day and a half to Portsmouth - in a time before motorways.

The main football magazine was the eagerly awaited *Charles Buchan's Football Monthly*, but there was also the weekly *Soccer Star* and various football annuals. We read and saw photos of riots at games abroad, with moats and fences round the pitches, and those 'in the know' said it could never happen here, though it later perversely became known as the 'English Disease'. We studied action photos and tried to identify the grounds from the stands in the background. We read comics like *The Hotspur*, *Adventure* and *Wizard* and collected cards of famous footballers, which were often issued with these publications. Every self-respecting schoolboy had his scrapbook with favourite players pasted in position. Some, myself included, put together books with match reports, news items and 'photopics' etc. for each season. Bert read mine on the way back from West Ham the next season and said to George Hannah, "This boy's got the makings of a journalist, George." (there were no fanzines in those days!). Praise indeed.

Manchester had the *Evening News* (M.E.N.) and *Evening Chronicle* newspapers. On Saturday night it was the *Football Pink* (Chron) and *The Green Un* (News), delivered in the street by newsboys shouting "Football Fee-nal!". Sundays *The Empire News*, *News Of the World*, *Sunday Pictorial*, *Observer* etc. Weekdays *The Guardian*, *Daily Herald* and *Daily Sketch*, *Despatch*, *Mirror*, *Mail* etc. No *Sun* or *Star*.

City's bookshelf comprised Frank Swift's *In The Goalmouth*, Peter Doherty's *In The Spotlight'*, Don Revie's *Happy Wanderer*, Roy Paul's *Red Dragon Of Wales* and Bert's *Steppes To Wembley*.

Various histories and season brochures had been published and the 1955 *Road To Wembley* is still a classic (miles better than Newcastle's), but wasn't repeated, sadly, in 1956, or 1969 for that matter, to the same standard.

With regard to City's history, I was totally uninformed. I'd no idea of the club's early struggles, name and ground changes, winning the cup in 1904, or the bribes scandal and losing four of our players (Meredith, Burgess, Bannister, Turnbull) to United in the early 1900s, or finishing runners up in the league in 1921, moving from Hyde Road to Maine Road in 1923, losing the cup final in 1926 and being relegated the same season. Losing the cup again in 1933, winning it in 1934, notching up a record attendance of 84,569 v Stoke in the sixth round, making it the biggest ground in England, and then securing the title in 1937 but going down the very next season despite scoring more goals than any other team in the division. I didn't realise we'd let United post war use our ground (astounding), when they recorded a post-war record low attendance of 8,456, but I knew we'd let them play European games under our lights. We'd come up (1947), gone down (1950), come up again (1951) and here I basically picked up in the mid 50s.

Of we go then.......

CENTURY CITY

CHAPTER ONE

CLOSE SEASON - 1957

City finished off the '57 season, with an away game at Birmingham which was drawn 3-3, to finish in eighteenth place with thirty five points. The Blues were never in any real danger of going down, but losing six on the trot in September and October caused a worry as the team plummeted down into twenty first spot. Results were gradually ground out and City pulled themselves clear, Cardiff and Charlton taking the drop with twenty nine and twenty two points respectively, being replaced by Leicester City and Nottingham Forest.

FINAL TABLE 1956/57 SEASON

	P	W	D	L	F	A	Pts
Man Utd	42	28	8	6	103	54	64
Spurs	42	22	12	8	104	56	56
Preston	42	23	10	9	84	56	56
Blackpool	42	22	9	11	93	65	53
Arsenal	42	21	8	13	85	69	50
Wolves	42	20	8	14	94	70	48
Burnley	42	18	10	14	56	50	46
Leeds	42	15	14	13	72	63	44
Bolton	42	16	12	14	65	65	44
Aston Villa	42	14	15	13	65	55	43
WBA	42	14	14	14	59	61	42
B'ham	42	15	9	18	69	69	39
Chelsea	42	13	13	16	73	73	39
Sheff Wed	42	16	6	20	82	88	38
Everton	42	14	10	18	61	79	38
Luton	42	14	9	19	58	76	37
Newcastle	42	14	8	20	67	87	36
Man City	**42**	**13**	**9**	**20**	**78**	**88**	**35**
Portsmouth	42	10	13	19	62	92	33
Sunderland	42	12	8	22	67	88	32
Cardiff	42	10	9	23	53	88	29
Charlton	42	9	4	29	62	120	22

In May United lost the F.A.cup final 2-1 to Aston Villa. Ray Wood suffered a broken jaw early on after a challenge by Peter McParland and this

MAY'S FOOTBALL MONTHLY

Villa's captain Johnny Dixon was on the front cover, and United's captain Roger Byrne leading out his team on the back cover.

Charles Buchan's editorial concluded that the camera can lie, when a goal by West Brom in a cup tie with Arsenal was allowed despite the linesman flagging for offside, and people's observations at the game, "whose view should be taken rather than those who watch it on TV", though he thought that TV is giving good service to the game. He also praised the Youth policies that teams, particularly United and Chelsea, are introducing.

Jack Dyson played in the England under 23 team in Glasgow on February 26 (14,000) 1-1.

Journo John Thompson thought that United may become, like Arsenal when they were successful, disliked by mean and jealous little men!

'No Mean Rivals' covered the "Bitter rivalry and firm friendship" - three pages of it - on City and United, including the furore when United's Frank Barson laid out Sammy Cowan in the '26 semi-final (City 3 United 0) condemned by F.A. Officials who took a "stern view". In Jimmy Scoular of Newcastle's article there's a pic of Jimmy Meadows, injured in the '55 final. Cup Final preview has a pic of the Queen presenting Roy Paul with the Cup in 1956 and CB tipping United to win it in '57. Wrong again!

was reflected on in the press with a call for substitutes, and no charging of goalkeepers. I had therefore won my bet with an older schoolboy who had boasted that United would win two out of the three cups they were challenging for, but, needless to say, he wouldn't pay up. A lesson learned for the future.

England played three World Cup qualifier games, beating Eire 5-1 at Wembley (52,000), Denmark 4-1 in Copenhagen (50,000) and drawing 1-1 with Eire in Dublin (47,000).

Scotland also played three W.C. qualifiers, beating Spain 4-2 in Glasgow (88,890), when the Real Madrid players Gento and Di Stefano were snuffed out - "a lesson to United who had lost to them in the Euro Cup semis last season", - Switzerland 2-1 in Basle (50,000) but losing to Spain 4-1 in Madrid (100,000) - they also beat West Germany 3-1 in a friendly in Stuttgart, (77,000).

Wales also played three W.C. qualifiers beating Czechoslovakia 1-0 in Cardiff (45,000), but lost 2-1 to the East Germans in Leipzig (110,000) and 2-0 to the Czechs in Prague (55,000).

Northern Ireland played just the one W.C. qualifier, beating Portugal 3-0 in Belfast (40,000).

Eire played just the two games home and away to England.

Czech U 23's 0 England 2 in Bratislavia (20,000).

Bulgaria U 23's 0 England 1 in Sofia (55,000).

Romania U 23's 0 England 1 in Bucharest (100,000).

In the F. A Youth Cup Final United had beaten West Ham 3-2 in the first leg, and 5-0 in the second. They had also won the Manchester Senior Cup, beating Oldham.

Falkirk 2 Kilmarnock 1 in the Scottish Cup final.

On May 8th the Blues embarked on a short tour to Spain and Germany, losing 3-2 in Barcelona at their old ground when dubious decisions went against City. The forty mile coach journey back to LLoret de Mar took three hours, including the driver refusing to drive under a bridge then driving through four feet of water with the roof creaking and cases being damaged! City lost 2-0 to an Eintracht Frankfurt XI, won 6-3 at SV Werder Bremen, lost 4-1 to Borussia Dortmund, then beat Lloret de Mar 9-0. Bobby Johnstone scored the two goals in Barcelona, the first straight from the kick off with a massive lob that soared over goalkeeper Ramallett. Bob had to return home for treatment to his troublesome knee. Jack Dyson was in the wars too for Lancashire with eye trouble.

A new pitch was being laid at Maine Road and the foundations for the stanchions for the new stand were being excavated. The residents of Thornton Road were surprised to observe that the new stand would square off the Kippax terrace and not follow the existing contour, the vertical columns rising to a tremendous height.

Roy Paul was wanted by Newport County, and Roy's fourteen year old son Robert was already living in Ton Pentre with relatives for health reasons.

John Charles was transferred from Leeds to Juventus for £55,000 plus a £10,000 signing on fee (they'd just signed Sivori from River Plate for £100,000) and the same terms were offered to United's Tommy Taylor by Inter Milan.

It was also rumoured they were after Matt Busby for £100,000!!

Players Union chairman Jimmy Hill had written to the Chairmen of Football League clubs regarding the imminent new deal for players and was urging a Blueprint be prepared for 1965.

In June...talent money amendments were advised for table placings, European cup rounds, and F. A. Cup rounds. Increases in footballers' salaries were proposed to £17 in season and £14 in the close season. The third divisions north and south would become the third and fourth divisions.

Birmingham's Roy Warhurst said he would sign for City and was pictured in the MEN at work in a Birmingham factory.

JUNE'S FOOTBALL MONTHLY

John Charles was on the front cover and Roy Warhurst leading out Birmingham City on the back cover.

In the editorial CB gives his opinion on the Sunderland situation re illegal payments in transfers. On page five there's a splendid colour photo of Bill Leivers in a darker City blue than normal. The cup final is reviewed, Villa deservedly winning it for the record seventh time. Peter McParland, dazed in his collision with Wood, recovering to score Villa's two goals. Future Blue Jimmy Murray tells how he and Peter Broadbent from the same street in a village in Kent made it to Wolves. Ex Blue Eddie McMorran is pictured on page thirty eight.

Sunderland director Ditchburn was given a life ban for payments to players in transfer dealings.

Duncan Edwards was demobbed from the army and the Italians had banned foreign players, so Tommy Taylor would not be joining Inter.

The famous ex Newcastle and Scotland International footballer, Hughie Gallagher, was found dead on a railway line. He was due to face trial the next day for assault, ill treatment and neglect of his fourteen year old son Matthew.

Roy Clarke, who received a five year benefit payment in '52 of £750, would receive £1000 for ten years' service in '57.

Lancashire and City player Jack Dyson was now suffering from an injured finger.

City were linked with Coventry's winger Ray Sambrook but the club had said no, though would maybe consider a part exchange plus a cheque.

Airdrie's Hughie Baird was also being considered for £15,000 (he later went to Leeds).

Johnny Hannaway was set to join Gillingham, George Thompson would go to Carlisle next week, a heat wave affected the Whit Walks and the club reported hundreds of new applicants for season tickets.

'Spidermen' were on strike wanting time and a third to finish the new stand. They were already working ten hours a day for John Booth and Sons of Bolton.

RUSH TO BEAT DEADLINE

Citv terraces closed

Oldham signed ex Blue Billy Spurdle from Port Vale.

Roy Paul had moved to Gell Pentre, his native village in the Rhondda. Roy would be joining non league Worcester City as player manager. He would train at Ton Pentre, was to be loaned a car to travel to Worcester, be paid £20 per week and the club would find him a part time job!

In July, it was announced that Dave Ewing, and not new signing Roy Warhurst, would be captain for the season, and City would continue with the deep lying centre forward plan. Elsewhere Trevor Ford, ex Sunderland now of PSV Eindhoven, was banned by the FA for three seasons, and Ernie Taylor of Blackpool was on strike.

Ex Blue, **Sam Barkas** was the new manager of Wigan Athletic and announced his ambitious targets as "to top the Lancashire Combination and gain entry to the Football League (shortly afterwards Sam joined City as scout). City announced a big profit for season 56/57 of £16,296, following on from £9,499 in '56; £3,776 in '55; £14,982 in '54; £5,589 in '53; £3,960 in '52; £8,986 loss in '51; £11,109 in '50; £21,382 in '49; £16,403 in '48; £6,655 in '47; and £9.767 in '46.

Jimmy Meadows, injured in the 1955 F.A. Cup final, was all set for his big day, targeting the opening day fixture further to his right knee recovery. United announced that all their games would kick off at 3pm or 7.30pm next season after completion of their £40,000 lights.

Sam Barkas

INS/OUTS

During the 56/57 season, first teamers, George Thompson, Billy Spurdle, Johnny Hannaway, Don Revie and Roy Paul left the club.

George Thompson was a goalkeeper signed from Preston for £7,500 in the close season of '56 as cover/back up whilst Bert returned to fitness. He lasted two games, the 5-1 loss at Wolves, where odious comparisons with Bert were made by fans, and the 2-2 draw with Spurs, when he broke his leg. In his second comeback game v West Brom for the reserves he snapped a collar bone. He moved to Carlisle in the summer, after five years went to Morecambe, retired to run a fish shop in Whalley, but died in 2004..

Billy Spurdle was born in Guernsey in 1926, signed from Oldham in 1950, and featured often for City as a forward in the early 50's. He played in the '55 cup final but missed out in '56, owing to a burst carbuncle on his elbow. He moved to Port Vale in Nov '56 and later re-joined Oldham before retiring in 1966 and returning to Guernsey.

Johnny Hannaway signed for City from Seaforth in April 1950. He played a number of games, at full-back, as understudy to Eric Westwood and Roy Little, from then until his transfer in June '57 to Gillingham. He spent three seasons with the Gills., returned North to Southport, retired in '65, and took early retirement from the building trade in '82, but died in August 2007.

JULY'S FOOTBALL MONTHLY

Frank Griffin (WBA) was on the front Cover with Johnny Hubbard (Rangers) and future Blue Andy Kerr (Partick Thistle) on the back cover. CB's editorial clarifies why Villa's second cup final goal was not offside. Colour pic of Bobby Charlton on page eight. Arsenal's David Herd tells of how he made his debut in May 1951 at Stockport in the same team as his father, ex Blue Alex; then how he was brought up in Moss Side, trained with the City players as a lad and played in the street with Dennis Viollet. John MacAdam changes his view and now thinks that fans deserve better facilities and that soccer on TV is now OK. Andy Kerr is there again in a pic on page nineteen. Ken Barnes is pictured at home with his missus Jean and kids Keith and Susan. Hugh Baird, of Airdrie then Leeds, had an article exclaiming "The Revie Plan? You can keep it". Perhaps that's why City didn't sign him?! Future Blue Peter Dobing didn't fall for the glamour of United and signed for Blackburn.

Roy Paul, The Red Dragon Of Wales, was signed from Swansea Town in 1950 for £19,500 after a short and unsuccessful time at F.C. Millionaros of Colombia. He was a colossus of a captain for the Blues, winning Welsh caps, leading us out at Wembley in '55, and vowing to return the next year to win it, which we did. He moved on to Worcester City as player/manager, then to Brecon Corinthians and Garw Athletic, before retiring and becoming a lorry driver. He contracted Alzheimers Disease and passed away in a Nursing home in Glamorgan in May 2002 aged 82.

Don Revie, 'The Happy Wanderer', signed for City from Leicester for £25,000 in 1951, being a regular, helping City to the final of '55, his name being given to 'The Revie Plan', winning England caps, and being voted Footballer of the Year. He helped City win the cup in '56, for which older Blues will always remember him, but moved to Sunderland later in the year after a disagreement with Les McDowall regarding going on holiday with his family for the first time in years, rather than on City's tour. Which is a bit strange because he rejoined City for their American tour of '58! He later joined and successfully managed Leeds, then England, and controversially coached the Arab Emirates side, then Egypt. Sadly, he contracted Motor Neurone disease and died at the age of 61 in '89.

The 57/58 Squad included: Trautmann, Leivers, Little, Barnes, Ewing, Warhurst, Barlow, Hayes, Johnstone, McAdams, Clarke, Fagan, Savage, Sear, Marsden, Branagan, McTavish, McClelland, Fidler, Phoenix, Fleet, Kirkman, Taylor, Cheetham, Hart. Other players on the books were - Bourne, Davidson, Faulkner, Grey, Horridge, Leigh, Matthews, Meadows, Murray, McDonald. McLardy, Pennington, Rucker.

Alan Douglas was Chairman, E. Gill, D.F.Hamer, F.R.Jolly, W Smith, were Directors. Les McDowall was manager, and Walter Crickmer was secretary. Backroom staff was Laurie Barnett (First team trainer), John Beeston (Physiotherapist), Fred Tilson (second team trainer) and Jim McLelland (Coach).

As for the season ahead, the best City could hope for was an improvement on last season. United, Spurs, Preston, Blackpool and maybe Arsenal and Wolves were expected to be strong again. Whilst the strugglers could be Portsmouth, Sunderland and Luton. Unknown quantities were newcomers Leicester and Forest.

Regarding the fixtures, it was traditional that if the first game was at home (Sheff. Wed.) then the next two would be away (Chelsea and United). Also the return with Chelsea would be mid-week, the next week, and they would then be out of the way, as would Preston, home and away in September. Apart from September, games were generally on a home and away basis, except for December when City would be

AUGUST'S FOOTBALL MONTHLY

Sheffield Wednesday's Albert Quixall was on the front cover and Sunderland's Billy Bingham on the back cover. CB's team of 1956/57 included Byrne, Blanchflower, Edwards and Berry of United, plus Harry Gregg of Doncaster Rovers in goal "for his coolness in all circumstances". Very astute!

There was a colour shot of future Blue Derek Kevan and also Jimmy Murray. John Savage, it's reported, once scored after being injured and moving to a forward berth (No record of this with City?). Results for last season and the full fixture list for 57/58 were included.

away for three on the trot, then home for three on the trot, four if we were drawn at home in the third round of the Cup. At Christmas we would play the same team away on Christmas Day, and home on Boxing Day. This year another short trip (Bolton the last two years) to Burnley (as opposed to the ridiculous long treks backwards and forwards to Chelsea, 51/52 and Plymouth in 46/47). A similar situation would occur at Easter, with three games over the Easter period, including Newcastle away on Good Friday and Easter Monday. Final game, v Villa, was also at home after Leeds, Sheffield Wed.

The division was made up of:
7 - Lancashire clubs: City, United, Preston, Blackpool, Bolton, Everton, Burnley
6 - Midland clubs: Forest, West Brom, Birmingham, Leicester, Wolves, Villa
3 - London clubs: Chelsea, Spurs, Arsenal
2 - Southern clubs: Luton, Portsmouth
2 - North Eastern clubs: Newcastle, Sunderland
2 - Yorkshire clubs: Leeds, Sheffield Wednesday

MANCHESTER CITY 1957-58

Standing: W. Leivers, K. Barnes, B. Trautmann, R. Little, R. Warhurst, D. Ewing.
Seated: F. Fagan, J. Hayes, R. Johnstone, W. McAdams, J. Dyson.

The photograph above shows City's handsome Blue team before the first Public Trial match, played on Saturday August 17th.

Once A Blue, Always A Blue

EDDIE from Worsley's story:

I lived in the Cheetham/Broughton area. My dad wasn't a football fan, he was always working and had no interest, so I was first taken to Maine Road after the war by a neighbour. We watched the likes of Andy Black and George Smith, but we also went to see Bolton, Bury, United even, when they were at Maine Road - I was in that record league gate v Arsenal - but I was never tempted to defect *(Ed - I've always said that gate was swelled with 50,000 City fans!).* City supporters club had a branch at The Waterloo pub and I remember Emptage, Linacre and Frank Swift visiting, though I was underage!

We'd travel on the 'specials' to Maine Road from Albert Square, arriving two hours before kick off to get a place on the wall or above the tunnels. I remember the 'invalid carriages' coming in at the Platt Lane stand, through the tunnel, and parking in front of the wall. United fans were quite disparaging of the way they were treated at O/T because the pitch was raised and therefore couldn't cope with the disabled in the same way that City could. Later I stood on the Kippax, where I used to get soaked. They'd come round the pitch with a board with the team changes, and half time scores were displayed on the perimeter wall, before the scoreboard was re-erected, and of course, as is now well documented, kids were passed overhead to the front, where they could watch the action better.

After games we'd go to the players entrance and wait for them to come out. Roy Clarke and Roy Paul used to tell us about playing for Wales. Eric Todd, the Evening Chronicle reporter, was very good with us.

I was 22 in '57 and working at the Francis Shaw engineering works. Mid week games we'd go straight to the match after work, meeting up with the same people. It used to be good mingling with away fans, chatting about how their team and players were doing. For away games it was the train. I remember travelling to Preston one time, going into Woolworth's, but as a mob of football fans we weren't liked (not surprisingly!). I never saw any trouble though, in fact the first trouble I ever saw was much later, in 1971 when a City fan nutted another Blue badly as he was moaning about Ronnie Healey letting in that softie v Chelsea in the Cup winners cup semi-final *(Ed - I moaned about that myself!).* Saturdays we'd go to the game and then on into town, Ping Hongs opposite the Gaumont where the United players would meet, or Belle Vue for the dancing, and we'd visit the speedway, or watch the wrestling. Bill Benny, the popular wrestler, was the doorman at a club off Market Street, in the centre of Manchester, that we'd also visit.

Sometimes we'd go to the Midland, leave our coats there, then go on to the Plaza where Jimmy Savile was the resident DJ (the first ever?). But we mainly went to the Ritz. You could get pass outs to go to the toilets which were outside the box office, and ten of us would work it so we went in for the price of two! But then it was a problem taking it in turns to go to the gents! Then we'd pick up the Pink and Green football papers, and the early Sunday papers, the Empire News, and a pie, whilst watching the women, in Piccadilly gardens! Sometimes it was the Grosvenor Hotel. We were into Trad Jazz and watched the Saints and occasionally the Mick Mulligan Band, with George Melly. *(Melly to Mick Jagger later: "Mick, you've as many facial lines as me." Mick: "Yeah but mine are laughter lines." Melly: "Mick, nothing could be that funny!").*

The United players, Duncan Edwards, Tommy Taylor and Eddie Colman, also went to the Ritz. Dave Ewing used to go to the Midland, a pub in Levenshulme near the Palais.

He'd tell us that the ball might get past him, but the man wouldn't!! Billy McAdams, what a centre forward he was. He had back problems but was totally fearless. He'd dive in for a header where the boots were flying.

Bert Trautmann was signed from St Helens Town and what a furore that caused - an ex German POW. The papers were full of letters, particularly from the Manchester Jewish community, City fans who would never go to watch the Blues again. But there he was, this big blonde handsome German, who proved to be a fantastic goalkeeper, and he won everyone over. Within a month the letters stopped.

I was in a bus queue near Richard Johnson and Nephew on Grey Mare Lane waiting for the 53 when I heard about the Munich Air Disaster. The papers were just coming out and news was passed by word of mouth.

I actually went to the first game after the disaster, Sheffield Wednesday in the Cup, at Old Trafford, which they won 3-0.

Things weren't as bad between City and United fans then. There wasn't the same aggro.

Eddie is a lifelong Blue and season ticket holder along with his son Graham.

JOYCE from Lytham's story:

I was born with a blue spoon in my mouth, in Cheadle. My father was a Blue, and so were my two brothers, Alan and Frank, who were quite happy to take their young sister to games from me being around six years old in the early 50's.

When Colin (Barlow) first came into the team I was at Boarding school in Abergele, North Wales. I had a schoolgirl crush on him, because he scored goals, lots of them, was very speedy, and he was extremely good looking. I wrote to him asking for a signed photograph, but when I didn't get a reply, a schoolfriend wrote separately on my behalf. Colin then sent me a registered letter enclosing a signed photo and a City blazer badge, which I still have to this day.

His father had a greengrocer's shop on Livesey Street, and dad and I used to call in. We became very friendly. Colin also had a sister who was a P.E. teacher. Later I saw an article in the newspaper announcing that Colin had become engaged to Eunice Rooney aged 18, a model, from Newton Heath, who had attended Notre Dame High School, but they didn't intend getting married for a long while yet. They met at a party in Blackpool which Colin had gone to with Ray Sambrook, were married on 16th June 1962, and the reception was at Belle Vue. I attended both the wedding and the reception at their invitation. There was a cine film of the wedding, later converted to video, which I still have. I left boarding school and attended St.Hilary's All Girl School in Alderley Edge. All the other girls thought I was very strange as I just lived for Saturdays. We went to the reserves too. Dad would drive from Cheadle where we now lived and park up at William Hulme's school. We went in the main stand, for first team and reserve games, where there were never any problems with me being female, and the language was always fine.

I'd wear my pencil slim skirt, high heels and sky blue and white scarf. I'd go down to the tunnel as the players came out and wish them luck. Dad had a furniture factory next to Louis Edwards' meat factory. He was trying to sell it but couldn't get a buyer. One day he was shaking hands at the entrance with a friend and a worried Louis spotted this and came scurrying over querying what was going on. Dad told him it was a buyer for the factory and he was going to turn it into a glue factory. Louis went white and told dad he'd top whatever price he'd been offered, so dad got a far better price than he could have hoped for in the end!

Joyce is a season ticket holder and has brought both her children, Louise and Richard, up to be Blues, even though their father was a West Brom fan!

DAVE from Mosley Common's story:

I lived in Heaton Chapel where my parents had Astley's newsagents on Manchester Road from 1947 until 1985. It was opposite the 'George and Dragon' near the traffic lights. Dad was brought up in Preston, and my grandad once raised the flag at the Preston Guild, which was a big honour. Dad supported Preston then, but my mum's family, from Marple, were United fans, as was my elder brother - we were two war babies, even though my Dad was in the Navy during the war, and me and my brother don't look a bit like each other!

I was taken to Old Trafford once when Preston played there and won and was impressed by the atmosphere, but obviously I had to do the opposite to what my brother did. So aged eight I went to City, stood on the open Kippax terrace, watched us beat Middlesbrough 2-1 and was hooked. There were no outside influences, I didn't have any City supporting mates, it was completely my own decision!

Saturday nights at the paper shop at six o'clock was one of the social events of the week. There was always a large queue of people waiting for the Pink or Green football finals to arrive, all swapping stories about the games. There was one City fan and he was a real moaner, no matter how well we'd done.

I was at Stockport Technical High School then *(Ed: we've worked out that we probably played against each other for the school teams!)* and I used to cycle down the A6, past Manchester Grammar, down Platt Lane and park my bike in a lovely lady's back yard for 3d. I'd leave the ground early, about half four, and belt back to my dad's to do my paper round. Naturally, I had the worst one! Then I'd catch the bus at twenty to six and Kay, my girlfriend, would be on it (we'd met at the local Youth club, St. Thomas's, where I was also in the choir) and we'd go to the The Savoy in Heaton Moor, sitting on the back row upstairs - in the double seats. Then we'd catch the bus to Reddish and I'd walk her home, then run half a mile to the 'Bulls Head' to catch the number nine back to Heaton Chapel. It all fizzled out though when I was invited to go on holiday with her family and declined as I thought it was a step too far at that time and she met someone else.

At first I used to stand in the corner at Maine Road, between the Platt Lane and the Kippax, just above the tunnel. Later I moved to the middle of the Kippax, just below the loudspeaker you could never hear. I didn't go to away games much but I remember going to Wolves one time and was appalled at the standard of the rail coaches they laid on, real cattle wagons. We were marched to the ground and I recollect Ted Farmer giving Bert some racist grief, standing over him sarcastically clapping after a Wolves goal, then Dave Ewing sorting him out. I don't think Farmer played much after that!! It was around this time that I met an old school friend, Dave Dutton, whose whole family were City mad. He got me a temporary job on a building site. We went all over the place in Britain, even to the friendly with Celtic at Hampden, but not to Europe.

I lived in the North East, Washington, from '67 to '70, a good place to be. I saw City win the league, and Newcastle the Fairs Cup, and drove down for the midweek cup matches. One time we beat Sunderland 4-0 and I went into the nightclub in Newcastle afterwards and the City players were in, clutching their half pints. Colin Bell was quite reserved, but Franny Lee, after two hours on the soccer pitch, was dancing the night away. Dave and I are still in touch, and our most memorable game was the Schalke one, 5-1.

Our Saturday routine was: in the pub, The Vine on Burton Road, sink a few pints of Wilson's, which went down well; out of the pub at ten to three, run down the back alleys, hope the queues weren't too big; get in for the start, all pumped up for it, and elbow our way down to our spot. It's all changed now, where you get to your seat and gaze round listening to the piped music.

Dave's a season ticket holder, together with his two teenage sons, Stephen and Andy, who sell a certain fanzine, though his missus is a red!

CHAPTER TWO

AUGUST 1957 - THE BIG KICK OFF

The big kick off loomed at last but first the friendly in Holland, then the Public Trial match, followed by Sheffield Wednesday and Chelsea at home, with Chelsea and United away, so hoping for a good start.

On August 10th Twente Enschede were beaten in Holland 4-1- Team: Trautmann; Leivers, Little; Barnes, Ewing, Warhurst; Fagan, Hayes, Johnstone, McAdams, Dyson.

Bobby Johnstone nabbed two, and Paddy Fagan and Billy McAdams one each.

Keith Marsden and Colin Barlow travelled, but Roy Clarke was left behind. Colin didn't play as he was suffering from the after effects of having tooth extractions, Bert staying with him in hospital.

The construction of the new roof over the Kippax was being hampered by strikes, and was only half cladded. News came through that ex Chairman and current director Bob Smith had died. Fans were told to watch out for an important new signing, but City were reported as not being interested in Johnny Haynes.

Jimmy Meadows was back after his '55 cup final injury for Saturday's trial match, and Jack Dyson would be at outside left, for the second time only in that position.

SATURDAY AUGUST 17TH 1957
K.O. 3PM: BLUES v MAROONS

It was the annual pre-season public trial match, Blues v Maroons.

Blues lined up with: Trautmann; Leivers, Little; Barnes, Ewing, Warhurst; Fagan, Hayes, Johnstone, McAdams, Dyson (trialled on the wing). This is the team whose photo appears in the early away programmes, with the players wearing black arm bands!

Maroons were: Savage; Meadows, Sear; Cheetham, Marsden, McTavish; McLelland, Kirkman, Faulkner, Phoenix, Clarke..

Blues won the game 2-1 with goals from Hayes and Johnstone. Kirkman replying for the Maroons.

Attendance: 10,839

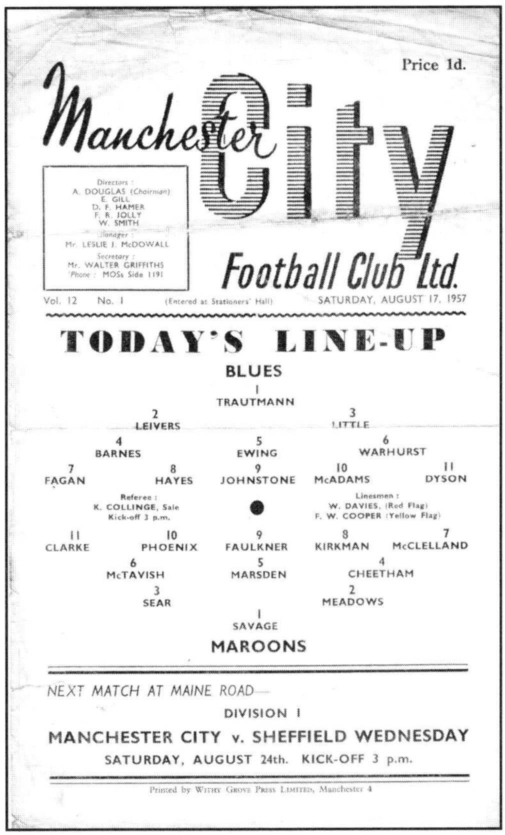
Price 1d.

Manchester City Football Club Ltd.

Directors:
A. DOUGLAS (Chairman)
E. GILL
D. F. HAMER
F. R. JOLLY
W. SMITH
Manager:
Mr. LESLIE J. McDOWALL
Secretary:
Mr. WALTER GRIFFITHS
'Phone: MOSs Side 1191

Vol. 12 No. 1 (Entered at Stationers' Hall) SATURDAY, AUGUST 17, 1957

TODAY'S LINE-UP

BLUES

1 TRAUTMANN
2 LEIVERS 3 LITTLE
4 BARNES 5 EWING 6 WARHURST
7 FAGAN 8 HAYES 9 JOHNSTONE 10 McADAMS 11 DYSON

Referee: K. COLLINGE, Sale
Kick-off 3 p.m.

Linesmen: W. DAVIES, (Red Flag)
F. W. COOPER (Yellow Flag)

11 CLARKE 10 PHOENIX 9 FAULKNER 8 KIRKMAN 7 McCLELLAND
6 McTAVISH 5 MARSDEN 4 CHEETHAM
3 SEAR 2 MEADOWS
1 SAVAGE

MAROONS

NEXT MATCH AT MAINE ROAD
DIVISION I
MANCHESTER CITY v. SHEFFIELD WEDNESDAY
SATURDAY, AUGUST 24th. KICK-OFF 3 p.m.

Printed by Withy Grove Press Limited, Manchester 4

The programme was a single sheet affair for a penny, which gave a brief tribute to ex Blues chairman Bob Smith who'd just missed his first AGM after attending forty consecutive meetings; he had died that week aged eighty three. He'd retired as chairman three years earlier because of fighting a losing battle against 'underhand methods in football', illegal transactions and all that, plus carrying the can for City's lost prestige and lack of success in recent years. Sounds familiar!?. He was still a Board member though.

We were also informed that 'due to circumstances beyond the club's control, the new covered stand - to be known officially as the Kippax Street Stand - could not be completed in time for this public trial match, but would be ready for next week's game with Sheffield Wednesday.'

Admission price was to go up by 3d to 2/3d, but the scoreboard side (end, surely !!) would reduce by 3d to 2s. The covered (but still unseated) Platt Lane end would be 3s, and Main Stand prices would be unchanged at 7/6d; 5/6d and 4/6d (cheap at twice the price).

Fixtures for First division, Central league and Lancs League "A", played at Shawe View Fields Urmston, were listed.

Tom Jackson in the MEN reckoned the league hat trick for United was 'in the bag' and looked as 'safe as the Bank of England'.

It was announced that the City v Wednesday game was off owing to the flu epidemic, and there was also a hitch with the erection of the floodlights on the new stand roof.

United announced a profit of £39,784, with £3,147 paid to City for Euro games.

SATURDAY AUGUST 24TH 1957
K.O. 3PM: BLUES v MAROONS

Again it was a single sheet programme for a penny which advised us that 'It's just one of those things' (familiar tale for City fans?!) Sheffield Wednesday, who were to be today's opponents, were gripped with the flu bug and both teams agreed to postpone the fixture. City asked the FA for help in organising continental opposition but time was against this, though it was 'not for want of trying', so a second public trial game was hastily arranged.

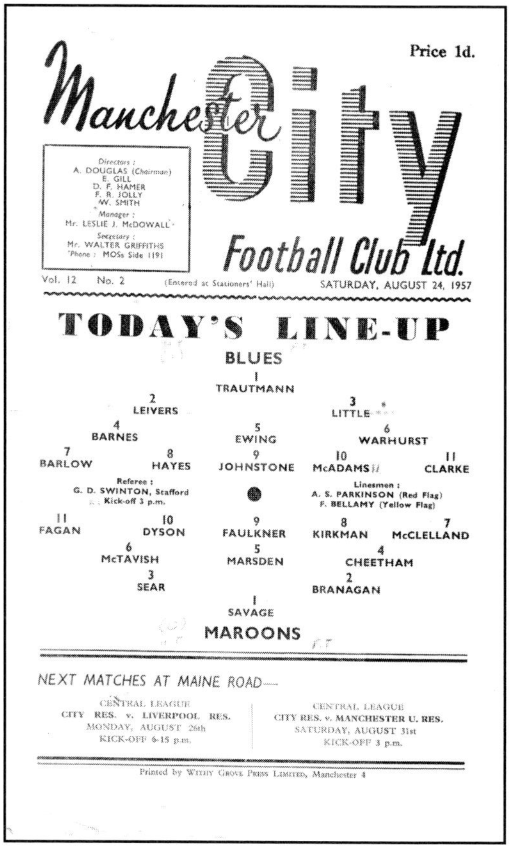

Price 1d.

Manchester City Football Club Ltd.

Directors :
A. DOUGLAS (Chairman)
E. GILL
D. F. HAMER
F. R. JOLLY
W. SMITH
Manager :
Mr. LESLIE J. McDOWALL
Secretary :
Mr. WALTER GRIFFITHS
'Phone : MOSs Side 1191

Vol. 12 No. 2 (Entered at Stationers' Hall) SATURDAY, AUGUST 24, 1957

TODAY'S LINE-UP

BLUES

1 TRAUTMANN
2 LEIVERS 3 LITTLE
4 BARNES 5 EWING 6 WARHURST
7 BARLOW 8 HAYES 9 JOHNSTONE 10 McADAMS 11 CLARKE

Referee : G. D. SWINTON, Stafford
Kick-off 3 p.m.

Linesmen : A. S. PARKINSON (Red Flag) F. BELLAMY (Yellow Flag)

11 FAGAN 10 DYSON 9 FAULKNER 8 KIRKMAN 7 McCLELLAND
6 McTAVISH 5 MARSDEN 4 CHEETHAM
3 SEAR 2 BRANAGAN
1 SAVAGE

MAROONS

NEXT MATCHES AT MAINE ROAD—

CENTRAL LEAGUE
CITY RES. v. LIVERPOOL RES.
MONDAY, AUGUST 26th
KICK-OFF 6-15 p.m.

CENTRAL LEAGUE
CITY RES. v. MANCHESTER U. RES.
SATURDAY, AUGUST 31st
KICK-OFF 3 p.m.

Printed by Withy Grove Press Limited, Manchester 4

Changes were made. For the Blues, Colin Barlow and Roy Clarke came in, replacing Paddy Fagan and Jack Dyson who lined up for the Maroons, with Ron Phoenix dropping out.

Blues: Trautmann; Leivers, Little; Barnes, Ewing, Warhurst; Barlow, Hayes, Johnstone, McAdams, Clarke.

Maroons: Savage; Branagan, Sear; Cheetham, Marsden, McTavish; McLelland, Kirkman, Faulkner, Dyson, Fagan.

Blues won again, 3-2 as expected, with goals from Barnes, Hayes and McAdams, with Kirkman and Dyson replying for the Maroons

For Jack Dyson this was an incredibly unlucky set of circumstances. Released early from cricket, but Wednesday down with flu, so another trial match arranged. This time he was picked for the Maroons, on the opposite side to Bill Leivers, and after scoring, broke his right leg in two places in a collision with Bill, after he nut-megged him.

Jimmy Meadows was included in the reserve team v Liverpool. In his MEN column, Bert warned that bigger wages would not raise soccer standards.

Billy Walker, Forest's manager, had enquired about Leivers, Little, Meadows, and any up and coming youngsters City might have available, but was told 'no deal'.

A 12,000 attendance was recorded at United reserves. *Next season I'd cycle back from City past United and walk up Cross Lane with a United girl I fancied, but never asked out!*

A hat-trick of titles again predicted for United.

1) WEDNESDAY AUGUST 28TH 1957 K.O. 7.30PM: CHELSEA (AWAY)

City's season kicked off a few days later than everyone else's with an evening game at Chelsea under their new lights, opened in the previous March against Sparta Prague. There were six sets of them, towering and impressive.

Chelsea, managed by Ted Drake, were formed in 1905, and in 1915 lost in the FA Cup final to Sheffield United 3-0, and would have been relegated to division two for the second time if the first division hadn't been increased to twenty two clubs. So they left that distinction, (first losing FA Cup finalists and relegation) to us in 1926. They won their first Championship in '55, with fifty two points, an all time low number! The reason being that there were a lot of good teams around that year!? Last season they were thirteenth with thirty nine points

The programme was a magnificent specimen. Dark blue cover with a ground view (no floodlights shown!) and the newish logo depicting a lion, which replaced the previous CFC one in 53/54 (and the pensioner in 52/53). Bet Middlesboro' and Millwall weren't impressed.

It was a 16 page effort with a full page on 'Our Visitors' and a team photo of City prior to the first Public Trial match. Bill Leivers and Jack Dyson being on the same side, and players wearing black armbands with respect to Bob Smith.

Page 11 included a classic line - **"WHAT MANCHESTER DOES AND THINKS TODAY THE REST OF THE COUNTRY DOES AND THINKS TOMORROW"** Wow, even the sadly departed Anthony H. Wilson, ardent promoter of all things Mancunian, would've been proud of that one!

Stamford Bridge once held 82,905 and rivalled Maine Road as the biggest in the country but I didn't make it there until April 1960, a 3-0 loss, Peter Bonetti's debut game. It was strange in that it had a greyhound track round the pitch which lost some atmosphere, and a smallish main stand, seats and paddock. Next to this was a giant double decker, the rest being open terrace apart from a small cover, yet to be named 'The Shed'. The whole place being completely rebuilt from the 70s onwards, slowly until 2002.

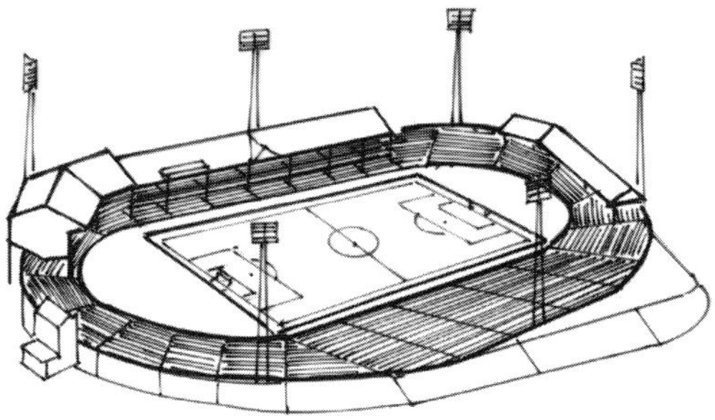

Pitch Size: 114 x 71 yds

In their first game they'd drawn at Spurs 1-1.

At Chelsea: Pre war we managed three wins out of twenty games, and post war we'd won three, drawn two and lost four, including the last two, but it was looking promising for tonight. Recent attendances ranged from 25,864 (48/49) to 64,396 (47/48) and it was the fifty ninth league meeting, plus two cup ties both at City.

From The Guardian's Special Correspondant: Hayes Leads Revival:

City's belated start to the season had a happy sequel at Chelsea. They won 3-2 though no one would have given a bean for their chances when, in a three minute spell divided by the interval, Chelsea went into a 2-0 lead.

But out of a slow beginning, came a powerful finish and none did more than Hayes at inside right to bring about the transformation.

Warhurst the newcomer from Birmingham, also played a considerable part in City's victory and to young outside right Barlow came the satisfaction of scoring in his first game in the first division. Ewing at centre half also had a fine game and behind him Trautmann made some saves that told he is back to the top of his class. With Greaves making his first home appearance for Chelsea and two new men in Warhurst and Barlow out for City the match had plenty of interest for both sides from the outset. All three newcomers left their mark on the game, most of all young Greaves. City's plan of attack with Johnstone playing mostly behind his inside forwards clearly had Chelsea a little puzzled. Mortimore and Saunders were regularly caught on the wrong side of their men, leaving Dicks at centre half with an unwanted choice of opponent to tackle.

Somehow Chelsea muddled through, relief coming to their defence from some tearaway raids by young forwards who, in their enthusiasm, however, repeatedly fell into City's off-side trap. But, seconds before half time, the trap for once did not spring and with the defence momentarily hesitating, **Lewis** headed home a centre from Brabrook, who had crossed to the left wing. Three minutes after the interval Chelsea were two up - the marksman **Greaves**, at close range from the persistent Allen's centre. So Greaves, scorer of 114 junior goals last season, had scored in each of his first two league games.

J. GREAVES

At this, Chelsea relaxed while their floodlights shone down on three City goals in fourteen minutes. First **Hayes** found a clear path through the middle on to Johnstone's pass, the goal coming off Matthews' body. Nine minutes later Warhurst deceived Matthews with a low shot that skimmed out of the goal-keepers hands giving **Barlow** an easy chance to equalise. With the Chelsea defence again in utter disorder, **McAdams** slipped a third goal past the hapless Matthews.

It was not the end of the excitement. In a seven minute period later, both goal-keepers were knocked out and so was City's left-winger Clarke. The injury to Matthews looked bad when he retired for treatment and Tindall took his place, but within a minute they were back to their normal positions, though with Matthews still in a daze.

FINAL SCORE: CHELSEA 2 CITY 3

Chelsea::Royal Blue (white collars) shirts/white knickers/black/blue and white tops stockings: Mathews; Whittaker, P. Sillett; Mortimer, Dicks, Saunders; Brabrook, Tindall, Allen, Greaves, J. Lewis

City: Sky blue/white knickers/sky blue and white hoops stockings: Trautmann; Leivers, Little; Barnes, Ewing, Warhurst; Barlow Hayes Johnstone, McAdams, Clarke.

Attendance: 43,722

Referee: J.G.Williams Notts)

Linesmen: JTW Bibby (Portchester), SJ Dant (Cambridge)

Goals For: 3 Against: 2

Reserves: Beat Liverpool 2-1 at home, Aug. 26th

For me, however, a very strange thing happened this night. My middle brother, Don, who had absolutely no interest in football whatsoever, advised me in no uncertain terms that he was taking me to Old Trafford on his motor bike and meeting up with his workmate from Gardners, Taffy, a red, to see them play Everton. Obviously, a boy's gotta do what his elder brother tells him, or risk a slap. Anyway, I thought it would be a good preview for Saturday, so I duly cocked on to the pillion and went to see what all the fuss was about. United won 3-0, but I was unimpressed - I never went for this City one week, United the next 50's type stuff, though I did occasionally go to Bolton, and sometimes to watch The Lions play rugby at Station Road. All I remember was walking to the ground in drab Trafford Park, standing on the Stretford End, thinking how exhausted David Pegg looked and being sarcastically addressed by Taffy from Gardners at the end of the game with "We've got your lot on Saturday, haven't we", and whilst I thought that was a bit disrespectful answered, "Yes, can I have a lift please?"

It's August 31st 2006 and I've just asked Don, my brother, for the first time, what that was all about, and he hasn't a clue?!

In the MEN United were branded as 'Big Heads' because they wouldn't do a BBC training film, as the £10 fee was considered too low!!

2) SATURDAY AUGUST 31ST
K.O. 3PM: MANCHESTER UNITED (AWAY)

Dawned the big day. Taffy picked me up, our Don had presumably had enough, the magic of United was obviously completely lost on him too. The expression on Taffy's face was a picture as I perched on his pillion resplendent in my sky blue and white City scarf, bob hat and rosette from the 1956 cup game with Everton.

Again it was the Stretford End for us, and I don't recall getting much stick as we went down 4-1, that would be reserved for Monday at school, no doubt.

United were formed in 1878 as Newton Heath. They won the league in 1908, and 1911 after nicking four of City's best players after the bribes scandal, plus the cup in 1909. Then they won nothing for the next thirty seven years, until the cup in 1948, but followed this with the league in '52, '56, and '57. They'd also reached Wembley last season, going down to Aston Villa 2-1. Additionally they'd reached the semis of the European Cup going out to the real 'Greatest Club in the World', Real Madrid.

Despite wanting to charge us exhorbitant rates for the use of Old Trafford when the Hyde Road stand was burnt down in the 20's, which we refused, nicking our old player Matt Busby as manager, being graciously allowed to play at Maine Road after the war as Hitler had cleverly guided a bomb onto Old Trafford, we were also soft enough to let them play their European games under our lights in Moss Side until they finally erected floodlights towards the end of that season.

The programme, the United Review, was pretty decent with a pic of the previous match on the front cover. It was priced at 4d for twelve glossy pages. It included a full page cartoon strip by Butterworth, chairman's message, pen pics of City players, review of certain past derbies with City by the pipe smoking Alf Clarke, United Topics by Tom Jackson, Matt Busby's message and all the usual fixtures, stats etc.

Old Trafford's (named after the cricket ground) record attendance was 76,962 for the F.A. Cup semi-final of 1949 Wolves v Grimsby. United fans had only ever mustered a maximum of 70,504 in there so Grimsby Town had always been a bigger attraction at O/T than Man. U.

Overall it was fairly bland, to be honest, though symetrical. A fairly standard seats and paddock main stand which curved round each corner onto the open terraces behind each goal, and a cover on the opposite side which strangely only kept two thirds of their fans dry, and was advertised as being built by Edward Wood. A terrace feature though was the white painted aisles and barrier supports, but it also had a rather old fahioned wooden perimeter fence with railings, painted, red and white. Oh and the pitch was at a raised level so players would fall off the edge when propelling towards the touchlines, and ball boys were needed. They did have stewards though to pack the crowd in. The ground was completely re-developed, once or twice over the years and now holds 76,000, all seated.

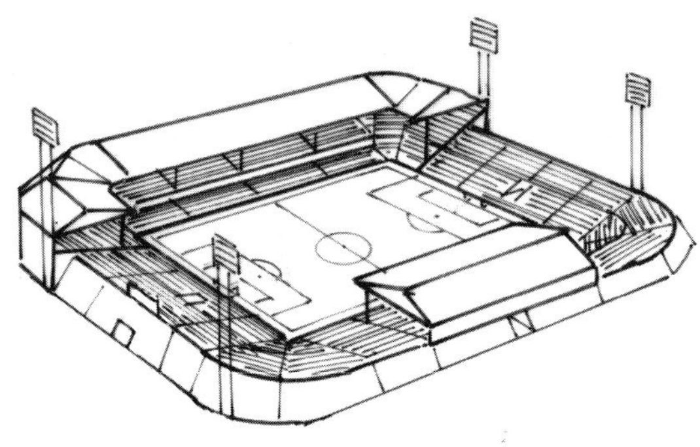

Pitch Size: 116 x 76 yds

United were of course managed by ex Blue Matt Busby. In their first two games they'd won 3-0 away at newly promoted Leicester, and by the same score at home to Everton.

At United: Pre-war we'd won four of the last five, including a 6-1. Post we'd won in '55, 5-0, but lost the last two 2-1 and 2-0. Prior to that there'd been five draws and one loss. Recent attendances at O/T ranged from 46,369 (53/54) to 60,956 (55/56) It was our sixty third league meeting plus a semi-final 3-0 in 1926, at Bramall Lane (46,450) and one cup tie and a Charity Shield game at City.

Team News: Unchanged

Taken partly from 'Old International' in The Guardian:
League Champions At Their Best - Feast of Splendid Attacking play

A huge crowd of over 63,000, a fine, still day for football, a pitch like velvet and five splendid goals, four to United, one to City - and an exhibition of football that tickled the palate and never palled from the first kick to the last - such was our portion at Old Trafford today.

The Manchester crowd was treated to a feast of smooth, resourceful attacking play, all five goals being perfect specimens in the art of goalscoring. Taylor played Ewing as skilfully and elusively as a mature player, Viollet and Whelan flitted to and fro, and wingmen Pegg and Berry gave City's hard working and resolute defenders Little and Leivers a sore trial. Edwards and Colman prompted their forwards, and, after interplay with Whelan, **Edwards** shot United into the lead. Shortly afterwards **Berry** made it 2-0, thrusting his head at a Pegg corner exactly as a tortoise pokes it's head from it's shell, and the result was a projectile akin to a violent shot.

Duncan Edwards

Colman, despite being repeatedly dispossessed by City players catching him in possession, then intercepted the ball and sent a forty yard pass beyond the City defence setting **Viollet** racing free and finishing with aplomb. **Taylor** was then on hand to stroke home the fourth goal when Trautmann only parried Pegg's shot. **Barnes'** sweetly struck drive, from a cleverly worked free-kick proved meagre consolation to a well beaten City team.

Yet, if any outraged City fan grabs you by the coat lapel and swears that if City's so and so forwards hadn't been a set of peg-legs they could have drawn the match or possibly won it, don't spurn him as a lunatic. The plain facts are that in the sixteenth minute McAdams gave Clarke a scoring chance on a plate. Result? A wild whiz-bang into the crowd. In the twenty first minute Edwards faltered momentarily and in a fit of abstraction, rolled a back-pass to Clarke instead of Wood. Result? A flurry of arms and legs in front of United's goal until McAdams eased the tension by aiming a shot at the half-time scoreboard. Barnes' beautiful goal followed from a slyly taken free-kick and then there were two dogged efforts by Hayes.

The last opening fell to Barlow, but his preference for violence as against placing sent another opportunity to the scrap heap. It was a sad day for City as a whole and a positive torture for the defenders. Leivers, Little, Barnes, Ewing and Warhurst fought gamely, but gameness was not enough.

Two lost points. Are City becoming so obsessed with offside tactics and neglecting the important consideration of defending in depth? If so, Viollet's breakthrough should give them food for thought. And is Fagan of such low value these days that his shooting would not have been useful on Saturday? - assuming, of course that he was not injured.

No doubt Taffy had a smirk on his face, but I never saw him again.

FINAL SCORE: UNITED 4 CITY 1

United: Red shirts/white knickers: Wood; Foulkes, Byrne; Colman, Blanchflower, Edwards; Berry, Whelan, Taylor, Viollet, Pegg
City: Blue shirts/white knickers: Trautmann; Leivers, Little; Barnes, Ewing, Warhurst; Barlow, Hayes, Johnstone, McAdams, Clarke.
Attendance: 63,103 **Average:** 53,412
Referee; F. B. Coultas (Hull) who refereed in the '57 cup final
Linesmen: R.C.Bladon (Burton on Trent) E.J.Daniels (Liverpool)
League position: 17th, having played 1 game less than the rest
Goals For: 4 Against: 6
Reserves: In the 'mini derby' City lost 4-3.

So Sunday morning at St. Peters Church choir was not a happy one for me, neither was Monday at school. The 'stick' started straight away, amongst other ribald remarks came "Doesn't say much for City if your half back had to score for you." "Oh yeah, what position does Edwards play?" United fans eh, but fairly tame really?!

LEAGUE TABLE

	P	W	D	L	F	A	Pts
Man Utd	3	3	0	0	10	1	6
Arsenal	3	2	1	0	5	2	5
Notts For	3	2	1	0	5	3	5
Wolves	3	2	0	1	11	2	4
Burnley	3	1	2	0	4	2	4
WBA	3	1	2	0	6	5	4
Luton	3	2	0	1	3	3	4
Everton	3	2	0	1	2	3	4
Chelsea	3	1	1	1	8	5	3
Portsmouth . .	3	1	1	1	5	5	3
B'ham	3	1	1	1	5	7	3
Newcastle . . .	2	1	0	1	4	3	2
Preston	3	1	0	2	5	4	2
Leicester	3	1	0	2	5	6	2
Blackpool . . .	3	1	0	2	4	5	2
Aston Villa . . .	3	1	0	2	3	4	2
Man City	2	1	0	1	4	6	2
Bolton	3	1	0	2	4	7	2
Leeds	3	1	0	2	2	6	2
Spurs	3	0	1	2	3	9	1
Sheff Wed . . .	1	0	0	1	1	2	0
Sunderland . .	3	0	0	3	1	10	0

SEPTEMBER'S FOOTBALL MONTHLY

Peter Farrell, of Everton was on the front cover, running out of what seems like the tunnel at Maine Road, and Pat Saward of Aston Villa on the back cover. There's a little pic of Bill Leiverson the inside cover, as part of an advert for the Soccer Gift book.CB's editorial claims it will be an exciting season in the third. He tips United to win the title for the third year running, and Preston and Blackpool to challenge them. Newcomers Leicester and Forest to hold their own. Villa and Arsenal to do well. City, Sheff. Wed., Leeds and Portsmouth to struggle. Colour pic of Dennis Viollet on page five. Jack Dyson has an article on page seventeen saying how he likes both playing soccer for City and cricket for his county.

FA Year book for 57/57 has Jack Dyson on the front cover challenging Jack Kelsey at Arsenal. Amateur 'who's who' is ex Blue Sid Cann, captain of Wycombe Wanderers. Future Blues manager Ron Saunders joined Gillingham.

CONCLUSION: First game postponed due to flu, so two away games to start the season. Barlow and Warhurst made their league debuts. Great come-back at Chelsea to win 3-2 but a demoralising defeat at Old Trafford, and a blow to the season with Jack Dyson's broken leg.

Once A Blue, Always A Blue

ALAN from Droylsden's story:

I was born a Blue and my granddad who I lived with was a Blue, as was my Uncle Joe. It was Uncle Joe who took me to my very first game when I was eight years old way back in 1946. Circumstances meant that Uncle Joe would move to London round about 1950 and trips to Maine Road would become less frequent because my mother wouldn't let me go on my own. I was about thirteen when my mother finally relented and she allowed me to go with my pal Mick Flint. We'd go on Mayne's' Football Specials' - double deckers from their garage at Clayton, and I would wear a blue and white scarf. It was quite difficult to find anywhere that sold them. We used to get there about half an hour before kick off, behind the goal where it was cheapest. My first game with Mick was 0-0 v Wolves. It was exciting, you could smell the Bovril, the smoke from pipes and the embrocation on the players.

I was nineteen in 1957 and it was the year I got married. The most predictable thing of that season was that you knew you were going to see goals. The only thing that you couldn't predict was which team would score the most or the result. There was excitement and drama of one kind or another in almost every game and each game was different. Les McDowall introduced the 'Marsden Plan', twin centre halves, in the home game with Preston which we were lucky to win 2-0. Then we beat Portsmouth 2-1 with Dave Ewing's famous long range goal. The return game with Preston was just a week later and Tom Finney turned us inside out as Preston handed out a 6-1 walloping. I was choked. It took just over twenty four hours to get this out of my system as I began to look forward to the weekend's game at West Brom. I remember going into the ground full of blind faith and hoping that the game against Preston would soon be forgotten. Little did I know that a worse nightmare was to haunt me. For the first hour or so of the game City held their own at 3-2 down and they suddenly collapsed conceding six goals inside the last thirty minutes. I came out of 'The Hawthorns' in a daze and shell shocked, hardly believing that my heroes had been beaten nine times. In fact the shock was such that somehow my memory in later years would always incorrectly recall Bert Trautmann being in goal that day when in fact it was John Savage, as Dave Wallace was quick to remind me! A similar thing happened at Leicester when City lost 8-4. Winger Derek Hogg and Jimmy Walsh ran us ragged and again I left the ground feeling bruised and battered. This time Bert was definitely in goal and It seemed a long way home to Droylsden.

Away games weren't all doom and gloom though. There was a particularly good win at Blackpool, 5-2 when Bobby Johnstone did to Blackpool what Jimmy Walsh was to do to us later in the season. Another treasured memory of those days for me was the 4-2 win at Leeds when Bert made a save that had to be seen to be believed. The Leeds centre forward, Hughie Baird was reputed to have one of the hardest shots in the game. He picked up a loose clearance and set off from his own half like a Powderhall sprinter. Then from about twenty yards or so he unleashed a rocket shot. Bert dived to his right in anticipation, the ball swerved in the strong wind and Bert back heeled the ball over the bar while horizontal and in mid air. At that particular time Eric 'Sketchbook' Thompson, a sports reporter for the 'Daily Mail', would report on the match and would usually include a sketched cartoon of a particular highlight and I remember his sketch of Bert and that incredible save. Sadly Eric Thompson died in the Munich air disaster.

The first inkling I had of Munich was on a newsagents billboard on Ashton New Road just up past the 'Mitchell Arms' on what is now the Beswick estate. It said 'United plane in crash' and when I got home I told my father-in-law who said, "has it buggery" Then it came on the news. For a good while I had been getting sick of all the United hype and press bias such as the time when Alf Clarke, who was the Evening Chronicle's United reporter and had been for some years, commented in a match report, "there was just a few minutes to go on the watch that United presented to me just before the kick-off" and he was supposed to be unbiased. The truth is that whilst I regretted the loss of all the victim's lives, but as far as it affected MUFC I had no real feelings about it.

I remember being in Manchester one Saturday morning, I'd finished whatever errand I had been on when I saw the Spurs players outside the Queens Hotel, they were playing United and I got the 'buzz' and decided on the spur of the moment to catch the special train to London where City were playing Arsenal. A good day out but as usual we lost at Highbury, the score was 2-1 with Billy McAdams scoring for us.

Bobby Johnstone was and still is my favourite player. He was magic, a Scottish 'tanner' ball player. He'd score with brave headers, he was hard and he could be naughty sometimes but he had phenomenal skill. He was Kinkladze plus, a different kind of player than Colin Bell my other outfield hero. Don Revie too. They said that Johnny Haynes was the finest passer of a ball but 'The Don' matched him. Ken Barnes had guile, Paddy Fagan, Joe Hayes, and Clarkey, were all great City players.

Away games were usually fine. I was never frightened. We'd banter with the home fans and take the piss out of each other with ribald remarks, depending on the scores and the result. Now and again it would threaten to boil over but the authorities soon had things back under control. The exception was Old Trafford where there was always a bad atmosphere and indeed still is and I was always glad to get out of the place.

CHARLIE from Sale's story:

I was an early reader of the football in the News and the Chronicle which whetted my appetite. Then dad promised to take me to the Wolves game, season 54/55 but it was postponed. This was followed by the F.A. Cup semi-final, which we didn't attend, City v Sunderland. My dad was City and my mum was from Sunderland so I decided to support whoever won the game! Luckily it was City, (preventing an all North Eastern final), who've been marginally more successful than Sunderland over the years! A few weeks later at Easter time, a few of the local lads said they were going to Maine Road, so I must have had enough money, one shilling (twelve old pence) at City (but only 9d at Old Trafford). So I went on the Good Friday. I was just nine years old. There were 57,663 there, I couldn't believe it, huge bowl, huge crowd, and this was going on just a mile from my home and I had never realised. The very next day, I must have got some more money from somewhere, it was Sunderland at home, and I went on my own. There were 60,611 there, City won both games, and were in the cup final. Then they lost 6-1 the week before the final to Blackpool, which I missed. Teams always took it easy before the final, which I watched on telly.

My grandad goes back to the Hyde Road days and was a friend of Horace Barnes, who lived near him in Withington. When Grandad came back injured from the first World War Barnes visited him in hospital. Horace was the first goalscorer at the new Maine Road stadium in 1923. Just another reason why I'm a City fan.

My dad only lived to the young age of forty nine, but he was fortunate to see both the '37 and '68 championship winning teams. I also got him a cup final ticket v Leicester in 1969, one year before his death in 1970. (A couple of months previously he and I saw on TV the great Brazilian team win the World Cup. What a way to go).

When the roof went over the Kippax in '57 I remember thinking how dangerous the steps at the back of the stand looked. Indeed these were replaced after the Ibrox stairway thirteen disaster in 1971. I always worried about the tunnels too, but there were no major problems over the years. Regrettably one of the other things I do remember from season 57/58 was Munich, and standing next to me in school assembly, were Alf Wood and Johnny Howarth, both United fans and footballers. Alf went on to play for City as you know, and both were absolutely devastated - which is why it upsets me when people go on about it as I think it's tremendously disrespectful - regardless of what we think of modern day arrogant United fans. .

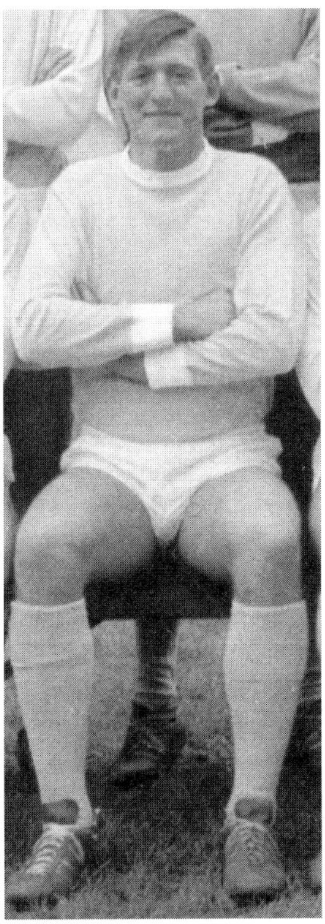

Alf Wood

Some of the players from that era were Cliff Sear, who was living above a shop in Yew Tree Road. John Savage was in a club house in Withington. I remember John McTavish, and Dennis Fidler, from United, who lives in Italy now and is a big friend of Peter Barnes, who goes over to see Dennis and his own daughters who live there. Bill Leivers, a lay preacher off the pitch but an assassin on it, with a temper. I once saw him leave the field and kick the centre flag into the stand, after a home cup tie loss with Norwich. I also remember the season before, Leeds at Maine Road with John Charles, six pm mid week kick off. John played centre half or centre forward. The Leeds young centre half, Jack Charlton, was injured and went to centre-forward, and Charles dropped back to centre half. So I saw him play in both his positions in one game. Other players that stood out were Dennis Viollet at United, who played in the street with David Herd when they were lads, (son of Alex Herd). Johnny Haynes whose passing appeared to be computer programmed. Peter Mellor, who I played with in John Gwynne's Sherwood Forest team, who later played for Fulham in the Cup Final of 1975.

The first 'incident' I remember was at Bolton, on the embankment when I got a toilet roll holder with a lump of wood in it on the back of my head. The second was a season or two later at Blackburn, early 60's, when I got chased back to the station. I can't remember why, but for some reason I've never worn colours, apart from my supporters club tie at functions.

Later I stood outside Maine Road's main entrance in 1963 when the crowd were shouting "Mac Out" (McDowall) and some were throwing pennies at windows. Myself and a friend were included in 'riot' photos in the Sunday Pictorial the next day??!!

Charlie's a lifelong Blue, and active supporters' club member

CHAPTER THREE

SEPTEMBER 1957 - THE MARSDEN PLAN

Chelsea, could we double them? Preston, Portsmouth, Spurs at home, Forest, Preston West Brom away.

3) WEDNESDAY SEPTEMBER 4TH 1957
K.O. 7.30PM: CHELSEA (HOME)

So to the first home game. A dash home from school, tea gulped down, met up with Jackie Phillips, one of half a dozen known Blues in Swinton at the time (Walt, Ged Morgan, Melv McGurk - who later played the organ at The Union pub in Manc. - and John Sharples being the others). We took the 57 or 77 bus to Piccadilly, then the 76x to Maine Road. An enthralling journey on the top deck of the bus which gave an insight to the poverty of Moss Side. Houses without curtains, lights without shades, just lone, low voltage light bulbs; people tended to sit outside on the steps in their vests, chatting with neighbours as the kids ran around barely dressed. An education, indeed and a world apart from 'poets corner' in Swinton, which itself was a bit sparse on millionaires in its council dwellings.

At Maine Road we stood on the open Scoreboard End, well actually I sat on the barrier half way up, as we viewed the newly completed Kippax Stand to our left, which somehow made that vast terrace look smaller. And the advertising hoardings, unlike on the other stands, didn't stretch the full length, but inexplicably were a series of six individual ones, displaying products I can't even remember now. Opposite was the Platt Lane covered stand behind the goal, with its curved covered 'apple pie corner' which met with the main stand. The main stand itself was magnificent, with three tunnels, and gable on the roof displaying the big advertisements, promoting amongst others, Stone-Dri, Lookers for Austin's, Savill's Pies, Red Rose Ales and Pakamac's.

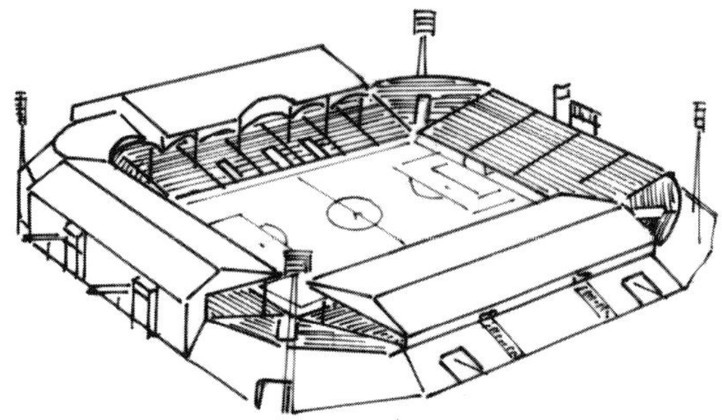

Pitch Size: 117 x 79 yds

City, had, of course, moved to Maine Road in 1923 from Hyde Road. Sheffield United were the first visitors and were seen off 2-1 in front of 56,993. The record attendance of 84,569 came in the cup tie with Stoke in 1934, probably before the Platt Lane was covered and extended with the addition of wooden terracing at the back. So the new Kippax stand was the first post war development. This was followed by the North stand, then the Main stand roof, the Platt Lane stand, new Kippax and the final desecration with the two temporary stands (Gene Kelly's) between the Kippax and Platt Lane, and Kippax and north stand, before the move to Eastlands.

First chance then to view the revamped **City programme**. There was a new front cover, which wasn't as impressive as the '55 to '57 one which included a great artistic ground drawing. This year it was a view from the scoreboard end, by Carrodus (not Frank?) where the stands looked too small and the floodlights weren't indicated. Also the goals were shown on the wall and not the goal-line, and, unbelievably, the main stand had the tunnels and stanchions in the wrong place. So a great chance lost then to show off the new Kippax (a chance taken up only in the 59/60 programmes onwards), but there was a proud claim for covered accommodation for 50,000, and an honours list.

It was a sixteen page edition with plenty of adverts - full pagers for Stone-Dri raincoats, 'Secure employment for Skilled men' at Metro-Vics., and British Railways back page advertising 10/3d to Nottingham, and 7s to Blackpool Illuminations. Plus several smaller ads for the Pink on Saturday, Burns Building Supplies, Gus Demmy, Red Rose Stout, Roy Clarke Sports, RAC motor insurance, Nunn for Ford, UCP restaurants, Finglands, Spears warehouse, Evening Chronicle, Empire News, Hilton Ready Mixed concrete, CH Radio services, Smiths wine and spirit merchants, a Carlsberg ad., and encouragement to read the Les McDowall - Matt Busby page in the Evening Chronicle Football Pink - "it's the talk of the soccer world".

No room for anything else then? Not a bit of it, an editorial reflecting on the match at Chelsea, Jack Dyson's injury and the voucher scheme, an innovative idea first introduced in August '55 to enable tickets to be purchased for all the big games which would surely come our way. The first being the '56 cup final. There was a 'Maine Road Gossip' column, portrait of the referee, half a page on 'Our visitors' where Greavsie was described as the seventeen year old 'season's sensation', and Chelsea's wonderboy. 'Sportsman's Corner' included fans' queries on all manner of football, and sometimes other sports related topics.

Guest journalist Arthur Walmsley, of the Evening Chronicle, had a one page article on the 'Luck Of the Game', commenting on Bert's and Jimmy Meadows' injuries and how they'd fought back, as an example to Jack Dyson, who "what others have done, he could do himself when the time comes"

There was 'the half time scoreboard', with facts about Chelsea, team line ups (Chelsea in red shirts, white knickers - always got a laugh that one) David Jack's (who scored Bolton's winner v us in the 1926 cup final) column on 'The New Chelsea' - where the club under Drake disregarded Chelsea's old style of artistic entertainers for a style of strength, speed and no frills, winning the '55 championship and leaving the Music Hall comics to look elsewhere - (though they didn't win anything else until the League Cup in 1965!) League tables, fixtures/results, results of First division games and our playing staff' completed the treasured document.

I must admit, however, that I saw an advert in Charles Buchan's Football Monthly which succeeded in tempting me to swap my complete set of home programmes for Don Revie's Happy Wanderer book, without a dust cover, but these have been lovingly replaced over the years for my delectation, and yours, in this publication!

The programme was, of course, only sold inside the ground.

Chelsea, managed by Ted Drake, were ninth with three points and City seventeenth with two points.

At City: Pre-war we'd only four losses in eighteen games, and post five wins, including an exciting 5-4 last season, four draws, no losses, so a home banker?

Recent attendances ranged from 20,733 (52/53) to 49,791(51/52) It was our sixtieth league meeting plus two cup ties, both at City 1915 third round 0-1 (32,000), 1948 fourth round 2-0 (45,059).

On the Saturday, after our Wednesday game last week, Chelsea had drubbed Birmingham City 5-1 at the Bridge so we were all set for a humdinger at Maine Road. Jimmy Greaves, however, was out owing to an injury sustained in a collision with Gil Merrick, Birmingham's goalie.

Team News: Fagan in for Clarke

From 'Old International' in The Guardian: Chelsea Suffer Heavy Defeat

The strange proceedings of tonight's game began with a novel appeal over the loud speakers for any registered referee or linesman to report to the office. After a second appeal a volunteer presented himself.

Chelsea went ahead through **Brabrook** in the second minute, when Bert misjudged a low shot, unprecedented in the great man's record, which accelerated over his shoulder into the net. Then came a real sensation which the crowd did not at first appreciate. After twenty five minutes Barnes was penalised for fouling Stubbs and indulged in a short altercation.

While the free-kick was being prepared, Bobby Johnstone was seen to leave the field and it transpired that he was sent off - for saying something naughty - to the ref.? - He thought the ref would then balance things up by sending off a Chelsea player, which he did! **Colin Barlow** smashed in City's equaliser on thirty four minutes, then on thirty six minutes MacFarlane made a flying tackle on Joe Hayes and was sent off.

Then immediately afterwards City scored two goals in two minutes, from the recalled **Paddy Fagan** and **Billy McAdams**, so 3-1 at half time.**Colin Barlow** netted the fourth in the seventieth minute, and my mate Jack assured me that there was no way we could lose, as **Lewis** hit back, then **Paddy** scored a fifth for City straight afterwards, just on full time.

FINAL SCORE: CITY 5 CHELSEA 2

City: Sky Blue/white: Trautmann; Leivers, Little; Barnes, Ewing, Warhurst; Barlow, Hayes, Johnstone McAdams, (Fagan in for Clarke, as proposed by The Guardian after the United game.)
Chelsea: Red shirts/white knickers: Matthews; MacFarlane, Sillett P.; Mortimore, Dicks, Saunders; Brabrook, McNichol, Allen, Stubbs, Lewis J
Attendance: 27,943 **Average:** 27,943
Referee: L.Tirebuck (Halifax)
Linesmen: H.Freeman (red flag) Godbehere (yellow flag)
League Position: 10th
Goals For: 9. Against: 8
Reserves: Lost 5-2 at Liverpool, Sept 2nd.

Chelsea finished the season in eleventh place with forty two points, and Ian McFarlane later joined City as first team coach. They went down in 1962, came back up in '63, won the league cup in '65, were FA Cup runners up in '67, winners in 1970, Euro Cup Winners Cup winners in '71, beating a depleted City team in the semi. League cup runners up in 1972, downs/ups in the 70's/80's, including a 5-4 Full Members cup win over City in 1986, finally reaching real finals in the 90's, winning cups and taking over the Premierhip in the 2000's

Jack and I walked it back to town singing Elvis's *Loving Teddy Bear*, a catchy song, which was out in the summer. But I hasten to add, as most of the United fans at school were Elvis fans too, always going for the obvious, I was a Buddy Holly boy, until he became trendy and later Roy Orbison's voice blew me away.

Bert looks to be out with an inflamed right shoulder for Saturday. Bobby Johnstone reckons he was sent off v Chelsea for telling Ken Barnes, who was complaining about being pushed by a Chelsea player to "push him back". Bob was considering quitting the game if he was to be further disciplined.

4) SATURDAY SEPTEMBER 7TH 1957: K.O. 3PM: NOTTINGHAM FOREST (AWAY)

City's third away game out of the first four.

Forest were formed in 1865, and won the F.A. Cup, their single trophy in 1898. They were promoted as runners up last season.

The programme was very red and a decent 16 pages priced at 4d with a ground photo on the front cover showing a terrace on one side awaiting the completion of a new stand, not quite yet in place.

The Chairman, rather pompously, advised the fans that their aim was to consolidate, that they were happy to be called Nottingham (not Notts.) Forest football CLUB - the only true club in the league, as they were run by a Committee, instead of a board of directors, with a happy family spirit.

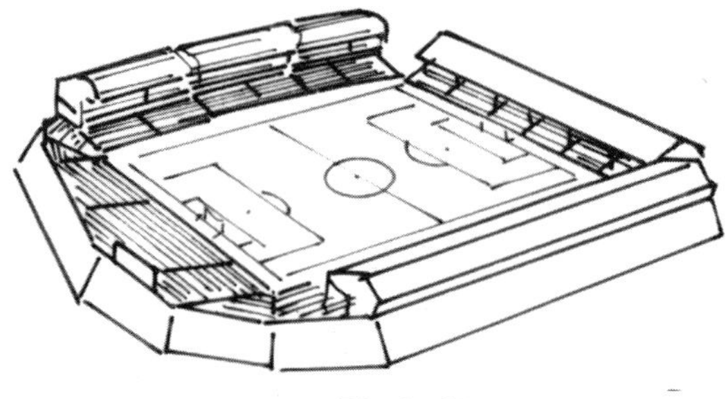

Pitch Size: 115 x 78 yds

The City Ground's current capacity was 45,000, soon to go up to 50,000 when the new stand would be opened in October v United. It comprised a Dutch barn style roofed seated main stand with a terrace in front (this burnt down in a '68 game v Leeds and was replaced). A small covered Trent End, and the new part seated/terraced stand along the length of the pitch. They also had a bit of a Kop which was strangely cordoned off in the middle by fencing, so that if you wanted to stand directly behind the goal you had to pay extra, which I found out on my first visit in 58/59 (lost 4-0). Floodlights were added in 1961, and the ground was almost completely re-developed during the 70's, 80's and 90's.

Forest, managed by Billy Walker had started in the first division with a great run of results, winning 2-1 at Sheff Wed., 2-0 at Birmingham, with a home win against Preston 2-0, and a 1-1 draw v Birmingham, making them joint top.

At Forest: Pre-war we'd won four, and drawn one of the last five, and post had just the one game a 1-0 win, played at Meadow Lane as the City Ground was flooded in 46/47. 32,194 attended. This was our thirty third league meeting plus two cup ties both at City.

Team News: Savage in for Bert, who was suffering from a shoulder injury received v Chelsea, Sear in for the injured Leivers.

From The Pink/Green:
Ill Luck Of the Irish Leaves City Gloomy

Forest, joint first division leaders, were first on the attack, with conditions perfect for football and watched by Forest's biggest crowd of the season, so far.

Wilson and Barrett threatened but were thwarted by Savage, Little and Ewing in turn, and Fagan brought out a great save from Thomson. After a shaky first fifteen minutes City were now coming more into the game, but Bailey came closest for Forest, though he was given offside. Forest then got the ball into the net from a Gray cross but Imlach was judged to have 'palmed' the ball through. Johnstone earned a round of applause for brilliant footwork in which he beat two men before back-flicking a glorious pass to Barnes who couldn't get Hayes away.

On thirty minutes Forest went ahead when Morley's sizzling thirty yard shot wasn't held by Savage who rolled it to **Wilson** who scored from five yards. This was tough luck on big John who until this unfortunate slip had played a fine game. Forest nearly went further ahead a minute later, Imlach beating Ewing for speed, but Savage came out causing him to shoot wide. City's attacking attempts were breaking down due to bad passing, and apart from an odd touch of brilliance from Johnstone.

City were making a modest Forest side look better than it actually was, as Savage made a couple of good saves to end the half. Forest continued to pile on the pressure, with Bailey outstanding, but City should have equalised in the fifty fourth minute when Johnstone put Barlow away. The winger cutting in beat his man but shot over. Then on fifty eight minutes, with City looking more dangerous, Fagan's shot was finger-tipped onto the cross-bar by Thomson and bounced away.

On sixty minutes though Forest went further ahead when, from Thomson's clearance **Barrett** resisted tackles by Ewing and Barnes to beat the advancing Savage with a glorious angled shot. Forest were playing good football now with the City defence at sixes and sevens, but it was City who scored the final goal, **Joe Hayes** netting two minutes from time, after running onto a short pass from Johnstone and flicking the ball into the net with his right foot as Thomson leapt forward despairingly.

BOB McKINLAY

FINAL SCORE: FOREST 2 CITY 1

Attendance: 37,041 **Average:** 48,005
Forest: Red shirts/white shorts: Thomson; Hutchinson, Thomas; Morley, McKinlay, Burkitt; Gray, Barrett, Wilson, Baily, Imlach
City: Sky blue/white: Savage; Sear, Little; Barnes, Ewing, Warhurst; Barlow, Hayes, Johnstone, McAdams, Fagan
Referee: A.W.Luty (Leeds)
Linesmen: D.H.Harrison, J.H.Hobson
League position: 11th
Goals For: 10 Against: 10
Reserves: Lost 2-1 at home to Huddersfield

Bert in his MEN column reckoned that subs should be allowed, but only for goalies! Stockport's Barrie Betts had now returned the £500 compensation he was awarded after injury was thought to have ended his career, but after battling back to fitness the football League wouldn't agree to let him start to play again, but would reconsider. Betts, did of course join City in 1960. Keith Marsden would be the mystery man in the new plan v Preston.

Barry Betts

5) WEDNESDAY SEPTEMBER 11Th 1957
K.O. 7.30PM: PRESTON NORTH END (HOME)

Home again, and mid-week again, so the usual routine for Jack and myself, though this was to be the last time we attended a game together, for no particular reason. (I met up with him again at a Swinton supporters club 'do' around 1997) Tonight, however, it was pouring down, so we paid our extra 3d and transferred to the Kippax, where it was lovely and dry. However, I'm almost ashamed to admit that whilst I was perched on the barrier half way up the terrace I had to make a quick descent as some pervert was trying to interfere with me, though my Dad hadn't told me of such people. Obviously it was a Preston fan.

Preston were formed in 1881, doing the double in 1889, winning the league in 1890, five times runners up, cup in 1938, four times runners up, last as recently as 1954. They were third last season with 56 points.

The programme's editorial headlined with 'This Form Upset The Pessimists', referring to the Northern Sportswriters who thought the game v Chelsea would be flat owing to Jimmy Greaves being missing. Then "one of these dismal Jimmies, (not Greaves, obviously!) after the game admitted he should have known better when City are playing!" The Ed goes on to praise the team's performance, especially without ace schemer Bobby Johnstone, sent off early in the game, and added that the Forest game was a disappointment, but reckons on the evidence so far, the pessimists are being premature, to say the least.

In Maine Road Gossip it was pointed out that City now have more covered accommodation than any other league ground, more than United, Everton, Spurs, Villa and Hillsborough. Also the ground committee are having their annual hot pot dinner and social evening at the Waldorf Hotel

In Sportsman's Corner, a United fan is corrected for thinking that they scored more goals than any other club in the league last season (if it ain't true, make it up, eh, they were at it even then!) . Spurs, Leicester, Derby, scoring more.

Arthur Walmsley suggested that fans would be more interested in seeing their club win a trophy than England winning the World Cup.
The Musical Programme by the Beswick Prize band was listed.

David Jack reflected on Len Shackleton's retirement from football. Len was a character and probably most famous for the blank page in his 'Clown Prince Of Soccer' book, with the caption "the average director's knowledge of football!"

The back page informed us that it was 4/9d to Preston, and 10/9d to Smethwick on the train

Preston, managed by Cliff Britton, were twelfth with four points and City were eleventh with four points also. They'd lost all three away games, but won all three home games so far.

At City: Pre-war they'd three wins out of the last four, and post-war six wins to City's three. So formidable opposition.

Recent attendances ranged from 20,002 (47/48) to 57,663 (51/52) It was the sixty fifth league meeting plus seven cup ties, all pre-war, three at City, 1902 first rd replay 0-0 7,000). 1915 first rd replay 3-0 (19,985) 1948 fifth rd 0-1 (67,494)

Team News: City's line up got the old tongues wagging, with Keith Marsden coming in for Colin Barlow and playing behind the forwards.

From The Guardian's 'Old International': Old Plan Rejuvenated

In the sort of weather that would make a duck billed platypus raise its eyebrows, a sizeable crowd took advantage of extra cover at Moss Side to watch City beat Preston. There was sufficient points of interest to induce the enthusiasts to brave the weather, for instance the prospect of rousing duels between Ewing and Finney, bovine strength as against feline stealth. There was also the intrigue of the new secret plan which amongst other things allowed Ewing to stick close to Finney and he could not have done this better if he was a belladonna plaster.

It was certainly a departure from the orthodox and it worried Preston as Hayes had three attempts at goal and one stupendous drive from McAdams sent the ball soaring upwards off Else's fists almost as high as the floodlight pylons. The next minute City helped themselves to a well deserved opening goal. Hayes shot, Cunningham saved on the goal line, the ball spurted upwards, and as it fell, **Fagan** had the distinction of scoring with his posterior.

There was a freshness and zeal about City's general approach, as effective as it was engaging, and the initial bewilderment of the Preston players in face of City's unconventional tactics certainly gave the crowd something to talk about, and their continued chatter proved how much the affair was going to their liking. What a pleasure it was after recent experiences to be able to sit back and enjoy a football match in Moss Side where skill was the final arbiter and not brute force.

One wondered what solution manager Cliff Britton would have for his worried players at half time. But whatever its ultimate merits may be The Plan had given City a more compact defence and had placed a decided stranglehold on Finney. Preston's best player was Thompson with a couple of shots and a superb header, and Dagger put over the crosses that Savage plucked out of the air with ease. Then after 68 minutes **Hayes** scored City's second, more or less ensuring that The Plan would get a further airing.

FINAL SCORE: CITY 2 PRESTON 0

City: Sky blue/white: Savage; Sear, Little; Barnes, Ewing, Warhurst; Hayes, Johnstone. McAdams, Marsden, Fagan
Preston: White shirts/black shorts: Else; Cunningham, Walton;, Docherty, Dunn, O'Farrell; Dagger, Thomson, Finney, Baxter, Taylor
Attendance: 24,439 **Average:** 26,191
Referee: R.Windle (Chesterfield)
Linesmen: H.Jolly, N.Methley
League position: Up to 10th
Goals For: 12 Against: 10
Reserves: Lost at Burnley 1- 0, Sept 10th

Eric Todd thinks The Plan will be a winner, but Tom Finney thinks it's too soon to judge. No personal hearing expected for Bobby Johnstone. 4-2-4 formation played by City v Preston. Bert should be back for tomorrow's game.

6) SATURDAY SEPTEMBER 14TH K.O. 3PM PORTSMOUTH (HOME)

A Saturday home game at last, and our second home fixture on the trot, surely another two points.

Portsmouth, formed in 1898, had won the cup in 1939, were runners up to City in 1934, and won the league in '49 and '50. They finished nineteenth last season with thirty three points.

The programme editorial headed, predictably, with "Give Plan a Chance". Never had such gasps been heard when it was announced that Keith Marsden would come in and drop back as though to keep a fatherly eye on John Savage". It was pointed out that the players were enthusiastic about The Plan, and the rest of us must just sit back now and await developments.

Directors :
Messrs. A. DOUGLAS (*Chairman*) E. GILL D. F. HAMER F. R. JOLLY W. SMITH
Manager : Mr. LESLIE J. McDOWALL *Secretary :* Mr. WALTER GRIFFITHS
'Phone : MOSs Side 1191

Vol. 52 No. 3 (Entered at Stationers' Hall) SATURDAY, 14th SEPT., 1957

GIVE PLAN A CHANCE

By THE EDITOR

MAINE-ROAD supporters are accustomed to surprises of one kind and another, but it is a long time since I heard such gasps as those on Wednesday night when the City team changes were announced. And when "Number 10," Keith Marsden, dropped back as if to keep a fatherly eye on John Savage, well . . .!

Conditions were deplorable, and Preston North End are not exactly the ideal team against whom experiments should be made—remember what happened at Deepdale when the deep centre forward plan was put into operation for the first time in a League match?—but the desired results were achieved in as much as City won and did not concede a goal. It may be said fairly, therefore, that the plan was successful, and that the long missing depth in defence was established.

It is obviously too soon to pass final judgment, but at least the City club, and particularly manager Mr. Leslie McDowall deserve praise for their enterprise. For the most part, City supporters and followers are among the most tolerant as well as loyal in the country, but when things are not going too well they do not hesitate to voice their feelings and suggest remedies most of which are untenable!

For obvious reasons all the advice cannot be taken, but the club are quite alive to the various needs, and when the occasion arises, they do their best to satisfy them.

Introduction of the new plan is a case in point, and it is up to everybody to give it a fair chance. The players are thoroughly enthusiastic about it, and after all that is the chief thing. The rest of us must just sit back now and await developments.

Voucher Scheme

The voucher scheme for the application of big match tickets will be in operation again this season and once again I give a brief explanation of how it works.

In every City programme, for first and second team matches, a voucher will appear in the corner of a page. You are asked to save these vouchers until called upon to send them to Maine Road in making application for big match tickets. Supporters who travel with the first team should save away programmes which will be accepted in lieu of vouchers.

Because demand exceeds supply the system does not guarantee receipt of a big match ticket but is aimed at a distribution of such tickets which will give regular supporters a fair deal.

Vouchers should be pasted in the appropriate numbered square on the pink sheet that accompanies this programme. This voucher sheet will appear for the last time in the programme at our next home game against Tottenham Hotspur, so mind you don't lose it—or your vouchers !

KEEP THIS COUPON and watch for ticket match announcements

MANCHESTER CITY F.C.
No. 6 14.9.57
TICKET COUPON

In Maine Road Gossip it was reported that Roy Clarke had received a benefit cheque for £1,000, and Jack Dyson £750. Also that the first public trial match had realised £634 6s to be distributed to local organisations.

Arthur Walmsley, in his column, praised City for The Plan saying it reflected credit on all at Maine Road, for attempting to tackle the early season problems instead of whinging about injuries, lack of top class signings and bad luck, finishing off with "such courage deserves a square deal from Lady Luck".

David Jack, in his 'It's suicide for some' column, was wary about the end of season split of the third divisions north and south into the third and fourth divisions, suggesting that clubs like Coventry, Palace *(who both eventually made it to the first!)*, Hull etc could be forced to 'put up the shutters'.

Back page advised 4/9d to Preston, 10/9d to Smethwick on the train.

Portsmouth, managed by Freddie Cox, were in sixth place with seven points and City tenth place with six points. They'd had a mixed start to this season, doubling Spurs, losing at Newcastle and Preston, drawing at home to Burnley, and beating Sheffield Wednesday.

At City: Pre-war they lost the last two. Post war they'd lost the last two, 5-1, and 4-1, so it was looking good.

Recent attendances ranged from 24,364 (56/57) to 51,490 (48/49). It was the forty first league meeting plus one cup final, City won 2-1, and one cup tie, 1936 third round, 3-1 (53,340) at City.

Team News: Bert was back, Leivers in for Sear,

From The Guardian's W.R.Taylort: Limitations Of City's New Plan

This was the second showing of The Plan which has the effect of reducing the attack to four forwards and having an extra centre half patrolling behind all the other members of the defence except the goalkeeper. With Marsden as the last line of defence, Ewing was left to haunt McLellan, Portsmouth's centre forward throughout the game, who became more useful as a decoy than a spearhead.

Flaws in The Plan became apparent when despite the promptings of Barnes and Warhurst, who worked like beavers, the attack was always a man short and goals will not always be presented as they were by Portsmouth. The weight thrown on the remaining forwards was enormous. It always will be so even if each pulls his weight all the time and this could not be said of Johnstone on Saturday. The Plan does not improve the game as a spectacle, and this match had little to commend it. The chill of autumn was in the air and the quality of the football did little to raise the temperature.

Jimmy Dickinson

There was precious little excitement in the first twenty minutes but Portsmouth were playing the better football and Trautmann finely turned a Harris header round the post. City went ahead against the run of play from a free kick on the centre line which Ewing lofted goalwards into the penalty area where it missed all heads and **Johnstone** hooked it into the net. There were misunderstandings in the City defence, then Warhurst had a point blank shot superbly saved. Portsmouth were looking highly vulnerable but **Harris** scored a beautiful equaliser after a fine movement with Gordon had left Marsden downfield.

The winning goal was the softest imaginable and again followed a free kick. **Ewing** no doubt heartened by his earlier effort tried again and lobbed the ball from 45 yards high into the goalmouth, this time against the wind. No one made any moves towards it. Barnett watched it placidly enough without exerting himself and it went into the net unmolested possibly pulled down by the wind at the last moment. No wonder Barnett squatted on his haunches in abject misery. The delighted laughter will ring in his ears for a very long time.

FINAL SCORE: CITY 2 PORTSMOUTH 1

City: Sky Blue/white: Trautmann; Leivers, Little; Barnes, Ewing, Warhurst; Hayes, Johnstone, McAdams, Marsden, Fagan
Portsmouth: Red shirts/white knickers: Barnet; Gunter, Wilson; Phillips, Rutter, Dickinson; Harris, Gordon, McClellan, Barnard, Henderson.
Attendance: 28,798 **Average:** 27,060
Referee: G.E. Oliver (Middlesbrough)
Linesmen: L. Horner, H.P.Hackney
League Position: Up two places to 8th spot.
Goals For: 14 Against: 11
Reserves: Lost 3-1 at Bury

I went to this game on my own, and had a fine moment on my way home. Picked up a Green at the Bull's Head corner in Swinton (still there).

Looked for United's result and saw they'd lost 4-0 at Bolton. So there I was, wearing my City scarf and bob hat with the biggest smile on my face in my life (after the '56 cup final win!). I looked up and there was the United coach stuck at the traffic lights, with Matt Busby in the front seat with the most miserable look on his face. Priceless. Naturally I waved, but no response from the miserable bunch.

Ray Sambrook from Coventry announced as a City target. Johnny Hart's leg is back in plaster, out for another five weeks. Recent Plan criticised for being dull and negative. Sheff. Wed. game re-arranged. Confirmed £20 per week for players and 2½% of some transfer fees.

A flu bug was still affecting players. We were advised 'Don't pan The Plan'. Stoke had made a bid for Billy McAdams

Sept 18: Lg Ireland 1 Scot League 5, at Dalymount Park 23,000.

7) WEDNESDAY SEPTEMBER 18TH 1957 K.O. 7PM: PRESTON NORTH END (AWAY)

The train left too early for me, 4.40 pm from Victoria, so a no go I'm afraid. Jack made it though and gave me a full run down on how hopeless City were.

Programme was a small A5-ish edition, of sixteen pages. Their 'Meet the Opposition' feature, made interesting reading. "Last week's rare victory over North End at Maine Road, gave City satisfaction but their line up bore little resemblance to that printed in the programme. (oh dear) Should this shake up appear again this evening then little may be gained by reference to the numbers on the backs of some of the Sky Blue shirts". Savage, Sear, Little, Barnes, Ewing and Warhurst are 'pen pictured'. Then "the fun begins with inside right Hayes on the wing, Johnstone will probably be number eight, but he'll pop up all over the place. Number nine will be Bill McAdams, Keith Marsden, the ex centre half, will probably spend his time roaming in the gloaming between his goalkeeper and the two full backs and Dave Ewing. Outside left will be Fionan Fagan, the only forward likely to stay put for any length of time. Other possibles were Colin Barlow and Roy Clarke". So Preston were obviously worried to death!

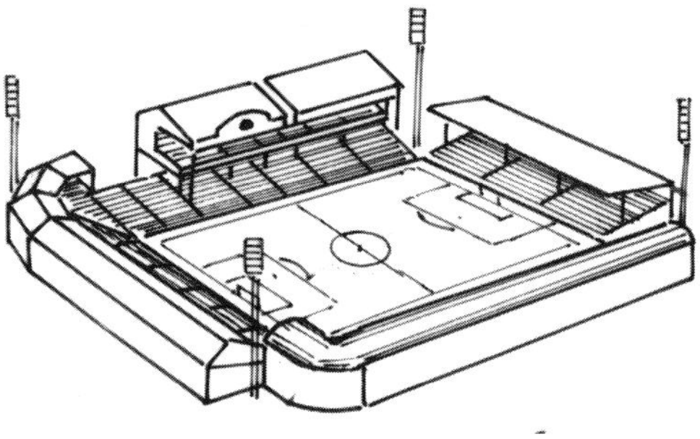

Pitch Size: 112 x 78 yds

The wonderfully named Deepdale's record attendance was only 42,684 v Arsenal in 1938. I first made it here in 58/59, for a 2-0 loss.

Main stand was small but distinctive, seats and paddock. Opposite was another small Dutch barn type roofed structure with loads of posts, seats and standing and curved round the terrace. One end was roofed, and the other partly roofed and also curved round the terrace.

They later utilised a plastic pitch, and redeveloped all three sides of the ground, leaving just the main stand, plus housing the National Football Museum.

Preston, managed by Cliff Britton, were thirteenth with six points and City were eighth with eight points. They'd had one game on the Saturday in between the City match and beat Spurs 3-1 at home.

At Preston: Pre-war we'd won twelve and lost seven. Post-war we'd won three but lost five getting walloped 6-2, 5-0 at the birth of the Revie Plan, and 4-0. So daunting?

Recent attendances ranged from 23,669 (53/54) to 37,083 (52/53). It was our sixty sixth league meeting plus seven cup ties, six at Preston: 1897 first round 0-6 (6,000), 1902 first rd 1-1 abd (10,000) and second replay 2-4 (5,000), 1903 first round 1-3 (8,000), 1912 first round 1-0 (15,000), 1915 first round 0-0 (14,000), 1925 first round 1-4 (24,536).

Team News: Savage in for Bert, Sear for Leivers, Johnstone out, Barlow in.

From The Guardian's 'Old international': City's Plan comes To Grief:

Tonight, Preston, who were so obviously playing in the light of their experience of The Plan in its first showing last Wednesday, seemed to be revelling in it this time, to such an extent that Tommy Doc, acting as a sixth forward, and Tom Finney, untroubled by Ewing's man marking, relished the gaps left in City's formation as Preston racked up six goals to City's one. Four of Preston's goals coming in the final half hour. City's forwards were non existent as the Preston forwards monopolised so much of the evening for shooting practice, and from close range too. By the sixty fifth minute proceedings became not only farcical but hilarious.

TOMMY DOCHERTY

By this time **Dagger** had opened the scoring on four minutes, after three successive corners. **Finney** with a great left foot shot made it two in the nineteenth minute with neither Ewing or Marsden around. Left winger **Taylor** swivelled and crashed home a low drive in the sixty third minute with City's defenders around but unable to move quickly enough to prevent it. Again with no City defender in sight **Thompson** banged in the fourth on sixty five minutes. Two wonder saves from bewildered goalie Savage, beating out shots from Finney and Thompson, then stemmed the rush of goals. It was debatable whether the score was a reflection of the plan or to Preston's brilliance or just to plain hallucinations. Certainly when Marsden, the lynch pin stopped a ball and left it for Thompson to smack home number five on seventy four minutes laughter just held its sides and continued when **Fagan** (the only forward to retain his position!) in the eighty second minute scored a goal of a lifetime from forty yards at least. Preston's sixth goal appropriately went to

Finney, and just beat the final whistle, to crown a great triumph for the Preston artiste.

That other teams will adopt the plan as unfolded tonight seems unlikely. As for Preston they would willingly pay money to have it tried on them every week.

FINAL SCORE: PRESTON 6 CITY 1

Preston: White shirts/blue shorts: Else; Cunningham, Walton; Docherty, Dunne, O'Farrell; Dagger, Thompson, Finney, Baxter, Taylor.
City: Sky blue/white: Savage; Sear, Little; Barnes, Ewing, Warhurst; Barlow, Hayes, McAdams, Marsden, Fagan,
Referee: G.Black (Kendal)
Linesmen: J.W.Bullough, J.A.Roberts
Attendance: 22,034 **Average:** 41,512
League position: 10th
Goals For: 15 Against: 17
Reseves: Beat Burnley 3-0 at M/R

Preston went one better than last season finishing runners up to Wolves with fifty nine points. They went down in 1961, reached the F.A. Cup final losing to West Ham in 1964, and have since stayed in the lower divisions.

O'Farrell managed Leicester when City won the Cup against them in '69, and like Docherty went on to manage United *(but badly)*.

8) SATURDAY SEPTEMBER 21ST 1957
K.O. 3PM: WEST BROMWICH ALBION (AWAY)

It was announced that City 'won't ditch the plan.' Things couldn't get any worse than a 6-1 loss at Preston, could they? You bet.

West Bromwich Albion were formed in 1879. They won the first division in 1920, the cup in 1888, 1892, 1931, 1954 (almost doing the double, finishing runners up to Wolves) so formidable opposition.

Programme had a strange front cover with a headless player shown in the ground viewed from one end. It was a threepenny job, twelve pages, covering the visitors, their Russian tour part three, and not much else.

The (beautifully named) **Hawthorns**' record attendance was 64,815 v Arsenal in 1937. I first made it for the cup tie in January. Main stand was small, seats and terrace. Opposite was a Dutch barn type roofed stand, some seats and uncovered terrace in front similar to that behind the goal, with M and B plastered all over, and an uncovered terrace behind the other goal. Ground, highest in the country, was completely re-developed in the 80's, 90's and 2000's.

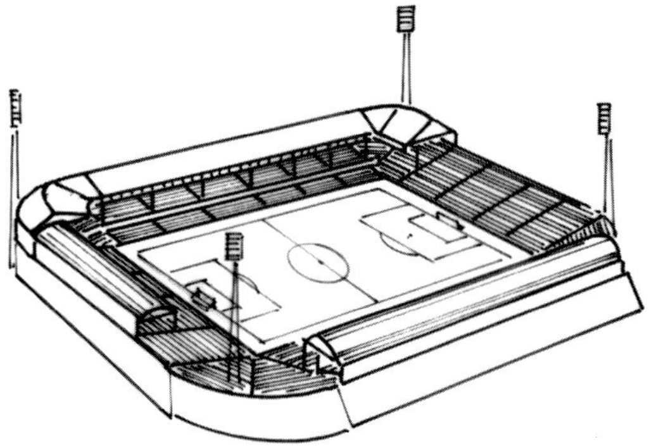

Pitch Size: 115 x 75 yds

West Brom, managed by Vic Buckingham (shouldn't he have managed Palace?), were fifth with ten points and City eleventh with eight points. They'd won two at home, drawn one and lost one to Arsenal. Away they'd won one drawn three (all 2-2) and hadn't lost.

At WBA: Pre-war we hadn't won any of the last sixteen games, post, just the solitary 4-0 win in '56 proving it could be done?!

Recent attendances ranged from 16,780 (49/50) to 38,567 (53/54). It was the sixty fifth league meeting plus one cup tie, 1901 first round 0-1 (16,000) at WBA

Team News: Branagan in for Sear, McTavish in for Warhurst , Barlow out, all with flu. Clarke in. Albert Bourne travelled as twelfth man. McDowall was away on a scouting trip.

For Albion Ronnie Allen's place was taken by Jimmy Dugdale, and Bobby Robson replaced Maurice Setters.

From The Pink/Green: Plan-less City Go Down like Ninepins

City retained the M-Plan, with Marsden standing only a yard or two away from Ewing, with only four forwards up. Even so, City's forwards produced the first attacking move of the match, going through Albion's defence but Fagan on the right running Clarke's cross over the bye-line. Ewing then partially headed a clearance which went to Horobin, whose long range right footed shot went wide of the post. Albion then gave some idea of how the plan could be beaten when Barlow sent a superb long-range pass from the half way line over Marsden's head for Robson to chase but Savage got there first. Kevan came close twice as did Whitehouse and Dudley, after Sanders had stopped McAdams' shot on the eighteen yard line.In the twenty first minute Howe moved up and let go a right footed drive from thirty five yards which was going past the post, Savage thinking so too, but it struck **Marsden**, again marking nobody, and trickled just inside the upright and over the line for one nil.

Dudley was twice inches away from putting Albion further ahead. Savage made tremendous saves and Kevan nearly blistered the paint on the cross-bar.But in the thirty sixth minute Albion did make it two, the direct result of this crazy clustered up City defence. Griffin beat Little and found Ray Barlow unmarked in the inside right position, who hit a right footer into the crowded goalmouth and the ball hit **Whitehouse** and was deflected past the helpless Savage, for another freak goal. Then three minutes later **Clarke** fastened on to a cross from McAdams to beat Sanders with a shot from twelve yards out, to pull one back. Two minutes later, on forty one minutes however, Ray Barlow laid on a pass to the right wing where despite City's packed defence, **Griffin** was unmarked and picked his spot from ten yards, to make it 3-1 at half time.

John Savage was cheered onto the pitch after the restart and within a couple of minutes City obviously decided that the M-plan was not for them today as Marsden moved up into the

Bobby Robson

forward line. It seemed to pay off as, after a couple of Albion chances Fagan made it 3-2 in the fifty fifth minute after a stinging shot from Marsden had been blocked.

But a minute later Griffin cut in and sent over a fierce cross which Savage, with a superhuman leap could only fist out to **Robson** who nodded the ball in, for 4-2. Bert, sitting watching on the bench must have felt for John.

Ray Barlow then brought Fagan down inside the area, but Barnes to his own horror and the disappointment of his team-mates side footed the resulting penalty to Sanders' right but yards wide. **Griffin** made it 5-2 with a spectacular dribble from just outside the penalty area going past four City defenders to hit a left footer into the net on fifty eight minutes giving Savage no chance.

Barlow hit the ball inches over City's bar and Hayes and Marsden then came close, but having tried nearly everything else the City backs resorted to offside tactics. However in the seventy first minute **Horobin** sent Savage the wrong way and into the net went number six. Still City pressed with McAdams and Hayes going close but Albion made it seven, **Howe** scoring from a penalty after an alleged foul by Ewing on Horobin, on seventy nine minutes. **Griffin** having moved over to outside left then hooked a beauty into the net from seven yards out in the eighty first minute. Five minutes from time McTavish took the ball full in the pit of the stomach and while he was lying doubled up Kevan went on only to be brought down by Ewing. This was too much for Savage who booted the ball high into the crowd. When it came back, **Kevan** scored number nine from the spot.

So it was 3-1 in the first half with the M-plan, and 6-1 in the second without it, City's biggest defeat since the 0-8 at Wolves in 33/34.

FINAL SCORE: WBA 9 CITY 2

W.B.A.: Navy blue and white striped shirts/white shorts: Sanders: Howe, Williams S.: Dudley, Kennedy, Barlow; Griffin, Whitehouse, Robson, Kevan, Horobin.
(Good job Ronnie Allen wasn't playing!)
City: Claret/black: Savage; Branagan, Little; Barnes, Ewing, McTavish; Fagan, Hayes, McAdams, Marsden, Clarke
Attendance: 26,080 **Average:** 38,4..
Referee: N.C.Taylor (Westbury)
Linesmen: D.King (Pontypridd) W.J.Madden (Bedminster)
League position: down four places to 14th spot
Goals For: 17 Against: 26
Reserves: Beat Chesterfield 5-1 at M/R

Fifteen goals conceded in the last two away games, the heaviest defeat since at Wolves in 1934, and surely the end of The Plan?

Much criticism of the new Plan in the press. Reckoned it was ditched at half time!?

Wales 4 East Germany 1, W/C qualifier in Cardiff (17,000).
England u-23's 6 Bulgaria 2, at Stamford Bridge (56,391).
Mac capped for N.Ireland v Scotland on October 5th.
Frank Swift became the first president of the supporters' club.

9) SATURDAY SEPTEMBER 28th K.O. 3PM: TOTTENHASM HOTSPUR (HOME)

Could the Blues bounce back from two humiliating defeats, or would they continue to crumble?

Spurs were formed in 1882 but didn't join division two until after the first war, winning the cup as a non league side in 1901. They won it again in 1921, and after their promotion in 1950, won the div. one title with Arthur Rowe's 'push and run' style of play in '51. They were runners up in '52, and also last season. Strangest transfer deal between the clubs was when Bert Sproston travelled up with the Spurs party, transferred to City for £10,000, and played against his old team on November 5th 1938, City won 2-0, and attracted a crowd of 47,998, the highest of the season.

B. SPROSTON (MANCHESTER CITY)

The programme's editorial was as shell-shocked as everyone and entitled 'What a Harassing Week'. It went on to say that there could be few genuine supporters who haven't sympathised with manager Les McDowall. Injuries and sickness upset his calculations, and his hope of a quiet weekend on his return from a 'scouting mission' to Scotland were shattered by news of the crushing defeat at West Brom, leading to numerous personal and telephone calls from people who wanted to know when the funeral of his new defensive plan would take place. No wonder he sought sanctuary elsewhere, and no wonder he had to wait until the last possible moment before deciding which team to pick and what formation to use.

Drastic, but not panic, action would be needed, after fifteen goals in two games, and it could have been more, but for the fine goalkeeping of Big John Savage. The future of the plan depends on whether Mac thinks he has the players capable of carrying it out.

We were also reminded that it would be the last appearance of the pink voucher sheet - cut out your vouchers (and ruin your programme!) paste them into the appropriate numbered square, and get ready to send them off to Maine Road. Front covers of away programmes would be accepted in lieu of reserve team vouchers.(no photocopiers in those days!)

Maine Road Gossip reflected on Spurs' good form at Maine Road. It also reminded fans that ex Blue Harry Anders, after his Port Vale spell, has settled at Accrington. Johnny Hannaway is Gillingham's popular captain, Errol Crossan who, after his time at Gillingham is now among the leading scorers at Southend, and Jimmy Gunning is at Lancs. Combination club, Nelson

Sportsman's Corner had no questions that were too scintillating.

There was no **Arthur Walmsley**, so page seven showed a photo of Bobby's goal against Spurs in the semi-final of 1956, which City won 1-0, despite Spurs' loud claims for a penalty though Bert later admitted holding George Robb's leg, instinctively, you understand!

Miss Sylvia Farmer was officially listed as the vocalist with the Beswick Prize Band, conductor, Albert Risby.

No **David Jack** either, so Derrick Collier penned a piece entitled 'the LSD *(pounds, shillings and pence, not the hallucinatory drug!)* of soccer', explaining that with the bank rate being at 7% it was a topical subject. He discussed Arsenal's finances, after their profit announcement of £39,011 and went on to explain that the costs of discovering and developing young players, which when totalled, amounted to a phenomenal figure, equivalent almost to a five figure transfer fee.

Train fare to Bordesley next week was 10/9d

Spurs managed by Jimmy Anderson, were eleventh with eight points and City fourteenth also with eight points. So far this season they'd won three including a 7-1 v Birmingham, lost one and drawn one at the Lane but hadn't yet won away, drawing one and losing three including a 1-5 at Portsmouth.

One Spurs Didn't Win !

Spurs have a very good record against City since the war, but one game they didn't get away with was the Cup semi-final at Villa Park in March, 1956. City supporters will remember the 40th minute when from Roy Clarke's centre, Bobby Johnstone headed the only goal. Our photograph shows the ball going in the Spurs' net. Bobby is not to be seen—but he was in the right spot when he was wanted!

At City: Pre-war, they didn't win one out of fourteen attempts, twelve losses, two draws. Post however, they won two, drew three, lost two, and won a cup tie. The programme for the '54 home game is one of the rarest post war home league programmes. Worth about £500 today!

Recent attendances ranged from 10,841 (53/54) to 41,645 (46/47) and 50,576 (53/54 cup). It was the forty third league meeting plus seven cup ties, four at City, 1909 first round 3-4 (20,000), 1914 third round 2-1 (36,256), 1930 third round replay 4-1 (37,716), 1954 fourth round 0-1(50,576), and the '56 semi 1-0, at Villa Park (69,788).

Team News: The M-plan was well and truly ditched and City were back to the deep lying centre forward plan!.

From The Pink/Green:
City Back on With Revie Plan

City shuffled the pack, after one of the most harassing weeks since before the '56 cup final. Leivers, after recovering from ankle injury, was now down with flu, Johnstone, Barlow Sear and Johnstone returned to the team recovering from injury and illness, replacing Little, McTavish, Clarke and Marsden, but Bert was still out, Savage retaining his place after two heroic displays against the odds.

Spurs had lost only one of their last seven games at Maine Road. Conditions were deplorable with light but insistent rain and mist driving the small crowd under shelter. City took time to become accustomed to the new formation with over-passing and a reluctance to shoot first time. In the twelth minute Spurs were unlucky not to take the lead when Medwin hooked the ball well out of Savage's reach but it hit the post and bounced back into the hands of the grateful keeper. Spurs were playing good football but were getting caught offside.

Branagan was first class in everything he did. After clever work by Johnstone, McAdams, then Barlow, came close. Sear did a good job keeping out Spurs. In the 19th minute Fagan tried a shot from close in which Reynolds parried some distance and the quick thinking **Johnstone** banged the ball into the empty net while Reynolds was still on the floor. City should have made it two when Johnstone pushed a gem of a pass down the middle. Hayes was bowled over as he tried to shoot and the loose ball went to Barlow who snatched it wide. Both City and Spurs spurned chances and Savage made a splendid full length save from Medwin. In the twenty eighth minute from Barlow's centre Fagan's shot hit Iley and went to **Hayes** who smacked it into an open net. Despite the heavy conditions the play was fast and interesting and McAdams was thwarted again by Reynold's desperate dive. City were playing with more speed and confidence than in the last two matches and were good value for their two goal half time lead.

After the break Spurs played good football and maybe deserved a goal, but City nearly went further ahead when Reynolds let the ball slip out of his hands from a Barlow centre. City missed other chances and at the other end Sear was becoming the popular hero. In the sixty first minute though Spurs pulled one back as Harmer pushed the ball through to Stokes who kicked it a little too far ahead as Savage came out and **Branagan** mis-read the situation and literally dribbled the ball into his own net. 2-1, as the rain came down pitilessly. It was a tragedy that everyone in the ground just hated to see as Branagan had been in such fine form right from the start. Reynolds made a good save from McAdams' flying header on sixty five minutes and after Savage made a brilliant save from Iley, Warhurst turned Stokes' effort over the bar, and Savage saved from Blanchflower. With sixteen minutes to go it was 3-1. From a long clearance from Savage, Hayes charged through before chipping the ball to **Barlow** on the right wing who chested it down and shot past the advancing Reynolds into the net.

Danny Blanchflower

In the seventy eighth minute McAdams took a corner on the right and **Hayes** jumping higher than anyone else headed City's fourth. Spurs were now well beaten and though Dunmore and Medwin tried hard they couldn't get past Sear. Two minutes from time **Johnstone** scored a fifth from Fagan's pass, with a straight short drive. At the end Terry Medwin, Spurs winger, clapped Cliff Sear off the pitch.

FINAL SCORE: CITY 5 SPURS 1

City: Sky blue/white: Savage: Branagan, Sear: Barnes, Ewing, Warhurst: Barlow, Hayes, Johnstone, McAdams, Fagan,

Spurs: White shirts/blue knickers: Reynolds: Baker, Henry: Blanchflower, Ryden, Iley: Medwin, Harmer, Dunmore, Stokes, Dyson

Attendance: 22,497 Average: 25,919

Referee: L.Howarth (Beverley)

Linesmen: G.F. Peverelli, S.Poulton

Position: 15th spot

Goals For: 22 Against: 27

Cliff Sear reflecting years later in *Manchester - The Greatest City*: "This was one of the club's greatest team performances. It was an afternoon of torrential rain, and it was about my third game in the first team. I got my chance because the regular choice, Roy Little had been left out. On the right Ken Branagan was also a last minute choice. In fact he was in the team so late he had to be pulled off the reserve team coach that was going to West. Brom. for a Central League game. It was a tremendous all round team performance by City and a good one for me too, despite a bit of a struggle I had in the first ten minutes or so."

Reserves: West Brom away, lost 1-0, Keith Marsden broke his leg.....

Confirmed no complications re Keith Marsden's broken leg. Wolves have turned down a City bid for Harry Hooper.

CONCLUSION: There were good home wins over Chelsea, Preston, Portsmouth and Spurs, but away it was a loss at Forest, then in surely the worst four days in the history of the club, the 6-1 loss at Preston and the 9-2 defeat at WBA as the plan was ditched. City dropped to fifteenth place and the goals for went up to 22 for and 27 against. Average home attendance was 25,919, away 38,426.

LEAGUE TABLE

	P	W	D	L	F	A	Pts
Notts For . . .	10	7	1	2	23	11	15
Wolves	10	7	1	1	27	13	15
WBA	10	5	4	1	27	14	14
Man Utd	10	6	1	3	28	16	13
Everton	8	6	1	1	15	9	13
Bolton	10	5	2	3	18	15	12
Arsenal	9	5	1	3	16	13	11
Luton	10	5	1	4	11	11	11
Preston	10	5	0	5	23	18	10
Newcastle . .	10	4	2	4	15	12	10
Chelsea	10	3	3	4	24	23	9
Leeds	11	4	1	6	13	20	9
Aston Villa . .	10	3	2	5	15	16	8
Spurs	10	3	2	5	22	26	8
Man City . . .	**9**	**4**	**0**	**5**	**22**	**27**	**8**
Portsmouth .	10	3	2	5	17	21	8
Sunderland . .	11	3	2	6	15	22	8
Burnley	10	3	2	5	13	24	8
Sheff Wed . . .	9	3	1	5	15	19	7
Blackpool . . .	9	3	1	5	10	16	7
B'ham	10	2	2	6	14	29	6
Leicester . . .	10	2	0	8	18	26	4

OCTOBER'S FOOTBALL MONTHLY

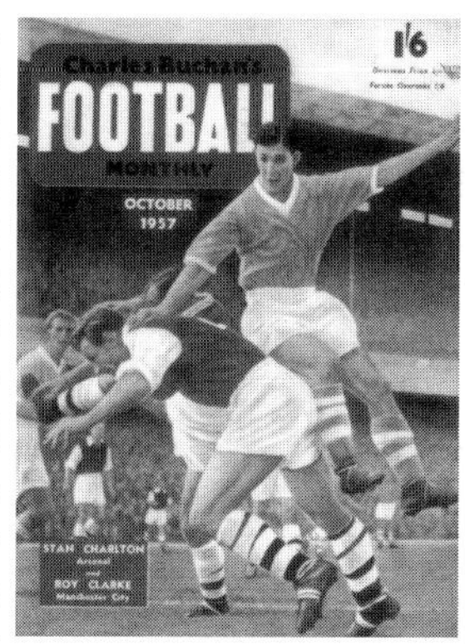

Would you believe, City's Roy Clarke was on the front cover, sat on Arsenal's Stan Charlton at last season's High-bury game (lost 7-3)? United's Bill Whelan is on the back cover (they had to balance things up didn't they?). CB's editorial looks forward to the World Cup next June. Cover point explains why Roy Clarke is unique. Wigan had three bosses last season, and Sam Barkas didn't last long this! Olympiakos and Panathinaikos teams had to have police intervention in the Greek cup final.

Once A Blue, Always A Blue

ALAN, from Gorton's story:

Born on the 2nd June, 1935, the middle child of Frank and Florence (Flo) Menzies dedicated Blues. Once a Blue, always a Blue, unlike Wayne Rooney.In season 1935/36 City finished ninth in division one when I was a babe in arms.

In 1936/37 we were Champions. I must have been a lucky charm, insisted mum and dad. Uncle George agreed. Uncle George and my dad used to cycle to away games at Sheffield, Blackburn, Bolton, Burnley and Preston. Reg Harris, eat your heart out. I found a cutting in my dad's scrapbook, going yellow, about City being the only team to be relegated the season after winning the title. Relegated after scoring eighty goals, the most in the division! Only City could do that. We finished fifth in division 2 in 38/39 before World war Two intervened until season 46/47 when we came back with a bang as division two Champions. I remember going to Maine Road with my dad and the name Dunkley comes to mind. If he had the ball I knew we were Ok. But is there anybody out there older than me who can complete the jigsaw?

My first taste of success. Sweet!

The years after were like Belle Vue Bobs. Plenty of ups and downs. Plenty of happy days following the Blues.

Demob happy in 1958 I secured a job at Horwich carpet shop, Regent Road Salford. It didn't last long. Well I had to work on a Saturday, so that was a no, no! Happy days and years followed as a bus conductor and driver.

Another bonus was that working on the buses provided a free pass to games at Maine Road. This was later abused, by drivers and guards using the passes when not working - they used to turn up in uniform at Maine Road. I know women like men in uniform, but in those days it was virtually men only, at football games.

I was working on February 6th, when a passenger informed me, at 'The Snipe', of United's plane crash. I was saddened by the disaster, as one of Gorton's own, Roger Byrne, perished, but didn't MUFCPLC milk it over the years?

I used to watch United at Maine Road when City allowed them to play there, after Uwe Rosler's grandad bombed O/T. Dad took me when United played Yeovil Town, in the F.A.Cup, which was an afternoon midweek game. My teacher at Stanley Grove was not impressed with the note from my mother explaining my absence. "What's the World coming to", he wailed. Charlie Mitten was a great penalty taker, like Ken Barnes. Charlie boy, always aimed for the stanchion, and never missed his target. But City were my team.

I have fond memories of Ray Sambrook in 1958, the only player I know who could play standing up asleep. I used to watch him with Sheila, my missus, play for the reserves, when he was left out of the first team.

Ray Sambrook played his part in a memorable game at Molineux as City gave them a jolt on the day!

I went to this six goal thriller at Molineux, and can remember Colin Barlow giving Billy Wright a torrid time, and not for the first time. Billy could never cope with the jet heeled Barlow. Pity that Colin sometimes forgot the ball!

Wolves went on to lift the division one title. Preston, with Tom Finney, were second, five points behind, on fifty nine points and City were fifth on forty points.

Alan is a lifelong Blue, and season ticket holder.

TED from Droylsden's story:

Bert was my hero and my ambition was to play in the junior school team, but I was only 5'4" and the lad holding the place was 5' 11" weighing in at around twelve stone. I was better than him, and annoyingly he was a United fan, Carl Bisley, and I remember him wearing United socks. Then I learned that he'd passed the 11 plus *(what, a United fan - Ed?!)* and was going to Chorlton Grammar School. I spent all summer with a tennis ball throwing it against the wall, and got another United fan, Keith Doyle, to shoot a casey at me day after day. I practiced and practiced and was so obsessed with Trautmann that I asked my pals to call me Bert, which really made my late mother laugh.

So 57/58 was my first year at Old Moat Secondary school in Withington, and the big day came at Hough End fields. Jimmy Scott was the other keeper in contention, slightly bigger than me, quite athletic, and - oh no - he turns up in a V neck red United shirt. Most of that team were United fans, others being Tony Durras, Terry Eden, Neville Davis, and a few others all pretending to be Duncan Edwards, Bobby Charlton, Tommy Taylor, David Pegg or whoever. I, of course, was Bert and only occasionally heard shouts of Bobby Johnstone, Joe Hayes, Ken Barnes, Paddy Fagan.

In 57/58 the first fixture was away at Chelsea and I was on holiday at Lymm, Heatley to be exact, staying at my mate's Post office/sweet shop as our family couldn't afford holidays in those days. At the rear of the shop they kept pigs and next door was an engineering works. On the day of the away game at Stamford Bridge one of the workers said "City always get a good result at Chelsea." Of course in 1957 there was no radio coverage or score flashes so we were ignorant of how the game was progressing. Next morning the same chap had a big smile on his face "What did I tell you son, City won 3-2." Oscar, my mate and I jumped up with glee. Almost forty years later Heatley post office in Lymm no longer operates and the works next door is now luxury apartments.

United had gained a lot of schoolboy support in sympathy after the Munich air disaster and some had actually been to Maine Road before with their dads to every home game. It was tragic, but I have never been tempted to change my colours.

United recovered and took five years to win the cup whilst we went from bad to worse getting relegated in the same year, 1963, though they only finished nineteenth.

I continued to play in goal after 57/58 and in actual fact my second most favourite goalie was Harry Gregg, who was magnificent and used to race to the edge of his area throwing himself at the ball. Matt Busby once told him to stay on his line but that was his game. However Bert Trautmann was and still is the greatest goalie I had the privilege to see. Eventually I grew a few inches and was a whisker away from playing for Manchester Boys. I actually heard through the grapevine that I was being watched by Mr Cassidy. Unfortunately my size went against me and that was that.

Yes 57/58 was an experience. I even went to night reserve games at Old Trafford if City weren't playing. Sometimes, or most times. I should say there were 15,000 or more fans watching. Our reserves at the time used to attract around 4,000. I used to catch an MCTD bus to Great Western Street and then a number 53 to Trafford Bar. The pie and gravy sold at the top of the Old Trafford paddock was delicious, not like today's. May I add that City's weren't bad either but I only bought a pie when it was a reserve game either at the back of the Platt Lane stand or where the curve was adjoining the main stand or at the scoreboard end. For the record Wolves won the league Championship in 57/58, and even in that season I got teased by my United schoolmates on a Monday if we lost and they won. Now I get it in the pub, or I used to as I don't take the bait as much now, I just count to ten.

During this time Roy (Nobby) Clarke lived on Victoria Road, Fallowfield which was a stone's throw away from where I lived in Eddisbury Avenue Withington. My mates and I used to pass his house and look out for him and he always acknowledged us. At the time he owned the Sports Depot in Princess Road in Moss Side where we bought our football gear - laces, studs and dubbin in the tin. Later he moved to premises on the corner of Dickinson Road and Wilmslow Road, which are now a wine bar. On match days when we could afford it my mates used to meet in the Avenue and off we went stopping on the way at Mr B's toffee shop, just past the old Cresta picture house. We usually bought penny Arrow Bars, or, if it was warm, a frozen Jubbly. I sometimes used to stand on the flagpole behind the goals at the scoreboard end. During this period the training was at Shawe View, home of our A and B sides. We caught the single decker 22 bus which ran from Levenshulme to Eccles, and sometimes during the school holidays we walked it. It was always sunny when we went to Urmston. We could smell the freshly cut grass which told us the season wasn't far away. I remember the central league games at Maine Road where every fifteen minutes the first team score was relayed on the scoreboard. One game in particular was the 9-2 drubbing at West Brom. on the 21st September 1957 and the scoreboard man put the wrong score up - he had us winning 2-0, and the crowd were elated only to be gutted when he changed it around. At the end of those games we used to all congregate outside the main entrance and usually the Commissionaire gave us the bad news, when we'd lost again!

Finally October 19th 1957 was my first ever away game against Blackpool at Bloomfield Road, and they had Matthews, Perry, Gratrix, Mudie, Mortensen, but we won 5-2. That day we caught the 102 Ribble bus from Mosley Street bus station to Blackpool and after the game we went on the fun fair, ate fish and chips from the famous Pablo's on the front and viewed the illuminations. All this after a great away win. Happy days.

Ted is a lifelong blue and season ticket holder.

CAROL of Leigh's story:

57/58 was my first full season of supporting the Blues and I can remember the players of that time more vividly than many since! My dad and I used to stand behind the Platt Lane goal, which was quite hazardous when Billy McAdams was kicking in before the match. None of those gentle little testing shots for him. Those which evaded Bert used to whistle past our heads like misguided missiles. Another hazard of standing in the Platt Lane was the noise from the Colin Barlow fan club. They were a group of glamorous, peroxide and fur bedecked women who used to shriek with ecstasy whenever their hero came within twenty yards of the ball. I considered him to be something of a whimp when compared with my own favourite, Ray Sambrook. Perhaps it was Sam's haggard face which made him look as though he was close to drawing his pension, or perhaps the way he held his back in agony after completing one of his stumbling runs, or the way hundreds of fans used to shout "Sambrook, get dressed!" which made me decide to support him!

CHAPTER FOUR

OCTOBER 1957 - STEADYING THE SHIP

So, were we now on the straight and narrow, or would we slip back into M-Plan type losses? Birmingham and Blackpool away, Sheff Wed, Leicester, Luton home.

Bert has broken down in training, could be out v Birmingham. Paddy Fagan has flu.

Wednesday October 2nd, WC Qualifier: Denmark 0 Eire 2 in Copenhagen (28,000).

Saturday October 5th, Home international: N.Ireland 1 Scotland 1 in Belfast, Billy McAdams played (58,000).

Martin Bakes

Roy Paul interested in signing Roy Clarke?

City have lost interest in Hooper, who was watched and had a poor game for Wolves reserves. Still interested in Sambrook from Coventry, Arthur Kaye from Barnsley, and Martin Bakes from Bradford City (who eventually went to Scunthorpe in June 1959!).

10) SATURDAY OCTOBER 5Th 1957
K.O 3PM: BIRMINGHAM CITY (AWAY)

Birmingham were formed in 1875 as Small Heath, and after seven promotions to division one were now in their second first division season finishing twelfth last season and being F.A. Cup runners up in 1931 and 1956.

Programme was smart with an impressive front cover, possibly one of the first exponents of an angled shot of the ground. It was 3d, and contained ten pages. There were a few City snippets - flu causing the Sheff. Wed. game to be postponed, Jack Dyson breaking his leg, and the M-Plan being shattered so comprehensively at the Hawthorns, opponents seeing the answer to it.

Congratulations were given to Mr and Mrs Jeff Hall, who were married at Wilsdon near Bradford last Saturday. England international Jeff sadly died a few years later from polio

St. Andrews' record attendance was 66,844 v Everton in 1939. I didn't make it there until the next season, a 6-1 loss (but we got them back the next day 4-1) It comprised a massive steep uncovered (Tilton) end, and a similar but partly covered side terrace. There was a newish main stand, seats and paddock, still in place today, but the stadium was let down by a tiny stand behind the other goal, the Railway end, later replaced with a stand similar to the main one. All three sides were then redeveloped in the 90's.

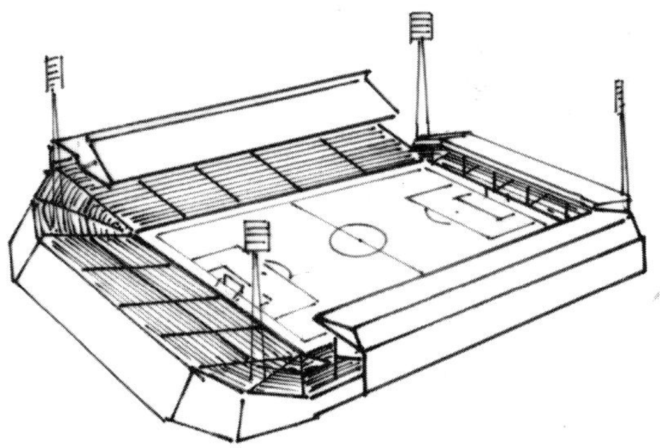

Pitch Size: 115 x 74 yds

Birmingham, managed by Arthur Turner, were twenty first with six points and City eleventh with ten points. Home form so far was two wins, two draws and two losses, and they'd had big defeats at Chelsea 5-1 when goalie Gil Merrick was carried off, and 7-1 at Spurs.

At Birmingham: Pre-war, we lost only one out of seven. Post though we'd had five losses and one draw, last season 3-3.

Recent attendances ranged from 23,747 (56/57) to 37,747 (46/47) (56,000 in the '55 6th rd cup game) It was the seventy first league meeting plus one cup final and seven cup ties, six at Birmingham: 1899 first rd 2-3 (15,399), 1927 third rd 1-4 (39,503), 1929 third rd 1-3 (25,005), 1947 fifth rd 0-5 (50,000), 1951 third rd 0-2 (30,057), 1955 sixth round 1-0, and the 1956 F.A. Cup final 3-1.

Team news: McAdams away on International duties, Leivers and Fagan out with flu, Clarke, McLelland in.

From The Pink/Green:
City Reel, Murphy Hits 3 in B'Ham Goal Rush

Les McDowall was away on his third scouting mission in a fortnight although a signing is unlikely. Two other of the club's officials were also out on scouting business - proof of the clubs ready-to-buy policy.

Roy Warhurst was captain for the day against his old club, and got a special cheer for presenting a brand new football to the tiny Blues mascot Paul Coudjre. Roy made a promising start by winning the toss, which was about as good as it got..

Only ninety seconds went by before Birmingham had the ball in the net, but it was ruled out when the ref. adjudged that Brown had handled. McLelland was brought down in the box by Green but the ref. waved play on. Before you could say 'Jack Robinson' Astall, Orrit and Murphy (the player involved in the injury to Bert in the '56 cup final) linked in a fast bout of interpassing and **Murphy** finished strongly with a low right-footer on three minutes. Only two minutes later Barnes attempted a short cross pass which was only half hit, the ball flying to Govan who fed **Murphy** who sidestepped Savage and fired into the empty net.

JEFF HALL

Birmingham continued to press with Barnes, Savage and Ewing coming to City's rescue, as the half continued in similar vein. A scuffle broke out on the terrace which required the intervention of several policemen but did little to enhance City's sporadic attacks which lacked Birmingham's aggression and power, City being lucky to be only two down at half time.

Only four minutes of the second half had elapsed when Astall (a tremendous bundle of energy) slipped a pass through to Orritt who flashed the ball across the goalmouth, Savage fumbled the ball to **Brown** who gently turned it in from six yards. The defence was equally as poor three minutes later when **Murphy** crowned a glorious down-the-middle dribble with a winning shot for the fourth goal. Clarke came close, trying to dribble round Merrick, but the keeper took the ball off his toes, and in the closing minutes Savage, showing great anticipation, leapt to bring off a fine save from Murphy. It was the only time City failed to score all season and overall the defence had a shocker.

FINAL SCORE: BIRMINGHAM 4 CITY 0

Birmingham: Blue shirts/white shorts: Merrick; Hall, Green; Watts, Newman, Neal; Astall, Orritt, Brown, Murphy, Govan
City: Claret shirts/white shorts: Savage; Branagan, Sear; Barnes, Ewing, Warhurst; McClelland, Hayes, Johnstone, Barlow, Clarke
Attendance: 28,059 **Average:** 36,698
Referee: R. Wood (Sunderland)
Linesmen: W.Williams, S.B.Stoakes
League position: Dropped to 13th
Goals For: 22 Against: 31
Reserves: Beat Stoke 3-0 at M/R

New move to speed Betts' come back, but the Football League Management Committee have refused to re-register as they do not think he's ready for the hurly burly of league football.

Fixtures for the Anglo-Scottish floodlit league announced: City v Partick Oct 14th; Hearts v City; Oct 21st; Partick v City Oct 28th; City v Hearts Nov 4th; City v Hibs Nov 11th; Hibs v City Nov 25th; Newcastle and Spurs the other teams competing. This competition was later 'scotched' by the Scottish League!

Everton have turned down City's £8,000 bid for Jimmy Gauld, but the Blues are confident of landing Harry Hooper from Wolves, and are also still considering a bid for Bradford City's Martin Bakes.

Oct 9th: F.League 3 Lg of Ireland 1 at Elland Road (13,000).

Scots Lg 7 Irish Lg 0 at Ibrox (35,000).

11) WEDNESDAY OCTOBER 9TH 1957
K.O. 7.30 PM: SHEFFIELD WEDNEDAY (HOME)

Yet another mid week game, the re-arranged fixture with Wednesday, and a chance to bounce back again.

Wednesday were formed in 1867, they won the title in 1903, 1904, 1929, and 1930, the Cup in 1896, 1907, and 1935, but had been up and down in recent years and were becoming known as the yo-yo team. Last season they were fourteenth with thirty eight points

Programme 's editorial was titled 'They Made No Excuses', and quoted the well known French expression, familiar to City fans, "Qui s'excuse s'accuse" interpreted as "Who excuses himself accuses himself" and if applied to football means "If you play badly and take a hammering, don't try and wriggle out of it by blaming the weather, the pitch or even injuries" then went on to say that after a merciless hammering in the last 3 away games, City got plenty of genuine respect for the sporting way they took defeat. (Well that's some consolation!) We were told that City were looking far and wide for new

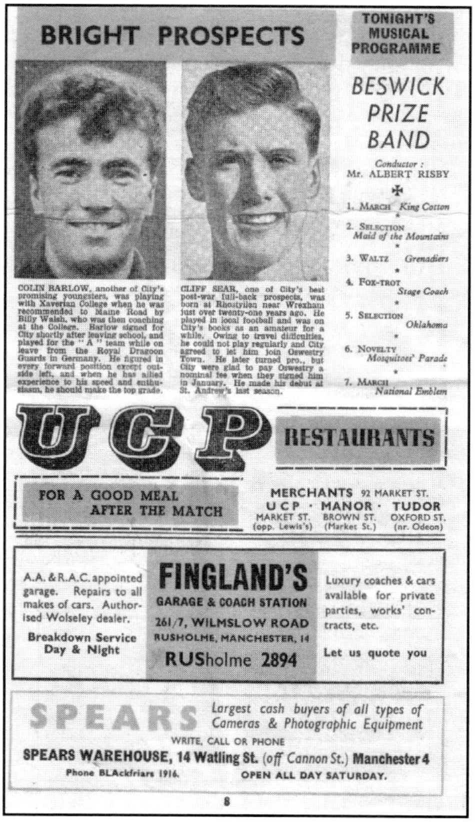

BRIGHT PROSPECTS

TONIGHT'S MUSICAL PROGRAMME

BESWICK PRIZE BAND

Conductor: Mr. ALBERT RISBY

1. MARCH King Cotton
2. SELECTION Maid of the Mountains
3. WALTZ Grenadiers
4. FOX-TROT Stage Coach
5. SELECTION Oklahoma
6. NOVELTY Mosquitoes' Parade
7. MARCH National Emblem

COLIN BARLOW, another of City's promising youngsters, was playing with Xaverian College when he was recommended to Maine Road by Billy Walsh, who was then coaching at the College. Barlow signed for City shortly after leaving school, and played for the "A" team while on leave from the Royal Dragoon Guards in Germany. He figured in every forward position except outside left, and when he has allied experience to his speed and enthusiasm, he should make the top grade.

CLIFF SEAR, one of City's best post-war full-back prospects, was born at Rhostyllen near Wrexham just over twenty-one years ago. He played in local football and was on City's books as an amateur for a while. Owing to travel difficulties, he could not play regularly and City agreed to let him join Oswestry Town. He later turned pro., but City were glad to pay Oswestry a nominal fee when they signed him in January. He made his debut at St. Andrew's last season.

UCP RESTAURANTS

FOR A GOOD MEAL AFTER THE MATCH

MERCHANTS 92 MARKET ST.
U C P · MANOR · TUDOR
MARKET ST. (opp. Lewis's) BROWN ST. (Market St.) OXFORD ST. (nr. Odeon)

A.A. & R.A.C. appointed garage. Repairs to all makes of cars. Authorised Wolseley dealer.
Breakdown Service Day & Night

FINGLAND'S
GARAGE & COACH STATION
261/7, WILMSLOW ROAD
RUSHOLME, MANCHESTER, 14
RUSholme 2894

Luxury coaches & cars available for private parties, works' contracts, etc.
Let us quote you

SPEARS Largest cash buyers of all types of Cameras & Photographic Equipment
WRITE, CALL OR PHONE
SPEARS WAREHOUSE, 14 Watling St. (off Cannon St.) Manchester 4
Phone BLAckfriars 1916. OPEN ALL DAY SATURDAY.

8

players but whilst the money was there they would have to be "the right man, or men." In Wednesday's squad they had a Walter and two Alberts plus Tom McAnearney (and his brother Jim) and as the old joke goes three players in one!

Maine Road Gossip reviewed previous City v Wednesday encounters.

Sportsman's Corner clarified City goalie Charlie Williams' goal from a goalkick which Sunderland goalie Doig fumbled into his net, April 14th 1900. If he hadn't touched it, it would have been a goal kick.

Arthur Walmsley was back, with his 'City's Silver Lining' piece, this time commending the club, after the recent three seasons of serious injury to players such as Johnny Hart, Bert Trautmann, Jimmy Meadows, and Jack Dyson. The club had paid for the best possible treatment for these players and he reckons the surgeons' bills wouldn't be far off the price of one star player 'in these days of inflated transfer fees!'

Cliff Sear and Colin Barlow had their mugshots in, being described as 'Bright Prospects.'

David Jack wrote about Wednesday's yo-yo years, and hoped it would be a long while before "the yo-yo travels down the string again", for them.

Train to Blackpool 7 shillings.

Wednesday, managed by Eric Taylor, were twenty first with seven points and City thirteenth with ten points. Form so far was no away wins and just two home wins.

At City: Pre-war was no wins for them in the last four. Post, no wins one draw and four losses, so a home banker!

Recent attendances ranged from 14,825 (54/55) to 55,485 (52/53) It was the fifty ninth league meeting plus two cup ties 1904 semi-final 3-0 at Goodison (53,000), 1934 fifth rd. replay 2-0 (68,614) at City. .

Team news: Leivers, McAdams, Fagan, Little in, Sear (down with flu), Branagan Clarke, McLelland out.

From The Guardian's 'Old International': Wednesday Go Down Fighting

Billy McAdams set off on his goal trail, when McEvoy tried to roll the ball back to his keeper Ryalls who, taken by surprise could do no more than allow the ball to bounce back off his shins to **McAdams** and the rest was child's play. How different it was for Wednesday when Finney closed in to hammer home a certain goal. Savage went down and brought off his second great save of the evening. Wednesday were forced to make four positional changes and were without their cleverest ball player in Quixall, and had been dogged with trouble from the start of the season, and did not deserve to be behind at the interval. Early in the second half **Barlow** put City two nil up with a most unusual goal, which was just like rubbing salt in the wounds.

A mild outbreak of exasperation by one Wednesday player was regrettable, though perhaps understandable, but the forwards channelled this frustration into their play and subjected City's goal to a veritable fuselage. Wednesday experienced desperate luck. Leivers scraped one shot from Finney off the line with Savage beaten, and O'Donnell hit the inside of a post and the ball bounced clear, while Savage had to use every inch of his phenomenal reach to tip Shiner's fiery shot upwards against the face of the bar and over.

ALAN FINNEY

Rarely will three such efforts amount to nothing. City won, but it's too soon to say whether the defensive problems have been solved. Game described as an apology for football, and at this rate City will need to buy spectators, not players!

FINAL SCORE: CITY 2 WEDNESDAY 0

City: Sky blue/white: Savage; Leivers, Little; Barnes, Ewing, Warhurst; Barlow, Hayes, Johnstone, McAdams, Fagan

Sheff. Wed: White shirts/black knickers: Ryalls; Staniforth, Bingley; Tom McAnearney, McEvoy, O'Donnell; Finney, Gibson, Shiner, Young, Greensmith.

Attendance: 24,036 **Average:** 25,542

Referee: E.R.Hill (Chester)

Linesmen: W.Crossley, W.L.Bennett

League position: Up 3 places to 10th

Goals For: 24 Against: 31

Reserves: No game

12) SATURDAY OCTOBER 12TH 1957
K.O. 3 PM: LEICESTER CITY (HOME)

Another home game and a chance to pick up some more points and balance up that goal difference.

Leicester were formed in 1884, had never won the league (but finished runners up in 1929), or the cup but were finalists in 1949 losing to Wolves, 'The Don' Revie missing that game for Leicester with a broken nose. So far they'd been promoted five times to the first (as opposed to City's seven!) to the first division and came up last year as Champs, seven points clear of Forest.

Programme's editorial asked 'Where Are The Crowds?' It went on to praise City's excellent home record, and a victory today would perhaps encourage the team to go and do likewise on tour. Maybe the erratic form, or the flu bug had kept crowds down, not one home crowd above 30,000 yet, and the club were astonished that last Wednesday, on a fine clear night, it was only 24,106. He then suggests that the supporters club should have to boost their propaganda work, if we are to get the 40,000 crowds we used to. Or is that the team's job?

There was more of the speculation of buying new players and how difficult it was!

Maine Road Gossip thanked those who contributed to the collection of £32 12s 10d on behalf of the RAF Association at the home game with Portsmouth. Visitors included ex red John Doherty, who later became a City scout.

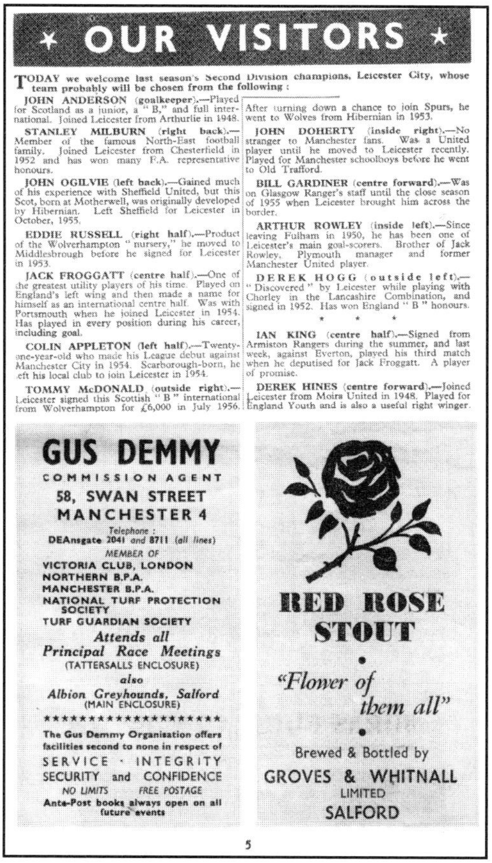

★ OUR VISITORS ★

TODAY we welcome last season's Second Division champions, Leicester City, whose team probably will be chosen from the following :

JOHN ANDERSON (goalkeeper).—Played for Scotland as a junior, a "B," and full international. Joined Leicester from Arthurlie in 1948.

STANLEY MILBURN (right back).—Member of the famous North-East football family. Joined Leicester from Chesterfield in 1952 and has won many F.A. representative honours.

JOHN OGILVIE (left back).—Gained much of his experience with Sheffield United, but this Scot, born at Motherwell, was originally developed by Hibernian. Left Sheffield for Leicester in October, 1955.

EDDIE RUSSELL (right half).—Product of the Wolverhampton "nursery," he moved to Middlesbrough before he signed for Leicester in 1953.

JACK FROGGATT (centre half).—One of the greatest utility players of his time. Played on England's left wing and then made a name for himself as an international centre half. Was with Portsmouth when he joined Leicester in 1954. Has played in every position during his career, including goal.

COLIN APPLETON (left half).—Twenty-one-year-old who made his League debut against Manchester City in 1954. Scarborough-born, he left his local club to join Leicester in 1954.

TOMMY McDONALD (outside right).—Leicester signed this Scottish "B" international from Wolverhampton for £6,000 in July 1956. After turning down a chance to join Spurs, he went to Wolves from Hibernian in 1953.

JOHN DOHERTY (inside right).—No stranger to Manchester fans. Was a United player until he moved to Leicester recently. Played for Manchester schoolboys before he went to Old Trafford.

BILL GARDINER (centre forward).—Was on Glasgow Ranger's staff until the close season of 1955 when Leicester brought him across the border.

ARTHUR ROWLEY (inside left).—Since leaving Fulham in 1950, he has been one of Leicester's main goal-scorers. Brother of Jack Rowley, Plymouth manager and former Manchester United player.

DEREK HOGG (outside left).—"Discovered" by Leicester while playing with Chorley in the Lancashire Combination, and signed in 1952. Has won England "B" honours.

* * *

IAN KING (centre half).—Signed from Armiston Rangers during the summer, and last week, against Everton, played his third match when he deputised for Jack Froggatt. A player of promise.

DEREK HINES (centre forward).—Joined Leicester from Moira United in 1948. Played for England Youth and is also a useful right winger.

In **Sportsman's Corner** Walter Ainscough of Collyhurst, questioned when we last conceded nine, and was advised 1906, 9-1 at Everton, and in 1941, also at Everton, 9-0.

Arthur Walmsley told the fans they should deal in facts, when urging the club to buy, and should take into consideration the injury situation.

David Jack's piece concentrated on Lancashire exile George Raynor, coach of the Sweden side. Jack suggested to George that they could be outsiders for the World Cup. George replied "yes, I fancy we've got a chance - playing at home" They were to lose in the final 5-2 to Brazil!

Leicester, managed by ex Blue Dave Halliday, were bottom with five points, and City tenth with twelve points. They'd lost every game on their travels, including a 5-1 loss at Villa . At home they'd won two, lost three, drawn one, so a good chance for the Blues to cash in.

At City: Pre-war, they'd not won in the last five. Post, one draw and two losses.

Recent attendances ranged from 13,648 (54/55) to 45,709 (46/47). It was the forty first league meeting plus one cup tie, at Leicester.

Team news: Bert back, and Sear in. Little and Savage out, so possibly our strongest team.

From The Guardian's W.R.Taylor:
City Just Win An Exciting Struggle

This was a game brimful of action, on a lovely day, in which there was hardly a dull moment.

City had been worried that they still hadn't had a crowd of 30,000, in spite of a 100% home record, but the remedy is simple. The brand of football they have been playing was the reverse of attractive, whereas if they can continue to be as entertaining as they were today, the missing thousands should roll back. Both City and Leicester tried to play attacking football and if at times the quality left something to be desired the consistency of the excitement more than compensated.

Blitzkreig was the order of the day and City eventually had the better of things, partly because of Hayes, both speedy and in great form, and Johnstone, playing very deep, supplying long accurate passes. Leicester's defence was struggling and showed plainly why they were nestling at the foot of the table, two of City's goals being the result of misunderstandings, while City looked better all round with Sear outstanding. For so slight a man he is a good back and if he fills out he could be a great one. City were ahead after five minutes, **Hayes** nipping in while Appleton and Anderson hesitated, his shot going in off a post. Trautmann saved at full length, McAdams went close twice and Fagan shot wide, but Hogg and

ARTHUR ROWLEY

Rowley combined for the equaliser. From Fagan's corner Barlow headed on, Anderson missed it completely, and **Billy Mac** tapped it in. McAdams missed another chance and Johnstone, with only the goalkeeper to beat was far too casual with a lob which Anderson caught easily, and seconds later instead of being 3-1 up City were pegged back to 2-2. A shot by Rowley was parried by Bert, Gardiner banged it back, Sear made a great one handed save and **Rowley** made no mistake from the spot.

It was end to end in the second half but when Johnstone put a long ball over the Leicester defence **Hayes** scored his second. Ten minutes later Joe was in a tangle with the Leicester defenders and **Barlow** took the opportunity to waltz round the lot of them to make it 4-2. From the restart though Leicester took advantage of a similar mix up and **McDonald** made it 4-3. The excitement continued however, both goals having narrow escapes, and in the end only the meanest of spectators could have complained that he had not had his money's worth.

FINAL SCORE: CITY 4 LEICESTER 3

City: Sky blue/white: Trautmann; Leivers, Sear; Barnes, Ewing, Warhurst; Barlow, Hayes, Johnstone, McAdams, Fagan
Leicester: White shirts/black knickers: Anderson; Milburn, Ogilvie; Russell, Froggatt, Appleton; McDonald, Doherty, Gardiner, Rowley, Hogg.
Attendance: 29,884 Average: 26,266
Referee: M. Dixon (York)
Linesmen: C.S.Wilkinson, E.Wain
League Position: Up two places to eighth spot
Goals For 28 Against: 34
Reserves: Won 3-1 away to Leeds, Oct 14th lost 2-1 at Sheff.Wed.

For this game I met up with John Cleaver from school, and a couple of his pals. We checked the back of the programme and spotted that it was only 7/6d on the train to Blackpool next week. It set off at twelve noon from Victoria, and stopped at Pendleton at 12.08, dead handy for us, Swinton and Broughton lads. Return was 5pm so not much time from the final whistle at twenty to five to get to Blackpool Central. We were up for it, discussing it all week at school, every day ad nauseum.

October 17th: Meadows quits and is to get £1500 nest egg and £17 per week until his contract is up on June 30th.
Bobby Johnstone, currently playing hide and seek from the club, transfer is on the cards, but Bob reckons he is to marry a girl from hometown Selkirk, find a business in Manchester with the help of the club, and settle in the area.
Johnny Hart denies rumours that he is quitting.
Plans announced to increase the strength of City's floodlights. City to play a friendly at Coventry under their new £15,000 lights on November 11th.
Ban lifted on Sunderland Director Mr S Ritson.
Oct 16th: England u 23 3 Rumania 2 at Wembley (40,000).
Saturday October 19th: Home International: Wales 0 England 4 in Cardiff (58,000).

13) SATURDAY OCTOBER 19TH 1957 K.O. 3PM: BLACKPOOL (AWAY)

Here we go. This was the real deal. Away games at Bolton and United didn't really count, this was a proper away game, train journey the lot! We all met up at Pendleton Broad Street Station, bought our tickets and leapt down the stairs, 3 at a time, to the platform. The train soon appeared. It was absolutely jam packed, bursting at the seams, and bedecked in Sky Blue and White. We were awestruck. We never dreamt that it would be full by the time it got to Pendleton and panic set in as we tried carriage after carriage to no avail. Nothing would stop us though and we finally managed to find a compartment with standing room only.

PETER DOHERTY
Manchester City F C

At Blackpool an hour or so later, everyone dived off the train, up the stairs and out on to the street, rattles a whirling. We were part of a vast Sky Blue and White army and it felt great. We had a snack in a café and read the local football green un which had us down as 'easy-peasy' for the Seasiders. Now I'd been past Blackpool's ground loads of times when out for a day trip or on holiday but I never realised that Bloomfield Road was a soccer ground - well it wasn't really, but still.

So we took our place on the wall at the front, down the side nearest to their main stand and chatted about how the F.A. Cup final win wasn't last season any more.

Blackpool were formed in 1887, and had their second promotion in 1937, after snaffling Stanley Matthews from Stoke, having previously transferred the legendary Peter Doherty to us. They changed their colours from light and dark blue stripes to tangerine, were losing finalists in the '48, and '51 cup finals, but won it in '53. They were runners up in the league in '56, and finished in fourth spot last season, so a biggish club, except in terms of support.

Bloomfield Road's capacity was 39,118 v United in 1932, and it was a hotchpotch. Main stand was seats and a paddock, unusually behind the goal. Opposite was the Kop, quite big. Down the side was a small covered terrace, and opposite a small stand along the length of the pitch with seats and terrace, each having 'Oh Be Joyful' on the roof!, In each corner of this stand were awkward little corner stands. The Kop later fell into disrepair, and was replaced by a modern stand in the 2000's which extended right round the length of the pitch. The other two stands were demolished.

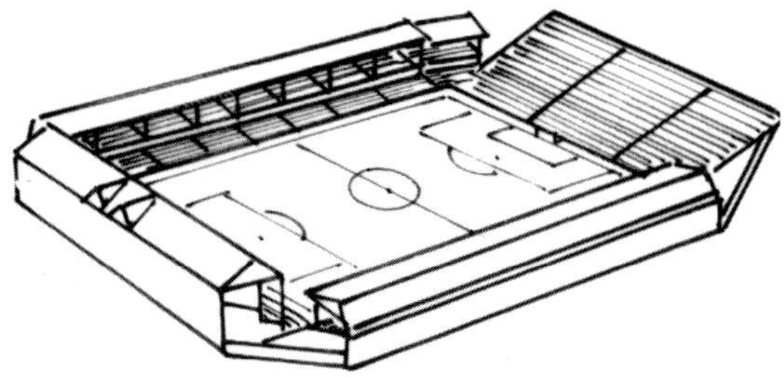

Pitch Size: 111 x 73 yds

Programme was a disappointment though, after the impressive pre-war job they produced. It was only twopence, but for eight pages. There was a brief review of 'Our Visitors' and plenty of adverts for the local theatres etc., for wrestling, films and shows. An interesting feature was the attendances given for central league games including 10,978 at O/T and 3,834 at home to Preston. First team home attendances varied between 21,099 to 34,181. 40,763 was the gate at O/T which they won 2-1.

Blackpool, managed by Joe Smith were thirteenth with eleven points, and City eighth with fourteen points. At home they'd won three, including a 7-0 over Sunderland, drawn one and lost two, including 4-1 v United. Away they'd won two, drawn one, lost two. We'd not won away since the opening game at Chelsea.

At Blackpool: Pre-war - we'd played ten won three, drawn five but lost the last two. Post- wins in '55 and '56 but lost 4-1 last season.

Recent attendances ranged from 17,014 (55/56) to 33,858 (51/52). It was our thirty ninth league meeting, with one cup tie at Maine Road.

Team News: For the first time since the opening week of the season City were able to announce the same team for two successive matches and they hoped this was a happy augury for their visit to Blackpool. Certainly an away point was overdue. Cliff Sear was facing his stiffest test to date being up against Stanley Matthews, who was almost twice his age!

From The Pink/Green (Charles Gleave): Blackpool Lights Go Dim Before Hayes-Powered City

City, with Alan Kirkman as the twelfth man brought along a strong contingent of several hundred supporters. Twenty eight fans flew over from the Isle of Man just to see Stanley Matthews and the lights were also an added attraction. When the game started in ideal weather the crowd appeared to be more than 25,000.

Opening exchanges were lively, with City facing the sun and after only two minutes **Barlow** headed in from a corner, Fagan placing the flag kick perfectly. Blackpool hit back and had a penalty claim turned down when Leivers was alleged to have handled, then Ewing headed a centre wide of his own post. The first time Matthews got the ball he was promptly robbed by Sear much to the delight of the travelling fans. There was certainly no lack of excitement and when Leivers passed back to Bert, who had come out of his goal, only a desperate clearance by Ewing prevented the ball going over the line. The City backs with the sun in their eyes were having difficulty clearing their lines and Blackpool deservedly equalised in the twelth minute. Perry crossed a low centre and Taylor was allowed to touch the ball aside to **Mudie** who gave Trautmann no chance from close range.

After twenty minutes Taylor, who had been limping, had to go to the touchline for treatment. Fagan came close, Hayes beat three men then slipped when about to score but in the twenty fourth minute City went ahead again. McAdams missed an open goal but **Hayes** shot the ball through from about six yards for 2-1. Warhurst was playing well for City and he sent Fagan away into the box who was promptly brought down by Armfield. **Barnes** made no mistake from the spot, scoring with a firm low shot to Farm's left. A minute later it was 4-1. Warhurst juggled with the ball lobbed it over to **Hayes** who brought it under control and in almost the same movement nearly broke the roof of the net with a tremendous right footer. Blackpool appealed for a penalty when Perry fell headlong as he jumped over Trautmann, but it was an obvious accident. The sun was now dazzling on that side of the field and Matthews repeatedly shaded his eyes whilst wondering where the ball was. Even allowing for Taylor's handicap there was no doubting City's superiority and they were full value for their interval lead.

Taylor was now hobbling on the wing and Matthews moved to inside right for the second half. McAdams was hit full in the face from a terrific clearance by Jim Kelly and went down like a log but trainer Laurie Barnett soon had him back on his feet again. Barnes was making the game look easy in attack and defence and Blackpool inexplicably kept giving the ball to Taylor who could hardly walk. Their only hope was Matthews who was here, there, and everywhere, showing a turn of speed which would have done credit to a man half his age. After fifty minutes though, **McAdams**, who'd had more than his share of criticism this season scored with a beautiful header from a long cross by Johnstone, to make it 5-1 at the Kop end. Only two minutes later Gratrix charged down the middle as City's defence were wrong footed and his shot was only parried by Bert to Mudie who scored easily to make it 5-2. Blackpool were putting up a brave fight, but Fagan broke for City and was blatantly obstructed by Armfield but the ref waved play on. Paddy missed a further chance, then Ewing brought Mudie down in the area but the spot kick was blazed over by Gratrix, the future City centre half, in the seventy sixth minute. Hayes had the ball in the Blackpool net again but the goal was disallowed.

STAN MATTHEWS

FINAL SCORE: BLACKPOOL 2 CITY 5

Blackpool: Tangerine and white: Farm; Armfield, Garrett; Kelly J., Gratrix, Kelly H; Mathews, Taylor, Mudie, Durie, Perry.
City: Sky blue shirts: Trautmann; Leivers, Sear; Barnes, Ewing, Warhurst; Barlow, Hayes, Johnstone McAdams, Fagan.
Attendance: 28,322 **Average:** 35,501
Referee: A.Holland (Barnsley)
Linesmen: H.Whewell, K.G.Hampson
League position: Up one place to 7th
Goals For: 33 Against: 36
Reserves: Lost 3-2 at Bolton

So an amazingly exciting day, though we hadn't the wit to catch a later train and spend a couple of hours in Blackpool! I went to bed that night with the sound of rattles in my ears. I just had to have one.

City's team who lost 2-0 at Leeds in the Youth Cup was: Guinn, Cooke, Sadler, Cheetham, Ashton, Shawcross, Fenner, Worthington, Lister, Hardman, Riley. Jimmy Meadows announced his retirement on October 22nd. Bert had a pop in his MEN column at the 'Know All' supporters.

Eire B 1 Rumania B 1 at Dalymount Park (20,000), Paddy Fagan played.
Scotland u 23 4 Holland 1 at Tynecastle (25,000).
Aston Villa winger Peter McParland, scorer of two goals in last season's cup final, and responsible for the challenge which broke Ray Wood's jaw was reported as receiving letters with Manchester postmarks suggesting he would be "signing his own death warrant " if he plays in the forthcoming Charity Shield game at Old Trafford on October 22nd. Peter played and Villa unsurprisingly lost 4-0.
Oct 23rd Ireland B 6 Rumania 0 at Belfast (10,000).
Eire B 1 Rumania 1, Dalymount Park (20,000).

14) SATURDAY OCTOBER 26TH 1957: K.O. 3PM: LUTON TOWN (HOME)

So an away win at last and surely a good chance to pick up another two home points. Or was it?

Luton Town were formed in 1885, joined division 2 in 1898/99, dropped out in 1900, joined div three in 1920/21 and were eventually promoted to div one in 1955. Last season they finished sixteenth with thirty seven points.

Programme's editorial headed with 'So Unpredictable' with fans querying, after the surprise result last week, the last time City scored five on an away ground. This astounded the Ed who thought the date was imprinted on the hearts of all Blues. It was February 12th 1955, and of course it was the 5-0 at Old Trafford. He goes on to applaud two players who've suffered from injuries recently, Billy McAdams and Bobby Johnstone who both gave first class performances.

He then says that City haven't had a draw all season, and the last at Maine Road was Villa on August 25th 1956!

Maine Road Gossip thanked all who contributed to the splendid collection of £63 7s taken on behalf of the National Spastics Society at the Wednesday game.

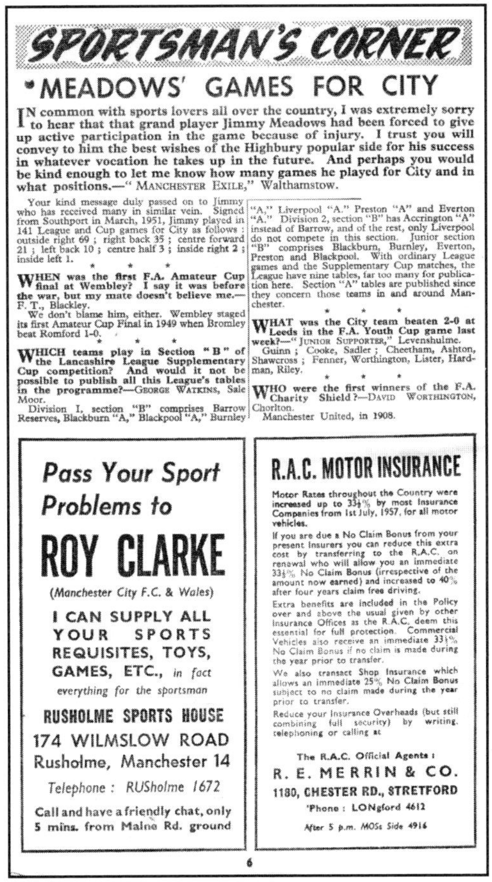

SPORTSMAN'S CORNER

"MEADOWS' GAMES FOR CITY

IN common with sports lovers all over the country, I was extremely sorry to hear that that grand player Jimmy Meadows had been forced to give up active participation in the game because of injury. I trust you will convey to him the best wishes of the Highbury popular side for his success in whatever vocation he takes up in the future. And perhaps you would be kind enough to let me know how many games he played for City and in what positions.—" MANCHESTER EXILE," Walthamstow.

Your kind message duly passed on to Jimmy who has received many in similar vein. Signed from Southport in March, 1951, Jimmy played in 141 League and Cup games for City as follows : outside right 69 ; right back 35 ; centre forward 21 ; left back 10 ; centre half 3 ; inside right 2 ; inside left 1.

* * *

WHEN was the first F.A. Amateur Cup final at Wembley? I say it was before the war, but my mate doesn't believe me.—F. T., Blackley.

We don't blame him, either. Wembley staged its first Amateur Cup Final in 1949 when Bromley beat Romford 1-0.

* * *

WHICH teams play in Section "B" of the Lancashire League Supplementary Cup competition? And would it not be possible to publish all this League's tables in the programme?—GEORGE WATKINS, Sale Moor.

Division I, section "B" comprises Barrow Reserves, Blackburn "A," Blackpool "A," Burnley "A," Liverpool "A." Preston "A" and Everton "A." Division 2, section "B" has Accrington "A" instead of Barrow, and of the rest, only Liverpool do not compete in this section. Junior section "B" comprises Blackburn, Burnley, Everton, Preston and Blackpool. With ordinary League games and the Supplementary Cup matches, the League have nine tables, far too many for publication here. Section "A" tables are published since they concern those teams in and around Manchester.

* * *

WHAT was the City team beaten 2-0 at Leeds in the F.A. Youth Cup game last week?—" JUNIOR SUPPORTER," Levenshulme.

Guinn ; Cooke, Sadler ; Cheetham, Ashton, Shawcross ; Fenner, Worthington, Lister, Hardman, Riley.

* * *

WHO were the first winners of the F.A. Charity Shield?—DAVID WORTHINGTON, Chorlton.

Manchester United, in 1908.

Pass Your Sport Problems to
ROY CLARKE
(Manchester City F.C. & Wales)
I CAN SUPPLY ALL YOUR SPORTS REQUISITES, TOYS, GAMES, ETC., *in fact everything for the sportsman*
RUSHOLME SPORTS HOUSE
174 WILMSLOW ROAD
Rusholme, Manchester 14
Telephone : RUSholme 1672
Call and have a friendly chat, only 5 mins. from Maine Rd. ground

R.A.C. MOTOR INSURANCE
Motor Rates throughout the Country were increased up to 33⅓% by most Insurance Companies from 1st July, 1957, for all motor vehicles.
If you are due a No Claim Bonus from your present Insurers you can reduce this extra cost by transferring to the R.A.C. on renewal who will allow you an immediate 33⅓% No Claim Bonus (irrespective of the amount now earned) and increased to 40% after four years claim free driving.
Extra benefits are included in the Policy over and above the usual given by other Insurance Offices as the R.A.C. deem this essential for full protection. Commercial Vehicles also receive an immediate 33⅓% No Claim Bonus if no claim is made during the year prior to transfer.
We also transact Shop Insurance which allows an immediate 25% No Claim Bonus subject to no claim made during the year prior to transfer.
Reduce your Insurance Overheads (but still combining full security) by writing, telephoning or calling at
The R.A.C. Official Agents :
R. E. MERRIN & CO.
1180, CHESTER RD., STRETFORD
'Phone : LONgford 4612
After 5 p.m. MOSs Side 4916

6

Sportsman's Corner included a best wishes letter from 'Manchester Exile' re Jimmy Meadows who'd just retired through injury.

Arthur Walmsley paid a final tribute to Jimmy Meadows by comparing him with a couple of City Greats, Sproston and Barkas.

David Jack questioned whether there are too many names in English football, with the Football League team meeting the Irish league next week, and wouldn't we be better allowing the near certs such as Clayton, Byrne, Wright, Edwards and Haynes to play in all representative games so that they could really get to know each other?

It was 30s (£1.50 in modern cuurrency) to Arsenal on the **train** next week

Luton, managed by Dally Duncan, were in tenth place with fifteen points and City seventh with sixteen points. Form so far had been good at home with five wins, two draws, and one loss, and two wins and four losses away.

At City: Pre-war we'd won one lost two. Post - won three and drew one.

Recent attendances ranged from 15,499 (55/56) to 57,592 (46/47). This was the fifteenth league meeting plus four cup ties, two at City, 1936 fourth rd 2-1 ((65,978), 1953 fourth rd 1-1 (38,411).

Luton went two goals up and it was so disappointing that City looked like they were going to lose their unbeaten home record, especially after last week's great result. They wouldn't have scored in a month of Sundays, so I left with five minutes to go, informing everyone in town that we'd lost 2-0. Then when I picked a Pink up in Swinton, I was astounded, gob smacked even, to find out we'd drawn 2-2 with late, late goals from Billy McAdams and Colin Barlow. So the first draw of the season and for nearly eighteen months at Maine Road, as almost predicted by the programme editor.

Team News: Nineteen year old Dennis Fidler - in for Fagan. Barnes recovered from a throat infection

From The Pink/Green:
Quick Fire Luton Had City In A Flat Spin

Luton were first away, but City replied quickly, then Sear showed his style and promise with a magnificent clearance. Johnstone was then treated by Fred Tilson, deputising for Laurie Barnett, the senior trainer and coach, who had gone to bed with a severe cold.

After fifteen minutes City provided a fine move finishing with Barlow heading just wide.Turner then let fly from ten yards but Trautmann beat it away. City replied through McAdams, but after Luton pressure they took the lead when after a short corner Jones' long ball was turned in by **Turner** on twenty nine minutes, with the City defence covering poorly.

Poor cover again led to Luton's second, **Pearce** getting all his weight behind a low sharply-angled drive which Bert only half parried and had to turn and watch it trickle slowly over the line into the empty net, which annoyed him no end. It was all Luton and the crowd began to boo.

Things didn't improve in the second half as very definitely Luton had the edge on City, in both defence and attack.

After fifty eight minutes though Luton were down to ten men when Dunne was stretchered off with a thigh injury after a close tackle with Fidler.

To the end Hayes strove and suffered, while Fidler had one of the most thankless debuts ever seen, his crosses meeting with deplorable response.

As the ground emptied City reduced the arrears, **McAdams** bustled the ball into the net from close range after latching on to Hayes' centre.

Then a minute later at the end of a tremendous attack, **Barlow** pushed home the equaliser with the Luton defence wide open. It was an exciting finish which City hardly deserved, but which preserved their unbeaten home record.

FINAL SCORE: CITY 2 LUTON 2

City: Sky blue/white: Trautmann; Leivers, Sear; Barnes, Ewing, Warhurst; Barlow, Hayes, Johnstone, McAdams, Fidler
Luton: White shirts/black knickers: Baynham; Dunne, Jones; Morton, Owen, Pearce; Adam, Turner, Brown, Cummins, McLeod

Attendance: 30,633 - first decent crowd and they nearly let us down. **Average:** 26,880
Referee: W.Clements (West Brom)
Linesmen: D.B. Hepworth, F.G.Perkins
League Position: Remained in eighth spot, with seventeen points same as United but six points behind leaders Wolves.
Goals For: 35 Against: 38

Reserves: Wolves away, lost 7-6. Apparently the game kicked off two minutes early, so by 3pm City were already two goals down! Scoring sequence then went 1-2, 2-2, 2-3, 3-3, 3-4, 4-4, 4-5, 5-5, 5-6, 6-6, 6-7. Scorers were Kirkman 3, McLelland 2, Bourne.

A full eight page programme was issued and Ivan Sharpe ridiculed Leeds' manager Raich Carter's proposal that substitutes should be allowed to come and go at any time during a match, covering all eleven positions. Ivan thought it silly. Blackpool, for example could keep Matthews for the second half of games, then as he got older just for the last quarter! As if!

City expressed alarm that gates were down by approximately 8,000 *(I make it 6,000).* On one occasion in the recent past there had been 28,000 at Maine Road and 14,000 for a reserve game at United.

It was announced that George Poyser had been appointed assistant manager and Chief Coach. John Kay writing in the MEN expressed delight that just when United were getting too big for their boots, along came Bolton, Blackpool, Wolves, Portsmouth, and West Brom to put them firmly in their place.

Oct 30th: Irish Lg 2 F/League 4, at Belfast, (18,000).

Future Blue Peter Dobing taken on by Lancs as a spin bowler.

PETER DOBING

Marsden, Dyson and Hart reported as recovering.

Four Monday night floodlit friendlies announced: Nov 4th Hearts away; Nov 11th Coventry away; Nov 18th Hibs home; Nov 25th Hibs away,

Partick Thistle and Hearts home were possibilities.

Oct 30th: Irish Lg 2, FL 4, Belfast (18,000).

CONCLUSION: A steady month, bad start with the heavy loss at Birmingham, great win at Blackpool, and two home wins v Sheff. Wed. and Leicester, but the100% home record went with the draw v Luton. There was a debut for Dennis Fidler. Average home attendance 26,880, away 35,501. Goals for went up to 35, against 38. Moved up from eleventh to eighth spot in the league

LEAGUE TABLE

	P	W	D	L	F	A	Pts
Wolves	15	10	3	2	40	17	23
WBA	15	7	7	1	37	21	21
Everton	13	7	4	2	24	19	18
Preston	14	8	1	5	29	19	17
Man Utd	14	8	1	5	37	25	17
Notts For	14	8	1	5	30	21	17
Arsenal	15	7	3	5	25	21	17
Man City	**14**	**8**	**1**	**5**	**35**	**38**	**17**
Luton	14	7	2	5	18	16	16
Bolton	14	6	3	5	24	25	15
Chelsea	14	5	4	5	30	27	14
Blackpool	13	6	1	6	24	22	13
Burnley	14	5	3	6	25	28	13
Leeds	15	5	3	7	17	25	13
B'ham	15	5	3	7	27	36	13
Portsmouth	14	5	2	7	24	26	12
Spurs	15	5	2	8	32	38	12
Newcastle	14	4	3	7	21	22	11
Aston Villa	15	4	2	9	22	34	10
Sunderland	15	3	4	8	18	38	10
Sheff Wed	14	3	2	9	18	30	8
Leicester	14	3	1	10	26	35	7

NOVEMBER'S FOOTBALL MONTHLY

Arsenal's Joe Haverty was on the front cover and Everton's Albert Dunlop on the back cover. CB's editorial 'opinion' covered signing on fees, players cuts from transfers, and refs should get more than £7 7s. United, who asked for fees for being televised doing training in working hours were sympathised with and though he thought that United would win the title he was surprised that people had them down as such after only a few games.

John MacAdam argued for substitutes provided players could be checked on that they weren't cheating to get substituted. Peter Doherty has an article bemoaning that modern players still play like they did in the old days.

Once A Blue, Always A Blue

JOHN from Denton's story:

I was living in the middle of nowhere, Shropshire, so I was a big Shrewsbury Town fan. I went to Wellington Grammar School and was mad on football and cricket, but as I lived in the Midlands I was hoping that Birmingham would win the '56 Cup Final. Then my dad, an accountant, got a job in Manchester, with the Education committee, so we moved to Fallowfield. Though it was a complete change for me and my five siblings, I was second eldest of six, I wasn't apprehensive, it was like going to heaven early, I could spend my summers at Old Trafford cricket ground, and winters at Old Trafford football ground. Don't forget that United had won the title in '56 and '57 they were in Europe, and there was something magical about the Babes. *(Ed - I'd forgotten!)*

But in August 1957 I went for a a walk with my sisters and little brother Brian who was in a push chair, through Alexander Park and via Maine Road on the way back. There was a match on, Blues v Maroons, so we decided to take a look, and I remember being at the back of the terrace, looking down and around from the scoreboard end at this massive ground, and saying incredulously "hey, that's Bert Trautmann down there, he broke his neck in the cup final". Impressive.

Then I started at Chorlton Grammar School in the second year, and I sat in front of Charlie Hadfield, who was a Blue and we caught the bus at the same place, the number 22, and we talked football. .

So I walked with Charlie to Maine Road to see City play Portsmouth, partly because I wanted to see the wonderful Jimmy Dickinson. City won 2-1 and Dave Ewing scored a goal from the half way line from a free kick, and I remember the Pompey goalie, Uprichard *(Ed - Barnett)*, seeing the funny side. That game made an impression on me, and I loved the sky blue.

I wasn't quite hooked even at that stage, but I went again, stood between the Kippax and the Platt Lane stand in that corner, when we played Sheffield Wednesday at night, with John Savage in goal, and we won again - those defeats at Preston and West Brom would have been enough to put anyone off, but not me.

I remember Munich vividly. On Thursday February 6th, in school we were bantering with United fans that morning, they'd drawn 3-3 in Belgrade the night before. It was only later that day when walking home down Wellington Road, just outside the Girls High School, I met my brother, Alan, he had his newspaper bag on his shoulder, it was his fourteenth birthday, and he said "guess what, United's plane's crashed". I said "you're joking" and he showed me the stop press, and it just happened to say that the plane had failed to take off, and I said "I tell you what, cos it's United knowing them, it'll be something of nothing". Then at ten past four the full impact started to come through. Alan had his birthday party that night, and I was still trying to come to terms with the disaster. There were other people killed at Munich other than the players, Frank Swift, journalists, stewards, passengers. The party went ahead, the music of the day playing and everyone having a great time, but I couldn't understand why everyone could be celebrating, I thought it was dreadful and kept disappearing upstairs lying on the bed crying my eyes out. I was devastated. I only saw that United team once, that was the 2-2 draw around Christmastime at Maine Road. My dad wouldn't let me go unless I was with an adult, so my next door neighbours' son, an avid United fan, who was about eighteen or nineteen and Welsh, Ewan Jones, took me. He had his red and white scarf and rosette on, and I sat on his shoulders in the 70,000 crowd wearing my blue and white one, plus my bobble hat and rattle. I must admit to finding it a thrill to see United run out at Maine Road, very special, but obviously wanting City to win, which we almost did. To put the game in historical context the Russians had just sent a monkey or a dog into space, first time something living. It was a great match and I remember Bert was brilliant and seeing Gregg racing out of his goal - City fans reckoned he was United's deep lying centre forward plan!

The rivalry at school was just as strong, but everyone in society was more tolerant then and there were never any fights, but one or two near ones. Some lads went to both grounds - I think that was maybe a throwback to ground sharing - first teams at M/R and reserves at O/T or The Cliff. We were very generous to them, (although we've had it thrown back in our faces since - Ed), we were first with nearly everything.

I don't think I went away until Sheffield Wednesday in '59, after the hot summer. I remember going through Woodhead on the train with Charlie, when all the reservoirs were empty in the Derbyshire hills. We scored and the ref gave it offside, with their full back and goalie standing on the line.

Bolton was my first local away game when Dougie Holden scored a goal. Trautmann claimed it had gone through a hole in the side netting. The linesman must have checked the nets before the match, but since then the linesmen have checked the nets even more thoroughly.

I'd actually been to a game at Molineux before all this, in the 56/57 season. A group of us from Wellington Grammar had a sporting weekend with a school who'd come up from Kent, and we had a trip to Wolves. We went in the North stand, there were about 40,000 there, the biggest crowd I'd ever been in, and I decided to try and get as close to Billy Wright as I possibly could. So I squeezed myself through the crowd, took about fifteen minutes to do it; down to the other stand; stood by the players' tunnel saw Billy Wright, and as he came past with the team I reached out and touched him. I touched Billy Wright. It was the dirtiest game I'd ever seen and Burnley won 2-1. Then I eventually went back to the North stand and no-one had noticed that I'd gone. Wolves were the team of the time, pioneers of European football, playing Real Madrid, Moscow Dynamo's, and a few used to go from where I lived but it wasn't really an option for me.

John's a lifelong Blue, radio/ TV commentator and after dinner speaker/compere.

John went on to explain 'The John McTavish story'.......

I (John Gwynne) started a football team in 1959, in Fallowfield where most of the kids lived in Sherwood Road, Street or Avenue, and near to the Sherwood pub. I was considered to be a bit of a poshie really because I lived in a semi-detached house on Wellington Road, and my dad was a professional man. Forest had just won the cup, so it was my idea to call us Sherwood Forest. We played friendly matches against Kingswood Rovers. One day they turned up with City winger Clive Colbridge as 'manager'

So I thought I'm not having this and we all marched along to Finchley Road, where I knew John McTavish lived, just round the corner from me. I was aged fifteen, plucked up courage, knocked on the door and asked his wife if Mr. McTavish lived here, yes, was the reply and John McTavish came to the door. I said "Clive Colbridge is Kingswood's manager and we wondered if you'd manage us" John said he couldn't make a decision right now but he'd give it some thought and I gave him my address. Within the week, obviously after he'd spoken to Clive, he came round to our house with a football and four corner flags from City. Flags with blue triangles - prior to this we'd had jumble sales to buy kits etc. Our kit was green shirts, white socks and shorts, because we were Sherwood Forest and he took an interest. Once we couldn't raise a team to play Bradford Rovers and had to call the game off. I told John, that we couldn't tell them as it was too far and John went all the way up there to tell their secretary - there were no phones in those days - he went out of his way. I don't know how long his commitment was, but John left City shortly after that. Never saw him again until May 11th 2003, the last game at Maine Road.

ALAN from Dukinfield's story:

At school it was about 50/50 City/United and I was a City fan because I didn't like United fans, simple as that. In 57/58 season I went to every match, bar two. I'd had a week away camping, when I must have caught the flu which kept me in bed. As it happens they were the away games at Preston (lost 6-1) and at West Brom (lost 9-2), not a bad couple of games to miss as it turns out. For home games I'd stand on the Kippax and we usually attacked the Platt Lane end in the second half so I'd move round to that stand and stand on the wall. You could walk all round the standing areas of the ground then, but you had to pay 3d from the scoreboard end to the Kippax. I'd sometimes go with Roland Jones from Stalybridge.

On the Saturday nights some of the away teams would have been based at the Grand Hotel in Piccadilly, so we'd hang around for autographs. I remember once walking down to London Road station with Ronnie Allen of West Brom. Bert used to make us queue up for his autograph and if it was raining he'd sit in his car to sign.

For away games we'd all meet on the stations, London Road, Central, Exchange and Victoria and soon got to know other Blues of similar age. We went from Central to Luton that day and on the way back coming down into Chinley station the signalman cocked up and our traindriver slammed his brakes on but couldn't prevent the train from ploughing into a train which was stationery at the platform, demolishing the last coach and the station canopy practically. I was stood in the centre aisle swinging on the seats, and was sent flying the full length of the coach, hitting the door at the far end. People were flung about, but no-one was badly injured. One bloke broke his glasses and some had cuts from flying glass. Sam, a well known Blue who had a trumpet at Derby games, used to walk round the pitch with it, suffered broken ribs. Apparently one bloke on the other train got up and moved from the last coach, which probably saved his life. We had to wait for a replacement engine to come and arrived back late at Central where there were a lot of people waiting to see if we were all right. There were about two hundred on the train and we were given free cups of tea which tasted bloody awful to compensate for the shock. I've never spoken to another City fan who remembers it?! I only suffered a bruised shoulder, so I was quite fortunate and it made the TV news the following night.

Most lads had a paper round to finance games and you could also collect empty returnable beer bottles for a small sum.

For London games we'd catch the early train, five in the morning, or the midnight special which arrived in London in the early hours. We'd then traipse around, playing football with a tennis ball in Downing Street or Hyde Park or take in the sights. We'd sometimes come home on the old Mancunian at 6pm, a non stop train which still took three and a half hours. It wasn't too expensive on the train in those days. Going to Spurs we looked at the Underground map and took the tube to Tottenham Court Road which you'd think would be near where Spurs were playing. When we got there we asked someone where the ground was and were told it was miles away, so we caught an overland train to Seven Sisters probably and missed the two minutes' silence for Munich. The crash was very, very sad. It gets on my nerves now, but I don't have any bitterness towards United, no real hatred, it's just the fans. But in the fifties you could go to Old Trafford with your sky blue and white scarf on and they'd come to Maine Road with their red and white scarves on without any bother. But they always complained, even if they were five nil up in games. Most away games I'd have a packed lunch in my duffle bag, and at places like Blackpool I'd sit on the wall at half time munching away!

Alan has been an active member of the supporters club since the 50's in the Ashton, Denton, Hyde and Dukinfield areas, as treasurer and travel and social events organiser.

Bert takes up his position at Highbury.

CHAPTER FIVE

NOVEMBER 1957 - ROCK 'EARTS AND 'IBS

Off to Arsenal, Leeds and Sunderland. Home games with Bolton and Wolves. Friendly games at Hearts, Hibernian and Coventry, with a home friendly v Hibs., so nine games in the month.

City were interested in Sambrook and Hooper, but no bid for Ernie Taylor. United reserves were averaging attendances between 9,000 and 13,000.

On City's missing thousands, fans' letters were printed in the MEN including the headline 'Give us quality' and: 'Lack of personalities, poor football, having to pay more for cover, colourless City side, accent on defence, and negative plans'. Crowds at O/T reserves up due to voucher scheme - one United fan who used to come to Maine Road when United were away also says he was now more entertained at United reserves. The fans are more choosy, and W. E. Abraham came up with this classic: **'Once a Blue, always a Blue'**.

15) SATURDAY NOVEMBER 2nd 1957 K.O. 3PM: ARSENAL (AWAY)

Arsenal were formed in 1886. They won promotion to the first in 1904 as Woolwich Arsenal, went down in 1913, finished fifth in division two in 1915 - but somehow achieved promotion ahead of Barnsley and Wolves, Chelsea staying in division one, but Spurs being relegated (though they came up the next year!) - as the first division increased to 22 clubs. They'd also moved from South to North London which brassed off Spurs even more!

They came to prominence in the late twenties, nicked Herbie Chapman off Huddersfield, won the title five times in the 'thirties, and the cup twice. They won the title again in 1948 and 1953, and the F.A.Cup in 1950 and were runners up 1952. Finished in fifth spot in 56-57 season.

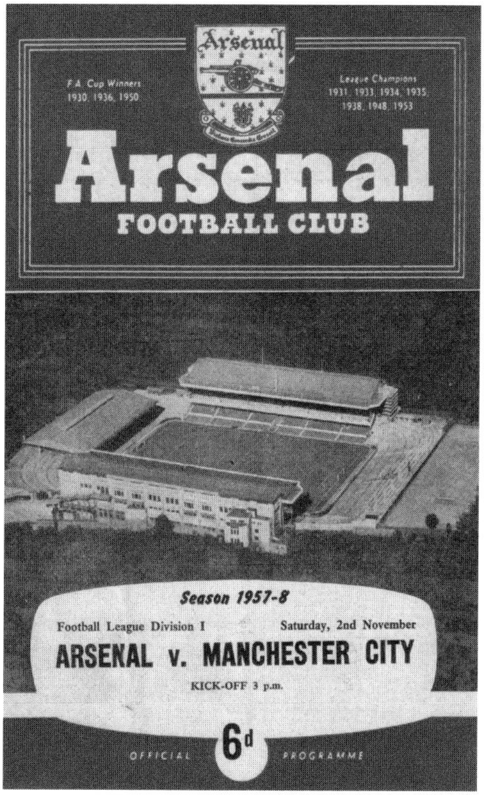

The programme was a magnificent effort which matched Chelsea's, being published and printed by the same company. It was of similar format, but with a red cover and ground picture of the elegant Highbury, priced at 6d for sixteen pages. It contained some good snippets on City, describing us as a team "which has been through many vicissitudes this season", having had more goals scored against us than any other team in the division, but were nevertheless in joint fourth spot due to our home form. We were, therefore, an enigma.

There were photos of Arsenal's previous games at Chelsea and Everton and the

Manchester players' pen pics were comprehensive. There was another page and a half devoted to City where a goal by hot shot Alec Herd was described. Goalie Charlie Williams' famous goal past Doig of Sunderland at Roker on fourteenth April 1900 was in there too. Apparently it wasn't directly from a goal kick so that's a myth. The full back, Bert Read, tapped it to Charlie who launched it. When Doig, who touched it in, was asked why he didn't save it he replied, "Well, as the blessed ball had already passed ten of you on the way, I hadn't the heart to stop it"- priceless.

The programme tells of Billy Meredith, working the night shift at the pit in Chirk, then playing for City the next day. Also the fact that you need the luck in football, and Arsenal's centre half in the '32 semi, admitting that he tripped Toseland in the box in the opening minutes, just as Ernie was about to score and it should have been a City penalty, but not given. Then a last gasp Arsenal attack, when City's full back (Billy Felton, promptly transferred to Spurs!) tried to shield the ball over the line, saw Arsenal's Lambert gain possession and cross for Bastin to score and put Arsenal into the final which they lost 2-1 to Newcastle.

Next was a full page black and white picture of the boys in Blue. One personal test I had as a youngster was to try and guess where team pics were taken. Some grounds were very distinctive, particularly Villa with its cinema balcony type gantry holding up the second tier of the main stand, or Maine Road with it's tunnels, and Spurs with its three tier stand. This one baffled me until now, having done a bit of research. It obviously wasn't Maine Road, looked like Birmingham, or Luton, where we hadn't yet played. We were wearing the sky blue, and Bert was in goal, so it could only have been Blackpool!! This was generally recognised as the team photo for 57/58 (until Ray Sambrook arrived) and was produced in colour by Soccer Bubble Gum's number two series of Soccer teams (see back cover).

Highbury's record attendance was 73,295 in 1935 v Sunderland and the ground was majestic. Two almost identical 'double deckers' along the length of the pitch which remained until 2006, when they moved to The Emirates. There was a covered North Bank and an open 'clock end'. All the stands had classy features, such as the Arsenal logo. The floodlights were amongst the first in the country and were situated along the roof of the East and West stands. So whilst there were no towering pylons to help you pick out from a distance where the ground was, it was a design later utilised by most football clubs when new and reasonably tall matching stands were built.

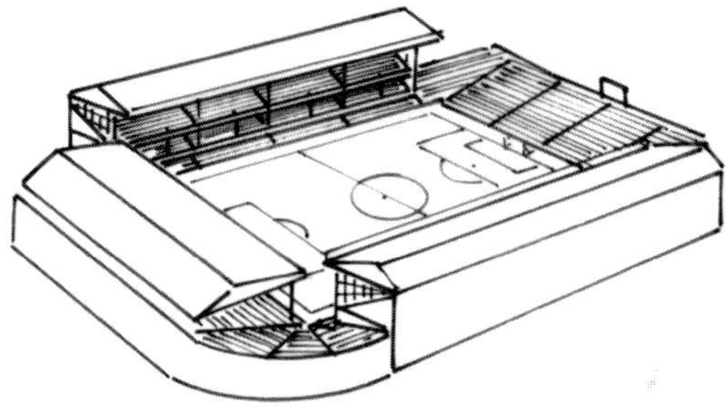

Pitch size: 110 x 71 yards

Arsenal, managed by Jack Crayston, were seventh with seventeen points and City eighth also with seventeen points. Their form so far was mixed, but they'd lost the last home game to Birmingham 3-1. Their full-back Charlton, once scored an own goal v Charlton to register the saying "When Charlton scored for Charlton, when Charlton couldn't score?"

At Arsenal: Pre-war - we'd lost the last one but doubled them in '36 and '37 when Frank Swift explained in his book *'From The Goalmouth'* that, "We only had a plan when we played Arsenal, but invariably we won." Post- war we'd had just the one win in '54, 3-2 when we went top for twenty four hours, otherwise four draws and two losses including a 7-3 in 56/57 ouch.

Recent attendances ranged from 30,864 (55/56) to 65,869 (53/54). It was the eighty third league meeting plus two cup ties, 1904 second rd 2-0 at Woolwich Arsenal (30,000), 1932 semi-final 0-1, at Villa Park (50,337), and one Charity Shield, 1934/35, 0-4 (10,888).

Team news: Fagan in for Fidler

From The Pink/Green:
City Muff Chances - Wonder Goal By McAdams

Arsenal manager Jack Crayston had torn a strip off his players pre-match after a disappointing 4-1 defeat in a mid-week floodlit cup game at Brentford. Notable absentee from the crowd was Max Woosnam who, now living in the south, invariably attends City's games in this part of the world. He was out of London this weekend however, but sent a letter of good wishes to chairman Alan Douglas. Also amongst the watchers were Johnny Hart and Johnny Hannaway, both taking a day off.

MAX WOOSNAM, Manchester City

City, who had Roy Faulkner as twelfth man, had one of their biggest followings of the season. Indeed so many supporters had come from Manchester that an extra train had to be put on to take them home. There was also such a tremendous interest in the game in London that fans were queuing for tickets before lunch. City kicked off with the strong breeze behind them, but the start was delayed as the referee had to advise youngsters behind the City goal not to let off any more fireworks. Play was fast and interesting with lively exchanges but it was Arsenal who took the lead in the seventh minute. Clapton beat Sear and from his centre **Tapscott** hooked the ball past Trautmann falling head over heels in the effort. The crowd had now increased to around 40,000 and they were generous in the applause for City's clever footwork. Bowen was inspiring Arsenal in attack and defence as their raids became more frequent, Trautmann making a brilliant save at the foot of the post which even the home players applauded.

JACK KELSEY

City's attacks were more infrequent and players were finding it hard to keep their feet after heavy rain in the night had made the surface greasy. In the twentieth minute Evans sent the ball whizzing over the bar, and a couple of minutes later McAdams only had to trundle the ball into the empty net but lost control and it was cleared by Charlton.

City couldn't complain about lack of scoring chances but it was Arsenal who went further ahead through **Bloomfield** in the fortieth minute, scoring with a well placed shot which seemed to go under Bert's body into the corner of the net.

Trautmann saved a pile driver from Holton and Clapton hit the post as Arsenal piled on the pressure.

Second half Bert made a super-human dive to save from Herd, but City persisted and **McAdams** made it 2-1 after forty nine minutes, Barnes lobbing the ball into the area and Billy nodding it past Kelsey giving him no chance.

City fought back well with McAdams and Hayes going close and Kelsey making great saves, but Arsenal had a penalty appeal turned down for hands. Twenty five minutes from time the floodlights were switched on although visibility was reasonably good as City fought hard for an equaliser. Trautmann made the save of the match from Clapton but on the second half showing City would not have been flattered with a draw.

Observer Newspaper Verdict: Bert was giving an oddly schizophrenic performance. Looking massively unbeatable, then for a weak shot from Clapton going down like some tottering heavyweight boxer, luckily the shot struck a post and bobbled tantalisingly along the line before being cleared. No one fought harder than Ewing, a great tree trunk of a centre half, and Johnstone, referred to as plump and perambulatory, prompted from a deep lying position.

So the good little run of three wins and one defeat was ended, but at least it wasn't a drubbing.

FINAL SCORE: ARSENAL 2 CITY 1

Arsenal: Red, white sleeves and collars shirts, white knickers, blue stockings, white rings white tops: Kelsey; Charlton, Evans; Holton, Dodgin, Bowen; Clapton, Tapscott, Herd, Bloomfield, Haverty.
City: Sky blue shirts, white knickers, sky blue and white hoop stockings: Trautmann; Leivers, Sear; Barnes, Ewing, Warhurst; Barlow, Hayes, Johnstone McAdams, Fagan
Attendance: 43,664 **Average:** 36,522
Referee: K.Howley Middlesbrough)
Linesmen: D.A.G.Baker (Bournemouth), C.W. Jenkins (Norwich)
League Position: Dropped two places to tenth
For: 36 Against: 40
Reserves: Beat Villa 5-0 at M/Rd.

15A) MONDAY 4TH NOVEMBER 1957 K.O. 7.30PM: HEARTS (away friendly)

After the trek down to London, it was a trip North to play Heart Of Midlothian in a friendly game.

City had previously played them at Tynecastle in friendlies in '56, won 4-3, and 50/51 lost 1-0; and in 53/54 at M/Rd won 6-3 (opening of floodlights). We went on to play them in the American tour at the end of the season, but didn't meet again until 1979, in the Skol Festival Trophy, drawing 1-1. Then in '94 we lost 5-1 in a pre-season friendly at Tynecastle!

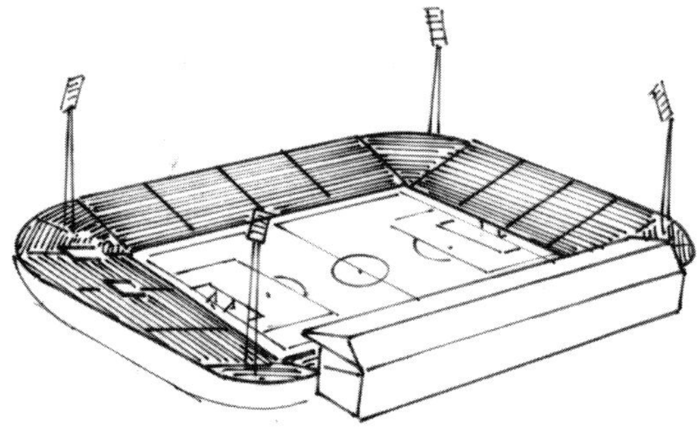

Pitch Size: 107 x 74 yds

I visited there for a European game in the 90's v Athletico Madrid, and the only change to the ground from the 50's when it had three open terraces and a main stand seats/paddock, was a cover over the opposite side to the main stand, which curved round the corner. It was generally run down.

As usual they did produce a nifty maroon souvenir **programme**, 3d for eight pages. **Notes from the Pavilion** penned:- 'The City' a name the Manchester club are more familiarly known as in the Midlands (?!), may not have the romantic glamour of their rivals M.U. but their football reputation has been built on the best traditions in the past. It goes on to describe the players, particularly Scots, and present Leicester manager David Halliday who the writer saw score a hat trick for City v Sheff. U at M/Rd (he scored three at Sunderland, and three at Birmingham in 31/32, but no trace of three in the Sheff. U. game!?) There were a further three pages on City including pics of Bobby Johnstone and Dave Ewing.

Report unearthed by Hearts historian David Speed:

It was **Murray** who opened Hearts' account on twelve mins, and then **Bauld** taking a through pass from MacKay scored with a tremendous drive which gave Trautmann no chance after sixteen mins. Towards the interval uncertainty in the Hearts defence brought reward for the City when **Hayes** had a shot deflected past Marshall by **Kirk**.

The Manchester team changed their tactics in the second-half when their deep centre plan came into action with a vengeance. Bobby Johnstone came prominently into the picture, and goalkeeper Trautmann helped the plan with several smart throws to unmarked colleagues. It was from one of his goal-kicks that City equalised ten minutes after the resumption. From a perfect Fagan cross, **Hayes** netted. Three minutes later, **Johnstone** lobbed the ball into the net in a breakaway which McAdams and he engineered. Hearts got on level terms in the seventy third minute when Hamilton squared a free-kick to Cumming whose drive was off the target, but **Murray** got the goal that mattered. Hearts defence was caught napping when, seven mins from the end, McAdams provided **Johnstone** with a perfect pass to restore the visitors' lead. Just on time, Hayes moved away up the right wing and lobbed the ball over Marshall's head for **McAdams** to place the ball into an empty net

FINAL SCORE: HEARTS 3 CITY 5

Hearts: Maroon shirts/white shorts: Marshall; Kirk, Thomson G.; MacKay, Gidden, Cumming; Blackwood, Murray, Bauld, Wardhaugh, Hamilton.
City; Sky blue shirts/white shorts: Trautmann; Leivers, Sear; Barnes, Ewing, Warhurst; Barlow, Hayes, Johnstone, McAdams, Fagan'
Attendance: 18,000 (receipts £1, 851)
Referee: W.M. Syme (Glasgow)
Linesmen: W.Geehan (Edinburgh) A.Dick !!! (Edinburgh)

Hearts went on to score one hundred and thirty two goals with twenty nine against to take the title with sixty two points, thirteen points clear of Rangers. They played City four times on the American tour in 1958. Won the title again in 1960, but only won cups after that. Dave MacKay was later signed by Spurs, and Alex Young became 'The Golden Vision' at Everton.

Unrest at United. After Doherty transferred to Leicester and Whitefoot to Forest, Freddie Goodwin and Eddie Colman put in a transfer requests (turned down). Eddie later admitted he was a bit hasty. Reserves Webster and Scanlon were also unsettled.

City crowds were down by 50,000 already. Bert reckons it's the United voucher system where programme sales number more than the reserve attendance. Jimmy Meadows is possibly to have a benefit game. Ernie Taylor on the transfer list at Blackpool, City may be interested at £8,000.

November 6th: Scotland 3 Switzerland 2, World Cup qualifier, at Hampden Park (58,811). England 2 N.Ireland 3, Home International at Wembley (40,000).

It was my dad's finest moment. If it wasn't bad enough hearing him gloat about Bolton, then this was the ultimate. The Northern Irish had achieved the impossible and beaten England. He had the afternoon off work and watched it at the Moorside Social Club, then came home drunk, slumped in his chair and repeated over and over "Belfast have beaten the whole of England" "What do you mean Dad, Belfast" "All the Irish players come from Belfast," he said, and without knowing, I couldn't argue. As a tribute here is the match report from January's Football Monthly:

England 2, Ireland 3.
(At Wembley, Wednesday, Nov. 6, 1957)

IRELAND beat England for the first time in 30 years and put an end to England's run of 17 games without defeat. They join Hungary and Scotland as the only teams to win at Wembley.

The Irishmen owed a lot to the superb goalkeeping of Gregg. But their team work and spirit were superior to that of a nonchalant, over-confident England.

They had in McIlroy the finest forward in the game; and the brothers Blanchflower, Keith—in his first international—and McMichael were strong defenders.

England's forwards failed and only Douglas and A'Court—deputy for Tom Finney—were up to standard. Haynes was completely outwitted by the clever Irish defensive tactics.

McIlroy, from a penalty-kick for a foul by Wright, scored the only first-half goal in the 32nd minute. A'Court equalised 13 minutes after the interval, but goals by McCrory (22 mins.) and Simpson (28) gave Ireland a winning lead.

Though England staged a strong rally, Gregg and his colleagues kept them down to a goal by Edwards (35 mins.).

ENGLAND: **Hopkinson** (Bolton); **Howe** (West Brom.), **Byrne** (Manchester Utd.), **Clayton** (Blackburn), **Wright** (captain) (Wolves), **Edwards** (Manchester Utd.); **Douglas** (Blackburn), **Kevan** (West Brom.), **Taylor** (Manchester Utd.), **Haynes** (Fulham), **A'Court** (Liverpool).

IRELAND: **Gregg** (Doncaster); **Keith** (Newcastle), **McMichael** (Newcastle); **D. Blanchflower** (captain) (Tottenham), **J. Blanchflower** (Manchester Utd.), **Peacock** (Celtic); **Bingham** (Sunderland), **McCrory** (Southend), **Simpson** (Glasgow Rangers), **McIlroy** (Burnley), **McParland** (Aston Villa).

REFEREE: B. M. Griffiths (Newport).
Attendance: 40,000.

Another gem he once came out with was when George Best flicked the ball out of Spurs goalie Pat Jennings' hands. "Only an Irishman could've done that," he said. "Dad," I said, "the bloody goalie's Irish"!

Clubs objected to United v Dukla Prague being on TV so plug pulled!

John Savage asked for transfer.

16) SATURDAY NOVEMBER 9TH 1957 K.O. 3PM: BOLTON WANDERERS (HOME)

A local derby, of the B list variety.

Bolton were formed in 1874, had never won the title and never would, but they were cup winners in 1923, 1926 (beat City) and 1929. Runners up in 1894, 1904 (to City) and in 1953, the so called Matthews final, though Stan Mortensen scored a hat trick. Bolton were 3-1 up with 20 minutes to go and virtually down to ten men but lost 4-3, goalies diving over the ball and stuff. Finished in ninth spot last season.

Programme editorial homed in on the 'Puzzle Of The Gates', these being 50,000 down on the corresponding time last year. The Editor states that City's form in Moss Side has been good, as have the performances, with six wins, one draw, and twenty two goals for, with nine against, so a puzzle indeed.

Last season, however, I would suggest we were still riding on the back of the F.A.Cup win at the start and at the end our loss of three out of four home games couldn't have helped the start of this campaign. Not to mention the weather, mid week games, the first home game being postponed v Sheff. Wed., and United hype.

Maine Road Gossip advised us that we should welcome units of the Royal Commando who will give a demonstration of unarmed combat at half time. Impressive it was too.

In Sportsman's Corner, H.Wilson, of Birmingham was 'fortunate to see the reserve game with Wolves at Molineux and supposed it would be impossible to tell him when was the last time the reserves scored six away from

IT JUST GOES TO SHOW

By ARTHUR WALMSLEY

(*Evening Chronicle Sports Columnist*)

SOCCER talking point during the week has been the circumstances under which Bryan Douglas scored for Blackburn Rovers last Saturday. Douglas had run out of the field of play over the dead ball line during a dribble, but when a Stoke defender passed back to his goalkeeper a few seconds later, Douglas, returning to the field again, intercepted the pass and scored.

Two seasons ago I saw Joe Hayes score a similar goal for Manchester City against Charlton Athletic at The Valley. Hayes had not run off the field, but had remained upfield to fasten a shoe-lace after a City attack had broken down, and was in a position between the Charlton full-backs and the goalkeeper.

A Charlton defender, obviously having forgotten Hayes' presence, swung round and passed back towards the goalkeeper, but Joe was in a perfect position to intercept, and had the easiest of tasks in scoring.

The spectators assumed Hayes was offside, and their impression was confirmed by the flagging of the linesman.

When the referee awarded a goal and pointed to the centre spot, the crowd's astonishment swiftly gave way to annoyance, and the referee, who had made a perfectly correct decision, was subjected to a protracted storm of booing.

In case, then, such an incident should happen at Maine Road and there are some among the spectators who may not be familiar with the section of the offside rule which covers both the Douglas and Hayes case, let me reprint it here :

Law 11, section (*c*) states that a man is not offside if the ball last touched an opponent or was last played by him. A footnote to the law states : "A player in an offside position shall not be penalised unless, in the opinion of the referee, he is interfering with the play or with an opponent or he is seeking to gain an advantage by being in an offside position."

Douglas ran out of play over the dead-ball line involuntarily and Hayes had stopped to fasten a shoe-lace. In neither case, then, could it be claimed they were seeking to gain advantage by being in offside positions.

But it all goes to show how easily the referee can be howled down from the terraces by spectators who haven't half his knowledge of the rules.

7

home and lost the match. He supposed right but was told that 'the Stiffs' beat Burnley 6-4 at Turf Moor last season when the goals were, as at Molineux, shared by Alan Kirkman, John McLelland and Albert Bourne.

Arthur Walmsley picked up on a Bryan Douglas (of Blackburn) goal where Bryan was off the field over the goal line after a dribble and when a Stoke defender passed the ball back to the goalie a few seconds later, Bryan nipped in, intercepted and scored. Arthur recalled a similar incident two seasons ago when Joe Hayes did exactly the same thing but the linesman flagged for offside. The referee overruled him and signalled a goal quite correctly and the crowd then subjected him to a prolonged storm of booing - it must have been at the Valley when we lost 5-2, November '55. Anyway, Arthur's point is, after explaining the rules, to show how easy it is for the referee to be howled down from the terraces by spectators who haven't half his knowledge of the rules. So there you go, referees are always right. Someone should have warned Andy Dibble later at Forest that time!.

David Jack in his column reckoned that the novelty of playing unknown foreign opposition in friendlies under the lights had now worn off, Plymouth only getting 7,000 v Red Star Paris, (not Belgrade?) moralising that attractive opposition will always fill the grounds, but a few lamps on pylons never will.

Bolton, managed by ex-Blue Bill Ridding were in ninth spot with seventeen points and City were tenth also with seventeen points. Away form so far included wins at Leicester and Sunderland, with big defeats at Wolves 6-1 and Birmingham 5-1. At home they'd won five, including 4-0 v United, drawn two, lost one. They'd also just beaten the Soviet Army side in a friendly.

At City: Pre-war, they won the last one, prior to that it was a draw and six losses, including a 5-1 and a 7-0, their record loss in 36/37 when they had Fred Swift in goal and we had brother Frank in ours. Post war they'd lost four and won four including last season's Christmas Day snowbound 3-1 and one was drawn.

Recent attendances ranged from 19,731 (56/57) to 46,648 (49/50). It was our sixty seventh league meeting plus two cup finals 1904 1-0 and 1926 0-1 plus six cup ties, two at City - 1905 second rd 1-2 (39,000) and 1947 fourth rd replay 1-0 (41,286).

Team News: Unchanged

From the Guardian's 'Old International': Bolton Disappoint, City Retain Record

NAT LOFTHOUSE

City won the game 2-1, preserving the unbeaten home record, with delightful goals from Hayes and McAdams, his sixth in six, Birch replying with a more unorthodox but equally delightful specimen for the visitors. Apart from the goals there was a headcracking contest between Lofthouse and Ewing and they both went off for treatment. (We took bets on who would return first) and, surprisingly, it was Lofthouse who returned after two minutes. Then eight minutes later Big Dave appeared to massive cheers with his head wound aided by a face towel.

Among the lesser known worthies of our age is the ex miner from Hindley who opened the score so beautifully for City in or about the twelfth minute. His name is **Hayes** and long may he remain the same simple loyal unassuming character we have always known him to be. Hayes comes in for a good deal of criticism and contumely at times, never let it be said for want of effort or trying but chiefly on the score of clumsiness. He seems to be the victim of his own impetuosity, or should one say of his frantic, hurried, pitter-patter running style. He picks his feet up and puts them down so rapidly that he finds ball control correspondingly difficult. So much more difficult than would a forward with the deliberate measured gait of a Carter or a Doherty. But on the rare occasions when Hayes can match his ball control to his marked powers of acceleration a goal of startling brilliance may result. Such was the case today. He picked up, gathered speed and forced home a long clearance from Sear like a master, leaving Higgins blinking with astonishment as he darted past him on the way.

The game didn't lack incident. Holden was outstanding for Bolton and it was not his fault that Parry failed to convert any of the scoring chances which Holden laid on. As for Johnstone not for long has one seen this Scottish footballer in such a serene and happy mood and so ready to demonstrate every facet of his footballing skills. His bland, unhurried commonsense distribution of the ball was an object lesson to everyone and was never better exemplified than when he dropped the ball onto McAdams' chest as if it had been a plain invitation to score. For once **McAdams** was willing and able to oblige after forty minutes.

Birch's goal for Bolton, the equaliser, had a flavour all its own. It followed a long chase along the touchline and then inwards towards the goal with Sear a zealous persuer. Trautmann advanced, leaving his co-defenders to cover the goal, which none troubled to do, so **Birch**, toe ended the ball coolly and impudently past Bert into the empty net. Bert then turned on Ewing and admonished him!

Bolton were generally disappointing, though youngsters Dean and Cunliffe played well. Dean kept goal with pluck and agility, growing in confidence as the game went on, saving the many hurricane shots hurled at him by Fagan, Hayes, McAdams, - the best being from a point-blank hook shot from Billy Mac and a violent shot from Barlow to which a coward would have closed his eyes and been cut in two.

On the whole the tussle between Ewing and Lofthouse ended with honours even. It was vigorous but frank and good humoured, and the knocking together of heads was purely accidental.

As for McAdams his goal was a good one and will be doubly valuable if it encourages him to shed the strange diffidence and mistrust which appears to afflict him nowadays whenever he catches sight of an open goal. The pearls from Johnstone which he lost through timidity today cannot be repeated indefinitely.

FINAL SCORE: CITY 2 BOLTON 1

City: Sky blue/White: Trautmann; Levers, Sear; Barnes, Ewing, Warhurst; Barlow, Hayes, Johnstone, McAdams, Fagan
Bolton: White shirts, blue knickers: Dean; Hartle, Edwards; Hennin, Higgins, Cunliffe; Birch, Stevens, Lofthouse, Parry, Holden
Attendance: 34,147 **Average now:** 27,799
Referee: A.Murdoch (Sheffield)
Linesmen: J.G.B. Peebles, D.R. Garside
League Position: Remained in 9th spot
For: 38 Against: 41
Reserves: Beat Derby away 1-0

So, my old fella's gloating was shortlived, if I could have found him, that is!
A friendly game then at Coventry who were wallowing in the third Division South and went into division four at the end of the season.

16A) MONDAY NOVEMBER 11TH 1957 K.O. 7.30PM: COVENTRY CITY (away, friendly)

We'd played them six times previously, all in division two, 38/39, 46/47, 50/51 winning five, drawing one and attracting 40,839 in the Maine Road 50/51 game. We also lost a friendly 2-1 in 48/49.

Dave Ewing was having further treatment to a head wound, and Ken Taylor could make his debut.

The programme was a smart four pager priced twopence. The front cover was of a reddish tinge, with a ground shot and a Coventry player wearing red and white broad stripes, even though the team were identified as wearing blue and white shirts, City playing in red (more likely maroon/claret). Obviously the notes said some nice things about our 'enigmatrical' (their spelling!) Blues deserving credit for giving the game a shot in the arm, despite being hit by injuries - five broken legs since the war and have always tried, with no little success, to play the football the crowds want to see.

On the back page was this little missive from Dan, Dan The Rhyming Man:

This soccer battle of the Cities
Evokes in thoughts a thousand pities
That underneath the floodlit sun
The game is not in division one

Well Dan only had to wait for another ten years....

Highfield Road's record attendance wasn't until 66/67 season, 51,457 v Wolves. I didn't visit until '68/69 when we drew 1-1. The ground looked odd, with a strange open Kop behind one goal, soaring up into the corner. A covered end behind the other goal, Dutch barn seated stand partly along one side with a terrace in front, and a short seated/standing main stand

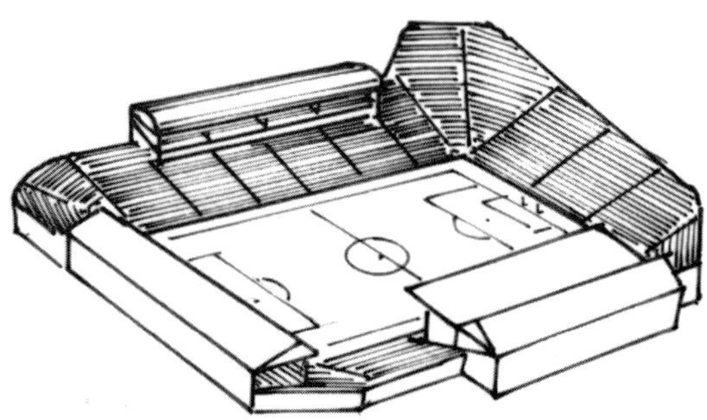

Pitch Size: 110 x 75 yds

with an extended roof. The ground was completely re-developed over the years before they moved to The Ricoh Stadium.

From Coventry's papers 'Nemo', John Davies: Young Spratt, Coventry's Hero

Hard on top of Coventry's six goal feast against Exeter, Highfield Road fans saw another heartening show against first division Manchester City and few of the crowd would begrudge their team's surprise win.

For long periods City were overplayed by superior football as Coventry, who had seventeen year old teenager Spratt to thank in the first half for a series of really magnificent saves which even had the high-powered City attack confounded, ran out worthy winners on the night.

In the first ten minutes alone Graham Spratt brilliantly kept out blazing shots from Barlow, McAdams and Johnstone (twice) - shots which would have left a lesser 'keeper than this agile teen-ager helpless. For a while it looked like City's cool and classic first division brand of football would bring the inevitable goals but Coventry's hard-working and composed defence kept cool. In the twenty third minute Patrick headed against an upright off a Sambrook corner, then Walters cleared off the line from the deep-lying Johnstone. Two minutes later a smart left wing move between Hill and the ever-menacing Sambrook saw Trautmann beaten by Patrick's header and **Jimmy Knox** was on the spot to shoot into an empty net. Both goalkeepers were kept busy before **Hayes** equalised after the ball ran loose following a goalmouth scramble and Joe scored from ten yards. For the second half City replaced Barlow with McClelland who nearly put City ahead. McAdams and Hayes then both hit the same upright but Coventry gradually took control on a 'gluepot' of a pitch. **Sambrook**, who looked dangerous every time he got the ball in the clear delighted the crowd with an ice-cool goal, when he side stepped the 'lanky' Leivers and beat Trautmann with an acute angled shot to put Coventry 2-1 up. Ten minutes from the end a devastating move between Rogers and Patrick got City's defence in a dreadful tangle and when the ball reached **Sambrook** he calmly shot into an empty net.

A minute later City got a penalty but Barnes could only put it wide of goal as he tried to side-foot it past Spratt. That was the end of the goalscoring attempts but City had enough of the ball in the first half alone to have scored a dozen.

RAY SAMBROOK

FINAL SCORE: COVENTRY 3 CITY 1

Coventry City: Spratt; Austin, Walters (Timmins); Jamieson, Curtis, Griffiths; Rogers, Patrick, Knox, Hill (P), Sambrook
City: Trautmann; Leivers, Little; Barnes, Taylor, Warhurst; Barlow (McClelland) , Hayes, Johnstone, McAdams, Clarke
Attendance: 8,480
Referee: (careful!) R.G.Warnke (Coventry)
Linesmen: D.R.Wildman, D,A,Moore

Coventry sold us Ray Sambrook, nicked the sky blue, made it to the first division in 66/67, won the cup in '87 (after seling us Bobby Mac and Tommy Hutch) but dropped into the (old) second in 2000/2001, where they remain.

November 13th: Scotland 1 Wales 1, Home International, at Hampden Park (42,918).

17) SATURDAY NOVEMBER 16TH 1957 K.O. 3 PM: LEEDS UNITED (AWAY)

Today's schoolboy game must have finished early for me, because I dashed home and tried to persuade my brother Don to take me to Leeds on his motorbike. "No, but we can have a run to Southport." Hmm so we went to Southport on his Velocette and I even got told off for leaning the wrong way when we went round corners. It was bloody freezing, Southport was shut, and the sea was out. Miles out.

So it was up to school pal John Cleaver to tell me about the game and mainly City's support which I was always fascinated by. "It was sky blue and white, all round the terrace behind the goal. Fantastic," he said.

Leeds were formed in 1904, as Leeds City, disbanded after a scandal in 1919 and were reformed as Leeds United in the same year. They'd never won anything, apart from promotions to the first in 1924, 1928, 1932 and most recently in 1956 so they were into their second season in division one after finishing eighth last term.

Programme was a classy looking sixteen pager for 3d. Front cover was a golden colour with a touch of blue, and a strange logo with owls and what looked like a well shagged sheep, and the motto 'Pro-Rege-Et-Lege', whatever that means?!

They'd just signed Wilbur Cush, from Glenavon in N. Ireland who was annoyed that his height was quoted as 5'4" and not 5'5" because that odd inch was important to him (and to most men Wilbur!?)

Some points about penalties were made, three penalties being awarded in Leeds' last home game in which Baird scored two for them. Apparently two players have scored three in a division one match - W. Walker for Aston Villa v Bradford City in 1921 and Charlie Mitten for United v Aston Villa in 1950.

During a third division north game between Crewe and Bradford in 1924, there were four penalties given in five minutes, a record. Scott, the Grimsby town goalie, saved three against Burnley in 1909, also a record.

They couldn't resist telling us that in the last match of season 25/26 City missed a penalty against Newcastle at 3-2 down. A draw would have saved us, but we took the drop.

Why am I relating this? Give it another few weeks.

There was also a quiz on the Blues, including:

1) What was Billy Meredith's transfer fee to United ? (A - £150, robbers)
2) Who scored the goals in the final of last year? (They meant 1956) (A - Hayes, Dyson, and Johnstone)
3) Who's the older club, City or United ? (A - United founded in 1885, City 1887)
4) What attendance records does Maine Road hold? (A - 84,569 v Stoke in F.A. Cup 1934. 82,950 United v Arsenal league 1948 - but 50,000 Blues cheering on Arsenal). Every other club has one record attendance, and I've never understood why at City it's split into Cup and league, though I have my suspicions.
5) When did a two-hundredth of a goal, prove costly to City? (A - 1927 when Portsmouth 1.7755 went up instead of us 1.7700 on goal average. It would have been us if it had been goal difference, 47 against 38).
6) Name as many as you can of City's '34 cup winning team (A - Swift, Barnett, Dale, Busby, Cowan, Bray, Toseland, Marshall, Tilson, Herd, Brook).
7) Who established City's individual goal scoring record for a league season (A - Tommy Johnson with 38 in Division 1 1928/29).

So you see, in the absence of any complete records about the Blues, we were learning all about the clubs' history from other club's programmes!

Elland Road's record attendance wasn't achieved until 1967 v Sunderland in the Cup, 57,892, just before Leeds played City in the sixth round. I made it there in 1959 when City won 4-0. It comprised a Dunlop and Rankin main stand, seats and paddock, still standing today, proudly shown on the back page of the programme and reputedly built with the money from the sale of John Charles to Juventus for £65,000. Opposite was the Lowfield Road stand and terrace. There was a small 'cowshed' at one end of the ground and a large Kop, yet to be concreted at the other. Floodlights looked like an exact replica of City's. The ground, with the pitch moved towards the Kop, was completely redeveloped over the years except for the main stand.

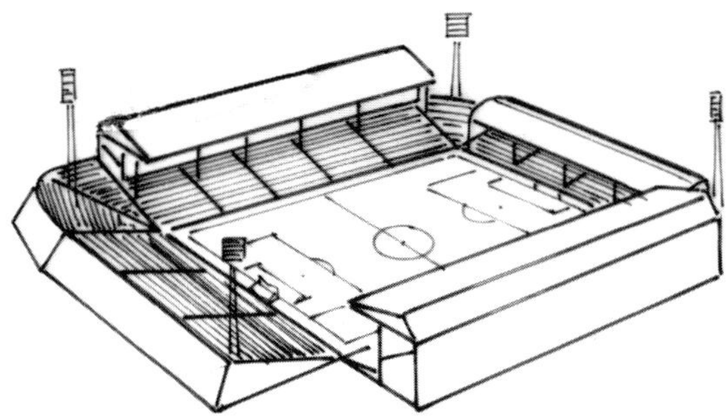

Pitch Size: 117 x 76 yds

Leeds, managed by Raich Carter, were in seventeenth place with thirteen points and City ninth with nineteen points. Form so far was mixed with four wins, including a 4-0 v Villa, two draws, and four losses at home. Only one away win, at Portsmouth, and a 5-0 drubbing at United.

At Leeds: Pre-war we'd won one out of the last nine, post-war, lost last season 0-2 (35.068) drew 1-1 in 50/51 (30,764). It was the thirty first league meeting plus one cup tie at City..

Team News: Little in for Sear, Phoenix for Johnstone, Clarke for Fagan. Yorkshire and England Cricketer Sir Len Hutton was in the crowd

From The Pink/Green
2 For Joe As City Lead 'Em A Merry Dance

Ron Phoenix was making his first ever appearance for City at centre forward, a position he'd been occupying with success for the reserves. It was a cold sort of day in Yorkshire, but the crowd was only about 22,000 at the start with the usual big following from Manchester.

Wilbur Cush

The pitch was greasy and mistakes looked plentiful. The light was poor, but City eyes were focussed on the opposition's Wilbur Cush, a City target who fellow Irishman Billy McAdams rated highly. Leeds kicked off and both teams pressed, though Leeds were on top in the early stages. City corners were cleared and Ewing twice checked Baird smartly. Leivers fired in a terrific shot which Charlton nearly turned past his own keeper. Ewing took a hard blow on the forehead, almost on the spot which was stitched last week and had to have treatment. From another corner Leivers 'cleared' the Elland Road stand with a terrific kick. The crowd then had a laugh when Phoenix, kicking the ball forward, hit the referee in the small of the back and knocked his whistle flying out of his mouth! City almost took the lead in the twenty first minute when Wood had to leap acrobatically to fist the ball over the bar, but it was Leeds who went ahead in the twenty ninth minute when Meek centred and with City claiming offside **Baird** slipped the ball into the net. The referee ruled that the ball had touched Leivers on the way and thus put Baird on side, Ewing's protests being in vain.

Hugh Baird

A minute later City were level when **Hayes** chased a long pass from Phoenix and gave Wood no chance with a great shot from close in. Bert then made two great saves fisting the ball over the bar each time. In the thirty fifth minute City went 2-1 up. McAdams chased a long pass through the middle and was in complete command when Charlton bowled him over as he prepared to shoot. Penalty, no doubt. **Barnes** made no mistake giving Wood no chance of stopping his hard low drive into the left hand corner of the net. It was all City now with Barnes and Warhurst prompting admirably. Five minutes before the interval Bert made one of the most fantastic saves ever seen from him. Baird unleashed a tremendous shot from twenty five yards and Bert slipped in the mud and stuck out a leg rather like a ballet dancer in the middle of an involved classical manoeuvre and the ball shot high in the air and was scrambled away. **We may never see such a save again**.

This was an isolated incident though, with City's class being up against Leeds' honest endeavour.

The floodlights came on for the second half with the City forwards giving Leeds problems. In the fifty seventh minute **Hayes** won possession about nineteen yards out from Ewing's free kick and rocketted the ball gloriously into the roof of the net for 3-1. Leeds were demoralised and Charlton was 'given the bird' when he passed back to Wood from thirty yards. In the sixty fifth minute City made it 4-1. From Trautmann's clearance Ewing combined splendidly with **McAdams** who tapped the ball home from close range.

Leeds had a little bit of fight left in them and after a persistent run by Cush, **Kerfoot** nipped in, shook off all attempts to stop him and shot past Bert from ten yards, after seventy minutes. City took command again with Phoenix going on his way rejoicing, always having the beating of the home centre half (Charlton, future World Cup winner!) and it was really amazing that City did not have more goals to underline their superiority. Leeds bucked up after their goal but had left it too late. Two minutes from time Ewing caught the headwound again but carried on, refusing treatment. So City won the match playing the orthordox game with Phoenix largely well forward and played it very well.

FINAL SCORE: LEEDS 2 CITY 4

Leeds: Blue and Gold: Wood (Roy); Dunn, Hair; Kerfoot, Charlton, Cush; Crowe, Ripley, Baird, Forrest, Meek.
City Claret and blue: Trautmann; Leivers, Little; Barnes, Ewing, Warhurst; Barlow, Hayes, Phoenix, McAdams, Clarke.
Attendance: 23,855 **Average:** 35,114
Referee: A.W.Sparling (Grimsby)
Linesmen: J.W.Hedley, Roy Harper - Roy became a first class referee and later reffed City's game at Sunderland in '68, 4-0 win and at Blackburn in the Cup in 1969, 4-1 win, and there may have been others. Roy was a great bloke, a sales rep. for a Sheffield company who used to visit the firm I was working at, George Robsons, still going today even though I left in 1969! He was a good friend of our '69 cup final referee George McCabe and obtained tickets for me from George for the final. Shortly after that final Roy collapsed and died refereeing a game at York City, which was a massive shock to all. A long time ago now but I will always be grateful to him for that act of kindness.

League position: Up three places to sixth
Goals For: 42 Against: 43 - so getting there!
Reserves: Won 3-1 home to Everton, bringing the goals tally up to 42, same as the first team.

17A) MONDAY NOVEMBER 18TH 1957
K.O. 7.30PM: HIBERNIAN (home, friendly)

Friendly time again, and tonight the turn of Hibs to visit Maine Road.

We'd previously played them at Easter Road in November 1955 when they beat us 2-1 and in March 1951 at Maine Road when they won 4-1. Later in 1960 we drew 1-1 at Maine Road, then in the 1979 Skol Festival Trophy drew 1-1, and in 1984 at Easter Road, we drew 0-0.

STARS OF EASTER ROAD

THEY MAY GIVE CITY HARD GAME

Gordon Smith | Willie Ormond | John Grant | Joe Baker

John Paterson | George Muir | Eddie Turnbull | Jim Harrower

UCP RESTAURANTS

FOR A GOOD MEAL AFTER THE MATCH

MERCHANTS 92 MARKET ST.
UCP · MANOR · TUDOR
MARKET ST. (opp. Lewis's) · BROWN ST. (Market St.) · OXFORD ST. (nr. Odeon)

FINGLAND'S
GARAGE & COACH STATION
261/7, WILMSLOW ROAD
RUSHOLME, MANCHESTER, 14
RUSholme 2894

A.A. & R.A.C. appointed garage. Repairs to all makes of cars. Authorised Wolseley dealer.
Breakdown Service Day & Night

Luxury coaches & cars available for private parties, works' contracts, etc.
Let us quote you

SPEARS
Largest cash buyers of all types of Cameras & Photographic Equipment
WRITE, CALL OR PHONE
SPEARS WAREHOUSE, 14 Watling St. (off Cannon St.) Manchester 4
Phone BLAckfriars 1916. OPEN ALL DAY SATURDAY.

8

Programme's editorial advised us that when a Manchester schoolboy was asked what is Edinburgh famous for he answered "Rock, 'earts and 'ibs". He goes on to review other Scottish teams' visits to Maine Road - Hearts, East Fife 2-1, 53/54, Aberdeen, 4-3 in 54/55,

Celtic 1-1 in 53/54, and Rangers won 4-1 in 55/56 to become the first team to beat City under the lights. Hibs. had won the Scottish cup twice and the Championship as recently as 48, 51, and 52.

Maine Road Gossip advised that Jack Dyson was a recent welcome visitor to Maine Road after having the plaster removed from his leg and hopes to be in action soon. Eighteen year old Blackley lad, Herbert Lister has also been signed on professional forms. Hibs line up included Joe Baker, who later went to Torino with Denis Law.

Arthur Walmsley waxed lyrical about Peter Doherty, whose son Paul was getting good reviews in his displays for the Army team in Germany. Paul, a newspaper reporter before being called up, didn't make it as a footballer but made it to Granada T.V., was the man behind the unofficial City magazine 'Out Of The Blue' in the 60s and edited City's programme for a while in the 70s. There were pics of the Stars of Easter Road 'They may give City a hard time'

David Jack reflects on the standing of English Internationals on the world stage. Top five listed by a Brazilian 'expert' were Di Stefano, Kocsis, Kubala, Kopa and Vukas. No Puskas, Matthews, Wright, Blanchflower or Charles, and David reckoned we'd have to demonstrate to the Continentals that we're over our post Hungary depression for our players to be rated again. Best way to prove this would be in the games against France, Scotland Yugoslavia, Russia and a yet unnamed team before the World Cup finals in Sweden.

From Tommy Wright, Hibs historian

Half a dozen English clubs were in attendance to watch Harrower of Hibs and for the first twenty minutes would gladly have paid top price for any of the visitor's attack. During this period Manchester City literally didn't know what had hit them as the five pronged Hibs attack left the home defence in a bewildered state. It was a pity that the Scots could not keep it up and in the end they were beaten by a goal that should have been avoided. Just after the break centre forward **Phoenix**, a replacement for Bobby Johnstone, fired a chance shot from twenty five yards that was in the net before goalkeeper Leslie was aware of it. For football craft Hibs were always the masters, but after that brilliant opening spell just couldn't find the essential finishing touch. Backed by the strong half back play of Turnbull and Baxter Hibs carved up the Manchester City defence at will and always looked capable of scoring an equalising goal, particularly with Ormond having the beating of Leivers in the later stages. How the English managers must have looked on in envy as seventeen year-old Joe Baker put on a polished display against a rugged Manchester defence and only a late punch off his head by Trautmann denied him the goal his play deserved. In the second half the home side tested the Hibs defence more often after changing their tactics, swinging the ball about and creating damage to great effect on numerous occasions. City's chief danger man was Hayes who almost scored but only succeeded in hitting the goalkeeper from close range.

JOHN GRANT

RESULT: CITY 1 HIBERNIAN 0

City: Sky blue/white: Trautmann; Leivers, Little; Barnes, Ewing, Warhurst; McLelland, Hayes, Phoenix, McAdams, Clarke. (Bobby Johnstone, the most famous signing between the clubs, didn't play)
Hibs: Green shirts, white knickers: Leslie; Grant, Muir; Turnbull, Paterson, Baxter; Aitken, Harrower, Baker, Preston, and Ormond.
Attendance: 13,511
Referee: K.Collinge (Sale)
Linesmen: F.W. Cooper, W.Davies

Hooper interest shown again. Arsenal's Eddie Hapgood has been paid £1,500 for libel and slander.

Harry Hooper

**18) SATURDAY NOVEMBER 23RD
K.O. 3PM: WOLVERHAMPTON WANDERERS
(HOME)**

Wolves were formed in 1876, were promoted in 1924 from the third, and in 1932 from the second. They were runners up in division one in '38. '39, '50, '55 and won it in '54. They were cup winners in 1893, 1908, and 1949, runners up in 1889, 1896, 1921 and 1939. Last season they finished sixth.

Programme editorial sympathised with the City club in that just as they were showing genuine form and getting into a challenging position, they were overtaken with a crop of injuries, six regulars being under treatment.

The win at Leeds had left City as having scored more goals away from home than any other first or second division team. Don't mention the 'against' column though, but nineteen of those came in three consecutive matches!!

Welcome arrival was Mr. George Poyser as Chief scout and assistant to Les McDowall. Poyser was considerably experienced in the game and had a reputation as a shrewd judge of a player.This wouldn't, of course, interfere with the long serving Mr Albert Kavanagh.

Maine Road Gossip informed us that we would be welcoming back Butlin's Young Ladies, who would treat us to another of their popular 'Keep Fit In Rhythm' displays.

Sportsman's Corner answers a query from R.McDonald of Openshaw, re a game in 1946 when we beat United 4-1 George Smith scoring four, three in seven minutes.

Arthur Walmsley gives credit to City for rising to sixth place, but says that people reckon we're only here because the teams below us are so bad. That is the sort of cynical, churlish comment which sounds clever but just emphasises the debits and ignores the credits. Our position is, he thinks, due to the speed and fleet footedness of the forwards Hayes, Barlow, Fagan and to a lesser extent Billy Mac. Hey and when the injury situation improves it could make City into a devastating outfit.

David Jack praises the old timers, Matthews, Finney and company and thinks despite his age Billy Wright will captain England in the World Cup finals in June

Train to Sunderland next week would be twenty one shillings.

Wolves managed by Stan Cullis, were having a great season. They topped the league with twenty seven points, City sixth with twenty one points. Away form was three wins, including a 5-1 at Birmingham, four draws and two defeats 1-0 at Everton (first game of the season) and 3-1 at Luton. At home it was seven wins and one draw, including a 6-1 v Bolton, 5-1 v Sunderland and 4-0 v Spurs. They'd regularly taken on foreign opposition in the 50s, including Moscow Dynamo under their lights, and had just beaten Real Madrid 3-2 at home and Hibs 3-2 away. They were also unbeaten in the last three games and were unbeaten at home. So no problem?!

At Maine Road: Pre-war Wolves won the last one, but prior to that lost thirteen on the bounce and there were some big City wins - 6-0, 5-0, 5-1, 4-0 and three - 4-1's. Post we won four they three, including last seasons 3-2, Bert's return after injury in the '56 cup final, with three draws.

Recent attendances ranged from 22,729 (53/54) to 67,800 (47/48). It was the forty ninth league meeting plus two cup ties, one at City, third rd. round finishing 2-2 in 1952 (54,497).

Team news: Fagan in for Clarke, Fleet the six foot, twenty year old Salford airman on a thirty six hour pass from RAF Bridgnorth, Shrewsbury, in for Bert.

From The Guardian's 'Old International': Wolverhampton's Last-Ditch Victory

The Molineux Juggernaut, better known as Wolverhampton Wanderers, crushed the life out of City in Moss Side.

If ever a defeat had its commendable side this was it. Even the croakers - the dyed in the wool variety - were stunned into speechlessness. For after falling one goal behind to a team of great physical strength and striking power, City produced, by a blend of speed and artistry, two of the finest goals Maine Road has ever witnessed, to be further augmented by a penalty goal and from a pinnacle of this 3-1 lead had begun to assume the aspect of conquerors.

But it is precisely at these moments that Wolves are most dangerous and staking their all on a series of full scale attacks produced three crucial goals in about eight minutes. By this time the floodlights were on (the credulous saw in that the secret of Wolves' recovery) and the yellow, baleful glare, intensified by the mist, lent to the old gold jerseys of the visitors something ghostly, eerie, Dantesque, as they sped about their devils work.

Barnes soon showed that he was going to be a very prickly thorn in the flesh to Wolverhampton, rampage as they might. He swept a dainty long centre in to McAdams and Bill forced Dwyer to make a thrilling finger-tip save. He sent Barlow scurrying away by a clever flick from a stray ball, while repeatedly, in the narrow confines of his own goalmouth, must have made young Fleet's hair stand on end by the cool, calm impudence with which he beat the various Wolves forwards with the ball, before tapping it back for safe clearances. The slightest slip, the faintest relaxation of vigilance one felt, and a goal must result. Sure enough it did. But not as a result of Barnes, but as a result of general slackness on the part of City's defence. Wolves took a quick, harmless-looking throw-in and **Murray** had three goes at it. His first shot hit a post, his second struck Leivers, and at the third attempt he stabbed the ball past Fleet.

Billy Wright

The next phase between the thirty third and the seventy seventh minute was all City's. It revealed that in Johnstone City have a peerless artist and a master distributor and in Barlow, Hayes, McAdams and Fagan as speedy a quartet of goal-poachers as can be found anywhere in the game. However this refers only to the speed at the disposal of the quartet, not to ball control or tactical resource generally. Were it otherwise they would be world-beaters.

Too often they have their thinking done for them and today Johnstone was ideally in the mood. The two exquisite passes with which he twice sent Barlow away could not fail to evoke answering responses in the shape of goals - one from **McAdams**, the other **Barnes**. And when Bobby was himself about to score had the supports brusquely removed by Harris. **Barnes** saw to it that the ensuing penalty kick was carefully credited to the account. This goal, taken so primly and precisely seemed to shock Wolves into action. Shadowy figures in increasing numbers pushed forward into the City goal area, relying on clever and persistent off-side tactics to eke out a thinned defence. But without a certain amount of contributory negligence on the City defenders part - or was it just crippling fatigue? - the three goals in eight minutes by **Murray**, **Mason** and **Broadbent** would not have been possible.

Alongside Barnes, Warhurst got through a prodigious amount of hard work, took his share of punishment without murmuring, and did his fair share of attacking bringing out the save of the match from Dwyer. Fleet, whose every touch was cheered all over the ground, promises well. He has clean hands, quick wits and a calm confident bearing. In the game's last phase, when the light was poor, his judgement was excellent, and he was in no way to blame for any of the goals that got past him. Sear, also showed commendable pluck and obstinacy for one so slender, and it is greatly to his credit that Deeley, Wolves' most waspish forward, caused no more trouble than he did. City were today up against a formidable trio of attacking marauders and Broadbent's method of dealing with Warhurst was peculiar and should have been preserved in a museum of Roman antiquities alongside the ballista.

FINAL SCORE: CITY 3 WOLVES 4

City: Sky blue/white: Fleet; Leivers, Sear; Barnes, Ewing, Warhurst; Barlow, Hayes, Johnstone, McAdams, Fagan
Wolves: Gold shirts, black knickers; Dwyer; Stuart, Harris; Clamp, Wright, Flowers; Deeley, Broadbent, Murray, Mason, Mullen - now that WAS an M-Plan!
Attendance: 45,121 **Average:** 29,724
Referee: P.Rhodes (York)
Linesmen: G.Ollerton, G.Ramage
League position: Stayed in 6th
Goals For: 45 Against: 47
Reserves: Lost 4-2 at Barnsley

I went to this game with a youth called Arthur, who fancied my older sister. He was a bit of a red and was well pleased when Wolves won, which I found really annoying. He didn't seem to notice the fact that Wolves went five points clear of United as it didn't bother him. Must've realised that they had no chance of winning the title that season and he had as much chance of going out with my sister, I'm pleased to say!

City eventually got their own back when at Maine Road in the early 70's in the league Cup. We were 3-1 down to Wolves with ten minutes to go and won 4-3.

18A) MONDAY NOVEMBER 25TH 1957
K.O.7.15PM: HIBERNIAN (away friendly)

Up to Edinburgh again, this time for the return friendly fixture with Hibs.

Programme was 3d for eight pages and had a smart green front cover with a pic of Hibs' recent game with Wolves, Malcolm Finlayson getting treatment for an injury.

There was good information on City's history, pics of Bobby Johnstone in Hibs' colours, and Bert smilingly saving a shot. We were advised that Maine Road held another record too (other than an international). This time the English midweek crowd of 80,407 for the semi-final replay between Derby and Birmingham in 1946.

Easter Road's record attendance was 65,850 v Hearts in 49/50. There was a main stand seats and paddock, with open ends behind each goal, and a huge open terrace opposite the main stand. The ground was partly redeveloped over the years.

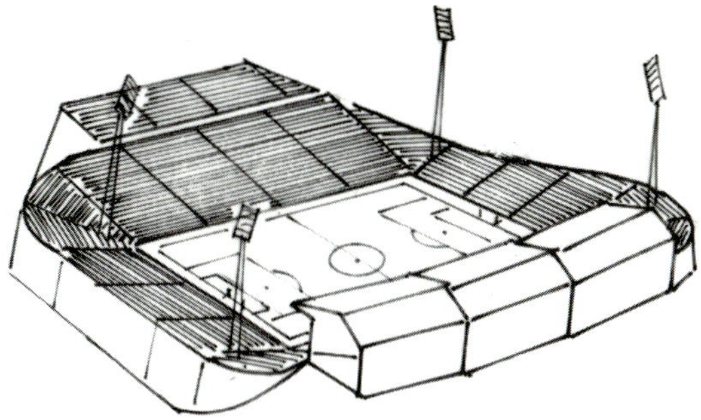

Pitch Size: 112 x 74 yds

From Tommy Wright, Hibs historian

The moaners who complain about two games in a week got their answer last night where a blistering first half blasted a Manchester side minus the services of goalkeeper Trautmann out of the picture and eventually finished handsome 5-2 winners. The home side were in no way dismayed when **Barlow** opened the scoring for the visitors in eight minutes via the right hand post. Paterson and company quickly closed ranks, and prompted by Turnbull began to turn the traffic City wise with penetrating dribbles and telling accurately placed passes. **Turnbull** gained an early individual reward with an equaliser after ten minutes when his thirty yarder screamed past Fleet. From then on the wing half put his mark on the game with a lively non stop role of attack supporting craft and when the occasion demanded fell back in defence to help his team mates with several timely interventions.

Hibs changed ends 4-1 to the good and it could well have been more had the Manchester defence not escaped the full penalty for their defensive indiscretions near the box. Ewing and his colleagues were in a flat spin by the speed in which Hibs swept into attack, the quick bewildering exchanges and the shoot on sight policy of Ormond and Harrower backed by the heavy artillery of Turnbull.

Leivers did not look English First Division class under pressure as Hibs supplied cut and thrust football while City struggled to get into top gear, Bobby Johnstone doing his best to supply zest and power. Leslie had several saves to make but by contrast City reserve keeper Fleet had little chance with four of the five counters, nor dare I say it would a fit Trautmann. The goalkeeper could blame the men in front of him who resorted to some heavy stuff in an effort to curtail the lively excursions of Ormond and Baker. The young centre had to receive treatment during the first half and was withdrawn with half an hour left to be replaced by Thomson. Hibs manager Shaw did the right thing here, as the young forward is far too good a proposition to aggravate an injury when the substitute law applies. All the others played their part in the victory to varying degrees of success, everyone contributing something to this really satisfactorily victory although Reilly appeared to slow down in the second half. **Barlow** opened the scoring in eight minutes, only for **Turnbull** to rocket in an equaliser minutes later, **Baker** putting Hibs ahead three minutes later with a header. After twenty minutes **Ormond** scored from a narrow angle just a yard from the bye-line past an astonished keeper. It was all Hibs now, **Harrower** netting Hibs' fourth with a twenty five yard shot. A momentary slackness in Hibs' defence allowed City to reduce the arrears five minutes after the restart through **Fagan** from a Johnstone chip. After seventy five minutes **Ormond** scored with a touchline special to seal City's fate who must have decided that it never rains but it pours even outside of Manchester. A game worth double the 15,000 gate.

JOE BAKER

FINAL SCORE: HIBS 5 CITY 2.

Hibernian: Leslie; Grant. Muir; Turnbull. Paterson, Baxter; Reilly, Harrower, Baker, (Thomson) Preston, and Ormond.
City: Fleet; Leivers, Sear; Barnes, Ewing, Warhurst; Barlow, Kirkman, Johnstone, Hayes and Fagan.
Attendance: 15,000
Referee: W.Brittle
Linesmen: A. McEwan, J.C.Ferguson

The unofficial table was led by Hibernian, followed by City, Hearts, Newcastle, Spurs and Partick Thistle

The games were classed as unofficial floodlit friendlies after failing to receive the permission of the controlling bodies on both sides of the border to play the competition as a competitive tournament. Although the advertising regulations of the time prohibited companies from sponsoring such competitions it is believed that "Schweppes'" were prepared to put up trophy and prize money amounting to £2,000. Representatives of Hibernian, Hearts, Partick Thistle, Manchester City, Spurs and Newcastle attended a meeting in Edinburgh on, I believe, Tuesday 13th September 1955, chaired by Hibs far seeing chairman Harry Swan. Coincidentally that same day the Hibs players left the city to play German side Rot Weiss Essen in the first ever European Cup game involving a British side. Rangers and Arsenal were also interested in the new floodlit competition which would feature only games between the respective countries, but in the end neither took part. Interestingly, Hearts did not, in the early 50's have floodlights of their own and played some games at Easter Road. Many unofficial "friendly" games took place over the next couple of years, the authorities still refusing to sanction the tournament on an official basis. Harry Swan insisted that the clubs would eventually be successful in their bid for legitimacy if they showed resolve, but Hearts, to Swan's everlasting disgust, eventually withdrew from the competition after the Scottish sides were threatened with expulsion from the league, and the tournament eventually died a slow death. At one point Partick Thistle even threatened to take the case to court, on the basis that it was unfair to allow both the European and Fair Cities Cups to proceed yet still prohibit the "Floodlit league," but this too eventually came to nothing.

Hibs finished ninth at the end of the season, and lost in the cup final 1-0 to Clyde. Whilst not winning the league again, they did manage a few cups over the years.
Goalie Lawrie Leslie went to West Ham., Joe Baker to Torino with Denis Law and then Arsenal and Forest. Later City signed centre-half Jackie Plenderleith from the Edinburgh club.

Nov 27: England 4 France 0 - friendly at Wembley (60,000). Hart was back playing in the reserves. Bert's shoulder was responding to treatment. Fagan received an ankle injury at Hibs. where Hibs' Liverpool born youngster Joe Baker went off, Hibs later denying it was due to City's tough play. Jack Dyson is back in light training.

19) SATURDAY NOVEMBER 30TH 1957
K.O 2.15 PM: SUNDERLAND (AWAY)

Sunderland were formed in 1879, joined the Football League in 1890/91 and were formidable until 1937, winning the league six times, runners up five times the cup in 1937, and runners up in 1913. Last season they finished twentieth, just three points clear of relegated Cardiff City.

The programme was a good one, 4d for sixteen pages. Front cover was red and white striped with a ground shot including floodlights, strange because today's game kicked off at 2.15pm. Manager Alan Brown thought it interesting that City and Sunderland would be employing similar tactics, a deep centre forward play, with Don Revie playing at number nine.

In **Soccer Gossip** the discussion is on the change in rules to allow youngsters to sign professional forms as young as 17. There's some info on City's history and that between the clubs, pen portraits and plenty of ads, so content-wise not too interesting.

Roker Park 's record attendance was 75,118 v Derby in the F.A. Cup 6 1933. I didn't manage a visit until the cup tie in 1983, a 0-0 draw. Ground comprised a double decker main stand along the length, seats and standing. Opposite was a seats/standing paddock type stand. Behind each goal was a huge terrace, where from the Fulwood (later roofed) end the Roker Roar would sound out. Floodlights looked on the small side. There was little change to Roker over the years, and they eventually moved to the Stadium of Light, where City were their first opponents in August 1997.

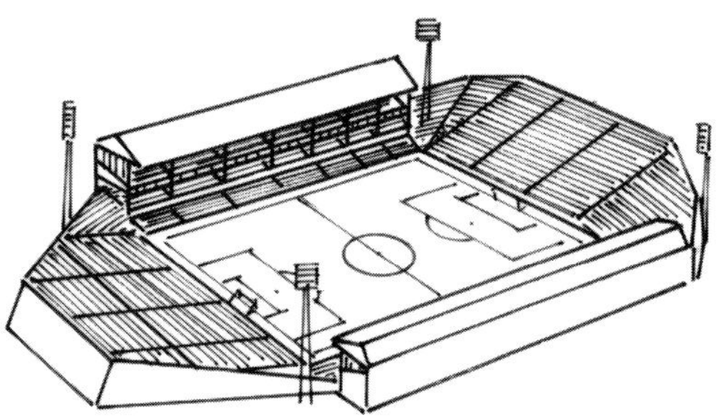

Pitch size: 113 x 74 yds

Sunderland, managed by Alan Brown, were seventeenth with fourteen points and City sixth with twenty one points. Their form so far was four home wins three draws, two defeats, to Arsenal and Bolton. Away they were shocking with one win at Birmingham, two draws, and seven defeats including a 7-0 at Blackpool, a 6-0 at Burnley, and a 5-0 at Wolves.

At Sunderland: Pre-war they usually beat us, but we did have five wins and seven draws out of the thirty one games. Post we'd won four lost three and drawn two, so not bad.

Recent attendances ranged from 33,733 (54/55) to 49,434 (53/54). In the Cup we'd won the '55 semi-final with that Roy Clarke diving header in the mud. It was our eighty first league meeting plus four cup ties, two at Sunderland 1913 second rd. replay 0-2 (27,974), 1928 fourth rd. 2-1 (38,658), and a Charity Shield game at City.

Team News: Bert was back after his shoulder injury, Clarke in for Fagan who had ankle trouble.

From The Pink/Green:
Late Rally Fails

Chief interest in the game centred on the appearance against his old club, of Don Revie, who couldn't play in the corresponding game last season because of injury. Under Revie's influence, at inside right, with the exploitation of the deep lying centre forward plan, Sunderland had been improving as their recent win at Birmingham testified. The early kick off kept the crowd down, under 20,000 at the start, but amongst them were the Italian Juventus team who had a match with Sunderland on the coming Monday night. Also with the Italians was 'Mr Moneybags' Gigi Peronace who chatted with McDowall and the City players but there was no mention of any transfer dealings (that was to come later with Denis Law!).

There were early raids by both Sunderland and City and in the third minute Revie crossed for Anderson to nod sideways for 17 year old Alan Spence to head over the bar. But a minute later Sunderland went ahead when a long clearance from Bert eluded Revie but Anderson kicked it back towards City's goal and as Bert came out. Revie coolly lobbed it over his head into the net. The game continued at a cracking pace with City having more of the play. Some of City's tackling incensed the home crowd and there was a good deal of booing, groans too as Spence nearly kicked the ball out of the ground from less than ten yards. Revie had seemingly taken over Shackleton's role, being here there and everywhere, lying deep one minute, appearing on the right wing the next and finally falling back to help his defence.

There are still very few better distributors of the ball. In the eighteenth minute a shocking lapse by Ewing whose hopeless mess of a pass back to Trautmann let Bingham in but his shot was saved by Bert who dived to his right and turned it for a corner. Ewing, no doubt, passed a silent vote of thanks to his goalkeeper. City were playing a short passing game which wasn't coming off, most of the passes being intercepted. Sunderland were finding their men but City were not and in the twenty seventh minute Sunderland went further ahead. A corner by Grainger was headed out by Ewing and when the ball came to **Anderson**, standing just inside the penalty box, he let fly with a thunderbolt and beat Trautmann to the world. On the half hour Barlow tried to walk the ball into the net but it was cleared after a scramble, though it should have been a City goal. City were nothing like as effective in front of goal as they have been. A shot from Johnstone, City's outstanding player, was charged down and at the other end Bert saved at point blank range from Bingham and then stopped a Revie lob, so the 2-0 half time score didn't flatter the Wearsiders.

DON REVIE

Sunderland were much quicker in everything they did but City had their chances with McAdams and Barlow coming close. Whilst playing good football City were generally too dainty and the finishing was dreadfully poor, though Sunderland enjoyed the run of the ball. City fans amongst the biggest away following of the season said, "Never mind, Billy Mac's yet to score."

At last McAdams barged his way through, won a corner, which was cleared, but City persisted and following a good run from Hayes, **Billy** tapped the ball home in the sixty sixth minute. That made it nine goals in nine consecutive games for the Irishman.

City now redoubled their efforts, though Trautmann made an incredible save from Bingham's red hot spinner. The lights were switched on as Hayes, McAdams and Clarke missed chances with Fraser making a miraculous save from Warhurst in the last minute. If City had shown such determination earlier they would have 'walked' this match.

FINAL SCORE: SUNDERLAND 2 CITY 1

Sunderland: Red and white striped shirts, black shorts, black with red top stockings: Fraser; Hedley, Elliot; Anderson, Hurley, Aitken; Bingham, Revie, Spence, Fogarty, Grainger.
City: Sky blue/white: Trautmann; Leivers, Sear; Barnes, Ewing, Warhurst; Barlow, Hayes, Johnstone, McAdams, Clarke.
Attendance: 35,442 **Average:** 35,145
Referee: A.E.Ellis - smiling Arthur, a Yorkshireman, went on to compere 'It's a knockout' with Stuart Hall and gave a few crucial decisions against City in future games at Bolton, Blackburn and at home to United when Dawson fisted the ball past Steve Fleet.

Linesmen: G.W.Ward, H.G.Wilson
League position: Down 4 places to 10th
Goals For: 46 Against 49
Reserves: Beat Sheff United 4-1 at Maine Road

CONCLUSION: Three away games gave us two losses and one win. At home we finally lost our home record against Wolves, but beat our local rivals Bolton. We completed four friendly games, three away, one at home. In the table we went from eighth to tenth. Goal difference went up to 46 for, 49 against. Average home attendance 29,714 away 35,145. There were debuts for Steve Fleet, plus Ken Taylor in the friendly at Coventry.

LEAGUE TABLE

	P	W	D	L	F	A	Pts
Wolves	20	13	5	2	50	23	31
WBA	20	9	10	1	48	28	28
Preston	19	11	3	5	41	25	25
Man Utd	19	11	2	6	46	32	24
Luton	19	10	2	7	28	24	22
Notts For	19	10	1	8	39	29	21
Blackpool	19	9	3	7	32	29	21
Everton	19	7	7	5	29	29	21
Arsenal	20	9	3	8	32	33	21
Man City	**19**	**10**	**1**	**8**	**46**	**49**	**21**
Spurs	20	8	4	8	44	45	20
Bolton	19	8	4	7	35	37	20
Burnley	19	8	3	8	40	37	19
Chelsea	19	6	6	7	41	37	18
B'ham	20	6	5	9	32	43	17
Sunderland	20	5	6	9	26	47	16
Newcastle	19	6	3	10	30	30	15
Portsmouth	19	6	3	10	32	36	15
Leeds	20	5	4	11	25	39	14
Aston Villa	20	5	4	11	30	45	14
Sheff Wed	19	5	3	11	29	40	13
Leicester	19	4	2	13	35	53	10

DECEMBER'S FOOTBALL MONTHLY

United's Eddie Colman was on the front cover and Birmingham's Noel Kinsey on the back cover. CB's editorial opinion commented on the FA trying to ban players from writing articles. CR Williamson identified players with weather names - Fogg, Lightning, Frost etc. John Thompson tells how Busby joined City whilst waiting for his visa to come through to emigrate to the USA.

Once A Blue, Always A Blue

EDDIE from Bristol's story:

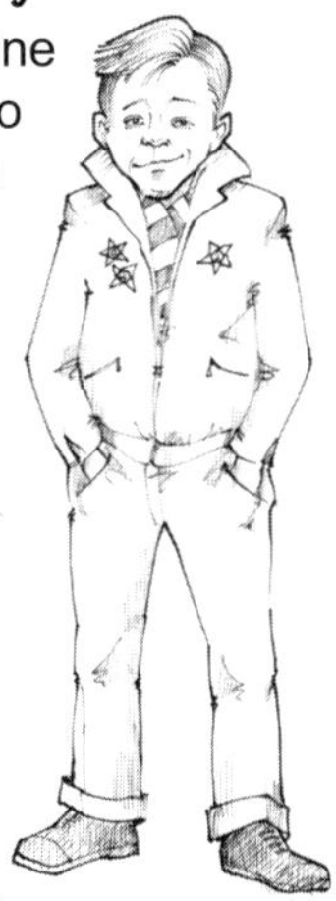

From April 1952 I lived on Maine Road. Our house backed on to the main car park, where every Sunday morning loads of us kids would play football, including a very young Neil Young. In those days there were lots of local derby games, Blackburn, Burnley, Bolton, Blackpool, Everton and of course United. We would wait for the coach to turn up on a Saturday morning to pick up the players and we would run over and start kicking a tennis ball around to show our heroes how good we were. Sometimes the players would join in, which of course was a great thrill to us. On one occasion

I scored a goal against Bert Trautmann and I think it was Ken Barnes that I beat for pace who was having a ciggie at the time. I kicked the tennis ball as hard as I could towards the middle of the two drainpipes that Bert was guarding, and as he bent down to pick up the ball it hit the kerb and sent him the wrong way, thudding against the brick wall that was our goal. Bert did not concede many at Maine Road so I was chuffed.

The players were very approachable in those days, most of them travelling on the bus to the ground on match days.

I remember so clearly the three derbies in '55 - 3-2 and 2-0 at Maine Road, one being a cup match and we beat United 5-0 at Old Trafford, when my pal and I stood behind the goal at the Stretford End where we cheered every goal and no one bothered us. How times change.

I got to know most of the players from the successful cup winning team of '56 including my hero Bobby Johnstone. I also got to meet Bob, and I have a photograph of him, me and Bert Trautmann. Do you know what, Bert did not remember that goal I scored against him. Great memories for me, and even though Maine Road has gone my house is still there.

Eddie is a lifelong Blue, and a first class entertainer.

JOHN from Bury's story:

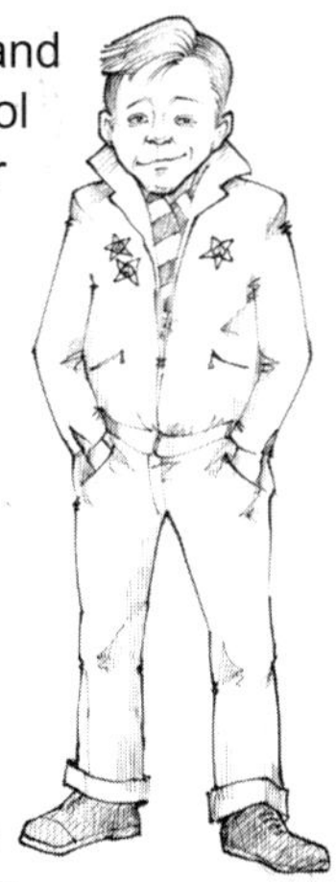

I lived in Salford, Broughton, and attended Lower Kersal school where the headmaster Arthur Gayle had played for WBA and managed Altrincham. My dad was a Geordie who came down to Manchester to work at Greengates in Trafford Park. He was a big Newcastle fan and in any football arguments we had, just used to say "get the record books out then John" We watched the 1955 cup finalon TV and after having Jackie Milburn rammed down my throat for years he went and scored an early headed goal, and *'Wor Jackie'* couldn't head a ball for toffee. That was the day I became a real City fan and I've never wavered since, even though Salford was all United, a sea of red. I mean, you couldn't follow the same team as your dad could you? Worse, my brother Andrew was a closet red, though he's never, ever been to watch them.

Liverpool player Roy Saunders, father of Dean, lived nearby, in his mum's council flat and played cricket for Cromwell Cricket club in the summer. When I became scorer for the team he'd give me lifts to games in his blue Ford Consul. Then he was transferred to Swansea, and Cromwell played their cricket team, which included Mel Nurse.

An early game I remember was a night match, a friendly v Hibs. City wom 1-0 but the player who impressed me most was Willie Ormond and I thought he was fantastic.

I went to secondary school at Salford Technical High, where they were practically all fanatical reds, one lad even, Brownie, sold programmes at O/T. They bragged that they had a reserve team full of internationals, so Munich didn't affect me too much. Some City fans depressingly changed to United at this time, for some astounding reason and so many reds would say "I haven't missed a match this season" then add ", since Munich". I remember them signing the likes of Bob Hardisty, Stan Crowther, Ernie Taylor, after the disaster..

To get to Maine Road I'd catch the number thirteen bus along Littleton Road to Victoria, walk it up past Thomson House (now the Printworks), then it was the 75 or the 76x to the bus depot near Maine Road. I always went on the scoreboard end. Coming home the Green 'un would be out in Piccadilly, then it was the 13 back home. Later I'd cycle it and pay my threepence to leave it in someone's back yard.

For away games we always went by train, queuing up at the station, sometimes the players would be on our train. Never saw any trouble, though once, coming back from an away game, the Everton fans' train was stationary on the middle track, as they'd wrecked it and were waiting for the police to arrive! I once had to walk it home from Piccadilly late at night wearing my colours but had no problems.

We had good wins at Blackpool, Everton and Leeds, but Birmingham, Preston, West Brom., and Leicester, oh dear, once you'd seen those defeats (4-0, 6-1, 9-2, 8-4) there was nothing anyone could throw at you! I attended a few reserve games too, Jimmy Meadows making his come back at home to Huddersfield with Denis Law and Ray Wilson in their team. At Leicester we stood on the half way line. I had a cowboy hat on painted sky blue and white, and a bloke tried to remove it but was discouraged by a big City fan!. I remember going to Nottingham the season after and it was the first time I'd heard about the Goose Fair. After leaving school I worked in Trafford Park as an apprentice toolmaker, jacked it in, joined the RAF and was posted to Aden - bomb alley and all that. I used to tune in to Reuters to get the results. Then I joined the Prison service. I was based near Cambridge for a while, and was taking a prisoner to London in a taxi and noticed the driver's ID, and it was ex Blue and ex-Cambridge manager Bill Leivers, who was having trouble with his legs at the time. We talked football and City all the way to London! I moved back to Manchester, Strangeways, and when I worked Saturdays and City had a goal against them the prisoners next door would bang on the wall and shout "Oh no, it's a goal!!", but all in good part. Football was a big emotional release for prisoners. We did get a few footballers in there, but mainly for non payment of maintenance and the like.

(Ed - I asked John if he ever wished he'd supported United. The response was swift and decisive "WHAT, get thee behind me…")

John's daughter Joanne is a staunch Blue also, after a freezing trip to Carlisle to watch the Blues lose! Why oh why! John recently became dis-illusioned with City and football, players wages etc, and let his season ticket lapse, but he's now back with a vengeance for 2007/08.

DENNIS from Crewe's story:

I attended my first game at Maine Road in April 1938, City 6 Leeds United 2. I was aged eleven and sat in the main stand with my pal Bobby Skews, and I marvelled at the skills of Peter Doherty and the electrifying runs of Eric Brook down the left wing. This was the last home game of the season, City were already relegated but finished in good style. In 1943 when I was fifteen I went with my two brothers Roger aged thirteen, and Peter aged eleven years, on the train from Heald Green to Mauldeth Road station. We were met by our school Sports master Mr Frank Moseley who lived in Burnage. He had played for City's junior teams in the 1920's and died at Maine Road in 1974. We walked to Maine Road but Mr Moseley had only one stand ticket which he gave to Peter. The rest of us went round to the Kippax and found an exit door ajar. So we went through and saw the game against Blackpool which ended 1-1. In the same year England played Scotland, winning 8-0 and my best memory was seeing Stanley Matthews coming towards us on the right wing and close to the touchline, beating two defenders, cutting inside and lobbing the ball over Crozier, the Scottish keeper, for the final goal. Absolute perfection, drawing the biggest cheer of the game.

I saw Manchester United play at Maine Road a couple of times also, both against City and other teams. They printed their own programmes with no reference to those games being played at Maine Road.

On 22nd April 1946 I had just turned seventeen years old and watched City lose to Blackpool in the Football League cup north semi-final second leg 2-1. I was on the school Easter break youth hostelling in the Lake District, and attended the game on my way home. I was in hiking gear with my rucksack. It was all standing on the Kippax on a beautiful sunny day with over 60,000 people packed in. The game was exciting though City lost, Peter Doherty scoring a blinder but then missing a wide open goal! The match finished and we were ready to go. I picked up my rucksack - it was all wet as were the terraces nearby. It had not rained therefore I concluded that people near and behind me must have urinated on it during the game - apparently a regular occurrence in the days of packed terraces.

Post war I came home on leave from doing National Service on Salisbury Plain and attended the England v Wales international, attendance 59,121, which England won 3-0 (scorers Mannion 2, Lawton) It wasn't a great game but the performance of Frank Swift that day was worth the entrance cost just to see him perform.

On the 23rd August 1947 City were back in division one and beat Wolves 4-3 in front of 67,800. It was an exciting game and Roy Clarke scored the winner with a ferocious shot which beat Bert Williams.

In August 1954, after losing 5-0 at Preston, City beat Sheffield United 5-2 at Maine Road. At the time and for the following few seasons or so I had made a 'pen friend' of Mrs Betty Wild who then worked in the City office and was the widow of the former manager Wilf Wild. She had been sending me City home programmes all these years, and invited me to the ground on the previous day to have a look round. Jim McLelland the then trainer/coach took me all around. In the boot room I met Bert Trautmann, who had a badly swollen right hand and so shook my hand with his left. But twenty four hours later Bert was in goal for the above game. I have always wondered how he got through that match as I could see no signs of holding back in his handling of the ball.

I have every home programme since 1946 and only 9 aways missing, and they include match reports from the early 50's.

Up to 2003/04, having lived away from the area for a while, on top of the 1079 games I have seen City play in I have also seen a further approximately 1000 games all over the country, visiting 122 grounds in total and 86 with City.

Pre-war programmes are becoming very rare and I have 189 City league and cup programmes including the 1926, 1933, and 1934 finals. Oldest programme is 1902/03 v Lincoln.

In the last season at Maine Road my programmes were used to feature articles on the opponents of the day, and I also assisted with the statistics for Polar Publications.

Dennis, sadly died recently at the age of 79

CHAPTER SIX

DECEMBER 1957 - THREE PENS FOR KEN

Another busy month ahead, Everton, Burnley, United at home, and Villa, Sheffield Wednesday, and Burnley away in the hectic Christmas period.

Bert was complaining about feeling tired. Back in August he thought "I was finished". In September he was in agony with his back, his shoulder was troubling him and so were 'the knockers'. He considered retirement but manager McDowall talked him out of it and he was now looking forward to receiving his £1,000 benefit in 1959. In the N.Ireland v Italy friendly in Belfast, the Irish fans booed the Italian National Anthem, Billy Mac was accused of assaulting their goalie, and the fans invaded the pitch at the end of the game, which ended 2-2, before 50,000.
MEN headline: 'United's title is slipping away' - now in fourth place on twenty four points, seven behind leaders Wolves, but with a game in hand.

20) SATURDAY DECEMBER 8TH 1957 K.O. 3PM: EVERTON (HOME)

Everton were formed in 1878. They'd won the title five times, 1891,1915,1928,1932,and 1939, were runners up six times, and had won the cup twice - in 1906 and 1933 (against City), runners up three times. They'd suffered relegation twice, in 1930, bouncing back in '31, doing well in the 30's and also went down in '51 but came back up in '54.

Most famous transfer between the clubs was Tommy Johnson in 1930.

Programme editorial looked ahead to City's three away games after today, then three home games, so the old computer can't be wholly blamed for today's daft sequences?! The Ed hoped for a home cup tie, which would then make it four homes on the trot!! He was also hoping for some good results, but thought it seemed reasonable to assume that City would enter 1958 in a sound position and certainly better than it looked after the WBA and Preston results. It could have been even better if points had been picked up at Highbury and Sunderland, where we'd played well and he thought that the home result against Wolves was the tragedy of the season.

Everton were welcomed and their performance in the first half of the 1956 cup tie "will never be forgotten by those privileged to see it".

I wasn't 'privileged to see it' however, for despite arriving at the ground at twelve noon, the perimeter wall was packed about six deep with kids, so my pals and I thought we'd get a good view from the back of the empty, at that time, scoreboard terrace. I was perched on a rear barrier and was a bit of a 'clever dicky' to a 'scouse Ted' who grabbed me by the throat after I'd told him Everton had no chance, and then he hovered me over the banking, not quite a shear drop, "You had your chance last year," he said, "Who's gonna win?"

Eventually, fearing for my life (though this was pre-Stanley knives, thankfully), I admitted it would be Everton. Then when he was almost out of sight, shouted "no, City!". After wandering round the ground outside of the terracing, we ended up watching the game perched on a barrier by the flagpole on the half way line at the back of the popular side (Kippax) and can be seen as shadowy figures in the pics of Bobby and Joe's goals. It was dismal until those goals came, with scouse urchins gloating and taunting "Trautmann never saw that one". 'Scousers' were everywhere, up the floodlights, on top of the half time scoreboard, with the lone copper trying to entice them down. Incredible, Thankfully, we won 2-1.

Oh, and they wrecked the trains on the way back to Liverpool!

★ OUR PLAYING STAFF ★

	Position	Height ft. ins.	Weight st. lbs.		Position	Height ft. ins.	Weight st. lbs.
Barlow, C. J.	O.R.	5 6	10 13	Leivers, W. E.	C.H. or R.B.	6 2¼	14 0
Barnes, K. H.	R.H.	5 9¼	10 10½	Little, R.	L.B.	5 9	11 4
Bourne, A.	I.R.	5 8¾	12 2	Marsden, K.	C.H. ...	6 1	12 8
Branagan, K.	R.B.	5 7¼	11 3	Matthews, F. R.	O.R. ...	5 10½	10 11
Cheetham, R.A.J.	W.H.	5 11	12 0	Meadows, J.	R.B.	6 0	12 5
Clarke R. J.	O.L.	5 9¾	10 12½	Murray, H.	O.L. ...	5 5	9 11
Davidson, D.	L.H.	5 9½	11 4½	McAdams, W. J.	I.R.	5 9½	11 7
Dyson, J.	I.L.	5 9	10 10	McClelland, J. B.	O.R.	5 8½	10 10
Ewing, D.	C.H.	6 0¾	14 0	McDonald, R.	L.B.	5 8½	10 10
Fagan, F.	O.R. or O.L.	5 6½	9 10	McLardy, B.	R.H. ...	5 8¾	11 13
Faulkner, R. V.	I.R. or I.L.	5 8½	11 7	McTavish, J. R.	R.H.	5 10	11 4
Fidler, D. J.	O.L.	5 9½	11 2	Pennington, J.	O.R.	5 0½	9 9½
Fleet, S.	Goal	6 0½	13 7	Phoenix, R. J.	I.L. or L.H.	5 8½	11 6
Grey, R. A.	I.R.	5 11¾	12 12	Rucker, N.	O.R. or O.L.	5 8	10 3
Hart, J. P.	I.R.	5 8½	11 2	Savage, J. A.	Goal	6 4	15 10
Hayes, J.	I.R.	5 7¼	10 11½	Sear, C. R.	F.B.	5 10½	10 1
Horridge, P.	R.B. or L.B.	5 9½	12 5	Taylor, K. V.	L.B.	5 11	11 12½
Johnstone, R.	C.F. or I.L.	5 5	11 2	Trautmann, B. C.	Goal	6 1½	13 13½
Kirkman, A. J.	I.L.	5 10	11 12	Warhurst, R.	L.H. ...	5 7	10 12
Leigh, P.	L.B.	5 7	11 0				

Are you reading the **Les McDowall—Matt. Busby** *page in the Evening Chronicle Football Pink—It's the talk of the soccer world*

14

Maine Road Gossip advised that City were to play an Army X1 at Park Hall Oswestry on December 16th K.O. 2.15 - you'd have thought we'd got enough games on over the next few weeks. The City supporters club Xmas Eve dance was cancelled, and replaced by a social evening at the Lord Lyon Hotel, Claremont Road, tickets 1/- each. They knew how to live then!

In Sportsman's Corner George White of Collyhurst asked what changes were made to accommodate the signing of Bobby Johnstone. He was advised that first Revie was injured, then Fagan was left out, and Johnny Hart broke his leg that day at Leeds Road, so the team selection resolved itself. An Ardwick City fan was irate about his mates' stupidity thinking Swift was in goal for City's home cup tie with Derby in 1950, lost 5-3. It was confirmed that Ronnie (or Tommy?) Powell was in goal.

Arthur Walmsley penned his sadness on Everton's Peter Farrell's absence from today's Everton team, having gone to Tranmere as player/manager. Arthur was present when Peter told Roy Paul, in a gentlemanly sort of way, at the training camp prior to the '56 cup tie that the losses in recent semi-finals would not be repeated that day. However after the game he was the first to wish our boys good luck in the semi-final. Aw.

David Jack listed the reasons given by fans on why gates have dropped this season as follows:

1) Standard of play has fallen and fans are not being entertained sufficiently by the players

2) Amenities at grounds are fifty years out of date in many cases, indeed, the facilities are primitive.

3) Transport, to and from the grounds is uncomfortable - and costly,

4) The game has practically no personalities of the calibre of Alex James, Peter Doherty, Len Shackleton or John Charles.

He concludes by suggesting that points 1) and 4) could be rectified when Professional Football is a more attractive career to teenagers than careers in other jobs and points 2) and 3) can be put right by the clubs. However he didn't think TV, knocked off for the International v France by the F.A., had any bearing on gates, and if the gentlemen who run soccer don't attend to these points and take action, then "the present slump will continue, and the consequences will be grave indeed". Admission prices didn't seem to be an issue.

Train 11/6d to Witton, and 6/- to Wadsley Bridge. Sounded good.

Everton were eighth with twenty one points and City tenth also with twenty one points. Their away form so far was four wins, one draw, and four losses. At home three wins, five draws, two losses.

At City: Pre-war they didn't win any of the last eight. Post, they won last season 4-2, lost the previous two.

Recent attendances ranged from 15,227(55/56) to 45,737 (54/55). It was the seventy third league meeting plus one final, 1933 lost 0-3, and two cup ties, one at City 1956 sixth rd.2-1, 76,129.

Team News: Fagan in for Clarke, Billy McAdams set to create a new goalscoring record for scoring in ten consecutive games.

From The Guardian's 'Old International': City Forwards Brilliant

On a wet December day no other explanation of this win was possible except that of sheer brilliance. Hayes and McAdams were holding the ball close, beating their men, and travelling at top speed with Johnstone plying them with passes in a manner which he rarely equalled and probably never excelled. Barnes had the unusual experience of scoring three goals - all from the penalty spot. What's more he seized the occasion to demonstrate how easily a goalkeeper may be beaten by the silkiest, gentlest of kicks provided due regard is paid to placing.

The awards themselves were proof of the pressure that Everton were under and rather than let City score what appeared to be certain goals they preferred to remove the supports of the players in the hope that one or two kicks might be saved or missed, but reckoned without Barnes, who gave the impression that he has made the art of taking penalties his special study. After about forty minutes City were three goals up, scoring two penalties within two minutes, the fifteenth and seventeenth and going like a forest fire. **McAdams** had also collected a pass from Johnstone, beaten his man on a sixpence, sprinted through a gap and scored handsomely on thirty five minutes. Hickson had managed a header which dropped onto the bar, but that was it from Everton until just before half time when **Harris** pulled two goals back, one from a narrow near post angle, the ball lodging between the stanchion and the side netting inside the goal.

The first half was also memorable for the Dave Ewing/Dave Hickson tussle. They'd been at it all game, and after an Everton attack, with the ball upfield, Salford born Hickson gave big Dave a smack, and the crowd roared its disapproval. Dave, naturally booted him up the backside just as the ref turned round to see what was going on, but he didn't send him off!

Within three minutes of the restart **Barnes** was asked to stroke home his third decisive penalty after another prompt and decisive decision by the referee who was under increasing pressure from players and was forced to take names. (I was standing right behind the goal when he scored the third and I'd no idea which side he was going to put it, so Dunlop had no chance and Ken told him so!)

McAdams scored City's fifth, concluding his goal trail, and the referee then sent off Hickson for too free an exercise of free speech. **Hayes** soon finished the scoring with a 6th and the only note of interest then was as to how petty and childish some professional footballers can become. It was nothing short of tragic that a game which promised so much ended so shabbily. It was clear from the start that certain players had the needle and seemed determined to pay off old scores and if the same teams play in the return game then maybe Hickson and Ewing should be sent into the gym pre match each wearing a pair of boxing gloves while the rest get on with the job. As far as football was concerned Johnstone again caught the eye as a perfect exponent of the deep centre forward game. His display was as near perfection as a modern inside forward is likely to reach.

FINAL SCORE: CITY 6 EVERTON 2

City: Sky blue/white: Trautmann; Leivers, Sear; Barnes, Ewing, Warhurst; Barlow, Hayes, Johnstone, McAdams, Fagan.
Everton: White shirts/black knickers: Dunlop; Sanders, Tansey; Donovan, Jones, Rea; Harris J., Temple, Hickson, Thomas, Williams G.

Attendance: 20,912, so despite covered accommodation for 50,000, the rain had kept the gate down to nearly half what was expected. **Average:** 28,843
Referee: R.J. Leafe (Nottingham)
Linesmen: V.Aldridge, R.Birkinshaw
League Position: Up five places to fifth spot
Goals For: 52 Against: 51
Reserves: Lost 2-1 at Blackpool

No sign of my '56 Teddy boy 'pal' today. Perhaps he was there at Christmas 1959. This was the day that we all arrived on the scoreboard end in dribs and drabs, to find that our territory had been usurped by Everton. Scuffles were breaking out throughout the first half, then at half time, with the score at 0-0, the more streetwise Blues, Jim, Tony Ashworth (met him at Arsenal, August 2007), Archie, Clive with the bowler hat, and company, started to heave the scousers out of our area with plenty of help from round and about. This was our territory, and we took it back. City promptly scored four goals in eleven minutes, Archie (I think) shouted, "If that's the effect that aggro has on the team, we'll have some every week". And everyone laughed in a good natured way, because that's the way things were then but was it a sign of things to come? Who knows. Would I have related this tale if it had gone the other way? Of course!?

In the F.A Cup third round draw City have a tough one away at West Brom. and the tie could be all ticket with a 58,300 limit. City are again linked with the newly demobbed twenty two year old Bradford City winger Martin Bakes.

21) SATURDAY DECEMBER 14th
K.O. 2.15 PM: ASTON VILLA (AWAY)

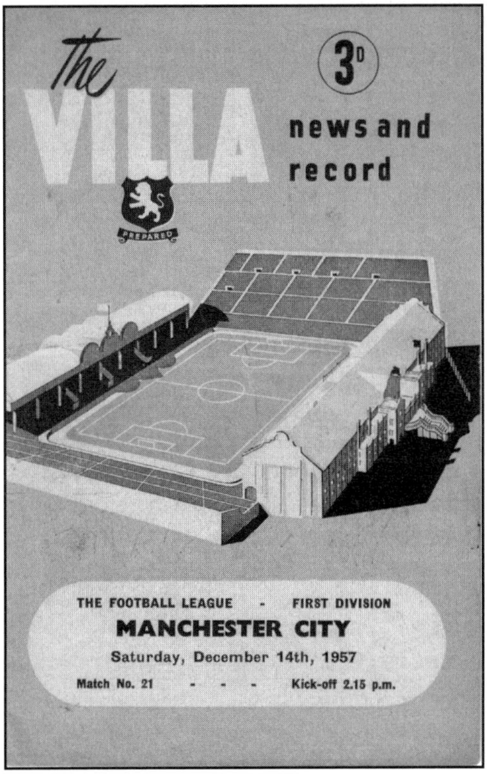

By this time I'd acquired a rattle. Not an easy task, even in Manchester - especially in Manchester, or Salford - it was hard enough finding a sky blue and white scarf. I made a drawing of one, but my woodwork teacher at school, Mr. Cameron, wasn't interested. So I ended up buying a dark blue and white one from a shop on Broad Street, for about 10/- (50p). I gave it my regards and went home and painted it Sky Blue, it took about ten coats and wasn't that loud! So I now had the full set, scarf, rattle, bob hat, lovingly knitted by my Aunty Matty. (But later nicked at an Old Trafford derby. The female United fans were very sympathetic about that - they always had more girl supporters than us Blues, mainly because of the 'oooh Bobby Charlton' adoration, which fell off when his hair did. Fickle females. I must also say though that I did have a kind word once from a United bloke after the 5-1 loss in 1960 in the 58 bus queue: "We won today but it could be your turn next" he said). Also, the plastic star lapel badges, with pics of our heroes in the middle, were an essential part of the kit, and now worth a bob or two, but I've lost mine.

Villa were formed in 1874, and won the league six times between 1894 and 1910, runners up eight times, between 1889 and 1933, plus the cup seven times including last season v United, and were runners up in 1892, and 1924.

The programme was twelve pages, numbered 129 to136, for 3d. Front cover was a lovely shade of sky blue, with a great artistic impression of their superb ground.

Notes reviewed the F.A.Cup draw. We'd drawn West Brom, away, where "we wouldn't have the happiest memories of what happened when we last visited The Hawthorns", they had drawn Stoke away. United were away at Workington. Ties to be played on Saturday January 4th, K.O. 2.15 pm unless the clubs agree to play the entire match under floodlights, then a K.O. no later than 7.30pm. Or if clubs agree to play the latter part only under lights, K.O. no later than 3pm. Teams and results next, and a Down Memory Lane feature on Villa's 1919/20 season. So absolutely nothing on City!?

Witton station was handily placed right next to the ground. Notices saying 'Beware Of Pick Pockets' were displayed at various vantage points.

Villa Park's record attendance was 76,588 v Derby F.A.Cup in 1946. There was a distinctive double decker main stand, its particular feature being the claret and sky blue cinema style balcony gantry, none of your old fashioned criss cross bracings here.

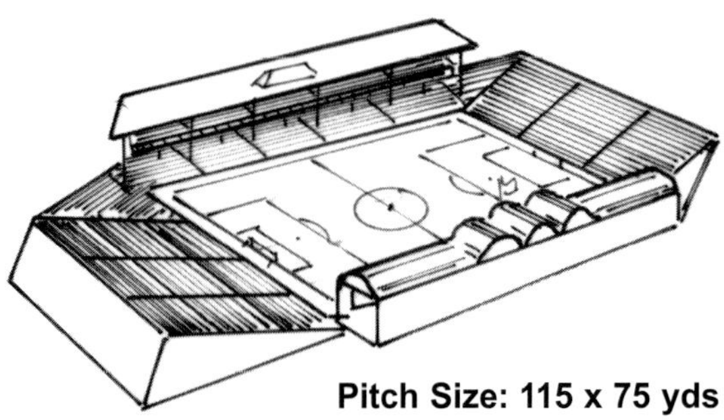

Pitch Size: 115 x 75 yds

Opposite was a barrel roofed Dutch barn type stand, seats and paddock with three gables on the roof. There was a big terrace behind one goal, and opposite was the massive Holte End. It was a regular semi-final venue, due to its location (especially later after the M6 was built), and City had won there twice recently, beating Sunderland in '55, on a quagmire, and Spurs in '56, both 1-0. The ground was completely rebuilt throughout the next few decades, retaining many of its distinctive features.

Villa were seventeenth with sixteen points, and City sixth with twenty three points. They'd won four at home including a 5-1 v Leicester, drawn two, and lost two. Away they'd won just one, last week at Sheff. Wed. 5-2, drawn two, and lost nine, including the F.A. Charity Shield 4-0 at O/T to United.

At Villa: Pre-war we'd won only one of the last fourteen visits, and once lost 7-1 in 1901. Post, we'd won two and drawn one of the last three.

Recent attendances ranged from 10,593 (56/57) to 50,614 (47/48). They were involved in the alleged City bribes scandal in 1904, and our biggest game was the '34 semi-final which we won 6-1 at Huddersfield (45,473). It was the seventy fifth league meeting plus four cup ties, three at Villa, 1900 first rd. replay 0-3 (20,000), 1910 third rd. 2-1 (45,000), 1938 sixth rd. 2-3 (75,540).

Team News: No changes

From Rob Bishop and Paul Vanes of Aston Villa, report by Cyril Chapman

City's defence was far from sound and Villa had much attacking play all through the game, but they found themselves in a vulnerable position where a late goal could mean defeat.

Villa looked capable of winning it in the first half an hour had Pace and McParland taken the chances given them by their new colleague Hazelden. He was the one bright spot as far as Villa were concerned. City had their chances too, the Villa defenders never getting used to the attacking scheme. Johnstone lay back very deep, with Hayes and McAdams playing more upfield than is usually the case. Dugdale did not follow Johnstone about but neither did he latch firmly onto Hayes and McAdams. Result was that Lynn and Aldis were frequently faced with a double threat from the City wings.

City's attacks slowly grew in momentum, provoking dangerous situations which Sims did well to relieve. But Villa had the most scoring chances even though their right wing flopped badly near half time. Crowther was troubled with a knee injury, and Smith could do nothing right. It was 0-0 at half time, strange considering the shaky defences.

PETER ALDIS

Sixteen minutes into the second half a sharp centre from Hayes on the right looked to be destined to be gathered by Sims, but **Aldis** interposed and headed it fairly and squarely into his own net.

Villa produced their usual honest endeavour and in the seventy first minute Smith crossed for **McParland** to head past Trautmann. A draw seemed likely but City's slippery forwards still had a trick up their sleeve. With a minute to go, after the ball had been switched from wing to wing **Joe Hayes** breasted in a cross from Fagan on the left. This defeat left Villa with what looks like being a tough struggle to stay in division one.

FINAL SCORE: VILLA 1 CITY 2

Villa: Claret and blue shirts/white shorts: Sims; Lynn, Aldis; Crowe, Dugdale, Saward; Smith, Crowther, Pace, Hazelden, McParland
City: Sky blue/white: Trautmann; Leivers, Sear; Barnes, Ewing, Warhurst; Barlow, Hayes, Johnstone, McAdams, Fagan.
Attendance: 24,767. **Average:** 34,201
Referee: J.V.Sherlock (Sheffield)

Linesmen: J.H.Brooks, D.H. Counsell
League Position: Stayed 5th
Goals For: 54 Against: 52
Reserves: Beat Blackburn 4-0

HALF WAY REPORT:

After twenty one games City were in fifth place with twenty five points, same as United, but ten behind leaders Wolves with one game in hand. At home we'd won eight including 5-2 v Chelsea, 5-1 v Spurs, 6-2 v Everton, drawn one v Luton, and lost just the one against Wolves.

Away we'd won four, including a 5-2 at Blackpool, drawn none, lost seven including the 6-1 at Preston, 9-2 at West Brom., and 4-0 at Birmingham. We'd introduced the M-Plan, promptly dropped, and played some good attacking football.

We'd had two players out with broken legs, Jack Dyson and Keith Marsden, and Jimmy Meadows had been forced to retire after the knee ligament damage he sustained in the '55 cup final.

There were debuts for Colin Barlow, Dennis Fidler and Steve Fleet, plus new signing Roy Warhurst.

The goals had come thick and fast, fifty four of them, from Hayes fourteen, McAdams thirteen, Barlow and Barnes eight each, Fagan five, Johnstone three, Ewing, Clarke, Aldis O.G. one each. Unfortunately we'd leaked a few, fifty two in fact.

Attendances at Maine Road ranged from 20,912 v Everton, and 45,121 v Wolves, averaging 28,843.

Away they ranged from 22,034 at Preston to 63,103 at United averaging 34,201

So looking at the goal tally of fifty four for and fifty two against, we couldn't possibly match that in the second half of the season, could we?

Ticket prices for West Brom announced: 750 seats at 7s 6d; 750 standing in the paddock 5s; groundside at 2s 6d. City could be playing in Claret and blue, Albion in all white.

22) SATURDAY DECEMBER 21ST 1957
K.O. 3 PM: SHEFFIELD WEDNESDAY (AWAY)

The second return game of the season, and chance of our second double, after the 2-0 win at Maine Road.

Programme was a twelve page edition for 3d, with a shadowy front cover, and inside it had a clear dark blue type face. Club News lamented the 5-2 loss to Villa two weeks ago, and told us that they'd tried to sign goalkeeper Harry Gregg from Doncaster, but instead settled for Mike Pinner, an amateur keeper from Pegasus. It was hoped that he'd go on to win full International honours with England as did City goalie J.F.Mitchell in 1925. 11 am kick offs were nothing new either, for they faced Preston on Christmas Day at home at this time.

Goal Trail Of Billy McAdams, reflected on Bill's eleven goals in ten matches, a run which started on the night City beat Wednesday 2-0 in October. Last time a run like this was achieved was in 1924/25 when Arthur Chandler of Leicester scored in sixteen consecutive

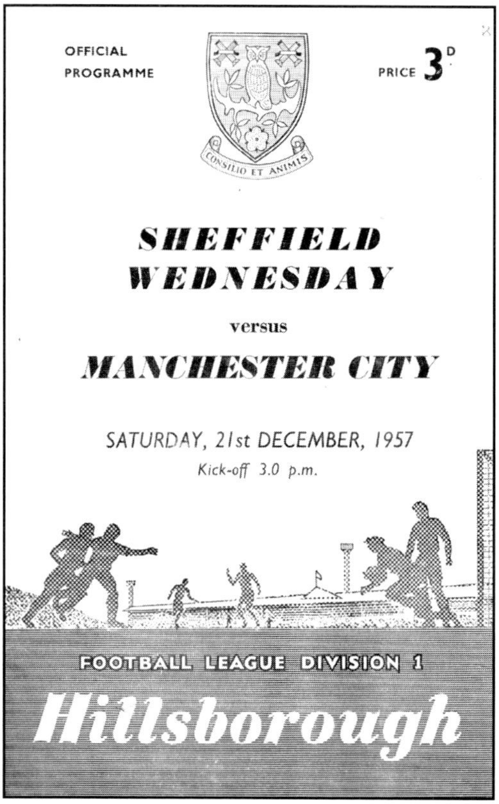

matches. City's remarkable 1936/37 season, was recalled, which was unremarkable until Christmas that year when we went on a twenty one game unbeaten run beating Wednesday 4-1 to clinch the title in April. Our upcoming game with WBA in the F.A.Cup was spotlighted and it was thought that despite the 9-2 reversal last October, when we were experimenting, Albion could be surprised on January 4th. Then there was a brief review of some of our players, including local boy Roy Warhurst.

Men And Matters mentions City's Ron Phoenix one of three brothers who once played together in the same team - Humphrey Park in the M/C Amateur league - Eric played for Gillingham, and Jack was an amateur with United.

Hillsborough's record attendance was against City - 72,841 in the F.A.Cup 5 1934, when some crowd casualties were reported. It was a fine ground and like Villa Park, regularly used for semi-finals. The Main stand was covered and seated with an open paddock in front. Opposite was a covered standing area, and behind one goal was a partly covered standing area. Behind the other goal was a huge wild hill of a Kop which would defy any attempt to cover it. But they did, as the ground was completely re-developed including an early cantilever stand, designed by a consultancy I later worked for, Husbands in Sheffield. The ground will, sadly, always be remembered for the disaster which occurred in April 1989.

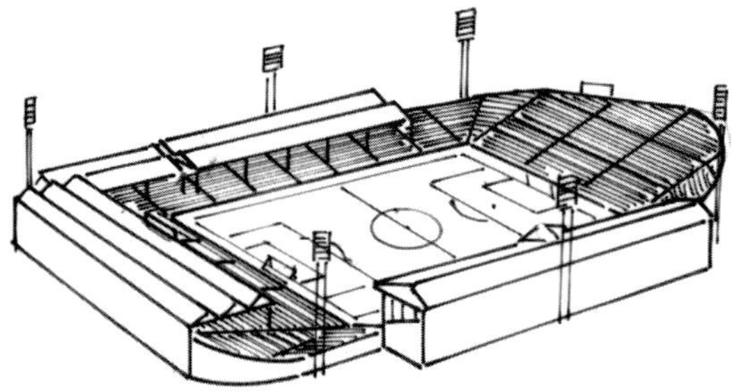

Pitch Size: 115 x 75yds

Wednesday were struggling, in bottom spot with thirteen points from twenty one games. City fifth with twenty five points. At home they'd won five including a 5-3 v Birmingham, drawn one, lost four including that 5-2 v Villa, plus a 3-4 in a friendly v Juventus. Away they'd not won any, drawn two and lost nine but ran Bolton, 4-5, and Wolves 3-4 close.

At Wednesday: Pre-war we didn't win a single game, including three - 5-1 defeats. Post, we won 4-2 in '54/55 drew two and lost two.

Recent attendances ranged from 11,271 (56/57) to 43,233 (52/53). It was the sixtieth league meeting plus the 1904 semi-final, 3-0 at Goodison, and the 1934 fifth rd. 2-2 (72,841).

Team News: Little in for Sear - pulled muscle, Kirkman in for McAdams- damaged back.

From The Pink/Green
Glory Goals After Double Injury Blow

City had high hopes of their second double of the season, Ron Phoenix was twelfth man, and transfer listed John Savage was on standby in case Bert didn't get back from last night's broadcast in London. In the event he did, so John was not required.

Conditions were perfect, in striking contrast to last season's game when there was a terrific snowstorm, but today's crowd looked poor.

Generally play was in favour of the home team, Hayes was brought down a few yards from goal but the referee waved play on. Wednesday swept to the other end and Shiner's five yard shot rebounded off the post and back into play. Barnes then needed treatment from Laurie Barnett, Trautmann let the ball slip from his grasp with Leivers making a timely clearance, then Johnstone fell heavily in the tackle and was carried off into the dressing room, leaving City with nine fit men and Barnes hobbling.

ALBERT QUIXALL

It came as no surprise when Wednesday took the lead in the sixteenth minute. Following a foul from Ewing, Quixall placed a free kick perfectly and **Froggatt**, jumping up, headed the ball into the corner of the net well out of Trautmann's reach. Leivers then had his name taken after a foul on Finney, and Johnstone returned to the field of play at outside right. Play was very scrappy and in the twenty fifth minute Trautmann made a brilliant save from Quixall's terrific free kick. Leivers was being booed every time he went near the ball, but City equalised in the twenty ninth minute. Little moving upfield slipped the ball nicely to **Hayes** who brought it under control, rounded Martin and beat Pinner all ends up with a magnificent right foot shot. Seconds later Bert saved brilliantly from Hill, then City took the lead on the half hour with a glorious goal. Fagan sent Hayes away on the left who centred hard and true as **Kirkman** flung himself forward and took the ball beautifully on his head giving Pinner no chance. On forty minutes the City goal had an extraordinary escape with Bert out of his goal Ewing mis-kicking and Leivers making a last ditch clearance. In the forty third minute City made it three when Curtis's mis-kick let in Barlow who centred and **Hayes** brought it down and fairly rocketed it home. A minute later it was 3-2 as **Shiner** scored from close range after a raid on the left. There was still time for Leivers to charge up field and let fly with a left footer that was off the mark before the half time whistle blew.

Although not needed, the floodlights were switched on after half time as Barnes took up his usual position, as we hoped he would not aggravate his injury. City took up the running and Pinner was applauded for making several good saves, the crowd getting good value from both goalkeepers. In the sixty first minute Wednesday equalised when **Wilkinson** nipped in smartly to score from twelve yards. City replied promptly, going ahead once more with **Kirkman** scoring his second in fine style. Twelve minutes from the end **Quixall** equalised again with an extraordinary goal. He was brought down by Little when going through, and as everyone stopped appealing for a penalty. He booted the ball towards goal, it flew towards the far post, rebounded along the line and was then cleared. To everyone's amazement the referee awarded a goal despite City's protests. So with only eleven minutes left City were really up against it, but got their just desserts in the eighty fourth minute when **Johnstone**, dribbling along the line and when nearing the flag he released a long spinning centre which dropped into the goalmouth and slipped from Pinner's grasp as Kirkman followed up just to make sure. So the nine fit men won the game.

FINAL SCORE: WEDNESDAY 4 CITY 5

The game was memorable for me due to a City fan and Wednesday bloke arguing with each other all through the game - "I suppose that was a foul too?" "Nothing wrong with that, a fair and square shoulder charge!" I think they shook hands at the end, and the Wednsdayite turned out to be Roy Barker, Works Manager of a firm I later worked at, the previously mentioned George Robsons, Sheffield, and you wouldn't mess with Roy!

Sheff. Wed.: Blue and white stripes, white knickers: Pinner; Martin, Curtis; McAnearney T ,Hill, O'Donnell,; Wilkinson, Quixall, Shiner, Froggatt, Finney.
City: Sky blue, white knickers: Trautmann; Leivers, Little; Barnes, Ewing, Warhurst; Barlow, Kirkman, Johnstone, Hayes, Fagan
Attendance: 22,042 **Average:** 33,188
Referee: K. Stokes (Newark)
Linesmen: F.W.Gallop, D..Garside
League Position: Stayed 5th
Goals For: 59 Against: 56
Reserves: Beat Sheff Wed 5-2 at home

Wednesday never really recovered from their start to the season when they were severely affected by the 'flu bug' and were relegated at the end of the season, finishing bottom with thirty one points. They came up in '59, and finished runners up in 1961 to the Spurs double winners. Any other season they'd have won it, then were rocked with the early 60's bribes scandal , Peter Swan, Bronco Layne and Tony Kay, who'd gone to Everton, all being suspended *sine die*. Albert Quixall the original 'goldenballs' went to United for £45,000 and they were winning the 1966 cup final 2-0 when Ken Wolstnholme allegedly cost them the cup by saying, "It looks like the cup's heading to Sheffield" just as Everton popped in three, and that fan, Albert Cavanagh(?), hilariously ran onto the pitch. We put them down in 1970, and they dropped to the third and back, won the league cup in 1991, but eventually descended back to the old third, and are now struggling to escape from the Championship.

23) WEDNESDAY DECEMBER 25Th K.O. 3PM: BURNLEY (AWAY)

Burnley were formed in 1882, were division one runners up in 1920 and went one better, winning it in 1921, but City stopped their record breaking run and finished runners up that season. They won the Cup in 1914 and were runners up in 1947. Last season they were seventh..

Programme was 3d for sixteen pages. Front cover was claret with a ground drawing. All their, (not ours?), supporters were wished a happy Christmas and a prosperous New Year. Turf Moor Mirror welcomed City as the visitors instead of their usual Christmas opponents, Preston. Last time they played us on December 25th, according to their programme, they beat us 1-0, even though Frank Swift had a stormer. Strange, because I can't find any trace of this one?! Nice things were said about Bert, and they were glad to see him back on duty. Next they thought that Manchester was awakening "in a somewhat mystified way to the fact that Old Trafford is not taking all the cream as it has done for a few years. Maine Road, after one of those unpleasant periods when it was regarded as the home of the poor relation, is back in the limelight and no doubt causing a flutter in

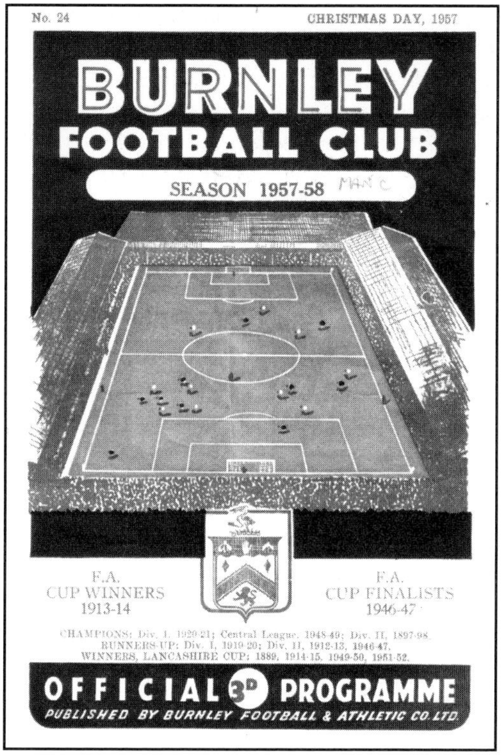

the other 'home' camp" Special mention was given to City's revival this season, and to Bobby Johnstone "a wonderful on the field pilot" and our other stars. Billy McAdams it turns out, was turned down at Burnley, after a trial, and still lives in Rawtenstall, "where he found himself a wife". The rest was mainly stats and adverts, including ex Blue Jackie Bray's Sport shop, and Robert Watson's of Bolton, advertising that they were responsible for the steelwork for the new stand and floodlight towers recently erected.

Turf Moor's record attendance was 54,755 v Huddersfield F.A.Cup third rd. 1934. I missed today's game, making my first visit in August 1958. 3-0 down at half time, won 4-3. There was a fairly standard seats and paddock main stand, a covered end behind one goal and an open terrace behind the other. The 'long side' had just been roofed and it was on a par, like Huddersfield, with the Kippax, but was just that bit steeper. The ground was eventually redeveloped in two phases, two stands in the 70's for the 'team of the 70's', and the other two in the more modern style of the late 90's

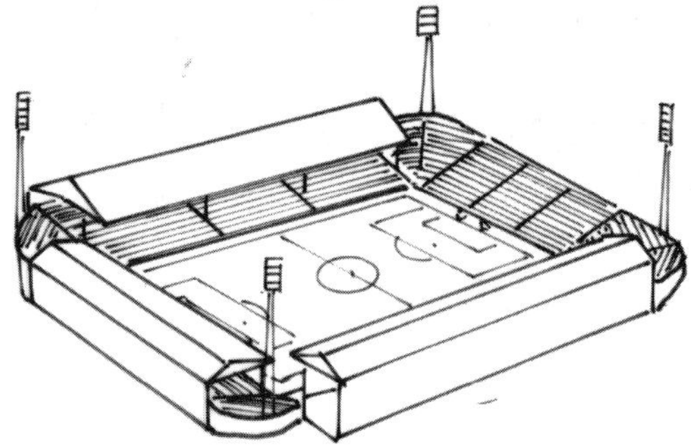

Pitch Size: 115 x 73 yds

Burnley were currently in eleventh place with twenty three points and City fifth with twenty seven points. At home they'd won nine, including a 6-0 v Sunderland and 7-3 v Leicester, (plus 6-0 v Lodz, and 0-1 v Blackburn, both friendlies) drawn one, lost one. Away they'd won one, drawn two, lost nine including a 0-7 at Forest, and a 1-6 at Chelsea within a couple of days in September - so it wasn't just us!

At Burnley: Pre-war we'd won two, drawn one, lost one of the last four, Post we'd won once, last season 3-0, but lost four and drawn four.

Recent attendances ranged from 16,746 (56/57) to 41,454 (47/48). It was the fifty third league meeting plus two cup ties both at Burnley, 1931 third rd. 0-3, (25,893),1933 sixth rd.1-0, (48,717).

Team News: Unchanged

From 'Sportsman' in the Burnley Express
Trautmann - and Burnley - were Brilliant

The game had something of a comedy start. A linesman on his preliminary examination discovered a hole in the net at the Bee Hole end and called the attention of the referee Arthur Ellis to the gap. Mr. Ellis inspected and Bert Trautmann borrowed a knife from a member of the crowd to assist in repair work. (Pity a similar action wasn't taken in the game at Bolton in September '58 when the Trotters popped one in through the side netting, missed by the same ref - Arthur Ellis!).

Previous Burnley/City matches had been something of a disappointment being more noted for their characteristics of grim, dour struggle rather than for pure football. However, this year the match hit the highlights. There has not been a better one this season, and indeed the goalless first-half came near to being a classic. It was worthy of the festive season with brilliant individual play, sparkling forward moves and the most dazzling display of goal-keeping it would be possible to witness anywhere at any time. The City have the reputation of being a tough team. They showed that they are fast to the ball and strong in tackle, but emphasised the all-important fact that they are capable of football skill which makes their position in the top half of the league understandable.

Burnley could have had a commanding lead at the interval if there had been a less competent goalkeeper to thwart their finishing, which had enough zest and accuracy to have made the game safe in their favour. Trautmann has distinguished himself at Turf Moor on previous occasions, but never with such amazing saves as today. His anticipation was uncanny and his split-second saves spectacular to say the least. Those he conjured out of the air from Shannon, Newlands, Pointer, Pilkington, in the first-half would have beaten a 'keeper of less calibre. He pursued his princely performance after the interval when Burnley continued to play the superior craft to which they allied speed and accuracy in distribution. The fear that they would not be able to clinch this excellence with goals was dispelled when **Pilkington** robbed Leivers and ended a solo corkscrew breakaway run by beating Trautmann at last. However the roar of delight was mingled with relief for in one of their best moves of the game **Fagan** had put the City in front nine minutes earlier and it looked as though it would develop into one of those matches, in which to quote one of the Turf Moor sages, the home team had "all the play and no goals"

RAY POINTER

The exchanges were at top speed with Shannon and Seith shining for Burnley in prompting attacks in which Pilkington starred. Adamson playing a thoughtful and shrewd tactical game against the City raids, inspired by the deep-lying Johnstone, and Barnes, being the mainspring of many of the Light Blues' wing raids.

Then eleven minutes from time **Cheeseborough** forced the ball past Trautmann from McIlroy to give Burnley the holiday points. Again Pointer pleased with lively and entertaining leadership which deserved a goal in celebration, but Trautmann was in no mood for distributing Christmas presents in the guise of free goals and never looked like being beaten from anywhere near the eighteen yard line.The awarding of thirteen corners to Burnley emphasises their attacking, persistent pressure. City gained four. Spectators are not likely to see a more worthwhile match with conditions all in favour of top-class football.

This was to be City's last ever Christmas Day fixture.

FINAL SCORE: BURNLEY 2 CITY 1

Burnley: Claret and blue: McDonald; Smith D., Winton; Seith, Adamson, Shannon; Newlands, McIlroy, Pointer, Cheeseborough, Pilkington
City: Light blue: Trautmann ; Leivers, Little ; Barnes, Ewing, Warhurst; Barlow, Kirkman, Johnstone, Hayes, Fagan

Attendance: 27,966 **Average:** 33,188
Referee: K.Stokes (Newark)
Linesmen: F.W.Gallop, D.R.Garside
League Position: fifth
Goals For: 60 Against: 58
Reserves: Beat Newcastle 4-1 at home

24) THURSDAY DECEMBER 26TH K.O. 3PM: BURNLEY (HOME)

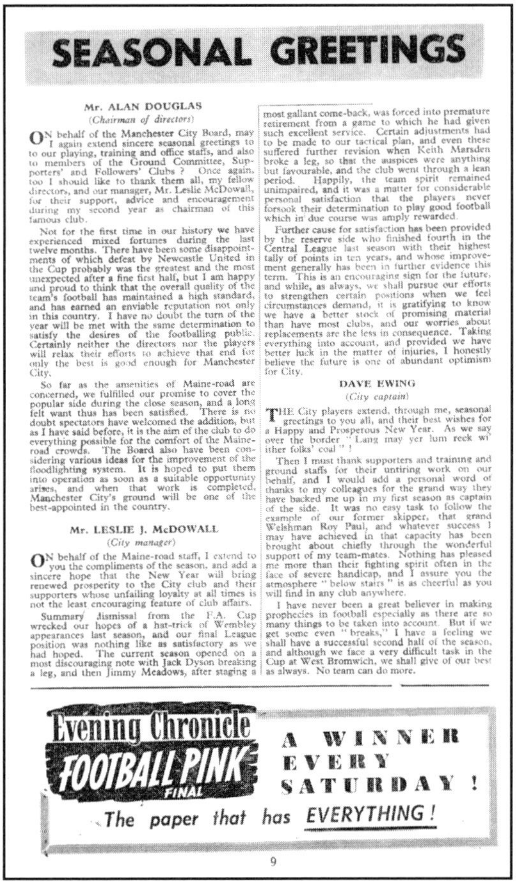

SEASONAL GREETINGS

Mr. ALAN DOUGLAS
(Chairman of directors)

ON behalf of the Manchester City Board, may I again extend sincere seasonal greetings to to our playing, training and office staffs, and also to members of the Ground Committee, Supporters' and Followers' Clubs ? Once again, too I should like to thank them all, my fellow directors, and our manager, Mr. Leslie McDowall, for their support, advice and encouragement during my second year as chairman of this famous club.

Not for the first time in our history we have experienced mixed fortunes during the last twelve months. There have been some disappointments of which defeat by Newcastle United in the Cup probably was the greatest and the most unexpected after a fine first half, but I am happy and proud to think that the overall quality of the team's football has maintained a high standard, and has earned an enviable reputation not only in this country. I have no doubt the turn of the year will be met with the same determination to satisfy the desires of the footballing public. Certainly neither the directors nor the players will relax their efforts to achieve that end for only the best is good enough for Manchester City.

So far as the amenities of Maine-road are concerned, we fulfilled our promise to cover the popular side during the close season, and a long felt want thus has been satisfied. There is no doubt spectators have welcomed the addition, but as I have said before, it is the aim of the club to do everything possible for the comfort of the Maine-road crowds. The Board also have been considering various ideas for the improvement of the floodlighting system. It is hoped to put them into operation as soon as a suitable opportunity arises, and when that work is completed, Manchester City's ground will be one of the best-appointed in the country.

Mr. LESLIE J. McDOWALL
(City manager)

ON behalf of the Maine-road staff, I extend to you the compliments of the season, and add a sincere hope that the New Year will bring renewed prosperity to the City club and their supporters whose unfailing loyalty at all times is not the least encouraging feature of club affairs.

Summary dismissal from the F.A. Cup wrecked our hopes of a hat-trick of Wembley appearances last season, and our final League position was nothing like as satisfactory as we had hoped. The current season opened on a most discouraging note with Jack Dyson breaking a leg, and then Jimmy Meadows, after staging a most gallant come-back, was forced into premature retirement from a game to which he had given such excellent service. Certain adjustments had to be made to our tactical plan, and even these suffered further revision when Keith Marsden broke a leg, so that the auspices were anything but favourable, and the club went through a lean period. Happily, the team spirit remained unimpaired, and it was a matter for considerable personal satisfaction that the players never forsook their determination to play good football which in due course was amply rewarded.

Further cause for satisfaction has been provided by the reserve side who finished fourth in the Central League last season with their highest tally of points in ten years, and whose improvement generally has been in further evidence this term. This is an encouraging sign for the future, and while, as always, we shall pursue our efforts to strengthen certain positions when we feel circumstances demand, it is gratifying to know we have a better stock of promising material than have most clubs, and our worries about replacements are the less in consequence. Taking everything into account, and provided we have better luck in the matter of injuries, I honestly believe the future is one of abundant optimism for City.

DAVE EWING
(City captain)

THE City players extend, through me, seasonal greetings to you all, and their best wishes for a Happy and Prosperous New Year. As we say over the border "Lang may yer lum reek wi' ither folks' coal " !

Then I must thank supporters and training and ground staffs for their untiring work on our behalf, and I would add a personal word of thanks to my colleagues for the grand way they have backed me up in my first season as captain of the side. It was no easy task to follow the example of our former skipper, that grand Welshman Roy Paul, and whatever success I may have achieved in that capacity has been brought about chiefly through the wonderful support of my team-mates. Nothing has pleased me more than their fighting spirit often in the face of severe handicap, and I assure you the atmosphere " below stairs " is as cheerful as you will find in any club anywhere.

I have never been a great believer in making prophecies in football especially as there are so many things to be taken into account. But if we get some even " breaks," I have a feeling we shall have a successful second half of the season, and although we face a very difficult task in the Cup at West Bromwich, we shall give of our best as always. No team can do more.

Evening Chronicle FOOTBALL PINK FINAL
A WINNER EVERY SATURDAY !
The paper that has EVERYTHING !

9

Programme editorial talked about school reports, new resolutions, and reflected on the season so far and on the vast improvement, compared with this time last year.

Injuries to Dyson and Marsden, who had received broken legs and Meadows being forced to retire prematurely, had not noticeably caused depression in the house. There were inexplicable set backs and horrible experiences at Preston, West Brom and Birmingham, though when City were not at full strength. So whether the second half of the season would give cause for equal satisfaction remained to be seen. With luck re injuries, and with similar team spirit, the programme Editor had every confidence for the future.

Maine Road Gossip reviewed previous City v Burnley tussles, and how we had "old scores to settle"

In Sportsman's Corner James Fuller of Eccles asked about City ending Burnley's unbeaten run in the 1920/21 season. Burnley opened the season with three defeats then went thirty games without defeat until City beat them 3-0 on March 26th. F.R.T. of Heaton Chapel's wife had chucked out all his treasured handbooks and asked for help on those for 1938 and 1951!!!!

Arthur Walmsley congratulated the Football League for paying to the Provident Fund raised by a 4% levy on gates, £74,986 to be shared among thirty five footballers aged thirty five or more who were retiring from the game.

Seasonal greetings were given by Chairman Alan Douglas who reviewed team performances and the work of the Ground Committee. Manager Les McDowall, finished his notes by stating that he honestly believes that the future is one of abundant optimism for City. Captain Dave Ewing felt that we'd have a successful second half of the season, that we'd give of our best as always, "no team can do more".

David Jack was worried about the England International team being in cold storage for four months (though he had this season down as 1956/57, World Cup season) with no Internationals lined up and reckoned they should fit games in against club sides in order to keep the international team in trim.

There was a **single sheet supplement** with teams and league tables in today's programme.

Train to Smethwick was 11/6d

At City: Pre-war, they hadn't won a game including an 8-3 and a 6-0 loss. Post, a bit different, finally winning in 1952, then again in '56 and '57.

Recent attendances ranged from 16,832 (51/52) to 67,672 (46/47) This was the fifty fourth league meeting plus two cup ties, both at Burnley.

Team News: Ron Phoenix in for Johnstone

From 'Sportsman' in The Burnley Express: Maine Road provided An Anti-Climax

The return match at Maine Road never touched the heights of splendour achieved the previous day and Burnley were a pale imitation of the side which gave City a football lesson at Turf Moor. This time the Manchester men were the masters and showed a whole hearted enthusiasm for the game. By contrast, Burnley played like a tired team. Their erstwhile spirit and sparkle had evaporated overnight and their football was listless and lacked method.

After his activities of the previous day Trautmann had what was tantamount to an afternoon off. Burnley with the exception of Pointer, and occasionally Pilkington, played as if they felt he deserved one.

From The Guardian's 'Old International': City Easily defeat Lackadaisical Burnley

Burnley demonstrated what an unhappy team they are away from home losing 4-1 to a much weakened City side.

The opening exchanges included much passing back to the goalkeepers and for the first half hour Bert must have wondered what had come over the Burnley forwards. They were anything but their usual nippy, zestful, energetic selves. McIlroy especially seemed dreamy and abstracted.

City's forward line was badly hit by Johnstone's absence and relied mainly on the speed of Barlow, Hayes and Fagan, though their finishing was hurried. But if City's line was jerky and disjointed, Burnley's was the last word in fecklessness, and one could only conclude that they must have burnt themselves out in their efforts at Turf Moor the previous day. Seven minutes before half time McIlroy missed the easiest of chances and it was no more than City deserved when **Barlow** snatched a goal from a goalmouth scramble just before the break.

From The Burnley Express:

JIMMY McILROY

After the interval both teams for some reason got the 'needle'. Phoenix, playing deep, began to achieve an accuracy in his passing which had been absent in the pre-interval period and his well-timed cross-field pass swept through the Burnley ranks to **Hayes** who had moved out to the left. Whether he was trying a centre or a speculative shot it is unnecessary to analyse, the fact remains that McDonald appeared to be under the mistaken impression that the ball would go over the bar and let it pass over his head. His chagrin can be imagined when it dipped into the far corner. However, one of the few Burnley players who retained his enthusiasm in adversity was **Pointer**, and it was fitting that he received just reward with a goal which could have put his side back in the game with a chance of saving it. Seith, sent a glorious pass down the centre and Pointer raced after it. Just as he was shooting with Bert advancing, he was brought down but had partially managed to kick the ball which beat the goalkeeper and bobbed with gentle reluctance slowly over the line. City, though, restored their two goal lead in the next raid, **Fagan** netting from close range. McDonald made timely saves and Shannon crashed in a great drive which had Trautmann helpless for once - but Little headed off the line for a corner (Burnley four, City eight). City were after the goals and were helped to make their total four by slackness in the Burnley defence. Then a long , ill-directed City pass looked like going out of play for a goalkick, but Barlow chased and whipped it across. A concerted rush, and **Kirkman**, from the near post and an almost impossible angle slammed in a shot which went in off the far upright. So Burnley's discomfort was complete.

FINAL SCORE: CITY 4 BURNLEY 1

City: Sky blue/white knickers: Trautmann ; Leivers, Little; Barnes, Ewing, Warhurst; Barlow, Kirkman, Phoenix, Hayes, Fagan.
Burnley: Claret and light blue shirts/white knickers: McDonald; Smith, Winton; Seith, Miller, Shannon; Newlands, McIlroy, Cheesebrough, Pilkington.
Attendance: 47,285 **Average:** 30,519
Referee: F.Collinge (Rochdale)
Linesmen: T.B.Edwards, H.P.Hackney
League Position: Fifth
Goals For: 64 Against: 59
Reserves: Lost 2-1 at Newcastle

Burnley finished in sixth position. They went on to win the title in their final game of the season at Maine Road in 1960.

City went into that game, on Monday 2nd May, in seventeenth place on thirty seven points and safe from relegation (Leeds and Luton taking the drop with thirty four and thirty points respectively) having won four of their last five games, at Newcastle, and Spurs, with home wins over Bolton and Preston after looking decidedly dodgy at one point, despite the signing of Denis Law in March. Burnley had to win the game to go above Wolves at the top of the table in the last match of the season.

There was a crowd of 65,981 at Maine Road and I remember jumping off the 76X bus and legging the last half mile to the ground rather than wait in the traffic jam. The game had kicked off and I ran round the back of the Kippax, as the vast punch of sound emanated from the tunnels. There was no chance of getting onto the Kippax, but I raced round to the corner between the Platt Lane and the Kippax where, amazingly, there was room to spare. I missed the first goal, Brian Pilkington after three minutes. Joe Hayes equalised after twelve minutes and Burnley clinched the title after thirty minutes through Trevor Meredith.

Wolves missed out on the double, beating Blackburn, (who were down to ten men when future Wigan supremo, Dave Whelan went off with a broken leg), easily 3-0 in the Cup Final.

Burnley were runners up in 1962 for both the league and F.A.Cup. Went down in 1971, came back in 1973, down again in 1976, then sunk to the fourth and nearly into the Conference. Now back in the Championship (old division two).

25) SATURDAY DECEMBER 28TH
K.O. 3PM: MANCHESTER UNITED (HOME)

Programme Editorial referred to the game as the 'highlight of the season', but saying it was a shame that the game came after one of the most exacting periods of the season, especially as the cup ties were only a week away but "both teams could be relied upon to produce a special effort, and give us plenty of entertainment".

Nice things were said about United and "just tribute to a fine club" was paid. (Those were the days, pre-Ferguson). However, the fans were warned that supporters should be grateful for all the good things they have enjoyed and not complain if there is an occasional drought. He then alarmingly says "if Manchester is to the fore, it doesn't really matter whether City or United have brought about that state of affairs" going on to state "there's room for two first class teams and I think we've got them". Then "City haven't had a drawn game with United at Maine Road since 1949/50 so well you never know!" Indeed.

Maine Road Gossip advertised a game between Manchester Boys and Sunderland Boys on January 1st at Maine Road. Fans were also advised that there was a reserve game at Maine Road on Saturday January 4th v Preston,

Maine Road Gossip

THIS IS DOUBLE VALUE

By THE EDITOR

MANCHESTER CITY, who have always taken an active interest in local schools' football, have given permission for the English Schools' Trophy match between Manchester Boys and Sunderland Boys to be played at Maine Road on Wednesday next, January 1st, kick-off 2-30 p.m. A keen game is anticipated, and we are hoping for a big crowd, especially as there are no senior matches in the immediate neighbourhood.

* * *

IN case you hadn't noticed it in the fixture list, may I remind you that City Reserves have a home game with Preston North End Reserves on Saturday, January 4th ? This game was arranged originally for Good Friday, but was brought forward in view of City's Cup-tie at West Bromwich. Supporters unable to travel to the Hawthorns thus will get double value for admission money—a match and a progress report on the Cup-tie.

ROLL CALL

(Including December 14th)

DIVISION I

Appearances.—Barnes, Ewing, Hayes 21 ; McAdams, Warhurst 20 ; Barlow, Johnstone 18 ; Fagan, Leivers 15 ; Sear 14 ; Trautmann 13 ; Little 10 ; Savage 7 ; Clarke 6 ; Marsden 4 ; Branagan 3 ; McTavish, McClelland, Fidler, Phoenix, Fleet 1.

Scorers.—Hayes 14 ; McAdams 13 ; Barlow, Barnes 8 ; Fagan 5 ; Johnstone 3 ; Ewing, Clarke, Aldis (Aston Villa o.g.) 1—54.

CENTRAL LEAGUE

Appearances.—Kirkman, McClelland 20 ; Phoenix, Taylor 18 ; Cheetham, McTavish, Branagan 17 ; Fidler 14 ; Fleet 13 ; Little 12 ; Savage, Clarke 9 ; Shawcross 7 ; Meadows, Marsden 6 ; Sear, Hart 5 ; Barlow, Murray 4 ; Johnson, Fagan, Faulkner, Horridge, Bourne, Davidson 3 ; Matthews, Leivers, Lister 1.

Scorers : Kirkman 14 ; McClelland 11 ; Fidler 6 ; Clarke, Phoenix 5 ; Bourne 3 ; Hart, Barlow 2 ; Murray, Branagan, Lister, Johnson, Fagan 1—53.

LANCASHIRE LEAGUE—DIVISION 1

Appearances.—Davies 12 ; Leigh 10 ; Bourne, Cooke, Pennington 9 ; Davidson 8 ; Horridge, Faulkner 7 ; Hibbert, Pike, Lister 6 ; Fleet, Matthews, Shawcross, Dixon 5 ; Worthington, Murray 4 ; Taylor, Rooney, Fidler, Johnson, Bradley, Hart, McDonald (R.), Cuthbert 3 ; Rogers, Clarke (M.) 2 ; Grey, Baxter, Phoenix (M.), Fenner, Jones, Senescall, Rucker, Hamer, Stringfellow 1.

Scorers—Faulkner 6 ; Johnson, Bourne 3 ; Worthington 2 ; Rooney, Fenner, Clarke, Stringfellow, Cuthbert, Lister, Davidson 1—21.

PORTRAIT OF THE REFEREE

WE hear a great deal about footballers' appearances, so by way of a change we'll mention those of Mr. Hugh Gerrard of Preston, who today makes his 276th League appearance "in the middle." It is also his birthday, so we extend sincere congratulations on both counts. Mr. Gerrard took up refereeing 22 years ago reaching the Central League via Preston junior football and the Lancashire Combination. Then followed a brief period on the Football League Supplementary list before promotion to the full list seven years ago.

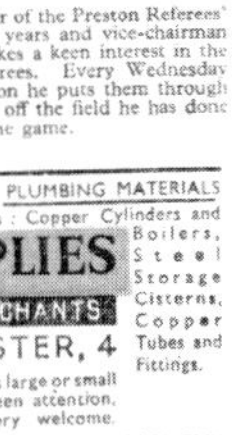

In addition to his League commitments, Mr. Gerrard had charge of the Scotland—Ireland amateur international two years ago, the Irish Cup final in 1954, and the Football League v. League of Ireland game at Maine Road in 1954. He has also been on the line at three full internationals at Hampden Park, but the match that stands out in his memory above all others was that between Manchester United and Blackpool at Old Trafford last year. "It had everything," he says.

Having been a member of the Preston Referees' Society for the past 23 years and vice-chairman for ten, Mr. Gerrard takes a keen interest in the coaching of young referees. Every Wednesday evening during the season he puts them through their paces, and on and off the field he has done much for the good of the game.

4

brought forward from Good Friday, so fans unable to travel to the Hawthorns would get double value for admission money - a match and a progress report on the cup-tie, hence 'double value'.

In Sportsman's Corner J. Guegan of Jersey was informed that Johnny Hart was the longest serving member on City's books but Roy Clarke had the most appearances.

Arthur Walmsley concentrated on the "purists who often express surprise that supporters can get enthusiastic about teams comprised of players from all corners of the British Isles - and perhaps beyond." He concluded, after telling us how lucky we are in Manchester, "and these have been golden post war years", by saying that there are no English, Welsh, Scots, Irish, or Germans on the field today for the cheering fans, there are just eleven men of City, and eleven United, and may the better eleven win.

Seasonal Greetings was a repeat of the same messages that were in the Burnley programme.

David Jack pondered on the fact that England, Ireland, Scotland and Wales would probably be represented in the final stages of the World Cup in Sweden next June. The President of the Italian F.A. thought that this gave us four chances instead of one and David thought he had a point and that a pooling of resources on a National scale would be a great thing for all concerned. He suggested an impressive line up, the sort that would demonstrate to the Brazilans, Hungarians, Russians, and Argentinians, that they are still learners at this game of Association Football. He concludes, though, that Britain could lick the World, but that's something he fears the Home Countries will never do as individuals.

Again there was a **single sheet supplement** in this programme with the teams, and up to date league tables.

Train to Smethwick 11/6d

United managed by ex Blue Matt Busby were third with thirty points, and City fifth with twenty nine points. Away from home they'd won four including 4-1 at Blackpool, drawn four including two - 3-3's at Birmingham and Everton and lost three including 4-0 at Bolton. At home they'd won nine, including 5-0 v Leeds and 4-1 v City, drawn none, lost four to Blackpool, Chelsea, Portsmouth and Spurs.

At City: Pre-war we'd won the last two, 4-1 and 1-0, post we'd lost last season 4-2 but won the previous four. In the cups we won the 1926 semi-final 3-0 at Bramall Lane (46,450) and the 1955 fourth rd. 2-0 (74,723), but lost the '56 Charity Shield, dubiously 1-0, when Bobby Johnstone's backheel direct from a corner was wrongly disallowed for offside.

Recent attendances ranged from 52,571 (51/52) to 78,000 (47/48) This was the sixty fourth league meeting plus two cup ties and one Charity Shield.

Team News: Johnstone back in for Phoenix. United were without Berry, Taylor, Whelan and Pegg.

An early Edwards shot flew past City's post and a United fan boasted to me "and that's just a start" - it wasn't, he didn't score.

From The Guardian's 'Old International': Trautmann Shows Gregg A Thing Or Two

Trautmann was at his magnificent best, and showed such a mastery of the art of positioning to make the impetuous Gregg at the other end seem in dire need of tutoring. Twice within the first five minutes Trautmann's agility alone, expressed in the form of two graceful swallow dives prevented Edwards and Scanlon from drawing first blood, and it was no surprise when **Viollet** put them one up in the sixth minute with a shot that kissed the post as it passed through.

Almost from the restart Johnstone lying deep punted a long high ball downfield with a carry well beyond United's defenders. **Hayes** went after it gazing upwards like a boy chasing a runaway kite and as the ball touched the ground he managed to trap it and flick it sideways past Gregg, who was fielding somewhere near to the penalty spot. Joe stumbled but recovered quickly and helped the bouncing ball into the net. 1-1.

Harry Gregg

Eight minutes later **Charlton** picked up a pass from Webster, and scored. United were on top until half time, City only managing some exquisite interplay between Barnes and Warhurst plus a shot from Fagan which narrowly missed the post with Gregg a noticeable absentee, so the score remained 2-1. After the break the game continued in a similar vein then fate took a hand. Foulkes saw Barlow break through on the right, show Byrne a clean pair of heels and whip a fast low centre past Gregg who had left his goal with what seemed more haste than judgement. As Foulkes raced back, perhaps a little panicky he was conscious of Fagan and Hayes closing in from the left and Kirkman hurrying up behind him, all intent on a rolling ball and a yawning goal in front of them. **Foulkes** acted quickly, but his attempt to hoist the ball into the crowd misfired and instead flew off his toe-end into the net.

The effect on City was extraordinary and whilst Bert defended his goal like a man possessed, Barnes, Warhurst and Hayes started to dominate the game and if Barlow had lobbed a twisting ball into another unguarded net instead of into the crowd, City could have won a last minute victory.

Some red shouted something derogatory about Bert having a hole in his body when they scored, and someone else (me. I'm afraid) shouted, "Well Gregg's got a hole in his a**e" prompting the inevitable, after a pregnant pause, from Jim, I think, "why, haven't you?"

FINAL SCORE: CITY 2 UNITED 2

City: Sky Blue/white: Trautmann; Leivers, Little; Barnes, Ewing, Warhurst; Barlow, Kirkman, Johnstone, Hayes, Fagan
United: Red/white: Gregg; Foulkes, Byrne; Colman, Jones, Edwards; Morgans, Charlton, Webster, Viollet, Scanlon.
Attendance: 70,483 **Average:** 33,850
Position League: Stayed Fifth
Goals For: 66 Against: 61
Reserves: Lost 4-0 at O/T

United lost eight of their players in the Munich Air Disaster in February. They finished the season in ninth place with forty three points, reached the semi-finals of the European Cup, losing to Inter Milan and the F A Cup final which they lost to Bolton 2-0. They went on to win the cup in 1963, the league in '65 and '67, European Cup in '68. City put them down with Denis Law's goal in '74, they were back up in '75, won the cup in '83 and '85, then finally after twenty six years won the newly formed Premiership, the end of football as we knew it. After that they won everything in sight.

CONCLUSION: Two good home wins, one commendable draw, two away wins, one loss giving a return of nine points. Up from tenth to fifth place in the table.Goals for up to sixty six, against sixty one. Wolves were six points clear of second placed Albion, and nine points ahead of City. Average home attendance 33,842 away 32,786.

LEAGUE TABLE

	P	W	D	L	F	A	Pts
Wolves	25	17	5	3	60	28	39
WBA	25	11	11	3	60	41	33
Preston	25	14	4	7	55	35	32
Man Utd	25	13	5	7	60	40	31
Man City	**25**	**14**	**2**	**9**	**66**	**61**	**30**
Luton	25	13	3	9	41	36	29
Notts For	25	13	2	10	53	38	28
Spurs	25	11	5	9	55	54	27
Bolton	25	11	5	9	45	49	27
Chelsea	25	9	7	9	56	52	25
Burnley	25	11	3	11	50	51	25
Everton	25	8	9	8	39	42	25
Arsenal	25	11	3	11	40	44	25
Blackpool	25	10	4	11	42	40	24
B'ham	25	7	8	10	45	56	22
Portsmouth	25	8	4	13	46	49	20
Newcastle	25	8	4	13	41	44	20
Aston Villa	25	8	4	13	41	52	20
Sunderland	25	6	7	12	29	56	19
Leeds	25	7	4	14	32	47	18
Leicester	25	7	3	15	47	66	17
Sheff Wed	25	5	4	16	44	66	14

JANUARY'S FOOTBALL MONTHLY

Newcastle's George Eastham was on the front cover and Wolves' goalie Malcolm Finlayson on the back. CB's editorial opinion condemns the England selectors for the team picked for the loss v N. Ireland. Page six has team photos of City and Preston before the Deepdale match (lost 6-1) John MacAdam applauds referees. Bert is pictured catching a high ball at Highbury, Double page colour centrefold spread of United. Programme swaps - J.Donohue of Manchester aged ten is in, is it him again?

Once A Blue, Always A Blue

FRANK from Clifton's story:

If you were in the boys choir at St. Peters, Swinton, you HAD to be a Blue, otherwise, at the very least, you got 'bushed' *(Ed - this was the initiation ceremony where you were forcibly pushed into the prickliest bush in the graveyard, and went home with cuts, scratches, grazes, and thorns in your flesh. Then, when you got home, you got a slap off your dad for messing up your Sunday best. Choirboys were NO Angels)* We took the 'boneshaker' tram from Albert Square to Maine Road and always sat on the whitewashed wall leading down to the touchline. At my first match, the fog came down, we saw 22 wraiths running about in the gloom, then a jinking run down the wing and a cheer - we saw nothing, but the ball was in the back of the net. Scorer was Dunkley, but I never saw him play again.

When I was young I used to go to City one week, Bolton the next and even United sometimes, but I was always a Blue. The United crowd was different, they'd move round at half time to be at the end United were attacking and I distinctly remember being there when they booed a young Bobby Charlton, off the pitch. It was always a more partisan atmosphere at United. In the 50's Bolton had a habit of beating both City and United particularly at Burnden Park. My dad used to gloat, he was a Bolton fan in the days of Tommy Banks, 'chopper' Hartle, Hennin, Lofthouse, Bobby Langton etc. If I went to Bolton with him he always wanted to walk to Farnworth, which was tiring for a kid who'd stood up all game. He only did that though so he could call in the pub for a pint or three. I was in the Navy from '51 to '53, and was stationed for a time near Portsmouth, where we'd go in our uniforms to Fratton Park.

I got married in 1957, (I was previously in the Scouts, my future wife in the Guides, not quite as embarrassing as my sister who met her hubby at the bellringing!) bought the house in Clifton, a semi, for £1,795. My mum was mortified at the mortgage I'd taken on! But I didn't go to many games that season as I was too busy with the house and garden. You could get the number 8 bus straight to Bolton so it would have been easier to watch them, but City were always my team. You picked your team when you were young (or 'bushed'!) and stuck with them. I went to Maine Road to see United play Dortmund in the European Cup in 56/57 and I saw City play Arsenal once but the crowd was that big that I didn't see a thing, not a thing, not one ball! At the time of Munich I was working at the District Bank in Ancoats and got a lift home on Alan Wolstencroft's motor bike. I remember seeing the placards about the air crash. My younger brother, ten years my junior and I never went to games together. David went and met up with his mates, and I went with mine, and we stood in different parts of the ground. Even if we went to games on our own we went separately, as I lived in Clifton and he in Swinton. If we met up at mum and dad's for Sunday dinner I'd say "I went to the game last week" and he'd say "So did I, what did you think?" and we'd discuss.

We only started to go to games together in the late sixties and the article I wrote for *King of the Kippax* issue 101 in January 2002 was the first time, in about 50 years, that we've reflected on the above. Incredible!

Frank is a lifelong Blue, season ticket holder, and my brother.

DAVE from Hebden Bridge's story:

Imagine....A brand new season ...and by the end of September we'd played nine, won four, lost five, scored twenty two with twenty seven against, twelve goals at home; we'd beaten Chelsea twice, lost games 9-2, 6-1, plus 4-1 at the Swamp; we'd had the same manager for seven years, and no-one was calling for 'McDowall out!'. City, as we know, have always been the same, but this was the start of the 1957/58 season, my tenth full season watching the Blues.

I was first taken to Maine Road at the end of March 1948 in anticipation of my third birthday. We beat Chelsea 1-0. Frank Swift was playing as was Roy Clarke.... Johnnie Hart made his debut two weeks later. But why was I taken to City? My father and his four brothers were Blues and always had been.

They were, funnily enough, brought up in and around Eastlands. So I wasn't given a choice! When I started going we lived in Chorlton, so it was the 85 bus and a walk along Lloyd Street to get there. I sat on the side of the tunnel wall

on the Kippax to the right of the centre line. The same people every week and crowds of 40.000+........it was very exciting. In the mid-50s one of my uncles aspired to a car... we could then leave Chorlton just after 2pm for a 3pm kick off and park in the side streets off Kippax Street. One of my uncles had an artificial leg so he and another uncle had season tickets...very occasionally you got to use them and it felt very posh in the main stand.

So by 57/58 I'd been through relegation and promotion and had cried on the steps after losing at Wembley in '55. Roy Clarke scored with a flying header against Sunderland in the semi at Villa Park played in monsoon conditions.

We won the Cup in '56 and I was given a midweek Wednesday afternoon off by the head teacher at our school to go to watch the third round tie against Blackpool.......Stanley Matthews and all. It had been abandoned on the Saturday due to fog. The head teacher was a great true Blue! I repaid him in '81 by managing to get him a ticket for the Paul Power semi at Villa Park. We also won 5-0 at the Swamp in February '55. We'd had the Revie plan, the Revie plan à la Bobby Johnstone and Revie and Roy Paul played their last games for City in 56/57.

By 57/58 I'm going with my mates, plus Dad and my uncles. My sister, my brother and two cousins were also going. We were now walking from Chorlton to save the less than 1p fare. We'd also go to see the reserves and anxiously await the score being put up every fifteen minutes. My Dad died in 1963 before the glory years. We buried him on May 15th and then went to see City v United and we were relegated at West Ham a few days later. He's buried in Moston Cemetery ...almost in earshot of Eastlands, if only we could make a Maine Road noise there.

I've been living in Yorkshire doing missionary work since 1963 so I drive past Moston Cemetery on the way to every home game now. I know he's really in heaven with his brothers but he's not answering our prayers.

My widowed mother Kathleen started going in the mid-60s and continued until the end of the season before last. She died happily and peacefully recently aged 86 years, and is also in Moston Cemetery. She has been a regular for forty years, had blue tinted glasses and hated reds and refs. We are going to continue with her name on the season card and not retire it. The family have TEN season tickets. We are me, my brother, sister and our children. The next generation, aged two, made his debut earlier this season....we've kept and passed on the faith.

So next season will see me celebrating - yes, celebrating, sixty years of watching City but let's go back to 57/58...

We finished fifth, six points ahead of the Rags, and qualified for the UEFA Cup. The problem was there wasn't such a competition as there is now. Away trips were achieved with York Motors of Chorlton. Before the midweek evening home match with Preston the team was announced with Keith Marsden, the reserve team centre half, and number five, playing twin centre half, but wearing a number ten shirt. It was another McDowall plan. Ahead of his time really.... playing 4-3-3...but someone in the crowd asked what was Marsden going to be doing? The answer came that every time Tom Finney got the ball Marsden was going to switch the lights out.

West Brom, Wolves...the big, bad Wolves.. and Arsenal were our bogey teams in the fifties.

Who was playing in 57/58? A lesson here. We had a settled team - eight players played thirty-plus games and another three played 28 or 29. We had the '56 Cup final defence, apart from Roy Paul, of Trautmann, Leivers, Little, Barnes, Ewing and no Paul, but Roy Warhurst from Birmingham. Roy Little was beginning to share the left back role with Cliff Sear. Up front it was Colin Barlow. His debut season and a particular favourite of ours since he went to our school. Then Joe Hayes, Bobby Johnstone, Billy McAdams and Paddy Fagan. Roy Clarke played five games and Ray Sambrook arrived on the scene - a typical City enigma who thrilled one minute and infuriated the next. Alan Kirkman, a regular reserve for some years, played four and scored three and Johnny Hart came back from another injury at the end of the season and scored three in five.

At Bolton on Easter Saturday we had a rare treat - seats in the stand!

In February '58 the Munich crash occurred. It was an awful thing to happen and I remember the bodies arriving at Ringway and being driven in hearses to Old Trafford. A very moving occasion. Matt Busby was a parishioner at our church, St.John's in Chorlton, so the whole thing was real and awful. I do hate the Reds but we shouldn't seek to diminish the memories of some really great players. Munich also caused a personal family tragedy. My cousin switched allegiance in sympathy.....now that if you are an Ansbro is unforgiveable.

The following season we escaped relegation by the skin ofour teeth....

Dave dedicates this article to his mother. RIP.

MATTY from Swinton's Story:

I was from an Irish Catholic family, brought up on the West coast of Ireland, and my parents came over to Manchester in the fifties to live in Cheetham Hill. My mum's sister was already in Manchester and she had married a Jewish fella, and City fan, who took me aged seven, to Maine Road for the first time. The date was December 28th 1957, it was the Manchester 'derby' and I was mesmerised. The biggest crowd I'd been in previously was at Church and here I was amongst 70,000. I asked my uncle who should I stick up for? "City of course!" he hissed. I was then passed down to the front, at the scoreboard end, over everyone's heads and I could smell the pipe tobacco and the liniment, and I remember it was a typical frosty, dark, gloomy, Manchester afternoon. I saw Bert Trautmann come down to our end and throw his cap into the net and it was obvious that he had a special relationship with the crowd. I don't remember much about the game, but the thing that struck me most was the sky blue shirts which City wore. To this day I also have a soft spot for teams like Lazio, Uruguay and even Argentina because of the sky blue. My dad wasn't a big football fan but he'd come to Maine Road with me if attractive teams like Spurs or West Ham were playing.

Later in the season I was aware of the Munich air crash and what a tragedy it was. United played their way to Wembley on a wave of sentiment and emotion. My Uncle Bernard had this big house, with a telly, and that day it was full of neighbours and friends. When Nat Lofthouse scored I cheered, and they made me go out of the room. When my dad, a big bloke, arrived he had a word and they let me back in just as Nat scored the second, but I thought I'd better keep quiet this time!

Matty's a lifelong Blue and still attends games on a regular basis

CHAPTER SEVEN

JANUARY 1958 - UP FOR T' CUP (AND OUT)

It was the turn of the year, and we wondered what the New Year would bring. Maybe some big signings, moving up the league, a good cup run, increased attendances, a century of goals to score, but hopefully not to concede, those big defeats being long gone!!?? Personally I'd be celebrating my fourteenth birthday, hoping for an early present with a win at West Brom. in the Cup - THE competition of the day, the glamour of Wembley always outshining the first division title race. Then it would be Forest at home, Portsmouth away and the fourth round of the cup, with a bit of luck.

JANUARY 3RD - CITY SIGN RAY SAMBROOK

City's first signing of 1958 was Coventry City's transfer listed winger, **Ray Sambrook**, bought for a fee of £15,000. Manager Les McDowall was on his way to Highfield Road within a few hours of hearing that the twenty four year old's transfer request had been granted, and quickly agreed terms with Billy Frith, Coventry's manager. McDowall arrived at the ground at 5.30pm and by 6.30pm had Sambrook (14 goals so far this season) signed and he was expected to make his debut in the home game with Nottingham Forest. Incidentally, Ray's dad Jack played for Wolves in the 20's. Other clubs interested were Cardiff, Birmingham, Preston and West Brom.

This signing torpedoed that of Swansea Town's speedy left winger, **Cliff Jones**, who City had watched on two occasions (though no previous mentions in the press?)! Cliff was a twenty three year old Frank Sinatra fan, a qualified plumber, just completing his National Service with the Royal Horse Artillery. He'd had seven seasons at Swansea winning Welsh caps and was described as a frail man, slightly bow legged, "who may well develop to be like Stanley Matthews". He joined Spurs the next month for £35,000, and enjoyed a brilliant career with the Londoners - oh what might have been!?

CLIFF JONES

At O/T Johnny Berry was reported as unhappy.

25A) SATURDAY JANUARY 4TH
K.O. 3PM: WEST BROMWICH ALBION (AWAY)
F.A.CUP 3RD Rd

City, three times cup winners, last in '56, runners up three times, taking on Albion, four times cup winners, last in '54, five times runners up. The sides had met only once before in the cup, the first round in 1901, which City lost 1-0 away in front of 16,000. General view was it would be different this time from the 9-2 league loss, but would it?

Well the trains departed from Mayfield station, which was next to London Road (now Piccadilly) at 9.55 am, 10.20, and 10.35. They would all be packed and we crowded together to have our photo taken by the Evening News photographer. I'm at the front, second from the right, wearing my bob hat and scarf, trying frantically to get my rattle out of my bag! Right behind me is my school pal John Cleaver wearing his school cap. I've no idea who the bloke is, he just put his arm round me in a fatherly sort of way as the photo was taken. Family game? How many women can you spot? I always wondered and hoped those fans would manage to see the happy times in the late sixties, and seventies

We arrived at Smethwick station, made our way to the ground and stood behind the goal, main stand to our right, on a cold, foggy day. Second half, every time they went up at the far end we heard a roar and knew they'd scored another.

The Hawthorns was as described in the September League fixture

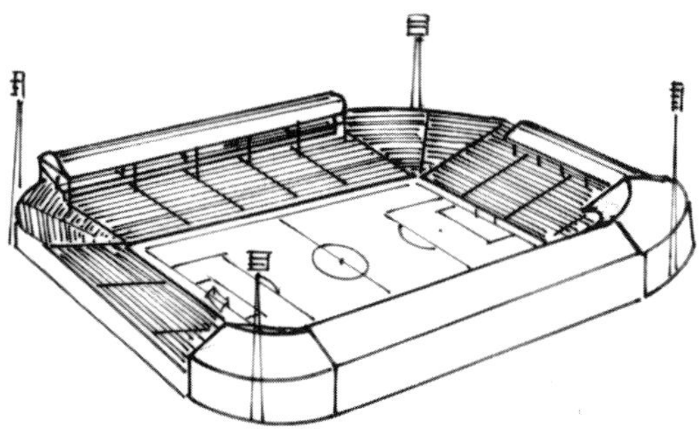

Pitch Size: 115 x 75 yds

According to **Eric Todd's 'Flashback' article** in the City programme of Dec '82 v Albion: "One match which does stand out was the 1958 F.A.Cup third round game at The Hawthorns. This, by the way, was round about the period when City and I were at loggerheads, and I was under self-imposed suspension. Anyway, I was not with the City party that day. Players and officials had been having a 'toning up' spell at Southport or some such place on that coast, and when things went wrong with the travelling arrangements, the players had to change in the coach and very nearly had to run straight onto the pitch. Little wonder that City were beaten 5-1. In spite of the score, City had the game's outstanding player in Roy Warhurst whose exploits included three goal-line clearances."

The programme was similar to the league programme with a section on 'Our Visitors' saying how our form was unpredictable at the start but we've now climbed the table steadily and last week got a 2-2 draw with our rivals United. "Both of these sides are poised to strike for the championship should opportunity arise". No mention of the 9-2, but plenty of time for that in the future....

West Brom had trounced City 9-2 in September, were second in the table, and after two defeats had just won at Birmingham 5-3 and at home to Burnley 5-1, Bobby Robson scoring four. Surely they couldn't put 5 or more past us, for their third successive game, could they?

Team News: Leivers failed a fitness test, Little and Kirkman were dropped, Sear, Branagan and Clarke came in, McAdams was still injured, and City were to play twin centre forwards, Johnstone and Clarke.

From The Guardian's 'Old International': WBA Butcher City - Barnes And Warhurst Have Nightmares

It was butchery - no less. And made no sweeter by the fact that the butchers light heartedly revelled in their task.

In no other way could one describe WBA's victory. Once City's gallant defenders had begun to wilt under their ceaseless, relentless, pressure, Albion's goal-hungry forwards cut them up wlthout mercy. Trautmann, of course, kept the flag of defiance flying by the splendour of his goalkeeping, as did Barnes and Warhurst in their respective spheres; but what were three among so many? Besides, in fairness to all City's defenders, it should be stated that rarely, if ever, was any relief or breathing space afforded them by counter pressure from their own side. City's attacks in the main were too fitfully made, too thinly pressed home, and too easily dispelled, for that. To Barnes and Warhurst in particular it must have been a nightmare. For no sooner was the ball worked clear and slipped forward, back it came, with a flutter of blue-and-white striped marauders following it.

Albion scored heavily because they have learned to extract from unorthodox moves the magical effect of the element of surprise. Allen's first pass being witness to that when he looked to be feeding the ball to the right but switched it left to the unchallenged Robson, who failed to score the quickest F.A.Cup goal of the round.

That pearl from Allen was a sample of things to come as he was here there and everywhere in Albion's formidable 5 man attack which relied as much on the intelligent anticipation and preparatory running into position of Griffin, Robson, Kevan and Horobin as on Allen's inspired prompting.

Naturally Albion take risks in thinning out their defence to augment their attack but only rarely was City's forward line speedy enough and determined enough to take advantage of this. Johnstone, playing deep, very deep at centre-forward seemed embarrassed by the fact that his colleagues, Clarke and Hayes, tended to play deep also so that he found unusual difficulty in placing his passes. Clarke, though once having a volley kicked off the line by Williams was scarcely a success at inside left, while Hayes gave only one example of his true quality with a glorious thirty yard burst which ended with a tempting pass to Barlow whose effort licked the foot of the post before trickling by.

How different the bombardment at the other end! Before the first ten minutes were spent Trautmann had made two saves of incredible celerity and sureness, considering the shocking light, while Warhurst, a grim fighter on this stricken field, had twice come to the rescue when Bert was beaten.

It could not last. **Allen** scored Albion's first goal by prodding through Robson's foozled shot with the sole of a boot on thirty five mins. **Ray Barlow** scored the next from a cleverly taken free-kick on fifty five minutes. **Griffin**, on fifty eight minutes took the third from a through pass by Horobin, while **Allen** in the sixty second minute, owed the fourth to a generous use of the advantage by the referee. In the last sixty seconds of the match two belated goals were added - one by **Hayes** for City and one by **Ewing** for Albion, much to Bert's disgust. Thus Ewing extracted one last wry smile even from tragedy.

FINAL SCORE: WBA 5 CITY 1

So the Wembley dream was over for yet another year and West Brom looked like they'd take some stopping.

West Brom: Blue and White striped shirts/white shorts: Sanders: Howe, Williams S; Setters, Kennedy, Barlow; Griffin, Robson, Allen, Kevan, Horobin,
City: Sky Blue shirts/white shorts: Trautmann; Branagan, Sear; Barnes, Ewing, Warhurst; Barlow, Hayes, Johnstone, Clarke, Fagan
Attendance: 49,669, compared with 26,080 in the league game.
Referee: B.M.Griffiths (Newport, Mon)
Linesmen: W.Briggs (Nottingham), R.Reddaway (Kettering)
City's next cup meeting with Albion was not until the third round of 1977, a 2-1 win at The Hawthorns after a 1-1 draw at Maine Road.
Reserves: Lost 5-2 at home to Preston

JANUARY 10TH

Joe Hayes, the man Bury, and Bolton let slip through their fingers, has been selected as reserve for England U 23's team to play Scotland at Goodison next week. Joe has scored eighteen league and one cup goal so far this season, bringing his total to nineteen and second only to Turner of Luton (twenty) in the division's goalscoring list.

Jack Dyson, who broke his leg in the club's public trial match last August may start playing again next month. He was told by the specialist that the fracture has healed perfectly. Jack was in full training at Maine Road today, showing all of his touches as he ran the ball up one leg across his chest and down the other leg, but he's still slightly worried about his speed off the mark.

Paddy Fagan, City's Eire winger has been dropped for tomorrow's game with Forest, and is wondering whether to put in a transfer request. He travels with the reserves for the fixture with Huddersfield.

At O/T Ray Wood has asked for a transfer which was refused.

Dave Hickson, sent off v City in December for remarks to the referee, was given a twenty one day suspension.

Roy Paul has given up as player-manager of Worcester City but will continue to play for them. Roy found it difficult to remain manager while living in Wales and didn't think it fair on the Directors to carry on.

Ex City, now Carlisle goalie George Thompson was sent off in the recent Carlisle v Workington fixture.

26) SATURDAY JANUARY 11TH 1958 K.O. 3PM: NOTTINGHAM FOREST (HOME)

So after the magic of the cup eluded City last week, it was back to league business with the return game with Forest, and a new signing to look forward too.

Programme announced a new feature ***'How City's Teams Fared'***. Needless to say it was a black Saturday last week when out of the five teams only the Juniors won!

As for last Saturday "City were well beaten by a splendid team and that's all there was to it. City must now aim for the top four and no taking things to heart like last year when after the Newcastle cup defeat City only took fifteen points from the remaining seventeen games and finished eighteenth with thirty five points. The challenge must be accepted by Ewing and his men".

New signing Ray Sambrook, was welcomed to the club as a strongly built player, a speedy winger and reliable marksman

Then finally it was congratulations to Joe Hayes, selected as a reserve for England under 23's against Scotland next week at Goodison.

Maine Road Gossip included complaints that supporters couldn't hear the P.A. from the main stand under the new roof of the Kippax, (a complaint that was being made until the day they demolished the stand in 1994!) and everyone was assured that it would be sorted. It was announced that the reserve programme would go up from 1d to 2d, but the number of pages would increase from two to four.

In Sportsman's Corner Walter Kingslade from Openshaw asked which first division teams had never won the F. A. Cup. He was advised Birmingham, Chelsea, Luton, Leeds, and Leicester. (Chelsea and Leeds first managed it in 1970 and 1972 respectively. In today's Premiership, 07/08, Reading, Fulham, Wigan, Middlesbrough and Birmingham haven't yet won it!))

Jimmy Fox, aged ten of Chorlton-on-Medlock asked who the Blue Devils were. It was the Scottish team sometimes known as the Wembley Wizards of 1928 who beat England 5-1. This was presumably long before Salford were known as the Red Devils and United became the, erm, self appointed Red Devils!!.

THE PERSONALITY BOYS

By DAVID JACK

(*Empire News and Sunday Chronicle columnist*)

ONE man doesn't make a team . . . so say the sages of Soccer. But if he's the right man he can make a tremendous difference. By that I do not mean a £30,000 import bought for the express purpose of winning a League championship. No, the players who really count in this game are the personality boys, the ones whose very presence on the field inspires their colleagues ; those, perhaps, not really noticed—until they have to miss a few matches.

Charlie Wayman was never the best centre-forward in England, yet his value to Southampton in 1948-49 could not be measured in terms of pounds, shillings and pence. In that fateful season for the Hampshire club, an eight points lead at the start of April seemed to have ensured promotion to Division I. Then Wayman was injured, and Southampton didn't win another game. They finished in third place and missed promotion by one point.

Ken Chisholm is not a star player. He's the first to admit that, but again, his value to the right team at the right time was inestimable. The team was Cardiff City, the season 1951-52. Promotion was on the cards, Chisholm was signed ; his goals made promotion a certainty. As Cardiff manager Cyril Spiers told me at the end of that season, " If Ken Chisholm never played another game for us, his presence on the field in the last half dozen games was worth £50,000 to Cardiff City."

Other names . . . other similar stories. Bristol Rovers lost Geoff. Bradford in 1955-56, and it cost them promotion. Newcastle United transferred Jackie Milburn, and they've never looked a good team since. Arsenal allowed Jimmy Logie to join Gravesend, and they've depressed supporters for years.

Which brings me to Eddie Baily, star inside-forward of Nottingham Forest, Manchester City's visitors today. Port Vale decided they could dispense with Eddie's services mid-way through last season, and for a relatively small fee, Forest were happy to sign him. Following Baily's departure, Port Vale hit a shocking spell with match after match being lost, ending in the final indignity—relegation to the Third Division.

Maybe the transfer of Eddie Baily wasn't entirely responsible for the decline and fall of the Burslem club. But it certainly helped.

11

Arthur Walmsley's column tried to ease the blow of the cup exit by praising Joe's selection as reserve for the under 23's. "Joe's performance in last month's 'derby' game particularly impressed when he displayed excellent dribbling and scheming qualities. These added to his existing ones of speed and power shooting make him one of the most dangerous inside forwards in the game today and on current form he is not flattered by his selection".

David Jack wrote in praise of the 'personality boys', those whose very presence on the field inspires their colleagues; those perhaps who are not really noticed - until they have to miss a few games. He then went on to name a few that clubs have missed, such as Eddie Baily (Port Vale), Jackie Milburn (Newcastle), Jimmy Logie (Arsenal).

Train to Fratton next week was to be 43/9d, 11-55pm Friday night, changing at Euston then Waterloo at 10.27am (Saturday) and we wouldn't return until some time on Sunday!

Forest, managed by Billy Walker were in seventh place with twenty eight points and City fifth with thirty points. They were having a decent season with seven home wins, including a 2-1 over City, 7-0 over Burnley, four defeats and one draw. Away they'd won six scoring four on three occasions, drawn one and lost six, but after leading the table in September had now dropped to seventh place. In the Cup they'd beaten Gillingham 2-0, but would face WBA in the next round.

At City: Pre war they'd only won once in fifteen attempts. Post, just the one game in 46/47 which they lost 2-1, with a gate of 26,354 . This was the thirty fourth league meeting, plus two cup ties, both at City, 1902 second rd 0-2 (16,000), 1924 first rd 2-0.(33,849)

Team news: City dropped three of the defeated cup team, Branagan, Clarke and Fagan, replaced by Leivers, McLelland and Sambrook. Hayes moved to inside left, Barlow to inside right.

From The Pink/Green/Guardian (W.R.Taylor): New Line Lacks Snap

Weather was crisp and dry, the pitch in tip top condition considering the amount of rain in the week. A special welcome was reserved for Sambrook, of whom great things were expected. Telegrams of good wishes from friends and relatives were waiting for him at the ground and all the players added theirs before the dressing-room tactics talk. It was a lively start by both teams. Sambrook was involved early on with a crossfield run, though Wilson had the ball in the net for Forest after five minutes, but the referee ruled that he had first brought the ball down with his hand. Baily was controlling the game as City were finding it hard to settle and Forest were superior in the opening stages. City's play thus far had been most disappointing and surprisingly devoid of enthusiasm, with Forest having the better of the exchanges. The first real threat came from Sambrook who was brought down just outside the box but the resulting free kick came to nothing. On nineteen minutes Imlach beat Leivers but his shot skimmed the crossbar. In the twenty fifth minute City took an unlikely lead when Hayes centred into the goalmouth to **Johnstone** who did a one two with McLelland, Bobby hitting it home with a short sharp rising shot into the roof of the net.

STEWART IMLACH

The Scot deserved his goal having done more work than the other four forwards between them. In the thirty second minute City nearly scored again, Thomson making an incredible save from Barlow's point blank shot. Sambrook was looking lively but Forest were defending well. Further chances were missed and City should have been three up by half time. McLelland, in addition to his speed, can cross low accurate centres and if persevered with could develop along useful lines. Judgement on Sambrook, who looked slow and indecisive, when he wasn't being starved of the ball would have to be deferred.The floodlights were switched on but the play was drab with mistakes on both sides. Even Johnstone was suffering though he continually fed McLelland, now closely guarded, on the right wing "spraying passes with the efficiency and accuracy of a machine gun, but to no avail, strangely ignoring the new man, and getting ironic applause when he finally passed to Sambrook".

At this stage there was a freak rainstorm which made conditions thoroughly depressing. Blown by a strong breeze the deluge swept across the pitch as both teams struggled. The rain stopped then started again stronger than ever. Sambrook was bustled off the ball as appeals for a penalty were turned down, and in the eighty third minute Gray's flag kick caused confusion in City's defence and **McKinlay** breasted the ball home from short range. Just before the end Hayes dribbling clear of the opposition, rolled the ball home into the net but it didn't count because the off-side whistle had already gone against him. Forest's diminutive winger Imlach lightened proceedings, after being continually fouled by Leivers when he squared up to big Bill, who laughingly pushed him away!

FINAL SCORE: CITY 1 FOREST 1

City: Sky blue/white: Trautmann; Leivers, Sear; Barnes, Ewing, Warhurst; McLelland, Barlow, Johnstone, Hayes, Sambrook.
Forest: Red shirts/white knickers: Thomson; Whare, Thomas; Farmer, McKinlay, Morley; Gray, Quigley, Wilson, Baily, Imlach.
Attendance: 34,837,:**Average:** 33,926
Referee: C. W. Kingston (Newport)
Linesmen: A.E.Wragg , C. Taylor
League position: Stayed 5th
Goals For: 67 Against: 62
Reserves: Lost 4-0 at Huddersfield

Forest went on to finish tenth with forty two points. They won the cup in '59, and remained in division one, being runners up in 1967, until taking the drop in '72. Under Brian Clough they came back up in '77, won division one in '78, won the league cup three times, the European cup twice and lost in the cup final to Spurs in 1991. They took the drop in '99, then went down again to division two (old three) and are now striving to climb back up.

JANUARY 15TH

Joe Hayes replaced the unfit Johnny Haynes of Fulham in the England U 23 team and scored the third goal in the 3-1 win over Scotland, before 19,327 at Goodison Park. It was Joe's first representative game but he did play for an F.A.X1 against the Army at Old Trafford last October.

Peter Doherty, Doncaster manager is reported to be interested in signing John Savage for £3,500, but is facing opposition from Walsall. Crewe are interested in Ron Phoenix.

Bobby Johnstone starred in a 2-2 draw with England behind closed doors at Edgeley Park. It was a thirty minute game only and couldn't be played at Maine Road owing to a frozen pitch and dense fog.

Matt Busby is to be Scotland's manager for the World Cup in June.

In Belfast it was N.Ireland 2 Italy 1 in a World Cup qualifier, and this time the 45,000 strong Irish crowd were exemplary and even cheered the Italian National Anthem.

Wales beat Israel 2-0 in a World Cup qualifier in Tel Aviv (55,000).

Still in dispute was the £3 appearance money for players which wasn't accepted, and the £20 weekly wage was now back to £12.

Massive blaze reported at Belle Vue.

Ex Blue Sid Cann Is the manager of the English youth team.

27) SATURDAY JANUARY 18TH 1958 K.O. 3PM PORTSMOUTH (AWAY)

Programme was 3d for eight pages with a nice shot of HMS Victory on the front cover. On the Blues they welcomed City with “Today we have great pleasure in welcoming our friends from Manchester City. They are having an excellent season and their football is always attractive, and I feel sure today’s encounter will certainly provide the usual entertainment between our two teams”.There were the usual pen pics of our players, but not much else.

Portsmouth were not having a good one. They were in eighteenth place with twenty points just a point clear of the relegation zone. City were fifth with thirty one points. At home they’d won seven, including a 5-0 v Luton, and a 5-1 v Spurs. Away they’d won two, 3-0 at United and 5-3 at Spurs, drawn one lost eleven including a 2-1 at City, 7-4 at Chelsea. They’d just won at Aldershot in the cup but would face Wolves at Molineux in the fourth round.

At Portsmouth: Pre war we’d won two, drawn three and lost six. Post, lost six drew one, but won the last twoo, so a good chance to achieve the double?

Recent attendances ranged from 24,286 (54/55) to 44,294 (49/50) This was the forty second league meeting plus two cup games, one at City, and the ‘34 final (won by City 2-1)

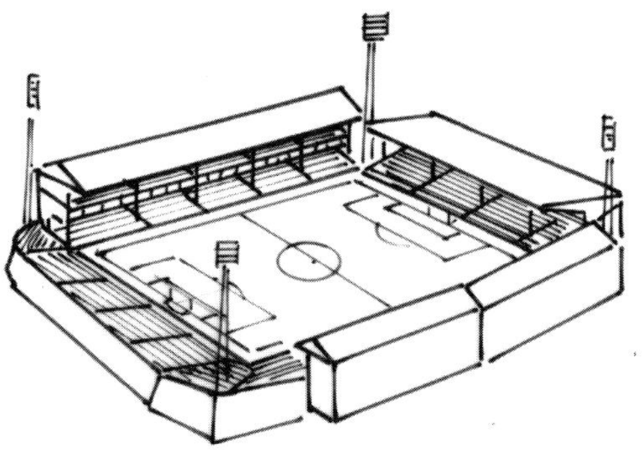

Pitch Size: 116 x 73 yds

Fratton Park’s record attendance was 51,385 v Derby in the FA Cup sixth round, 1948. It was the first ground to stage a floodlit league match, on Wednesday Feb 22nd 1956, a re-arranged game with Newcastle. There was a double decker seats and paddock main stand, with a mock Tudor main entrance. Opposite a partly angled seated stand with a terrace in front, later given an extended roof. Open end behind one goal, with what was known as a ‘Boilermaker’s hump’ in the far corner! Behind the other goal was a covered standing enclosure, eventually replaced. (I didn’t manage a visit until 1985, a 2-1 win setting us up for promotion). The ground was virtually the same and has hardly improved in the last fifty years, though it’s now all seater, and there’s now a roof over the open end

Team News: Warhurst out with a cold and McTavish in.

From The Portsmouth Evening Mail by 'Nimrod' (courtesy of Ian Cunningham) Victory Goals by Crawford - Costly Slip By Trautmann

Derek Dougan

For Portsmouth Derek Dougan was making his first appearance at inside left, and Ray Crawford returned to lead the attack (unfortunately for City!). A small party of City supporters who had left Manchester in the early hours welcomed the official party at the ground before the start. The pitch which was soft and muddy was heavily sanded over large areas, as Crawford kicked off towards the Fratton End. Ewing soon had the crowd jeering as he volleyed into touch but up front Barlow was looking dangerous. Johnstone, being marked by Dickinson, slipped his marker but shot wide, as did Hayes on a couple of occasions, and Uprichard saved well before Pompey went ahead after nine minutes with a glorious goal from Crawford. After a first time pass by the Pompey centre forward to Harris, the winger picked up the ball on the touchline and raced clear of Sear. His cross found **Crawford** racing into the area top speed and he volleyed the ball into the roof of the net. A cross drive from Newman beat everyone but touched the far post and flashed out for a clearance.

After some brief City pressure Pompey attacked with great gusto, causing Ewing to head towards his own net but luckily it went a foot over the bar. The crowd roared for Trautmann as he brought off one scintillating save after another, including racing thirty yards out of his goal to put the ball in touch. City conceded four corners in five minutes but Bert was making saves which would have beaten any ordinary keeper.

Dickinson was acting as a sixth forward but City came close with efforts from the fleet footed forwards Barlow and Hayes causing Uprichard to receive treatment. Sambrook came close as did Dougan and Harris, then with three minutes of the half remaining City, who had been attacking with a will, levelled the score. A tremendous crossfield clearance by Leivers found **Sambrook**, who was giving Gunter an anxious time and went round him in the area, drew Uprichard, then shot past him for his first City goal.

As the teams came off at half time the crowd reserved special applause for Trautmann, who had completely won them over and well he deserved it for the way in which he had carried City through Pompey's opening onslaughts.

Second half City nearly took the lead after Barlow nipped in to intercept Albury's back pass and gave the ball to Sambrook who was thwarted by Uprichard rushing back towards his untenanted net and tipping it over the bar.

Pompey were now having to defend gamely in the treacherous conditions, Gordon was having a bad time of it and Harris's crosses were lacking direction.

Newman could have scored but shot tamely for Bert to collect, and Harris saw his shot hit the upright and bounce back into play. In spite of driving rain and the heavy going the pace never slackened, both teams missing chances.

With ten minutes to go Pompey took the lead in extraordinary fashion. Gordon backheeled the ball to Newman whose shot was double fisted out by the City goalie straight to **Crawford** standing on the edge of the six yard box. The

Pompey forward had time almost, as it were, to scratch his head in perplexity at being given such an opportunity, before banging the ball into the roof of the net, as poor Trautmann beat the ground in despair. City certainly crowded on full sail in the dying moments of the game and Pompey had to defend desperately to keep them out, with Hayes blazing over the bar..

FINAL SCORE: PORTSMOUTH 2 CITY 1

Verdict was McLelland must challenge harder, Sambrook to be faster off the mark, and Ewing to forget the worries of being captain.

Portsmouth: Royal blue shirts/white knickers: Uprichard; Gunter, Wilson; Albury, Rutter, Dickinson; Harris, Gordon, Crawford, Dougan, Newman

City: Red (claret) shirts/white knickers: Trautmann; Leivers, Sear; Barnes, Ewing, McTavish; McLelland, Barlow, Johnstone, Hayes, Sambrook

Attendance: 26, 254 **Average:** 32,320

Referee: K.G.Aston

Linesmen: G.W.Thorpe, E.E.Booth

League position: Dropped one place to 6th

Goals For: 68 Against: 64

Reserves: Beat Bury 5-0 at M/Rd

Portsmouth stayed up at the end of the season on goal average, took the drop in '59, then eventually fell to the fourth before climbing slowly back to the Premiership in 2003, where they've consolidated. Ray Crawford went on to win a league title with Ipswich and Irishman Derek Dougan achieved celebrity status at Wolves, in particular.

JANUARY 18TH

John Savage, the tallest goalkeeper in England was transferred to Walsall for a fee of £4,000, he'd been on the transfer list for some time as he could not gain a place in City's reserve team.

Peter Doherty has quit Doncaster, possibly for Bristol City.

JANUARY 27TH

Matt Busby, new Scotland manager recalled **Bobby Johnstone** to play in the trial next Monday, Scotland v Scottish league, for the World Cup finals in Sweden next June. Bob last played for Scotland two years ago, but struggled against injury after the 1956 Cup Final.

Plans for a summer tour of the USA were announced.

CONCLUSION: Only three games in the month, and no wins. Out of the F.A Cup, a home draw and an away loss in the league and a postponed friendly at Derby on the 25th January due to the poor state of the ground. But we did sign (Ray Sambrook) and sell a player (John Savage) .In the league we stayed in sixth place. Goals for: 68 against 64 Average home attendance 33,918 away 32,320

LEAGUE TABLE

	P	W	D	L	F	A	Pts
Wolves	25	17	5	3	60	28	39
WBA	25	11	11	3	60	41	33
Preston	25	14	4	7	55	35	32
Man Utd	25	13	5	7	60	40	31
Man City	**25**	**14**	**2**	**9**	**66**	**61**	**30**
Luton	25	13	3	9	41	36	29
Notts For	25	13	2	10	53	38	28
Spurs	25	11	5	9	55	54	27
Bolton	25	11	5	9	45	49	27
Chelsea	25	9	7	9	56	52	25
Burnley	25	11	3	11	50	51	25
Everton	25	8	9	8	39	42	25
Arsenal	25	11	3	11	40	44	25
Blackpool	25	10	4	11	42	40	24
B'ham	25	7	8	10	45	56	22
Portsmouth	25	8	4	13	46	49	20
Newcastle	25	8	4	13	41	44	20
Aston Villa	25	8	4	13	41	52	20
Sunderland	25	6	7	12	29	56	19
Leeds	25	7	4	14	32	47	18
Leicester	25	7	3	15	47	66	17
Sheff Wed	25	5	4	16	44	66	14

FEBRUARY'S FOOTBALL MONTHLY

Jackie Mudie of Blackpool on the front cover and Ron Stitfall of Cardiff on the back cover. CB's editorial opinion thought that charging of goalies should be banned after the Ireland v Italy game (a disgrace), for the World cup finals only.

It was reported that Sam Cowan became City's manager in November 1946 and left after only seven months in June 1947, just after he'd steered City to promotion.

Peter Murphy of Birminham has an article where he states that the 'Iron Men' were crushed (in the 1956 cup final) because they were too cocky. Blimey, not one colour pic of a United player in there this month!

B.Sutton of South Uxbridge Street, Burton-On-Trent, sought a pen-pal who supported City - his own age was fourteen. I think I replied to this one, but can't be sure. Anyway, he thought Brazil were great winning the World Cup in 1958 and patriotically I didn't (!!) and he never wrote again!

Once A Blue, Always A Blue

PAT from Davyhulme's story:

I was fifteen and it was shortly after the war when my cousins insisted that I became a Blue.

I started to go to City with a friend, Theresa, but we couldn't afford to go very often and my mum didn't like me going anyway. I was at school with Colin Barlow and Nobby Stiles. Brian Kidd and Bernard Manning were also from the same area. I used to go dancing to the Plaza, on Oxford Road and would dance with a red haired lad called Bobby Whelan. But seeing him out of context at the dancehall I didn't realise he played for City's 'A' team or reserves. There was nothing in it though as he wasn't a free agent, just having a night off from his girlfriend and we were simply dancing partners

He'd get me tickets for the reserves and in fact introduced me to Ron (Phoenix), so he has a lot to answer for! But Bobby wasn't retained at the end of that season. Anyway one thing led to another and Ron and I were married in 1954. Ken Branagan was best man. I didn't really see it as a big deal marrying a footballer, he was only a man after all! We went to live with my mum and dad, as it was a big step buying a house in those days. They thought the world of him. We were sat on a beach at Lytham St Annes in 1960 when this man, called Marshall, approached and said "I've been looking all over for you, I've heard City aren't keeping you on, and I want you to come and play for Rochdale". So Ron then played for 'Dale and we moved to Davyhulme where we bought and ran the hardware shop, with Ron doing it part time whilst playing football.

We've two sons, Matt is forty three, he played some football but had trouble with his knees, but is a keen City fan. Simon, who is forty one, lives near Ipswich and is a Professor of Physics and a musician. He hasn't really got the City bug!

It hurts when people ask if we resent the modern day footballers and the money they earn, because Ron was well paid in his playing days compared with the ordinary working man, so no, we don't at all.

IAN from Didsbury's story:

I was born a Blue, one of six generations. My grandad, Andrew, played for Dunfermline in the 1900's and came to live in Manchester, on Hyde Road, in Mrs Gaskell's house. He knew Peter Hodge who managed City in the 1920's. I went to Ducie Avenue school, as did Robert Donat, the famous actor, and later Fred Eyre, and John Thaw, but I played football for Dickenson Road Presbyterians. Later Bill Leivers was a lay preacher there. Remarkable, he was so tough on the pitch, what a contrast.

After being one of the fortunate far east 'veterans' (we were by the time we returned) to be eventually repatriated to the UK in 1946, I eventually obtained a position with Richard Johnson and Company (wire manufacturers). I mention this as little did I then know I was on the site where my beloved City would, nearly sixty years later re-house themselves! I was christened 'the City nutter' in that it appeared the entire Manchester section of the O/T support were employed by R.J. and N. Ltd. Of course we were bang in the centre of the homes of Stiles, Kidd etc., with the HQ of the Louis Edwards meat emporium on the opposite side of the road (Forge Lane). In fact, come 'derby games' I pretended to be a red, visiting their offices to obtain tickets and did so until I was 'outed'! However by that time I could afford season tickets in H block of the main stand. I went to the Everton v Liverpool semi final at Maine Road in the early fifties, standing on the open terrace and someone urinated down my back. I always went in the seats after that.

I first met Bobby Johnstone in the 'Lord Lyon' pub on Claremont Road, Rusholme (a stone throw from Maine Road) and he assisted me, along with Frank Thomson and my uncle Andrew Niven, to form the Rusholme branch of the supporters club in 1955.

Another City supporter was Mabel Thomas (resident pianist at the 'Lord Lyon') who was to become the grandmother of footballer Geoff Thomas, and she was a gem with her City songs.

Following Roy Clarke's flying headed goal to beat Sunderland in the dying minutes of an epic semi-final in '55 (Roy was carried off injured and missed the Wembley final) we headed home - '12 City nutcases' in a Hackett's mini coach (this I hired for the majority of away games in 54/55) . Pub number four, five, or six found us in Stafford with a surprisingly welcoming licensee who not only supplied us with sandwiches but allowed our 'pianist' to play the piano. This was the first occasion I had heard a 'Johnstone and Clarkey' song - I certainly knew all the words by the time we had departed that Stafford pub! Here goes:

A Johnstone for me, a Johnstone for me
If you don't know Johnstone, you're nae use to me
Stan Matthews is brae, Willie Waddell and awe
But our wee Bobby's the pick of 'em all

Who said City couldn't play
City couldn't play, City couldn't play
Who said City couldn't play
City couldn't play football

After the ball was centred
After the whistle blew Clarkey got his temper up
And down the wing he flew
He passed the ball to Johnstone
And Johnstone passed it back
Clarkey took a flying leap
And in the net it went

Who said City couldn't play.....

We persuaded Bobby to move to my home in Hamilton Road where he settled in comfortably and unobtrusively, spending time kicking a ball in Crowcroft Park with Ian and Olivia, my two young children. I was told that Ian was selling Bobby's autograph at school - true or false - I do not know (Ian didn't strike me as a future entrepreneur) The 'Lord Lyon' was the centre of many happy City memories, especially on a Sunday. Seven days after the '56 cup win, I headed there at lunchtime to behold a scene of the F.A.Cup on Mabel's grand piano - sing song in full flow, including Roy Paul, Bobby, Ken Barnes (with usual Cheshire Cat smile), Doug Mimmo (Head of C.I.D.), his fellow officers (didn't have many reds in the police hierarchy in those days). Harry Smith (the licensee) kindly suggested I collect my young children and bring them to touch the F.A.Cup. This I did speedily in my Ford 'Pop'. When I returned, Bobby, Roy Paul, and Ken each gave Olivia and Ian two half crowns, a small fortune in those days for children and their joy was complete when we eventually took Ken (and the Cup) home to Burnage.

Footballers did not have their own cars at that time (Bobby Johnstone being an exception, he had a Sunbeam Talbot so that he could visit his family in Scotland at the weekends). Ken left the Cup with me enabling me to take it to the office the following day to laud in front of the reds. I put blue ribbons on it, got photos and showed it off in the office, on the 'City nutter' desk.

I did a similar thing in '69, Malcolm lent it me this time. I had it on the wall in the 'Fletcher's Arms', where I'd moved to and put it under the bed at night.

The middle fifties were heady times following City, with the two cup finals.

My own 'cup final' was a game in Fog Lane Park for City supporters. I scored a goal and we won. I had played in Stoke, Inverness, Paris, Norwich, Luckmow, New Delhi, but the Fog Lane game is the one I'd choose (I played in Bobby Johnstone's boots!).

I got a phone call from a friend, a United supporter at the time of Munich and I, a staunch Blue, was in tears. That's why I don't like the songs some fans sing, it's not City's style.

Ian is a lifelong Blue, and ex Director of the club, now a Life President

David from Derby's story:

Like most City fans, I guess, I was first taken to Maine Road by my dad. I bet 20,000 other City fans would say the same. It was either '48 or '49 and we were playing Middlesbrough, we lost 1-0. I remember Wilf Mannion broke his leg in that match, well my dad told me so *(it was Billy Linacre - Ed!)* and really I was hooked. I remember that match, not particularly for the match itself, but more for the atmosphere of it, the feeling of belonging to something special. There were about 60,000 fans there, which ain't gonna happen again, and I remember people being kind to me, and lifting me up. We were right at the very top of the old Platt Lane stand, which was a large stand then. I wanted to go again, but not just because of the football. I liked the sky blue shirts, we were the only club to wear those colours at that time. Later Coventry imitated the blue because one of their directors saw us play in it in the 1955 cup final, liked the colour and adopted it in the sixties.

I was living in Cheetham Hill, where I'd catch the bus into town and change buses to go to Maine Road. The poverty in Moss Side didn't surprise me, because that was the norm. Seeing my mum take the washing in a pram to the wash house. Looking back it was archaic, but that's what everyone's mum did, that's what happened, and as a kid the norm is what you see at that time, not what you can't see.

I didn't go to City with my dad for very long, I then used to go with a pal, strangely enough it was Joe Lewis, who is the father of the Bury MP Ivan. For the 1955 cup final I queued up all night on my own and got a 3/6d ticket. My dad had had a heart attack at a City game towards the end of that season and was in hospital. I remember vividly going to see him after getting my ticket and when he said "let me see it" I said "Dad, you can have it" but he replied "No, I just want to see it so I've seen one (1934) and touched one". He died that year and those words have stayed with me ever since, but the bad news was mother and father wouldn't let me go to the game. They didn't want me to go on my own at that age. So I did the only thing I could and ran away from home.

I hitch-hiked down to London and remember there were no motorways at that time. It wasn't as hard as it appeared though because I had my City scarf on and I picked up a lift quite easily. I stood behind the goal, but Meadows went off, and there were no substitutes then, and we lost 3-1. I got in so much trouble because mum and dad didn't know for sure where I was, though they made an educated guess. I'd set off for Waterloo Road school on the Friday but I'd had no intention of going. I got plenty of earache, but I wasn't sorry, just sorry about the result.

But I remember most, even more impressively, the Roy Clarke header in the semi-final v Sunderland at Villa Park. I arrived there very early waiting for the gates to open in the pouring rain. We used to enjoy the couple of hours before kick off in those days, watching the crowds come into the ground,

The next year City, just like in 1934, reached Wembley again and won it 3-1. The club had started the voucher system, through which I obtained my ticket and I was allowed to go to that one. I went on the coach, enabling me to look around London, and I stood in the same place at Wembley as the year before. So I was there when my hero Bert broke his neck and I think it was Dave Ewing who did it, after the Murphy incident, when he took a hell of crack. Joe Hayes, Bobby Johnstone and Jack Dyson scored the goals, and I can tell you that later on, Mary, my future wife, dumped Jack Dyson for me!

I went to away games, when I could afford it, on the train. I remember going to Blackpool and I was so surprised about how tiny the ground was and they were a big club then. I also went to Bolton and Old Trafford with the horrible little railings - a big club with a garden fence round the pitch *(and gnomes on it - Ed)*. There was an announcement on the tannoy, “a special mention to all Manchester Shitty supporters” which went down like a bag of sick - but that was the day we beat them 5-0 I think.

So I was a second generation Blue and I’m now delighted to say that my grandson, Zac, aged three, is now a fourth generation Blue. One of the things that gave me as much pleasure as anything else was when I made him the first known unborn season ticket holder at City, even before his birth. I had no choice as the seat next to ours became available and I had to invest and buy it.

But I always feel that my personal fate is tied to City with a bond. So many significant things have happened to me and City at the same time. If we lose it can be a disaster. For example: in 1981 City got to Wembley v Spurs and I was leader of the opposition party on Derbyshire County Council, but we won the election from the Tories and took control, so Labour had won Derbyshire back. It was so very memorable. In 1983 I was Labour Parliamentary Candidate for the Amber Valley. The Labour Party lost the election, I lost my seat, and City got relegated, it seemed to ding dong like that. Then in 1987, City got relegated again and I lost my seat in the general election again. Then lo and behold in 1989 we re-won Derbyshire and City won promotion.

In the year 2000 I was told I had to have a heart by pass, so I thought if we get promoted I’ll have it. We won 4-1 at Blackburn. I had the operation, then a year later we were relegated and I got the glorious news that my by pass had failed. So I take very seriously any kind of tragedy that comes to City, which happens all too often.

I have to go on now until someone switches the light out, so I make hay while the sun shines.

One of my worst moments was when a scout from United, who was watching my son John, knocked on the door, and John was actually offered apprentice terms. So I promptly rang City, who he then signed for, and that made it all the better, so whatever happened later with John, *(Ed - he died tragically from cancer in 2006)* that was a proud moment. He scored the winning goal for us in the curtain raiser for the Full Members cup final, that mad house at 5-4, our kids v Chelsea’s kids, which we won 2-1,

I was at the Swindon game (8,015) with 25,000 other City fans, I’ve never met anyone who wasn’t there *(Ed - I must be the only one who wasn’t there, as I was playing in the Eccles and District League, at Littleton Road that day)* and significantly that was the first game to which I took my daughter Susan (Bookbinder). She was all of two years old and we had very good seats in the main stand, a good time to go as there was hardly anyone there. At the first game in the old third division, Bernard Harding from Cheadle, who I sat next to, shook my hand saying “another nine months of misery”, but it didn’t quite turn out like that though.

Every game for me is a trip down memory lane. We all have our worries and problems, but the beautiful thing is that the minute I get in the ground, no matter what happens, the phone is off and if I were to get a message saying the house is on fire I’d say ‘Well let the bloody thing burn, I’m at the match, sod off’. I’ve got to admit that if they opened up Maine Road I’d still be back there, but no question Eastlands is the future and I’ve got great seats that I wouldn’t swap with anyone. So I’m very happy there, but my home is still Maine Road. What I can’t have at Eastlands are the memories which came with me to every single game.

Maine Road could have been developed better. It was disrespectful what they did to it. When it opened in 1923 with one covered stand, the rest standing, you knew you were going to a stadium. City then ruined the bloody place, and in the end they desecrated it. My temple, I loved going. Platt Lane, the scoreboard end, it was deliberate, planned destruction. They ruined it, four stands, all completely different, then there were the 'Gene Kelly' *('Singin' in the Rain' - geddit?)* stands. Whoever designed them needed a brain scan, ridiculous. They don't deserve the fans they've got. We put up with it because we have no choice. When we went down in the sixties the crowds went down, but they went up in the nineties. The fans defy logic. We're all nutters, but for all the other things that have happened I wouldn't have it any other way. Thirty one years and we're still here, says it all.

David is still a big Blue together with his daughter Susan and grandson Zac.

CHAPTER EIGHT

FEBRUARY 1958 - CITY AND MUNICH

Off we go, then, looking to double Spurs, and Leicester whilst hoping to avenge heavy defeats by West Brom and Birmingham....

28) SATURDAY FEBRUARY 1ST 1958
K.O. 3PM: WEST BROMWICH ALBION (HOME)

LEAGUE TABLES

DIVISION I
(Including January 18th)

	P	W	D	L	Goals F	Goals A	Pts
Wolves	27	17	6	4	63	32	40
Preston N.E.	27	15	5	7	61	39	35
West Brom.	27	12	11	4	64	45	35
Man. United	27	14	6	7	68	43	34
Luton Town	27	14	4	9	45	37	32
Man. City	**27**	**14**	**3**	**10**	**68**	**64**	**31**
Nott'gh'm F.	27	13	4	10	55	40	30
Chelsea	27	11	7	9	61	54	29
Burnley	27	13	3	11	55	53	29
Blackpool	27	12	4	11	48	44	28
Tottenham	27	11	6	10	58	59	28
Arsenal	27	12	3	12	43	47	27
Bolton W.	27	11	5	11	49	59	27
Everton	27	8	10	9	41	46	26
B'ham City	27	8	8	11	49	60	24
Portsmouth	27	9	4	14	50	54	22
Aston Villa	27	9	4	14	46	57	22
Newcastle U.	27	8	4	15	43	48	20
Leeds United	27	7	6	14	34	49	20
Sunderland	27	6	8	13	32	62	20
Leicester C.	27	8	3	16	50	69	19
Sheffield W.	27	6	4	17	49	71	16

CENTRAL LEAGUE
(Including January 25th)

	P	W	D	L	Goals F	Goals A	Pts
Man. United	28	19	4	5	98	48	42
Wolves	28	19	3	6	70	40	41
Everton	26	16	4	6	69	37	36
Huddersfield	27	14	4	9	58	42	32
Barnsley	27	13	6	8	56	50	32
Sheffield W.	26	12	5	9	48	40	29
Bury	27	12	5	10	58	56	29
Liverpool	25	13	2	10	62	43	28
West Brom.	28	11	5	12	50	55	27
Stoke City	28	11	5	12	44	52	27
Man. City	**29**	**13**	**0**	**16**	**70**	**62**	**26**
Derby C.	27	11	4	12	45	58	26
Chesterfield	27	10	5	12	45	45	25
Newcastle U.	29	12	1	16	45	63	25
Preston N.E.	28	10	4	14	49	54	24
Bolton W.	27	9	6	12	47	52	24
Sheffield U.	28	10	4	14	49	57	24
Blackpool	26	9	6	11	37	46	24
Aston Villa	28	11	2	15	46	67	24
Burnley	26	8	5	13	31	50	21
Leeds United	26	6	4	16	37	56	16
Blackb'n R.	27	7	2	18	38	79	16

LANCASHIRE LEAGUE-Supp. Com.
(Including January 18th)
DIVISION I—Section "A"

	P	W	D	L	Goals F	Goals A	Pts
R'dale Res.	10	7	2	1	43	11	16
Bolton 'A'	9	6	1	2	19	12	13
Bury 'A'	9	5	0	4	36	22	10
Man. City 'A'	**8**	**4**	**1**	**3**	**18**	**15**	**9**
Man. U. 'A'	9	2	2	5	23	17	6
Oldham 'A'	9	0	0	9	6	68	0

DIVISION II—Section 'A'

	P	W	D	L	Goals F	Goals A	Pts
Man. City 'B'	**9**	**8**	**0**	**1**	**35**	**11**	**16**
Bury 'B'	9	4	1	4	15	18	9
Man. U. 'B'	6	3	2	1	17	9	8
Bolton 'B'	8	3	2	3	12	15	8
Stockport 'A'	9	2	2	5	19	34	6
Rochd'le 'A'	9	1	1	7	14	25	3

JUNIOR DIV.—Section 'A'

	P	W	D	L	Goals F	Goals A	Pts
Stockport 'B'	8	6	1	1	26	15	13
Bury	8	4	0	4	28	16	8
Man. City	**8**	**3**	**1**	**4**	**16**	**19**	**7**
Bolton	8	3	0	5	16	20	6
Rochdale	8	3	0	5	10	26	6

THIS SEASON'S FIXTURES

LEAGUE 1st Division

1957	Opponents		Res.
Aug. 28	Chelsea	A	3-2
31	Manchester United	A	1-4
Sept. 4	Chelsea (7-30)	H	5-2
7	Nottingham Forest	A	1-2
11	Preston N.E. (7-30)	H	2-0
14	Portsmouth	H	2-1
18	Preston N.E.	A	1-6
21	West Brom. A.	A	2-9
28	Tottenham H.	H	5-1
Oct. 5	Birmingham City	A	0-4
9	Sheffield Wed. (7-30)	H	2-0
12	Leicester City	H	4-3
19	Blackpool	A	5-2
26	Luton Town	H	2-2
Nov. 2	Arsenal	A	1-2
9	Bolton Wanderers	H	2-1
16	Leeds United	A	4-2
23	Wolverhampton W.	H	3-4
30	Sunderland	A	1-2
Dec. 7	Everton	H	6-2
14	Aston Villa	A	2-1
21	Sheffield W.	A	5-4
25	Burnley	A	1-2
26	Burnley	H	4-1
28	Manchester United	H	2-2
1958			
Jan. 4	West Brom. (Cup 3)	A	1-5
11	Nottingham Forest	H	1-1
18	Portsmouth	A	1-2
Feb. 1	West Brom. A.	H	4-1
8	Tottenham H.	A	
15	Birmingham City	H	
22	Leicester City	A	
Mar. 1	Blackpool	H	
8	Luton Town	A	
15	Arsenal	H	
22	Wolverhampton W.	A	
29	Leeds United	H	
April 4	Newcastle United	A	
5	Bolton Wanderers	A	
7	Newcastle United	H	
12	Sunderland	H	
19	Everton	A	
26	Aston Villa	H	
May 3	F.A. Cup Final		

Central League

Maine Road

1957	Opponents		Res.
Aug. 26	Liverpool (6-15)	H	2-1
31	Manchester United	H	3-4
Sept. 2	Liverpool	A	2-5
7	Huddersfield T.	H	1-2
10	Burnley	A	0-1
14	Bury	A	1-3
16	Burnley (7-30)	H	3-0
21	Chesterfield	H	5-1
28	West Brom. A.	A	0-1
Oct. 2	Preston N.E.	A	1-5
5	Stoke City	H	3-0
12	Leeds United	A	3-1
14	Sheffield Wed. (7-15)	A	1-2
19	Bolton Wanderers	H	2-3
26	Wolverhampton W.	A	6-7
Nov. 2	Aston Villa	H	5-6
9	Derby County	A	1-0
16	Everton	H	3-1
23	Barnsley	A	2-4
30	Sheffield United	H	4-1
Dec. 7	Blackpool	A	1-2
14	Blackburn Rovers	H	4-0
21	Sheffield Wed.	H	5-2
25	N'castle U. (11 a.m.)	H	4-1
26	Newcastle United	A	1-2
28	Manchester United	A	0-4
1958			
Jan. 4	Preston N.E.	H	2-5
11	Huddersfield T.	A	0-4
18	Bury	H	5-0
Feb. 1	Chesterfield	A	
8	West Brom. A.	H	
15	Stoke City	A	
22	Leeds United	H	
Mar. 1	Bolton Wanderers	A	
8	Wolverhampton W.	H	
15	Aston Villa	A	
22	Derby County	H	
29	Everton	A	
April 5	Barnsley	H	
12	Sheffield United	A	
19	Blackpool	H	
26	Blackburn Rovers	A	

Lancashire League "A"

(Shawe View Field, Urmston)

1957	Opponents		Res.
Aug. 24	Preston N.E. 'A'	H	0-1
31	Bolton W. 'A' (S.C.)	H	1-2
Sept. 7	Rochdale Res. (S.C.)	A	0-3
28	Blackpool 'A'	A	5-2
Oct. 5	Everton 'A'	H	1-2
12	Liverpool 'A'	A	1-1
19	Barrow Res.	A	1-2
26	Man. U. 'A' (S.C.)	H	0-0
Nov. 9	Bolton W. 'A' (S.C.)	A	2-1
16	Everton 'A'	A	2-3
23	Blackpool 'A'	H	1-2
30	Burnley 'A'	H	0-3
Dec. 7	Bury 'A' (S.C.)	A	2-1
14	Blackburn R. 'A'	A	5-2
21	Blackburn R. 'A'	H	1-3
26	Bury 'A' (S.C.)	H	4-2
28	Oldham A. 'A' (S.C.)	H	8-0
1958			
Jan. 4	Rochdale Res. (S.C.)	H	1-[illegible]
11	Barrow Res.	H	1-2
18	Rochdale Res.	A	4-1
Feb. 1	Bolton W. 'A'	H	
8	Burnley 'A'	A	
15	Bury 'A'	A	
22	Rochdale Res.	H	
Mar. 1	Man. United 'A'	H	
8	Man. United 'A'	A	
15	Liverpool 'A'	H	
22	Bury 'A'	H	
29			
April 4			
5	Oldham Ath. 'A'	H	
7			
12	Oldham Ath. 'A'	A	
19	Preston N.E. 'A'	A	
26	Bolton W. 'A'	A	

12

Programme editorial reflected on past City and West Brom games, the cancellation of last week's friendly at Derby and indeed no other City matches being played. Ray Sambrook was congratulated for his goal at Fratton, but the team were scolded for throwing away the points: "that were there for the taking and not for the first time this season". With regard to keepers, now that John Savage had gone to Walsall, great things were expected from Steve Fleet, for whom a great future was forecast. He had signed as a full time pro, further to demob from the RAF. Roy Dixon had signed similarly, having done well in the 'A' team .

Other newcomers were welcomed too: Arthur Sadler, full back on the ground staff and Norman Fairweather, amateur outside left from St. Helens.

Finally Bobby Johnstone was congratulated on his return to the Scottish representative scene and it was hoped he would make the World Cup side.

Maine Road Gossip advised that Jimmy Meadows' registration had been cancelled; thanked all who put to the recent collections of £194 for M/C and Salford District Hospitals Commentaries' Association and £78 10s 6d for the St John's Ambulance Brigade.

City have given permission for M/C Boys to play London Boys at M/Rd under floodlights on Wed April 2nd KO 7.30pm.

Sportsman's Corner - William Anderson of Davenport asked if any league club had the same ground name as another. Answer - Swindon and Northampton, The County Ground; Aldershot and Chesterfield The Recreation Ground, not to mention, which 'Sportsman' didn't, Newcastle and Exeter having St James' Park, and Old Trafford is also a cricket ground, plus Stirling Albion have Annfield with two n's, so not quite Liverpool's Anfield!

Arthur Walmsley reckoned that today's fixture, apart from United's was the most eagerly anticipated, and could turn out to be the best of the season.

Lancs born, Essex educated, moved to Durham, now a Londoner, **David Jack** lamented the poor form of London first division clubs this season. Shame!

It was 30/- to London for next week's game at Spurs, **train** departing 11.55pm Friday night, returning Euston 6.05pm or 12.30 am Sunday!

West Brom, managed by Vic Buckingham, were having a good one and were third in the table with thirty five points. City were sixth with thirty one points. They'd only lost one at home, 2-1 to Arsenal, had won nine with big wins v City 9-2, Burnley 5-1, and drawn three. Away though they'd won three, drawn six and lost three including a 5-1 at Luton. In the cup they'd beaten City 5-1 in the 3rd round, drawn with Forest 3-3 and won the replay 5-1 and would play Sheff. Utd in the 5th round.

At City: Pre-war we'd won four of the last five, including a 7-1 win in '37/38. Post they lost 5-0 in 46/47 drew 1-1 in 49/50, won three, '52, '53, '54 and lost the last three, so all set.

Recent attendances ranged from 13,933 (51/52) to 57,663 (54/55) It was the seventy sixth league meeting, plus two cup games, both at West Brom..

Team news: Warhurst and McAdams back in for McTavish and McLelland.

From The Guardian's 'Old International': City Win Easily But Only Trautmann Saves A Deluge

Albion pounded the City defence, and Bert could only parry a point blank Horobin shot, **Kevan** following up to slot home in the ninth minute. Bert though, was having a stormer, and by his extraordinary judgment, anticipation and agility, pulled City back from the brink of disaster. His goalkeeping genius kept watch and ward, saving City from being cut to ribbons. Barnes and Leivers played magnificent football, as did Warhurst but smeared his best work with too many 'transgressions of the laws'. In the later stages Sear made heroic tackles as he flung his snake like body across the turf, or thrust forth a telescopic leg to thwart the Albion forwards. Ewing made last ditch clearances, symbols of a refusal to capitulate.

DEREK KEVAN

City thundered back and **Billy Mac.**, who'd had a stinker so far, finished off a Barlow/Hayes passing move, letting the ball pass between his legs before side footing home a deflected shot off Dudley in the twentieth minute. Griffin hit the post, then Sambrook started to get involved, left Williams in his wake, and crossed for **Barlow** to score in the fifty second minute. Ray was at it again and crossed wickedly which Joe helped on and **McAdams** lunged forward, crocodile fashion to head in the third on fifty five minutes. Fourten minutes later **Billy** completed his hat trick when he tapped home a centre from Hayes. Only then could City assume the port and call of conquerors. For a quarter of a century City fans have been entertained by some of the finest goalkeeping to be seen anywhere in the world. Today both keepers were in action. Trautmann on the field, Frank Swift in the press box. Swift's eyes gleamed at Bert's performance, experiencing that pleasurable overture which only goalkeepers know.

Revenge then, but Jim Sanders in the Albion goal looked so dejected that I actually felt sorry for him.

This was Frank Swift's last visit to Maine Road and Don Davies' (Guardian's Old International) last report on City, both died at Munich.

FINAL SCORE: CITY 4 WBA 1

City: Sky blue/white: Trautmann: Leivers, Sear: Barnes, Ewing, Warhurst; Barlow, Hayes, Johnstone, McAdams, Sambrook
WBA: Sanders, Howe, Williams, Dudley, Kennedy, Barlow R, Griffin, Whitehouse, Robson, Kevan, Horobin
Attendance: 38,702 **Average:** 34,267
Referee: J.W. Topliss (Grimsby)
Linesmen: V.J.Batty, D.H.Harrison
League position: Stayed in sixth place
Goals For: 72 Against: 65
Reserves: Won 3-2 at Chesterfield

Derek Kevan joined City in 1963, Bobby Robson went on to manage Ipswich and England, Don Howe went on to manage Arsenal, Maurice Setters who didn't play, later moved to United. Albion won their last match of the season to pip City for fourth place. They had future success in the League Cup in '66 and the F. A. Cup in '68, when they also doubled us but beat United 6-3 at The Hawthorns to set us up for the title, but they did lose to us also in the 1970 League Cup final, 2-1. After that they had many years in the second division and just the odd appearance in division one or the Premier league.

FEBRUARY 3RD

Bobby Johnstone was injured in the West Brom game, so was unable to play in the match for Scotland today and only 50/50 for Saturday, but later declared fit. Peter Doherty was appointed new manager of Bristol City. Birmingham had named Pat Beasley and Arthur Turner as joint managers.

In a World Cup qualifier Wales beat Israel in Cardiff 2-0, 35,000.

FEBRUARY 6TH

I went on an errand for my Mum to the local shop in Lower Sutherland Street, Swinton, owned at the time by Horace Rees around 5pm-ish. I'd been in before, loads of times on my way to and from City, fully bedecked, sky blue scarf, bob hat etc. however I was greeted with "you're a United fan, there's been a plane crash".

The first news coming through was that the plane bringing the United team back from Belgrade had crashed at Munich at 3.10pm. Harry Gregg and Bill Foulkes were not hurt, but among the dead were Roger Byrne, Tommy Taylor, David Pegg, Eddie Colman and Mark Jones. Matt Busby had only a 50-50 chance, and Duncan Edwards would not walk for years. Also amongst the dead was News Of The World journalist Frank Swift, ex City and England goalkeeper.

FEBRUARY 7TH

The morning papers listed the twenty one dead. Additional to these were Geoff Bent and Billy Whelan. Secretary Walter Crickmer, trainer P.H.Currie, H.Whalley coach. Journalists Alf Clarke (MEN), H.D.Davies (M/C Guardian), Geo. Follows (Daily Herald), T.Jackson (MEN), Archie Ledbrooke (Daily Mirror), Henry Rose (Daily Express), Eric Thompson (Daily Mail). W. Satinoff (M/C business man), W.T.Cable (steward), B.Miklos (travel agent).

Survivors were: Jackie Blanchflower, Bobby Charlton, Ken Morgans, Albert Scanlon, Dennis Viollet, Ray Wood and Johnny Berry, but with injuries. Two stewardesses, two wives and a young baby also survived.

United's game with Wolves the next day was postponed obviously, but all other games were to go ahead with flags at half mast and players wearing black arm bands,

Reference was made to the entire Torino team wiped out in a plane crash on March 4th in 1949 when their plane crashed into Superga Basilica. Also in March 1950, eighty rugby supporters died when the plane carrying them back from the Ireland v Wales international crashed at Llandow, South Wales.

Ironically, the FA only lifted a flying ban last year.

There was a plea to award the FA Cup to United and a Disaster fund was to be set up.

At our school some of the toughest lads were in tears but I did overhear someone say "pity it wasn't City 'cos their players are no good".

29) SATURDAY FEBRUARY 8TH 1958
K.O. 3PM: TOTTENHAM HOTSPUR (AWAY)

The photo opposite shows the City players lined up during the two minutes silence, heads bowed before the game. Whether this had any effect on the team we don't know but City did suffer a crushing, though extremely unlucky defeat. The team had travelled down to London the day before, and it was reported that they attended the local cinema where they possibly saw the newsreels of the disaster.

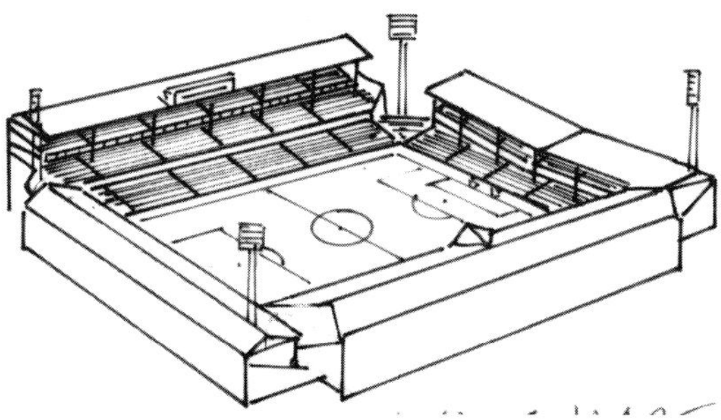

Pitch Size: 110 x 73 yds

The programme was disappointing. It was a large four page issue, a bit like a reserve team programme. There was no mention of Munich as it was printed before the day of the crash. There is a brief history of previous encounters, and of the club plus a round up of the divisions. Wolves being firmly established in the lead in division one with a useful clear points margin over their nearest rivals Preston North End. The following three pages included match reviews and the usual statistical information.

COPYRIGHT ALL RIGHTS RESERVED

TOTTENHAM HOTSPUR

FOOTBALL AND ATHLETIC COMPANY LIMITED

Official Programme

AND RECORD OF THE CLUB

Secretary: R. S. JARVIS
Team Manager: J. ANDERSON
Medical Officer: Dr. A. E. TUGHAN

Chairman: FRED. J. BEARMAN
Vice-Chairman: FREDK. WALE
Directors: F. JOHN BEARMAN, D. H. DEACOCK, S. A. WALE

PRICE TWOPENCE

VOL. L. No. 39 SATURDAY, 8th FEBRUARY, 1958

MANCHESTER CITY HERE TODAY

This afternoon we give a hearty welcome to Manchester City who are our visitors in the League for the return match played at Maine Road on September 28th when they were the winners by 5 goals to 1, their scorers being Hayes 2, Johnstone 2, and Barlow, with one of their defenders giving us our goal.

The City's last success at Tottenham was in 1951-52 season, but they have since drawn here on two occasions in the League, and we can expect a stern test this afternoon. Last Saturday the "City" were avenged for their defeat in the Cup by beating West Bromwich by four goals to one after Albion had opened the scoring. It was pleasing to hear that their goalkeeper, Trautmann, is now back in best form after his injury, and gave an outstanding performance for them.

Manchester City's history is closely linked with that of the Football League; in their first two seasons they competed under the name of Ardwick, and then from 1894 onwards under their present title in either the First or Second Divisions. The considerable amount of success they have enjoyed is shown by the fact that they have had 37 seasons in Division One to their credit with one Championship in 1937.

Their other major honours are: Division One Runners-up 1903-4, 1920-21. Division Two Champions 1898-99, 1902-03, 1909-10, 1927-28 and 1946-47. Division Two Runners-up 1895-96 and 1950-51.

F.A. Cup Winners in 1904, 1936 and 1956. Defeated Finalists in 1926, 1933, and 1955.

In season 1925-26, when they lost to Bolton in the Final they had the misfortune to be relegated, surely a most unusual experience for Cup Finalists, and this despite the fact that they had scored 89 League goals. And in the following season their luck regarding goal average reached its climax. They were running neck-and-neck with Portsmouth for promotion and had scored over 100 goals in the process. On the last day of the season they had the same number of points as their rivals with goal averages almost identical; both clubs won their matches, but Portsmouth scored five goals, and when the averages were worked out Manchester City were pipped by less than a 200th part of a goal.

IN LEAGUE AND CUP

With the season now two-thirds completed Wolverhampton Wanderers are firmly established in the lead in Division One, and have a useful clear points margin over nearest rivals, Preston North End who are closely followed by Manchester United and West Bromwich. The pace is still a hot one, however, and last Saturday of the first seven clubs in the table West Bromwich were the only one to lose—to Manchester City, our visitors to-day. Wolves are the only club in the First or Second Divisions who have not suffered defeat at home, a distinction which is shared by Swindon and Plymouth Argyle in the Third South.

In Division Two a keen fight is in progress for the honours of the Championship, and for promotion. London is well placed with Charlton in first place with 37 points, one point ahead of West Ham, who have the same lead over Blackburn Rovers with Liverpool and Fulham still well in the hunt.

In the Third Divisions there are two keen contests in being, first at the top of the table for Championship honours which is still wide open, and also in the middle of the table to avoid the last 12 places which would mean relegation to Division Four next season.

In the Fifth Round of the Cup the First Division is some-

IN THE INTERESTS OF GROUND CONDITIONS, PLAYERS ON EITHER SIDE WILL NOT SIGN AUTOGRAPHS ON THE FIELD

Printed by Thomas Knight & Co. Ltd., The Clock House Press, Hoddesdon, Herts.

White Hart Lane's record attendance was 75,038 v Sunderland in the FA Cup 6 1938. It comprised the massive triple decker along the length, with seats, the shelf and press box on the roof. (now looks small!) Opposite was the main stand, seats and paddock, with two similar stands, covered seats and standing behind each goal. The ground was completely re-developed over the years from 1980 to 2000. I didn't make it here until 1986, won 2-0.

Spurs managed by Jimmy Anderson were in eleventh spot with twenty eight points. City sixth with thirty three points. They'd had eight home wins including a 7-1 against Birmingham, two draws, and three losses including a 3-5 v Pompey. Away they'd won three drawn three and lost eight including 5-1's at City and Portsmouth. They'd gone out of the cup in the fourth round to Sheffield United.

The players observe a two minute silence before the game at White Hart Lane.

At Spurs: Pre-war we'd won the last one, drawn the one before but lost seven before that. Post, three draws, three losses and only one win in 51/52, 2-1. We did win the '56 semi at Villa Park 1-0 though.

Recent attendances ranged from 31,622 ('56) to 58,163 ('52). It was the forty fourth league meeting plus seven cup ties, three at Spurs 1922 third rd 1-2 (53,000), 1930 third rd 2-2 (37,000), 1935 third rd 0-1 (48,983)

Team news: Unchanged

From The Pink (Paul Burden)/Green: Beat-The-Mud Hayes Rattles Spurs - Bert saves Pen. - Lucky Spurs Snatch A Hatful

It was a grim faced City team which drove to Tottenham from their London hotel today for the return league game at White Hart Lane. All the players wore black arm bands in memory of the victims of the Munich Air Disaster and two minutes silence was observed before the kick off. The flags on Tottenham's stands flew at half-mast and all the Spurs players came out in black shirts for the silence.

Just before the start it was overcast and cold as a heavy rainstorm burst over the ground drenching all the spectators and leaving the pitch in a slippery state.The Spurs players took off their black shirts and immediately went into action. It was an entertaining early phase in which first Spurs and then City took charge though finishing was generally below average - not surprising on a ground giving such a poor foothold.

Bert was getting cheers from the Spurs fans, one shouting "what a goalkeeper", but in the twenty fifth minute City had a let off when Brooks' shot smacked against the far upright and bounced clear. It was cut and thrust all the time with every man fast off the mark. After thirty four minutes Sambrook made a good run and put across a head-high centre. Up went Hayes with a flying header. The ball hit the bar, bounced down, and appeared to go over the line before Ditchburn collected. Three minutes later Sambrook, having his best game to date, weaved his way through the Spurs defence then suddenly squared the ball inside from close range. Ditchburn and Norman missed it and the ball ran on to **Hayes** who netted from three yards out. Barlow was then pulled back in the penalty zone by Norman but the referee refused a penalty and in fact lectured Johnstone for over reacting.

City were the better team for most of the first half. Spurs set the pace on the resumption but twice Barlow was pushed off the ball when through in the penalty area but the referee refused to give City any award. Then when Tottenham took up the challenge referee Mr

Westwood gave them a penalty which surprised everyone - even the home supporters. It was awarded after a goalmouth melee, with a Spurs player appealing for a penalty, after a great tackle by Ewing on Robb. Up stepped Harmer for the shot whilst the City players were still arguing about the decision. He went for the far corner hard and low as Bert threw himself down with a magnificent dive and checked the ball which slithered out of his grasp to safety. However on the fifty eighth minute **Brooks**, cutting in sharply from the right, found the bottom far corner of the net for the equaliser. On the sixtiethh minute Johnstone fed Barlow who dribbled around the full-back and then lobbed it home. The referee disallowed it leaving everyone gasping with astonishment.

Bobby Smith

There had been some amazing incidents in this game in which Spurs, it seemed, got away with everything and City with nothing. This caused the Blues to lose heart in the last thirty minutes, Spurs taking advantage of these 'lucky' breaks moved down en masse and then **Smith** shot them a second goal from close range in the sixty second minute. Spurs went on to take two more goals within a five minute period. The first coming from a Ewing back pass which stuck in the mud letting in **Smith** who had little difficulty firing it in the net on seventy four minutes. Five minutes later after a goalmouth melee **Smith** stabbed the ball home from only two yards out. So after being 1-0 up City were now 4-1 down and to cap it all they were well and truly 'robbed' when schoolmaster **Robb** got Spurs' fifth, closing in smartly from the right and giving Trautmann no chance with a cross-drive.

FINAL SCORE: SPURS 5 CITY 1

Letters were later printed in the MEN from Spurs fans condemning the refereeing decisions and non decisions that went against City

Spurs: White shirts/blue knickers: Ditchburn; Hills, Henry; Blanchflower, Norman, Ryden; Medwin, Harmer, Smith, Brooks, Robb

City: Blue shirts/white knickers ; Trautmann; Leivers, Sear; Barnes, Ewing, Warhurst; Barlow, Hayes, Johnstone, McAdams, Sambrook.

Attendance: 37,539 **Average:** 32,668

Referee: A.E.Westwood (Warwick)

Linesmen: D.J.Farrow (Suffolk), J.M.Hall (Warwick)

League position: remained in sixth.

Goals For: 73 Against: 70

Reserves: Drew 2-2 at home to West Brom

I visited the United museum a few years ago and they had a reproduction of the Pink (or Green) with a back page headline of City's 5-1 loss. So United fans could mourn Munich and have a gloat at City at the same time. Sometimes I really do wonder about the dignity and mentality of that club but we rise above it. It wasn't until years later that they did anything for the victims of Munich and their families.

Spurs went on to finish third that season and were moulding a great side, going on to win the double in 1961 when we were the first team to take a point off them (after beating them at WHL in 1960 when Bert parried a pen right on half time and the ref blew up before Jones netted the rebound!) They won the cup again in '62 and were the first British team to win a European trophy, the Cup winners cup in '63, and had continued cup success in the 60s, 70s and 80s (spit) but nothing much since. Manager Keith Burkinshaw, when he left in the 80s glanced back as they became more and more corporate saying "there used to be a football club there".

It was reported that Hungarians Puskas, Czibor, and Koscics might sign for United and the lads at school, slowly becoming accustomed to the Munich situation were now becoming excited at the prospects of all the new signings.

Frank Swift's funeral took place at St Margarets Church Whalley Range, attended by 300 or so mourners.

United's chairman Harold Hardman and secretary Les Olive were to attend the match at Maine Road tomorrow as guests of the club and City had agreed a collection. Ernie Taylor signed for United for £8,000.

20,000 Stoke fans were travelling to Bolton for the cup match.

It was crisis day for Duncan Edwards.

Cliff Jones signed for Spurs for £35,000

Paddy Fagan considered he had no future at City and could sign for United.

Ron Phoenix is a target for QPR but the price tag of £10K looks to be too much.

30) SATURDAY FEBRUARY 15TH 1958 K.O. 3PM: BIRMINGHAM CITY (HOME)

It was pouring down. I didn't switch to the Kippax, but watched it from the perimeter wall at the scoreboard end. The band played Abide With Me (I think) and all in the main stand stood up removed their hats and sang it with heads bowed. It made the hairs on the back of your neck stand up. The rain continued unabated and the game was called off in the fortieth minute, the pitch a quagmire. It was as though the heavens were sending a tearful message of sympathy to Manchester.

The programme had dedications to United from The Editor, Chairman Mr Alan Douglas, Manager Leslie McDowall, Secretary Mr Walter Griffiths, Trainer Laurie Barnett, Captain Dave Ewing, supporters club chairman Bill Miles, and former captain Roy Paul.

In Memoriam

Here are pictures of the eight journalists; Mr. W. Satinoff and the steward Mr. W. T. Cable, who were among those who died in the Munich disaster.

FRANK SWIFT (News of the World)

ALF CLARKE (M/c Evening Chronicle)

W. SATINOFF (M/c business man)

HENRY ROSE (Daily Express)

GEORGE FOLLOWS (Daily Herald)

TOM JACKSON (M/c Evening News)

ARCHIE LEDBROOKE (Daily Mirror)

W. T. CABLE (Steward)

DON DAVIES (M/c. Guardian)

ERIC THOMPSON (Daily Mail)

NUNN BETTER FOR FORD

DISTRIBUTORS OF FORD CARS THAMES COMMERCIAL VEHICLES AND FORD INDUSTRIAL ENGINES

282 BURY NEW ROAD · MANCHESTER 7 · Telephone BROUGHTON 2201

7

One page **IN MEMORIAM** had photos of the players and officials who died, another was dedicated to the journalists, passenger and steward.

Arthur Walmsley gave a poignant dedication to his missing press colleagues.

Birmingham, managed by Arthur Turner/Pat Beasley, were in fifteenth spot with twenty four points and were only three points above the danger zone. City were sixth with thirty three points. They'd got four home wins, including a 5-1 v Bolton and a 4-0 v City, three draws and six defeats, including a 5-1 to Wolves. Away they'd won four, drawn four and lost six, including an 8-0 at Preston and a 7-1 at Spurs. They'd gone out of the cup in the third round at York, and added one time City target Harry Hooper to their squad.

At City: Pre-war, they had no wins out of their last eight visits. Post war lost five drawn one, so looking good?

Recent attendances ranged from 21,005 ('56/57) to 44,777 ('55/56) This was the seventy second meeting of the clubs plus eight cup ties, one at City 1913 first rd 4-0 (16,442).

Team news: Sear in for Little,

They took the lead in the fifteenth minute when Roy Warhurst's back pass stuck in the mud and Orritt crashed it past Bert, with Billy Mac equalising in the twenty eighth.

FINAL SCORE: CITY 1 BIRMINGHAM 1
(abandoned after forty minutes)

City: Sky blue/white: Trautmann; Leivers, Sear; Barnes, Ewing. Warhurst; Barlow, Hayes, Johnstone, McAdams, Sambrook.
Birmingham: Red shirts/white knickers:Merrick; Hall, Farmer; Larkin, Smith, Watts; Hooper, Orritt, Brown, Murphy, Govan
Attendance: 23,461
Referee: E.S. Oxley (Pontefract)
Linesmen: N.Methley, E.T.Nottingham

League Position: remained sixth
Reserves: Drew at Stoke 2-2

Birmingham won the league cup in 1963, took the drop in '65 and generally struggled, dropping to the third, battling back to the Premiership, winning nothing to date, and are now back in Prem. after a season in the first (old second).

Shock news was that Fagan and McTavish could be transferred to United.
David Meek was introduced as the new MEN reporter for United
Manchester Boys v London Boys at Maine Road, 50% of proceeds to United fund.
Bob Lord, Burnley Chairman upset United by stating that other clubs shouldn't sell their stars to them. Stan Crowther signed from Villa for United.
United groundsman reported as stealing £300 from the club.
Jack Dyson is to play for the 'A' team v Rochdale reserves at Shawe View, Urmston on Saturday at inside left in a Lancs league fixture.

February 21st, fifteen days after the air crash, Duncan Edwards died peacefully at 2.15pm.

30) SATURDAY FEBRUARY 22ND K.O. 3PM: LEICESTER CITY (AWAY)

Chance of a double? On the coach to this game Billy Mac was supposed to have remarked to Bert "time you let another seven in". Bert responded by saying "I've never been on the losing side to Leicester"

The programme had a smart, if dull, blue and white front cover. It was fourpence for eight pages but had a cracking illustration and review of City's history, though little else.

Filbert Street's record attendance was 47, 298 v Spurs in F.A. Cup 5th rd. in 1928. It had the usual seats and paddock main stand and a small covered standing area opposite. There was a double decker behind one goal, known as

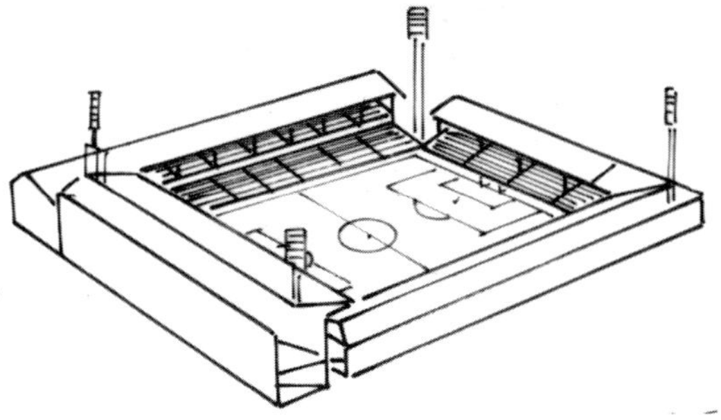

Pitch Size: 112 x 75 yds

The Kop, and a small covered standing area behind the other goal. It pretty much stayed the same, a few boxes added in a new stand behind the goal and a new main stand built, before they moved to The Walker Stadium in 2002. I first made it here in 1960, a 5-0 loss!

Leicester were struggling in eighteenth spot with twenty two points. City were sixth with thirty three points still. Away from home they'd won two, drawn one and lost twelve including three 5-1s, 4-3 at City and a 7-3 at Burnley. At home they'd won seven, including a 6-1 v Villa, drawn three, and lost five. They'd gone out of the cup in the third round at Spurs 4-0.

At Leicester: Pre-war we'd won three and drawn one of the last four. Post we'd won the last three, so looking good. Recent attendances ranged from 28,017 (46/47) to 32,825 (54/55) This was the forty second league meeting, plus one cup tie, 1920 second round 0-3 (23,041) . Brace yourself!

Team news: Little and Fagan replaced Sear and Sambrook

From The Pink/Green:
An Avalanche Of Goals

Leicester lined up experimenting with a double centre forward plan as continuous snow made the pitch heavy. After a hectic defensive spell City slipped into the lead with a fourth minute goal from **Johnstone**. Little, moving forward centred towards the Scot who nodded the ball home. In the tenth minute Leicester levelled through the lively **Walsh** who evaded Ewing and saw his shot bounce back from the far post into the net. Hayes missed a sitter and Warhurst was warned by the referee for clattering Walsh and Bert won applause for collecting centres and clearing his lines. Leicester were pulled up time and again for offside as the snow continued and one of the linesmen was pelted with orange peel and a banana skin by home fans!

In the twenty eighth min. young Riley scored a simple goal after Hines' scoring pass was blocked when Bert ran out to close the gap. The ball skidded away and **Riley** had time to pick his spot and score. Two minutes later City's defence got in a tangle in the area and the ball finally ran loose to **Walsh** who hit it home from six yards. It had been all Leicester for a considerable period but Fagan fluffed a good chance swapping the ball from left to right foot and finishing weakly in the thirty fifth minute. City had an incredible escape five minutes before the interval when Walsh's shot was deflected over the bar by Bert's outstretched leg. But after forty three minutes **Johnstone** reduced the arrears when he dribbled past everyone and into the penalty area before scoring. City couldn't hold out, however, though

Derek Hogg

Hayes missed an open goal and poor defensive covering let in **Hines** who scored from comfortable range. City though could easily have been on level terms or even ahead if only the inside men had been in shooting form.

After only seventy seconds of the new half Fagan was grounded by Russell and **Barnes** stepped up to beat Anderson easily with a penalty shot which swung slightly away and into the bottom corner for 3-4.

City were pressing hard and when Barlow centred Russell handled but no penalty was given. The Blues went further behind in the fifty seventh minute against the run of play when Leicester were awarded a penalty after Walsh fell heavily after tussling with Ewing, **Riley** scoring from the spot.

Up the Blues came again and Hayes' beautiful centre was headed home by **McAdams**. in the fifty ninth minute. It was little consolation though as Leicester scored a sixth in the sixty second minute, **Walsh** jumping on a loose ball and smacking it home from ten yards. City had further chances, but twelve minutes from the end **Hogg** sent a low one across the goalmouth which eluded Warhurst and Little stood on the line for number seven. Then with only three minutes remaining **Walsh** scored a magnificent goal with a rising cross-drive from eighteen yards.

FINAL SCORE: LEICESTER 8 CITY 4

Leicester: Blue shirts/white knickers: Anderson; Cunningham, Baillie; Morris; King, Russell; Riley, Walsh, Hines, Walker, Hogg.
City: Trautmann; Leivers, Little; Barnes, Ewing, Warhurst; Barlow, Hayes, Johnstone, McAdams , Fagan
Attendance: 31,017 **Average:** 32,564
Referee: K. Howley (Middlesbrough)
Linesmen: S.K.Kinnear, R.D.Kirk
League Position: Dropped from sixth to tenth place
Goals For: 77 Against: 78
Reserves: Won 5-1 at home to Leeds

In the crowd a spectator collapsed needing hospital treatment.

Verdict: Bert was left exposed and Ewing was helpless in the mud as Leicester's twin centre forwards Hines and Walsh had a field day and the Scot could only flounder as they passed him by, his height and weight looking better suited for the Highland games at Braemar! Dave's colleagues were of little help having enough problems of their own as Leicester racked up at least twenty scoring chances.

From The Guardian's Special Correspondent:

A wedding party, passed on the way to a match, is regarded as a happy augury by the more credulous of our footballers. City, who were beaten 8-4 by Leicester, saw such a party on Saturday. The orange-coloured dresses of the bridesmaids off-set the drabness, which is Leicester's London Road station on a cold snow-swept evening, but by that time City were on their way home.

Trautmann, the goalkeeper, looking wistfully to the opposite platform was heard to observe ; "They are four hours too late"

For Trautmann had received the biggest jolt to his pride since he first appeared for City more than eight years ago although he could not be held responsible for the rout.

Leicester finished the season in eighteenth place, with thirty three points, having scored 91 and conceded 112. They went on to lose in the cup finals of 1961 and 1963, but won the league cup in 1964. They also lost the 1969 cup final to City, Peter Shilton failing to stop Neil Young's rocket, after which they were relegated. They struggled in the years after that but finally won the league cup again in 2000, after Martin O'Neill took over, but are now in the first, old second.

At school: "Trautmann can't be that good Wallace if he let in eight"

City could have three players in the World Cup squads - Sear for Wales, McAdams for Northern Ireland, and Johnstone for Scotland. However the hot news is that Scotland have overlooked Bobby as they've misunderstood the letter re City's end of season tour to America. McDowall has denied that all three players were committed to City's American tour.
City will play Bolton in the Manchester Senior Cup Semi-Final at Maine Road.
One time City target Martin Bakes may sign for United and Bob Hardisty, the Bishop Auckland stalwart, has come out of retirement to assist their reserve team.

LEAGUE TABLE

	P	W	D	L	F	A	Pts
Wolves	30	20	6	4	76	36	46
Preston	30	18	5	7	74	40	41
WBA	30	13	12	5	70	53	38
Luton	31	17	4	10	57	42	38
Man Utd	29	15	7	7	74	48	37
Notts For	31	14	5	12	61	46	33
Chelsea	31	13	7	11	68	61	33
Burnley	30	15	3	12	61	58	33
Spurs	31	13	7	11	69	67	33
Man City	**30**	**15**	**3**	**12**	**77**	**78**	**33**
Blackpool	30	13	6	11	55	48	32
Bolton	31	12	7	12	55	66	31
Arsenal	30	12	4	14	52	58	28
Everton	30	8	11	11	44	52	27
Leeds	30	9	6	15	40	52	24
Leicester	31	10	4	17	67	81	24
B'ham	29	8	8	13	50	73	24
Newcastle	29	9	5	15	47	51	23
Portsmouth	30	9	5	16	52	60	23
Aston Villa	30	9	5	16	49	67	23
Sunderland	31	6	9	16	38	78	21
Sheff Wed	30	7	5	18	55	76	19

CONCLUSION: A sad month in all respects. One home win, two heavy defeats, an abandoned game, down to tenth place and the Munich Air Disaster. Goals for: 77 against 78. Average home attendance: 34,260 Away 32,564.

FRANK SWIFT 1913-1958

The man we'll miss but not forget, by the Sports editor of The News Of The World (an obituary from the NOTW following Frank's death in the Munich Air Disaster. Frank had been following United in Europe for the Sunday Newspaper).

The Munich plane disaster touched us all. And to-day I have a melancholy duty. Our sports pages carry no feature article by Frank Swift. Instead I have to write of Frank Swift, the man we knew.

A melancholy duty it is, yet I am grateful that I can at least pay a tribute from The News Of The World to a wonderful personality, who gave so much to the soccer public, spectators and readers.

Swifty collected countless friends everywhere in his playing days and then with his writings. He was that sort of man. You liked him and you respected him. His make up was reflected in what he wrote for us and for you. Bright, genial, easy to get along with and without an atom of malice or resentment.

The NOTW and its readers will miss him, but they won't forget him.

For the past two days telegrams, letters, messages and tributes have poured in to our offices - from individuals, from organisations, from overseas, and from all parts of Great Britain.

"Frank Swift, the goalkeeper and newspaper man, was a man loved by everyone," says secretary Alan Hardaker, in a message on behalf of the Football League.

This so well sums up the feelings of all those who wanted to pay their tributes, from Senor Bernabeau, President of Real Madrid - to the two anonymous girls - "just two football fans" who called with a bunch of daffodils to place on Frank's grave.

In the NOTW it was John Hepburn of our Northern sports staff who was most closely associated with Frank Swift. So let John Hepburn speak for us all:-

Genial Jester

"Big Swifty is no more. The empty seat across the desk keeps staring at me, forcing me out of the numbed disbelief of the past two days. The unopened fan-mail adds stark emphasis.

I mourn a close personal friend and respected colleague. But my loss is unimportant. Football has lost one of the all time greats- a showman who put back into the game far more than he ever got out of it.

To me Frank Swift will be remembered not so much as the greatest goalkeeper I ever saw but as the big, genial jester whose ready wit and pleasant personality were loved by millions.

Though he had hung up his boots nine years before, he was still escorted to his car after every match he saw by dozens of young autograph-hunters, some of them too young to ever have seen him play. "I'll worry when they don't ask me" he would say, after signing the lot.

I shall never forget the day at Windsor Park, Belfast, when Frank was being pressed for his signature in the midst of more than 50 Irish schoolboys after the Ireland - England match. Twenty yards away the England players were allowed to file into their bus - unmolested - and unnoticed!

Another unforgettable incident at Madrid last year showed that our leading footballers were Swift fans too. Frank and I were watching Manchester United training for their European cup match at the Real Madrid stadium when he was dragged out onto the field by Bobby Charlton, Dennis Viollet and Billy Whelan so that they could be photographed with 'The Big

Fella' as his great friend Matt Busby always called him.

Officialdom gave Frank the same Royal welcome in board rooms all over the country - and confided in him most of soccer's secrets. The confidence was not misplaced.

Frank Swift hated flying. He often confessed his fears when we were airborne. But he would not let his apprehensions interfere with his desire to follow the fortunes of Manchester United who he was convinced would win the European Cup. It won't be the same without Big Swifty."

Frank Swift signed for City from Fleetwood and made his debut on Christmas day 1933. Six months later he played at Wembley in the 2-1 win over Portsmouth, as a nineteen year old. Despondent at half time, at 1-0 down and blaming himself for the goal, Freddie Tilson told him not to worry as he'd pop two in during the second half. Fred did, but Frank fainted at the end, much to his embarrassment.

His brother Fred Swift played for Bolton.

In 1937 he was City's number one as the title was lifted but he was robbed of his greatest professional years when war broke out. He won nineteen International caps, fourteen war time caps and was the first England goalkeeper of the twentieth century to captain his country. He retired in 1949, but made a brief return owing to Alec Thurlow's illness in 49/50, before Bert took over. There were problems over his registration with City until the mid fifties, and at the time of Munich, aged forty four, he was the Official Supporters Club President and always a very popular and welcome figure at Maine Road. Indeed he was present in the press box at City, on the Saturday before Munich for the league game v West Brom. (won 4-1).

MARCH'S FOOTBALL MONTHLY

United's Duncan Edwards was on the front cover and Bryan Douglas of Blackburn on the back cover. There was an insert stating that the edition was produced some days before the tragic air crash occurred and hoped that the front cover would be taken as a tribute and a reminder of happier days.

CB's editiorial opinion thought that there should be no charging of goalies and that the goalie should only be allowed to handle inside the goal area. *(CB had obviously never played in goal!)* Maximum wage of £17 plus £3 appearance money instead of £20 had been sanctioned by the League Management Committee. This means that a player out of the first team would lose £3 a week. Bill Curry of Newcastle recalls the 5-4 cup tie win over City in 1957. Future Blue Roy Gratrix of Blackpool explained how he was settled at centre half "and I like it". Soccer scrapbook for 1934, naturally includes City's magnificent cup win over Portsmouth..

Once A Blue, Always A Blue

FRED from Worsley's story:

I was taken to Maine Road in the early fifties from Blackley, by my dad who'd had a special box made for me which I stood on leaning against the perimeter wall at the scoreboard end. I remember one game in particular, City v Preston, about 51/52. Dave Ewing miscued the ball which went for a corner at our end. As Angus Morrison placed the ball for the kick, Tom Finney took up a position at the near post. This was just too much for me. I couldn't believe that the great Ton Finney was only two feet away. To my father's horror, in front of 52,000 people, I jumped over the wall and asked Tom for his autograph. At this point did Tom say:

1) Clear off kid, can't you see there's a game going on here.

2) Call the one policeman over who was sitting in his special little dug-out near the corner flag.

Or did he:

3) Sign the kid's autograph book, ruffle his ginger hair and lift him back over the wall to his mortified father.

I still have the autograph, but this was an age where superstars behaved like superstars.

I remember those players from that era vividly and I used to go to Old Trafford every other week to watch, not support, all the great players because in those days, without much TV coverage, you only got chance to see the likes of Finney, Matthews, Shackleton, Milburn etc. once a season, so that was a sensible thing to do.

At fifteen years old I was playing for the school and for Manchester Schoolboys hoping that City would want to sign me. It was just about the time of the Leicester game in '59. City had to win this to stand a chance of staying up and if City were going to offer me a contract, I thought they might not want me if they went down.

Wilf McGuinness was the big star in Blackley, we all looked up to him. Other Blackley lads were Brian Kidd, who was younger than me, Colin Barlow, who drove around in an open topped Ford Consul, though I didn't know him then., Nobby Stiles, who captained England Schoolboys and who we saw getting off the 112 bus, going to games - with a very distinctive walk - and I played with Bert Lister, and Joe Dean in Boggart Hole Clough.

In my early days at the club there were some remarkable characters. 'Shuffling Sam' (Ray Sambrook) was amazing, he'd shuffle in, with steel tips on the toes and heels of his shoes like Fred Astaire. He lived in digs above the cobblers shop at the back of the Kippax with Mike Pearson. He later helped out Keith Marsden who owned the 'Poco - Poco' club in Stockport, but he was the most unlikely bouncer imaginable. His greatest game was the Newcastle 5-1 where he skinned the Newcastle full back Whitehead time after time and scored two goals.

Manager Les McDowall was a poor communicator and the other members of the backroom staff were difficult to connect with. Fred Tilson was the trainer and he used to sit in the dressing room and pick his horses, then stand at the end of the tunnel supervising the laps round the pitch. Mondays it was five laps - run one, walk one, four laps, run one walk one etc. It was all I knew and in the afternoons we were told to "bugger off home" if we came back for extra training.

Jimmy Meadows attempted a further come back for City in the reserves at Derby. Kev.

Walsh and myself travelled with the team, and sat on the bench. Jimmy was captain and centre half, but he'd forgotten his boots, and actually played in mine. Paddy Fagan was playing for Derby then, and he was clipped from behind by Gerry Baker. He turned round and whacked him, then was sent off. Afterwards Cliff Sear told me that Paddy thought it was him. I remember thinking, why would anyone want to whack Cliff Sear!

Fred remains a big Blue, he is an accomplished writer and a BBC Radio Manchester pundit, after dinner speaker etc.

John from New Zealand's story:

For me, it all started in the early fifties when my dad, an old Hyde Road' man, started to take me to see Bert, Bill, Dave, Bobby, Roy, Jack, Don and Ken Barnes. Yes, I was right behind the goal when he scored his three penalties against Everton - first one to the left, then to the right, then to the left again. Another early hero was the strongly built crew-cut wearing Billy McAdams - I remember him scoring a hat-trick against WBA when they were at their peak. He came from Distillery, the Irish League club I was later to play for, coming up against another great City post war centre forward, Alex Harley, towards the end of his career.

By the time I was ten years of age, I was going to first team and reserve games. Every Saturday leaving Stretford on my bike, going through Chorlton and Whalley Range, where it was rumoured that several City players lived in club houses, but no matter how slowly I went past, I never did see any of them.

I would often arrive before the turnstiles opened and be one of thousands to leave my bike in one of the many back yards down the entries (alleyways) between rows of terraced houses adjacent to Maine Road itself. For three old pence, we were given a numbered raffle ticket, to ensure we went home on the bike we came on. When I could afford a match programme, I too distinctly remember that lovely fresh paper smell and the joy of devouring its every fact, figure and photograph. I remember gazing up at the tall floodlights, counting each bulb, happy that 'the other lot' didn't have such cathedrals in the sky.

Ball boys were still a thing of the future and I vividly remember the great Roy Paul retrieving the ball just in front of me and at that moment the marvellous cocktail of embrocation and Brylcreme entered my memory bank.

In these early fifties, our 'fanzine' was a verbal one, which emanated from a group of several hundred fans who congregated outside the main entrance after every match. These sessions would last until well after six o'clock and I was the spellbound observer sharing the passion, knowledge and intensity of these fully grown men airing their frustrations and glorying in the triumphs. There was also the extra delight when United's adverse result sometimes filtered through. Many of the same faces were again present after reserve games, and yes, the tangible expectation as the man at the scoreboard gave us the fifteen minute updates from the first team away match. At these gatherings one eye was always kept on the players' entrance so that when one of our heroes came out, the animated conversation would come to a temporary stop whilst we all looked in admiration and some brave soul would shout out 'There's Steve!' followed by 'Well played!', and my dropping the bike to rush over and get another autograph. Steve Fleet would always have a smile and a quick word and it must be said nearly all the players willingly gave their signature. My greatest hero Bert Trautmann would always give his autograph and even when I saw him years later still looked every inch the Greek god. By contrast, I can also remember with absolute clarity the great and wonderful Bobby Johnston outside the players' entrance in a navy suit and Brylcreemed hair with hands in pockets and looking slightly overweight. If only he was with us today taking charge of the midfield! I used to sometimes get on that bike of mine and cycle to Boundary Park just to see Bobby, Bert Lister (how we could do with him now as well) and Bill Spurdle with Oldham before their careers ended.

John is now exiled in New Zealand from where he follows the Blues

IAN from Cheadle's story:

I was influenced by my father from a very early age, and remember being taken on the Kippax virtually as a baby, in my mothers arms. Dad told me, before I could speak, that United fans were not nice people. According to him they were all thieves and burglars with big black bushy beards and moustaches and all the City people were nice and clean shaven. I believed him big time. Still do.

Mum was City, dad married three times and they were all City. He married the right ladies. I can't remember my first game, not a clue, but I remember from 53/54, players like Roy Paul, Billy Spurdle, and Ken Barnes. I thought it was fantastic that you could buy the little blue plastic star things on the fore court with the black and white player photos in the middle, I'd add to my collection on my bobble hat every week. I always had my rattle with me, can't remember where I got it, but I had to paint it, about seven times, and I remember later Stan Gibson (City's long-serving groundsman) standing under the City mosaics before kick off, his work done, and he'd say hello and chat to me.

We lived on Hamilton Road in Longsight which is the other side of Platt Fields, Birch Fields, so I'd walk in the early days, like Derek Jeffries with his boots under his arm, down Dickenson Road. We were dead posh in the 50s because my dad got a Ford Pop, one of the earliest cars, and we'd chug along to the 'Lord Lyon' and park down the side. Dad would leave me outside and bring me a bag of peanuts while he went in for a quick drink - it was the hotbed of City support. Then we'd park the car up and trot down. It was magical to me because I always remember, even at that age, you got a tingle as a young lad walking to the ground with your dad, it was fantastic. I always went with my dad because I had seven main school-pals in my life and six of them supported 'Stretford Rangers' and I was the seventh. So I could never go to football with my pals - they were rough and I was the clean cut one of course.

I went to Birchfield Primary School on Birchfield Road, not too far from the ground. The City/United ratio was typical too, I was in a class of 11 boys and 22 girls so every boy was in the school football team and I was the only boy in a blue and white kit on games day. That's why I'm so strong because when you've come through school with ten red and white kits against one, you've had a tough time. Luckily, I'm not just saying this, but I can't dance, I can't swim, I can't sing, but I can play football and that helped.

Then I went to Ladybarn High, Parrswood Road, and experienced a similar sort of thing, but it got even tougher from eleven to seventeen, but I always played for the school teams so I got respect that way.

I lived for football. We used to play at the Dairy on Beresford Road, used to stand there for hours just kicking the ball and heading it into the tin barricade just because you loved the crack of when you hit the goal. We'd play football there till it was pitch black every night but you don't see that as much now because of the modern world, but we played out all the time. I lived in Longsight which is now completely changed, but it was lovely in those days, there were hardly any cars (apart from my dad's Pop!), so you could play in the street and I remember getting our first telly - black and white, obviously.

We used to put green pieces of transparent colour slip over it to watch it in green so we'd have colour telly or we'd have a blue night. "Shall we watch it in blue tonight?" Happy days. We had no money, lived in a terrace house which was painted sky blue, white and maroon. Players of that era were all great heroes, but I preferred Tom Finney, who I thought was a better player, to Stan Matthews.

My dad's dentist was a United fan and he didn't use his season tickets much, so when it was too far to watch City away we'd go and sit with their ticket holders and cheer for the opposition. That's how fanatical we were, quite mad. In the end I think we were reported. *(Ed: funny when we do it, but out of order when they do it!)*

Derby games I've never missed one, home and away, testimonials, the lot in fifty years. We usually went in the main stand at City, season ticket holders, A block, H block centre, then down to the posh B block, and we were there in H block on the day we played Swindon Town.

Ian's a season ticket holder, has brought up his kids the same way, and still a fanatical Blue

DENIS from Stretford's story:

I was in a family of seven, two girls and five boys. Dad wasn't a football fan but two of my brothers were, Rob was a Blue and Jack a Red. They'd argue, sitting at opposite ends of the dining table. Cups were flying and I remember once dad was half shaved and chased them down the street, and gave them both a belt when he caught up with them!

Later on, however, after he was de-mobbed, Jack moved to Levenshulme and as it was nearer for him to go to City then, he supported the Blues. Another brother, Ronnie, was a City fan and emigrated to Canada from where he follows City on TV. We lived in Stretford where there was a mix of fans but mainly reds because people, like Jack, went to their nearest ground, but often went to City one week, United the next.

Tilly, later to become my wife, was a PT instructor in the army, based down south, and she stayed on after the war for a couple of years as a comptometer operator. She'd go to Millwall one week, Charlton the next, with her mate. They'd pick up tomatoes and mouldy fruit from the grocers on the way and they would throw them at the players for a bit of fun! Imagine the furore that would cause today!

We'd known each other since we were five, lived in the same street and were very competitive in sport, particularly athletics. But in my teens I contracted a condition which affected the bone marrow in my leg and I was consequently turned down by the Merchant Navy. Penicillin arrived too late for me. I was off work for two years. Frank Swift was my idol, and I wrote to him when I was in hospital, and he sent me a photo. It wasn't up to much and my brother Bob went and 'had a go', so I got a better photo!

I worked Saturday mornings, caught the 53 bus from Trafford Bar to Lloyd Street, Moss Side. I went with a mate and we'd stop off at a herbalist on King Street, where we hung out before games. We used to go on the scoreboard end, but walked round to the end City were kicking towards.

After the match we went straight home for our evening meal, top deck of the bus. There would be plenty of banter, but it was always fun, light hearted stuff.

Where we lived in Stretford was one of the main walking routes for United fans. If they lost a game I'd stand at our gate and torment them by keep asking the result.

Denis is a devoted fan, as is his son Colin, but stopped attending when City left Maine Road.

CHAPTER NINE

MARCH 1958 - MOVING ON UP

After only three games in January and three in February, a busy month loomed for March, with four homes, Blackpool, Birmingham, Arsenal and Leeds, then Luton and Wolves away plus an away friendly at Derby…..

31) SATURDAY MARCH 1ST 1958
K.O. 3PM: BLACKPOOL (HOME)

The programme's editorial - 'All Have An off Spell' dwelt on last week's incredible game at Leicester where City didn't take all their chances and the result didn't fairly reflect the run of play. Not quite how Eric Todd recalled it in his 'Do You Remember?' column of the City programme v Leicester September '72. Eric reckoned if Leicester had taken all their chances they would have had double figures by half-time, City being completely outplayed.

Changes were expected for today's game. The club had been inundated with suggestions, but "whilst genuine supporters have the interests of the club at heart the amateur advisers should remember that there are few teams in the history of the game who have been consistent and brilliant."

It was predicted that Dave Ewing, who's had a lean time recently (not the only one), could possibly do with a rest "the man with the big heart and unlimited courage, if dropped should be back before long."

In Maine Road Gossip, the chance of a double was aired, and thanks were given to City fans for the collection of £489. 5s at City's home game with Birmingham. It was taken by members of United's supporters club for the dependants of those who lost their lives in the Munich Air Disaster and will be part of a central fund.

In Sportsman's Corner, George Mintern of Eccles, queried Bert's comments of last week, letting seven in on three occasions (Derby '49/50; Wolves '52/53 and '55/56) and was told that John Savage was in goals when we lost 7-3 at Highbury, and 9-2 at The Hawthorns. HRG of

Results of First Division Games

(Including February 22nd)

CLUB		Arsenal	Aston Villa	Birmingham City	Blackpool	Bolton Wanderers	Burnley	Chelsea	Everton	Leeds United	Leicester City	Luton Town	MAN. CITY	Manchester United	Newcastle United	Nottingham Forest	Portsmouth	Preston North End	Sheffield Wednesday	Sunderland	Tottenham Hotspur	West Bromwich A.	Wolverhampton W.
Arsenal	H	★	4-0	1-3	2-3	1-2			2-3	2-1	3-1	2-0	2-1	4-5	2-3		3-2	4-2		3-0	4-4	2-2	
	A		0-3		0-1	1-0	1-2	0-0	2-2		1-0	0-4		2-4		0-4			0-2	1-0	1-3	2-1	
Aston Villa	H	3-0	★	0-2	1-1			1-3	0-1	2-0	5-1	2-0	1-2		4-3		2-1	2-2		5-2	1-1		2-3
	A	0-4		1-3	1-1		0-3	2-4	2-1	0-4	1-6	0-3		1-4		1-4			5-2	1-1		2-3	1-2
Birmingham City	H		3-1	★	0-0	5-1	2-3	3-3					4-0	3-3	1-4	0-2		3-1		2-3	0-0	3-5	1-5
	A	3-1	2-0				1-3	1-5	2-0	1-1	2-2	0-3			2-1	1-1		0-8	3-5		1-7	0-0	1-5
Blackpool	H	1-0	1-1		★	2-3	2-4	2-1		3-0	5-1	1-2	2-5	1-4			2-1		2-2	7-0	0-2		3-2
	A	3-2	1-1	0-0		0-3			0-0	1-2	1-2	0-2		2-1	2-1	2-1			3-0	4-1		1-1	1-3
Bolton Wanderers	H	0-1			3-0	★	2-1	3-3	1-5	0-2	2-3	1-2		4-0		2-0	1-0		5-4	2-2	3-2	2-2	1-1
	A	2-1		1-5	3-2				1-1	1-2	3-2	0-1	1-2	2-7	2-1		2-2	0-3		2-1		2-2	1-6
Burnley	H	2-1	3-0	3-1			★	2-1		3-1	7-3	1-2	2-1		0-2	3-1	3-1	2-0		6-0	2-0	2-2	
	A			3-2	4-2	1-2		1-6	1-1			2-3	1-4	0-1		0-7	0-0	1-2		3-2	1-3	1-5	1-2
Chelsea	H	0-0	4-2	5-1			6-1	★	3-1	2-1	4-0	1-3	2-3		2-1		7-4	0-2	1-0		2-4	2-2	
	A		3-1	3-3	1-2	3-3	1-2		0-3				2-5	1-0	3-1		0-3	2-5	3-2	2-2	1-1	1-1	1-2
Everton	H	2-2	1-2	0-2	0-0	1-1	1-1	3-0	★		2-2	0-2		3-3	1-2	1-1			1-1	3-1		1-1	1-0
	A	3-2	1-0			5-1		1-3			2-2	1-0	2-6	0-3	3-2		2-3	1-3		1-1	1-3		0-2
Leeds United	H		4-0	1-1	2-1	2-1				★	2-1	0-2	2-4	1-1	3-0	1-2	2-0	2-3		2-1		1-1	1-1
	A	1-2	0-2		0-3	2-0	1-3	1-2			0-3	1-1		0-5		1-1	2-1		2-3	1-2	0-2		2-3
Leicester City	H	0-1	6-1	2-2	2-1	2-3			2-2	3-0	★		8-4	0-3	2-1	3-1		1-3	4-1	4-1		3-3	2-3
	A	1-3	1-5		1-5	3-2	3-7	0-4	2-2	1-2			3-4	0-4			0-2		1-2	2-3	4-1		1-5
Luton Town	H	4-0	3-0	3-0	2-0	1-0	3-2		0-1	1-1		★		2-2	0-3	3-1		1-3	2-0	7-1		5-1	3-1
	A	0-2	0-2		2-1	2-1	2-1	3-1	2-0	2-0			2-2	0-3			0-5	0-1		0-3	1-3		1-1
MAN. CITY	H					2-1	4-1	5-2	6-2		4-3	2-2	★	2-2		1-1	2-1	2-0	2-0		5-1	4-1	3-4
	A	1-2	2-1	0-4	5-2		1-2	3-2		4-2	4-8			1-4		1-2	1-2	1-6	5-4	1-2	1-5	2-9	
Manchester United	H	4-2	4-1		1-2	7-2	1-0	0-1	3-0	5-0	4-0	3-0	4-1	★		1-1	0-3		2-1		3-4		
	A	5-4		3-3	4-1	0-4			3-3	1-1	3-0	2-2	2-2		2-1	2-1		1-1				3-4	1-3
Newcastle United	H			1-2	1-2	1-2		1-3	2-3					1-2	★	1-4	2-0	0-2	0-0	2-2	3-1	3-0	1-1
	A	3-2	3-4	4-1			2-0	1-2	2-1	0-3	1-2	3-0				3-2	2-2		0-1	0-2	3-3	1-2	
Nottingham Forest	H	4-0	4-1	1-1	1-2		7-0			1-1			2-1	1-2	2-3	★	2-0	2-1	5-2	2-0	1-2	0-2	
	A			2-0		0-2	1-3		1-1	2-1	1-3	1-3	1-1	1-1	4-1		4-1	0-2	2-1		4-3	2-3	0-2
Portsmouth	H					2-2	0-0	3-0	3-2	1-2	2-0	5-0	2-1		2-2	1-4	★	0-2	3-2		5-1		1-1
	A	2-3	1-2		1-2	0-1	1-3	4-7		0-2			1-2	3-0	0-2	0-2		0-4	2-4	1-1	5-3	1-3	
Preston North End	H			8-0		3-0	2-1	5-2	3-1			1-0	6-1	1-1		2-0	4-0	★	3-0		3-1	3-1	1-2
	A	2-4	2-2	1-3			0-2	2-0		3-2	3-1	3-1	0-2		2-0	1-2	2-0		4-4	0-0	3-3	1-4	
Sheffield Wednesday	H	2-0	2-5	5-3	0-3			2-3		3-2	2-1		4-5		1-0	1-2	4-2	4-4	★	3-3	2-0	1-2	
	A				2-2	4-5		0-1	1-1		1-4	0-2	0-2	1-2	0-0	2-5	2-3	0-3			2-4	1-3	3-4
Sunderland	H	0-1	1-1		1-4	1-2	2-3	2-2	1-1	2-1	3-2	3-0	2-1		2-0		1-1	0-0		★	1-1		0-2
	A	0-3	2-5	3-2	0-7	2-2	0-6		1-3	1-2	1-4	1-7			2-2	0-2			3-3			0-3	0-5
Tottenham Hotspur	H	3-1		7-1			3-1	1-1	3-1	2-0	1-4	3-1	5-1		3-3	3-4	3-5	3-3	4-2		★		1-0
	A	4-4	1-1	0-0	2-0	2-3	0-2	4-2					1-5	4-3	1-3	2-1	1-5	1-3	0-2	1-1			0-4
West Brom. Albion	H	1-2	3-2	0-0	1-1	2-2	5-1	1-1					9-2	4-3	2-1	3-2	3-1	4-1	3-1	3-0		★	
	A	2-2		5-3		2-2	2-2	2-2	1-1	1-1	3-3	1-5	1-4		0-3	2-0		1-3	2-1				1-1
Wolverh'ton Wanderers	H		2-1	5-1	3-1	6-1	2-1	2-1	2-0	3-2	5-1	1-1		3-1		2-0			4-3	5-0	4-0	1-1	★
	A		3-2	5-1	2-3	1-1			0-1	1-1	3-2	1-3	4-3		1-1		1-1	2-1		2-0	0-1		

13

Higher Ince asked if City couldn't put pen pics in of OUR players, and was told "We'll do what we can." (See Chapter 12, Class of 57/58!)

Arthur Walmsley paid tribute to Stanley Matthews in his column and how difficult Roy Little generally found it to mark him.

David Jack asked if relegation was disastrous, quoting that it gave teams a chance to rebuild without the same pressure, and attendances often rose when the team would be doing better, provided no more than three seasons were spent there! He finished by saying that four up and four down was long overdue, but that was another story!?

Train to Luton next week would be 25s

Blackpool, managed by Joe Smith, were eleventh with thirty two points, a place behind City on thirty three points. They'd had seven home wins, including a 7-0 v Sunderland and a 5-1 v Bolton, two draws, and six defeats, incuding 5-2 to City. Away they'd won six, including 2-1 at O/T and 4-1 at Sunderland, drawn four, and lost four.

At City: Pre-war we'd won the last three, 7-1, 5-1 and 2-1. Post we'd won three including 5-0 in 52/53, drawn two, and lost four including 6-1 the week before the '55 cup final.

Recent attendances ranged from 22,515 (53/54) to 63,925 (55/56) This was the fortieth league meeting, plus one cup tie in '56, City won 2-1(42,517) after 1-1 (32,577) abandoned. .

Team news: Sear in for Little, Sambrook in for Fagan, Ken Taylor, only other game at Coventry in the friendly, in for Ewing *(programme editor must've been tipped off)* - McTavish in for Warhurst. Ken Barnes took over the captaincy from Dave Ewing.

From The Pink/Green:
Freak Goal Helps City

Bert, the baffling, brilliant Trautmann smashed attack after attack by Blackpool though it was City who had the ball in the net on fifteen minutes but Hayes was given offside. Blackpool slipped into the lead in the twenty fourth minute when Hugh Kelly sent a neat ball inside to **Perry** who, as Trautmann came out fired straight and hard into the far corner of the net. Garrett left the field with a nasty cut over his eye as Blackpool pressed certainly knowing where the goal lay. City had chances too and the elusive goal looked to be arriving when Jimmy Kelly handled in the box in the thirty ninth minute. Barnes sent the penalty to the left hand corner but Farm dived the right way and saved. Blackpool then raced to the opposite end and Bert conceded a disputed corner. Harris swung the kick into the middle and **Perry** nodded it in on forty one minutes. Two minutes later City were awarded another penalty when Garrett, who had just returned with a plaster over his eye, held Johnstone and this time **Barnes** made no mistake.

City resumed in great style but in the sixty first minute **Durie** beat Leivers and scored with a deflected shot off Sear taking it beyond Trautmann. In the sixty ninth minute City reduced the arrears through **McAdams** whose close range shot went in off Wright. A minute later it was 3-3. **Johnstone** placed a free kick perfectly, and the ball, after apparently running down Kelly's body trickled into the net. Three minutes from time Sambrook sent in the perfect centre and **Barlow** scored the winning goal.

FINAL SCORE: CITY 4 BLACKPOOL 3

City: Sky blue/white:Trautmann; Leivers, Sear; Barnes, Taylor, McTavish; Barlow, Hayes, Johnstone, McAdams, Sambrook
Blackpool: Tangerine shirts/white knickers: Farm; Garrett, Wright; Kelly J., Gratrix, Kelly H.; Harris, Mudie, Charnley, Durie, Perry
Attendance: 30,621 **Average:** 34,024
Referee: J.S.Swain (Cleethorpes)
Linesmen: A.Edge, J.Hall
League position: Up to 7th
Goals For: 81 Against: 81
Reserves: No game

Jack Dyson scored (Stringfellow in some reports?) for the 'A' team after ten minutes in the 1-1 draw with United, said he was feeling fine and looking forward to next season..

Blackpool held their own until 1967 when they took the drop, were promoted in 1970, but took the drop again in 1971 and were destined to be a lower division team, though they surprised us a couple of times in cup ties. Their centre half Roy Gratrix was sussed out in the programme as being 'on the small side'. Needless to say City didn't and signed him in 1964.

Roy Gratrix

Liverpool fans were described as soccer ruffians and ran mob rule at Blackburn at the sixth round cup tie. United fans suggested that the 'new team' shouldn't be regarded as second best.
European Cup semi- finals were fixed so United didn't need to fly and they will face either Dortmund or Milan in the semi.
Evening Chron were running a 'What's wrong with City feature.' Fans letters included 'don't pick on Dave, we have no full backs like Sproston and Barkas'
United backlash was beginning. One fan wrote that he was fed up with all the bunkum written about them. Additionally journalists were having to defend the 'prolongation of the agony which seemed to have gone beyond the bounds of genuine sorrow and sympathy'.

32) WEDNESDAY MARCH 5TH K.O. 7.30: BIRMINGHAM CITY (HOME)

The re-arranged fixture from the abandoned February 15th game.

The programme's editorial commenced with: Manchester City never have been noted for making a song and dance about their activities although there have been many occasions on which they would have been fully justified in doing so.

The quietness did not mean that Mr George Poyser, new chief scout and co. haven't been busy, oh no, for a number of promising youngsters will soon be given trials. Roy Clarke, loyal clubman, is playing with the reserves and 'A' team, and he is quite happy helping the youngsters along.

Maine Road Gossip welcomed Birmingham again. Executive committee of Manchester City supporters Club have sent a donation of 25 guineas to the Munich Air Disaster Fund sponsored by the Mayor of Manchester. Collection for the Children's Sunshine League realised £74 12s 2d at the West Brom home game.

HOW CITY'S TEAMS FARED

DIVISION I, March 1st.—City 4, Blackpool 3.
CITY : Trautmann ; Leivers, Sear ; Barnes, Taylor, McTavish ; Barlow, Hayes, Johnstone, McAdams, Sambrook.
BLACKPOOL : Farm ; Garrett, Wright ; Kelly (J.), Gratrix, Kelly (H.) ; Harris, Mudie, Charnley, Durie, Perry.
Scorers : **City**—Barnes (pen.), McAdams, Barlow, Kelly, H. (o.g.). **Blackpool**—Perry (2), Durie. *Attendance :* 30,621.

CENTRAL LEAGUE, February 22nd.—City Reserves 5, Leeds United Res. 1.
CITY RESERVES : Fleet ; Branagan, Horridge ; Phoenix, Taylor, Shawcross ; McClelland, Kirkman, Hart, Clarke, Fidler.
Scorers : **City Reserves**—Clarke (3), Kirkman (2). **Leeds Reserves**—Ripley.

LANCASHIRE LEAGUE, DIVISION I, March 1st.—City " A " 1, Manchester U. " A " 1.
CITY " A " : Dixon ; Horridge, Leigh ; Cooke, Davidson, Shawcross ; Pennington, Stringfellow, Dyson, Clarke (R.), Fairweather.
Scorers : **City " A "**—Stringfellow. **United " A "**—Mooney.

LANCASHIRE LEAGUE, DIVISION II, February 22nd.—Accrington S. " A " 2, City " B " 2.
CITY " B " : Dowd ; Rucker, Hibbert ; Scowcroft, Rooney, Ashton ; Nichol, Worthington, Lister, Faulkner, Murray.
Scorers : **Accrington " A "**—Bennett, McCreadie. **City " B "**—Faulkner, Worthington.

LANCASHIRE LEAGUE, JUNIOR DIVISION, February 22nd.—City 5, Rochdale 2.
CITY : Marsland ; Edwards, Dootson ; Swann, Stevenson, Nortley ; Nelson, Hardman, Woodward, Richardson, Bradshaw.
Scorers : **City**—Hardman (2), Woodward (2), Nelson. **Rochdale**—Owen, Martin.

14

Sportsman's Corner advised Lawrence Mason of Harpurhey that City's last abandoned game before Birmingham was the '56 cup tie v Blackpool.

Arthur Walmsley gave tribute to Roy Clarke and particularly his display in the '55 F.A. Cup semi v Sunderland.

There was a pic and history of **Gil Merrick**, who sported a moustache, not popular in those days despite film stars like Errol Flynn and Clark Gable.

David Jack, prompted by the FA Cup semi final draw this week, criticised the ticket allocation to fans of only 15,000 to each club for the final. Time for a complete overhaul, David says - quite rightly.

Train was 25s to Luton next week.

Birmingham since the abandoned game had managed a couple more matches, Wolves away, 5-1 loss, and Arsenal home 4-1 win. They were in fifteenth place with twenty six points, City seventh with thirty five points.

Team news: Big Dave was back replacing Ken Taylor, Warhurst replaced Barnes who had flu.

From the Guardian's 'Special correspondent': City Held - Both Sides Finish Inaccurately

Poor finishing by both sets of forwards restricted the score to 1-1. Johnstone was in fine form until fading with a knee injury and City were left without a connecting link as Barnes was missing. McAdams fluffed a chance and both goalkeepers made good saves, though Bert was injured plucking the ball out of the air after a shot by Brown from short range. An offside decision by the linesman robbed City of what would have been an excellent goal as Barlow got the better of Murphy and coolly placed the ball past Merrick. Just before half time McAdams headed against the Birmingham crossbar. Early in the second half Bert had no chance of reaching a low shot by Brown, which Leivers kicked off the line. Then Sambrook cut inside Hall and centred to Hayes who dummied letting the ball go to **Barlow** who scored with a craftily taken cross shot in the fifty fifth minute. Five minutes later **Murphy** with seemingly little power drove a centre from Hooper low and just inside a post. Bert misjudged the pace of the shot and dived just too late. Then Bert was stranded outside his box as Astall shot into an empty net but Ewing chased back and breasted the ball away. It was all City in the closing stages but the score remained at 1-1 just like the abandoned game.

FINAL SCORE: CITY 1 BIRMINGHAM 1

City: Sky blue/white: Trautmann; Leivers, Sear; Warhurst, Ewing, McTavish; Barlow, Hayes, Johnstone, McAdams, Sambrook
Birmingham: Red shirts/white knickers: Merrick; Hall, Green; Larkin, Smith, Neal; Astall, Orritt, Brown, Murphy, Hooper
Attendance: 30,655 **Average:** 33,813
Referee: E.S.Oxley (Pontefract)
Linesmen: E.T.Nottingham, N. Methley
League Position: 6th
Goals For: 82 Against: 82
Bert Lister scored 5 v United 'B' team in the 5-1 win

For me it was Choir practice the next night, the anthem, 'Olivet To Calvary'. A couple of the United lads couldn't get in at O/T for the cup tie with West Brom last night, so went to Maine Road to support Birmingham and delighted in telling us how they took the mickey.

"Who's catching you up in the league then?"

"Well, (indignantly) we've had Munich."

So there we were, us Blues, feeling sympathy and compassion for United's situation, giving money to the cause, and these idiots didn't have the good grace to respect even that. Typical.

Fans queuing from noon, and thousands locked out of O/T at last night's game v WBA in the cup, which could have caused disaster. A car ran into fans in Peel Green who then tried to overturn it. Munich fund now standing at £22,000. Official support withdrawn to the Lord Mayor of Manchester to visit Munich and the cost of £75 for the two would have to be stood by the Lord and Lady themselves.

Johnny Hart, last injured v Spurs in '56 set to make his comeback at Luton and Roy Cheetham could make his debut, as Ken Barnes has gland trouble. City will get 25,000 tickets for the semi final at Maine Road. (Using the voucher system I got one for my dad.)
Ken Taylor is to have an operation.
Ray Wood dropped his transfer request at O/T.
City report no interest in Huddersfield's Ron Cockerill

33) SATURDAY MARCH 8TH 1958
K.O. 3PM: LUTON (AWAY)

LUTON TOWN F.C.

FOOTBALL LEAGUE — DIVISION 1
LUTON TOWN
v
MANCHESTER CITY

Official Programme
Price 3d.
SATURDAY, 8th MARCH, 1958

17in. murphy Console with "tambour" doors which roll away out of sight

Tambour!

- Beautiful modern cabinet veneered in West African walnut.
- Easiest ever programme selection — "Spot-on" at one click of the switch.
- Perfect centring and unique unmasked tube-mount giving biggest possible picture on 17 in. screen.
- ¼ in. Armour Plate glass front.

Williams & Richardson
Proprietor: H. R. WILLIAMS
YOUR murphy DEALER
174, BISCOT ROAD · LUTON
Phone: LUTON 6897/8

V310D 17 in. Console £105.0.0

The programme was a large white edition with a brick wall and boater on the front, eight big pages for 3d.

Club notes made reference to the Munich Air Disaster Fund, all clubs being asked to make collections at their grounds and Luton's was scheduled for today.

There was a brief review on City as the most free scoring team in the first division with eighty two goals to date. However it must not be overlooked that they had also conceded eighty two, which should make for an entertaining game of attacking football today. The rest of the programme was made up of adverts and statistics.

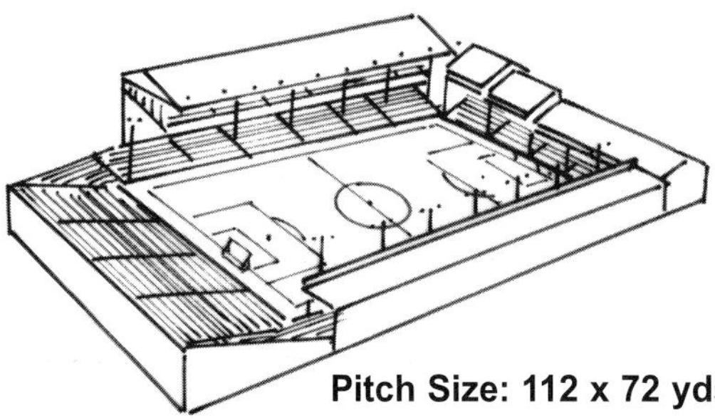

Pitch Size: 112 x 72 yds

Kenilworth Road's record attendance was only 30,069 and that came the year after in the F.A.Cup sixth round at home to Blackpool.

I didn't make it there until the cup tie of '61 - yeah that one. Down 2-0 after fifteen mins, 3-2 up at half time. Two drunken Luton fans scrapping with each other over the merits of Denis's third, in the pouring rain. 6-2 up twenty minutes to go and referee K.R.Tuck, of Chesterfield, good rhymimg slang eh, abandoning it then, instead of at half time and we lost the replay, of course (though it's hardly ever mentioned that we were down to ten men with Ken Barnes a passenger on the wing).

It was a dump. Small 'bobbers stand' down one length, half a main stand, seats/paddock down the other. Small covered terrace behind one goal and an open Kop behind the other. Floodlights on poles. No wonder Millwall fans tried to wreck it years later, causing the away fans ban. There's been a few cosmetic changes since, plastic pitch in then out, roof over the 'Kop', but it's still a dump.

Luton, managed by Dally Duncan, were in fourth place with thirty eight points. City sixth with thirty six points. Away from home they'd won six, drawn two, and lost eight including a 5-0 at Portsmouth. At home, they'd won ten including a 7-1 v Sunderland and a 5-1 v West Brom, 4-0 v Arsenal, drawn two, including 2-2 at Maine Road, lost four. In the cup they'd lost 3-0 at Stockport in the third round.

At Luton: Pre-war, we'd lost two and won one of the three meetings. Post-war two draws and two - 3-2 losses..

Recent attendances ranged from 12,087 (50/51) to 22,796 (46/47). It was the sixteenth league meeting plus four cup ties, three at Luton, 1938 fifth rd 3-1(21,099), 1953 fourth rd replay 1-5 (21,991), 1955 fifth rd 2-0 (23,104).

Team news: Debut boy Roy Cheetham, the seventeen year old local lad who had been waiting for this chance since joining up at Maine Road when his schooldays were over, came in for Ken Barnes, and it was an emotional return for Johnny Hart who replaced Bobby Johnstone, out with leg bruises. Sear fit after a cold scare.

From The Green:
Late Rally By Blues

The Luton pitch was a dreadful mess of snow and mud and Luton were first away but City were soon back in it though neither goalkeeper was ever seriously troubled in the first quarter of an hour. The boo-boys started early giving McAdams a round for a sharp tackle on Turner. Weaknesses in defence were giving Luton too much room, but Bert was on his toes and Cheetham made a timely clearance. There was an appeal for a penalty on McTavish but it was turned down by the referee. There was little other incident in the first half and City were lucky to be level at 0-0. The second half started much the same and it was tough on Baynham trying to keep warm with nothing to do for long spells; on the other hand Bert was constantly in action, both in the air and on the ground.

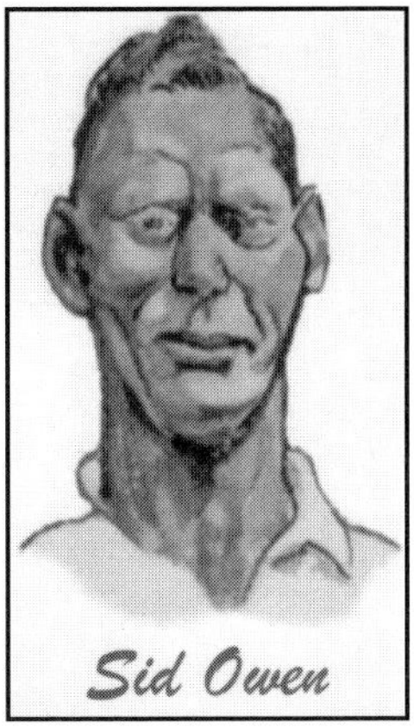

Barlow hit the ball against the foot of the post and at the other end Trautmann continued his good form. Two strange offside decisions rubbed out successive efforts from first McAdams, who scored from close range when seemingly perfectly positioned and then Hayes nodded home but got the same treatment. Anyway, the Blues continued to improve and slipped into the lead in the seventy third minute. Hayes dribbled though the Luton defence and pushed it to **Barlow** who hit it on the half turn. The ball crashed against the inside of the far post, came out, struck Dunne and rebounded into the net. Then two more goals came in the next two minutes. **Pacey** notched the first from close range at the height of a goalmouth struggle. Then at the other end Sambook rounded off a nice move with a straight drive from five yards. Luton claimed a penalty when Sear checked and brought down McLeod but the referee would have none of it.

FINAL SCORE: LUTON 1 CITY 2

Luton: White shirts/black knickers/ black with white top stockings: Baynham; Dunne, Hawkes; Groves; Owen, Pacey; Adam; Turner, Brown, Rowland, McLeod
City: Sky blue/white: Trautmann; Leivers, Sear; Cheetham, Ewing, McTavish; Barlow, Hayes, Hart, McAdams, Sambrook.
Attendance: 16,004 **Average:** 31,591
Referee: J.V.Sherlock (Sheffield)
Linesmen: C.W.Jillings (Romford), D. D. Juggins (Romford) - so Jillins and Juggins!
League position: Up to 5th
Goals For: 84 Against: 83
Reserves: Drew at home with Wolves 3-3

Note: The soccer special was involved in a collision when it ploughed into the back of a stationary train at Chinley station, five passengers being injured. Apparently a signal stuck at Chinley and signalman Jack Shirt was accused of being negligent in his duty and not for the first time. When asked what he had to say for himself later in court by the judge he replied "nothing Sir".

Luton went on to finish in eighth spot. They reached the cup final in '59 losing 2-1 to an eventual ten man Forest team, Elton John's Uncle Reggie breaking his leg (I won't go breaking my, I won't go breaking my...) They took the drop in 1960, down to the fourth and back, we relegated them in '75, they us in '83, had a good spell in the 80's with the plastic pitch and away fans ban, winning the league cup in '88 and runners up in '89. Down in 91/92 and became a lower league club, again.

Bert played in a benefit game for Sheffield United's Jimmy Hagan. In Bert's regular MEN column he tells that just before kick off last Saturday a Post Office boy arrived at the ground with a telegram to Johnny Hart reading "good luck on your return to the game." It was from Joe Mercer, then Sheffield United's manager and future Blues manager.

J. MERCER (EVERTON)

Ken Taylor who was injured in his debut match is to have a cartilage operation. Jack Dyson is to lead the reserves against Derby if the pitch is suitable. It was and City won the game 5-1 on March 12th and Phoenix, Fagan and Kirkman were watched by Wolves and Walsall scouts.
Bobby Johnstone is being watched and could have a good chance of playing v England at Hampden on April 19th.
John Kay in the MEN was being criticised by United fans for commenting on the mass hysteria from the terraces after Munich and was told, amongst other things to "go and jump in the lake"

34) SATURDAY MARCH 15TH 1958
K.O. 3PM: ARSENAL (HOME)

The programme's editorial praised the form of eighteen year old Roy Cheethan in his debut last Saturday at Luton. He explained that supporters' letters, many of them, and most containing sound common sense, are received on team selection, concluding that this is best left to the Manager! "Mr McDowall has never hesitated to introduce 'new blood', and I am sure much more will be heard of such as Cheetham, Shawcross, Taylor, Fidler, Stringfellow and Fleet."

Maine Road Gossip reminded us of our poor form v the Gunners at Maine Road.

Condolences were given to City Manager **Les McDowall**, whose father died in Glasgow this week aged 85.

In Sportsman's Corner, PD of Moss Side asked when the Platt Lane stand was built. It was completed for the start of the 1935/36 season.

Arthur Walmsley was pleased that City beat a high flying Luton Town last week with a City team, which on paper at least, looked to be below strength, but showed that the club's second line strength points the way to bright seasons ahead. Johnny Hart's return after an eighteen month lay off with injury - broken leg, broken knee cap, broken ribs, strained ankle ligaments - made happy news too and Arthur hoped Johnny would be around for many years to come.

David Jack again reckoned that the Football League team to face the Scottish League at Newcastle on March 26th should be made up of the probable England team, now unsettled with the loss at Munich of Byrne, Edwards and Taylor. He argues that local players, Clough, Eastham, Stokoe, should not be picked just to boost the attendance, and pander to local tastes, but suggests the following team: Sanders (WBA)

in place of Hopkinson (Bolton); Howe (WBA), Langley (Fulham), Clayton, (Blackburn), Wright (Wolves), Clamp (Wolves), Matthews (Blackpool), Finney (Preston), Charlton (United), Haynes (Fulham), Pilkington (Burnley), leaving out his favourites Harmer (Spurs), Douglas (Blackburn) and Barlow (WBA) but hoping that places could be found for them!

Train to Newcastle 21s and Aintree 7/6d

Arsenal, managed by Jack Crayston, were fourteenth with nine home wins, including a 4-0 v Villa and 2-1 v City, two draws, and six losses, including 5-4 to United the week before Munich. Away they'd won four, drawn one, lost nine including 4-0's at Luton and Forest. In the cup they'd lost 3-1 at Northampton in the third round.

At City: Pre-war they'd won the last one but lost three and drawn one prior to that. Post we'd only won once, 2-1 in 54/55, drawn two lost four.

Recent attendances ranged from 20,782 (47/48) to 48,367 (51/52). It was the seventy eighth league meeting, plus two cup ties, one at Arsenal, the 1932 semi-final and a Charity Shield game in 1934 at Highbury.

Team News: Bobby Johnstone came in for Johnny Hart, Little in for Sear and Paddy Fagan came in for Billy Mac. Ken Barnes was in the reserves after his illness and Warhurst was suffering with a groin injury.

From The Guardian's W.R.Taylor: Arsenal Enjoy Themselves - City's Sorry Defence

Bogey team Arsenal had a field day with the City defence being deplorable. City now look to be about to set a most peculiar record finishing in the top half of the table with eighty six goals for and eighty seven against. If the trend continues we could be both scoring and conceding one hundred goals. Only Southampton with ninety have scored more so far, but the fans will no doubt grouse bitterly about the goals on the debit side. The defence was at twelves and fourteens rather than sixes and sevens, Clapton in particular being given the freedom of the park. Arsenal cantered home comfortably and City missed Barnes and Warhurst languishing in the reserves but were handicapped in the second half with injuries to Hayes, the best forward, and Little. Johnstone had an off day and the City attack was disjointed.

Arsenal took advantage of a cold wind and **Bloomfield** lobbed the ball over the advancing Trautmann in the third minute after great gaps had appeared in the defence. Arsenal were well on top but were pegged back by a great goal from **Hayes** in the eighteenth minute. McTavish sent a through ball to Barlow whose centre was struck with speed and accuracy by Joe, to make it 1-1, and that was as good as it got. City made chances but Bert completely missed a pass from Groves and **Bloomfield** rammed the ball home in the 44th minute. Second half with the crowd shouting "shake it up a bit" City showed more initiative, but, with Hayes limping on the wing and Little hobbling, Arsenal took control. Leivers brought down Nutt in the penalty area and **Herd** scored with an explosive shot on the hour. Despite Arsenal taking it easy **Bloomfield** dribbled past two defenders and shot past Bert for 4-1. Leivers, by now frustrated was repeatedly sweeping upfield, had a shot kicked off the line and **Barlow** scored from the rebound in the eighty ninth minute. In the closing minutes Bill had shown such power and determination in attack that it might be well worth trying him up front to add some punch and surely there'd be nothing to lose under the present circumstance.

D. HERD

FINAL SCORE: CITY 2 ARSENAL 4

City: Sky blue/white: Trautmann; Leivers, Little; Cheetham, Ewing, McTavish; Barlow, Hayes, Johnstone, Fagan, Sambrook.
Arsenal: Red and white shirts/white knickers: Kelsey; Charlton, Wills; Ward, Fotheringham (ooh I say), Petts; Clapton, Groves, Herd, Bloomfield, Nutt.
Attendance: 31,645 **Average:** 33,686
Referee: R.Wood (Sunderland)
Linesmen: K.G.Hampson, S.Gandy
League Position: Stayed in 5th place
Goals For: 86 Against: 87
Reserves: Won 3-0 at Villa, beat Huddersfield 5-1 at M/Rd (March 12th)

Arsenal went on to finish twelfth. Success eluded them throughout the 60's, though they always did well against City and they even had a couple of embarrassing league cup final defeats. That changed with the Fairs Cup win in 1970, followed by the double in 1971, then the trophies have flowed regularly to the present day.

34A) MONDAY MARCH 17TH DERBY COUNTY (away, friendly)

This was the re-arranged friendly game with Derby from January 25th. They'd been relegated from the first division in '53, and were presently sixteenth, which is where they finished at the end of this season in the second division. In the cup they'd gone out at Middlesbrough 5-0 in the third round.

Their only honour to date was the F.A. Cup in 1946. Pre-war we'd played each other forty four times, City winning twenty one, drawing nine losing fourteen. Post we'd played ten with good home form, four wins, one draw, no losses but at Derby we'd won one, (3-1 in 51/52), drawn one, and lost three, including a 7-0, and a 5-0. Though we did win in the F.A.Cup third round in 1955 3-1 (23,409). Recent attendances v City at Derby ranged from 15,618 (52/53) to 31,275 (47/48). Peter Doherty was the most famous transfer to Derby from City.

I had a pen pal at the time from Burton On Trent, contacted through the pages of Football Monthly, who supported Forest, hated Derby, and got me a copy of the programme. It was sixteen pages for 3d of poor quality paper. There was a pleasant section on 'Our Visitors', the league's leading scorers with eighty four goals (no mention of eighty three against!). The rest was ads and statistics.

The Baseball Ground didn't have its record attendance of 41,826 until 69/70 v Spurs. I didn't make it there for ages. First visit being in '84 for the 1-0 loss. Only change from the 50's was the double decker along the length of the pitch, the Ley stand replacing a standard covered terrace. There were two double deckers, one behind each goal, seats and paddock and a covered seats and paddock main stand. They moved to Pride Park in 1997.

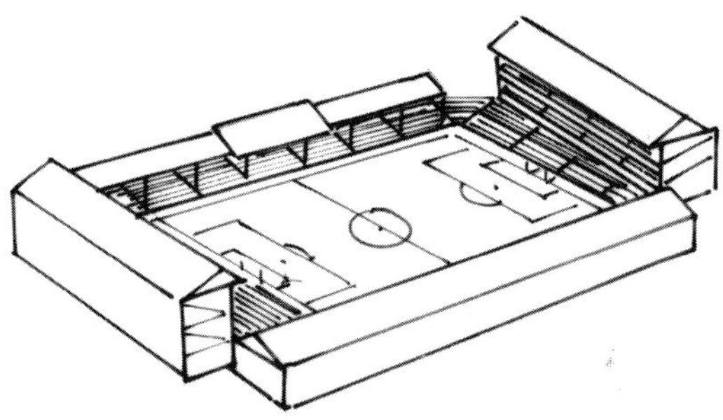

Pitch Size: 110 x 71 yds

Team News: Peter Leigh was in for Roy Little, Warhurst for McTavish, Hart back in for Johnstone.

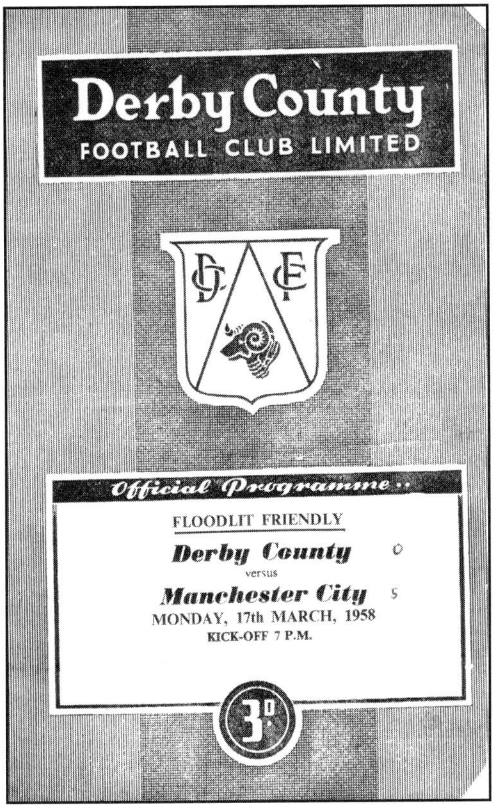

From The Derby Friendly Daily Paper: Those City Slickers Slam Derby

City's zip-along speed merchants hit a sluggish Derby County for five and they did it with six reserves in the team.

Bewildering inter-changing of positions had the Derby defenders in constant trouble. Centre-half Martin McDonnell was so perplexed he did not know where to go and who to follow. It was fast, fluent football and the home defenders had no answer. Albert Mays and Frank Upton tried valiantly to muster some cohesion in the home rear guard but Upton spoiled his efforts with poor distribution. Jack Parry was the only forward to trouble a solid, competent City defence with goalkeeper Bert Trautmann at his best. It would be unfair to judge young Derby debutants Tim Womack and John Bowers on this showing - they were playing in a demoralised side.

All the City men deserved credit. They showed Derby just how far they have slipped in the four seasons since they left the senior league.

City won easily with goals from Billy Mac in the fifteenth minute, Colin Barlow on forty five and seventy eight minutes. Johnny Hart on fifty minutes and Ray Sambrook on eighty five minutes

FINAL SCORE: DERBY 0 CITY 5

Derby: White shirts/black shorts: Oxford; Barrowcliffe, Smith; Mayes, McDonnell,Upton; Bowers, Ryan, Parry, Darwin, Womack.
City: Sky blue/white: Trautmann; Leivers, Leigh; Cheetham, Ewing, Warhurst; Fagan, Barlow, Hart, McAdams, Sambrook
Attendance: 8,296
Referee: R.H.Windle (Chesterfield)
Linesmen: . M. A Gilbert (Chaddesden), L.D.Maddocks (Allestree)

Derby, later, under Brian Clough, were promoted in '69 and won the title in '72 (which City should have won). Cloughie left and they won it again in '75 under Dave MacKay. They went down in 1980, and since then they've had their ups and downs, but the Baseball was always a bogey ground to us.

After United's game at Burnley their chairman Bob Lord denied he'd called them 'teddy boys'. He also advised that his club were sympathetic about Munich. Pearson was sent off - "six of one, half a dozen of the other" - reported David Meek, starting as he was to go on - but Gregg, despite being astride Shackleton, hitting him with his fists, was not. Pearson was reported as making derogatory remarks about Bob Lord. Funnily enough a few days later Jimmy Murphy made 'Pancho' shave off his sideboards - to put an end to that taunt??!!'

From The Burnley Express March 17th:

Greaves and Crowther 'trying to ride roughshod' over both laws and opponents. Neutrals came to express sympathy, but left disappointed.

It was more in the nature of a tragedy the decline of a cause and the shaming of a famous name. On this display some members of this gallant young team which has arisen from the wreckage of Munich have a long way to go to be worthy of the rich heritage of sportsmanship bequeathed to them by those who'd gone before.

One was left with a feeling of regret and the fervent hope that when Mr Matt Busby returns to duty he will discipline these 'angry young men' to the path of great traditions from which they have so lamentably strayed.

Letters to the Chron from United fans pointed out that Mr Lord was just jealous of United and concluded that, "It's just plain jealousy" - W. Burton of 82, Oxford Street, Old Trafford. (Burnley went on to win the title in 1960, so they were obviously very jealous!?). It turned out that the refreshments sent in by Burnley after the match were sent back uneaten by the United squad!.

Three City players are refusing to fly during the five week tour of the USA and Canada in the summer. The squad will sail there and back, but owing to the busy schedule will make internal flights.

March 17th: Lg of Ireland 2 Irish Lg 2, Dublin, 20,000

March 19th: Bolton res. 0 City res 1

35) SATURDAY MARCH 22ND
K.O 3PM: WOLVERHAMPTON WANDERERSS (AWAY)

The programme was 3d for eight pages, and in truth the front cover wasn't as impressive as previous Wolves programmes, with a ground view taken from the Kop end of the stadium.

'Notes' by Wanderer commented on City's heavy recent losses at Molineux but concluded that there was nothing to indicate that the present day City could be taken lightly - the most fantastic goal average in the league is testimony to that.

Today's topical talk brilliantly written by Ivan Sharpe estimated that Wolves needed eleven or twelve points from the remaining games to become worthy champions of England in next year's European Cup.

After reviewing Wolves' season he went on to welcome today's guests. "If you want anxiety with your enjoyment, follow Manchester City", a statement said by others this season. At the time of the M-Plan Ivan said that he liked our double defensive system if it had been executed by the right players. Why? Because the game can do with new notions, especially at a time of falling attendances at most places.

He commented on today's semi-finals. Bolton, without Nat Lofthouse, an orchestra without a leader, at Maine Road, v second division Blackburn, who would be inspired by Ronnie Clayton and could qualify for their eighth final, one more than Wolves. (Ironically they both met in 1960 to make it eight all!)

At Villa Park it was second division Fulham v United. Ivan thought that Fulham heading for their first final could crack under the strain, a great deal depending on Haynes and Bentley.

Equally, everything hangs on how the tremendously-limelighted United team emerge under ordeal as this is their supreme test to date. At Burnley last Saturday Ivan wasn't surprised to find that cracks in temperament were appearing (they lost 3-0), but if they can keep their heads, and make the most of Ernie Taylor's promptings, they may yet see Wembley - flukes permitting.

The English team for next week's League international includes Wright and Clamp from Wolves and surprise choices Langley of Fulham, Pearce of Sunderland, and Kevan of WBA - so the World Cup team is still wide open.

The rest was tables, results, statistics etc, but Ivan's notes alone were worth the 3d.

Molineux's record attendance was 61,315 v Liverpool FA Cup 1939. I didn't make it there until the next season, a 2-0 defeat, when two drunken Wolves blokes made it very threatening and uncomfortable, shall we say. Built on a hill it comprised an angled main stand, seats and paddock which followed the contour of the road. Opposite was the very distinctive multi-span structure, again seats and paddock. There was a covered terrace behind one goal and opposite, taking advantage of the hill was a huge Kop, partly covered. The perimeter wall was a low one and players often went over it into the crowd - as did Mike Summerbee in '65. The ground was completely re-developed over a long period of time.

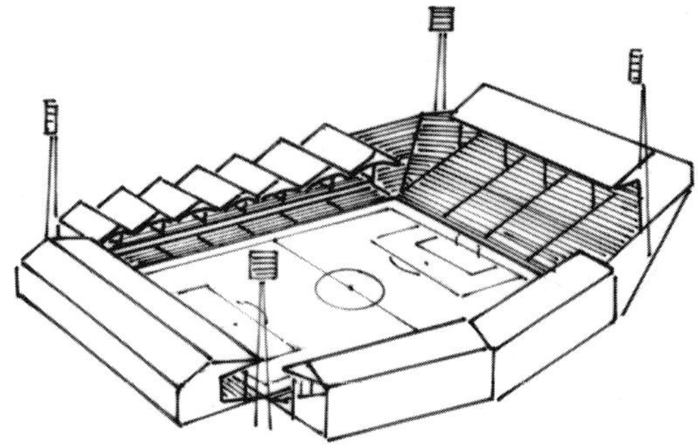

Pitch Size: 115 x 72 yds

Wolves, managed by Stan Cullis, continued their terrific season. They were top with fifty two points, City fifth with thirty eight points. Away they'd won eight, including 4-3 at City, biggest win being at Birmingham 5-1, drawn three, and lost four. At home they were invincible winning fifteen including 6-1 v Bolton, 5-0 v Sunderland and drawing two. In the cup they'd gone out in the sixth round 2-1 at Bolton.

At Wolves: Pre-war, they'd won the last five including a 5-0 and an 8-0. Post, just as bad - we'd lost six, including a 7-3, 7-2, and 5-1, with three draws, giving a faint glimmer of hope.

Recent attendances ranged from 27,606 (53/54) to 44,735 (49/50). This was the fiftieth league meeting, plus two cup ties, two at Wolves 1911 second rd 0-1 (25,000), 1952 third rd replay 1-4 (42,865).

Team News: From last Saturday's game, Sear was in for Little, Barnes in for Cheetham, Warhurst in for McTavish, McAdams in for Hayes, who injured an ankle in the Arsenal game.

From Eddie Griffiths:

Wolves will want to charge Bobby Johnstone with larceny after this game, because if ever a man dictated how the game should go and stole a point from championship-chasing Wolves, Bobby did. We have seen a number of deep-lying centre forwards since the Continentals gave us a preview, but this man Johnstone is 'tops'. A master tactician, he was all over the place and with Colin Barlow and Bill McAdams forming a two-pronged spearhead, the Wolves defence did not know who to mark and there were times when the slide-rule passes by City's Scottish International had them flat footed. Certainly Billy Wright has not been given such a run around for a long time. He and his partners did not know who to mark and in the end were rather fortunate to save a point. Yet when Wolves put on pressure they looked good, but only in spasms....

From Harry Palmer:
A Penalty Missed, Two Own Goals

Jimmy Murray

Wolves, whose last home defeat was a year ago, went straight on the attack, but within fourteen seconds City were a goal up. **Stuart** intercepted a through ball from Johnstone and then put it back for Finlayson to clear. The goalkeeper missed the ball and his late dive failed to stop it trickling over the line. Wolves seemed completely demoralised for a few minutes and when they did get on the move passes went astray. For City, Johnstone, Barlow and McAdams spurned chances and for Wolves, Murray, Mason, and Clamp were dangerous. Wolves' pressure paid off in the thirty fifth minute when **Ewing**, trying to clear Deeley's harmless looking shot, put the ball into his own goal, to cloud a fine performance. Next, Deeley was brought down in the box after thirty seven minutes by Sear but Bert dived to save his penalty, the fourth Wolves had missed this season. Two minutes from the interval Wolves went ahead when the dynamic **Deeley** went round Sear and flicked the ball into the net (one report had it as a Deeley header from a Clamp centre?).

Shortly after the interval, on forty seven minutes, City equalised. Sambrook's corner was fisted away by Finlayson, but Sambrook put the ball back into the goalmouth where **Barlow** scrambled it over the line. City kept up the pressure and in the fifty fifth minute went ahead when **Barlow** scored from a McAdams cross. City's goal now came under fire. Mullen hit the post and all their forwards pressurised. In the seventy third minute after Murray's shot was pushed out by Bert but only to Mason, he tapped it to **Mullen** who scored the equaliser.

Wolves were on top in the closing stages and Mullen hit the woodwork, but Barlow nearly had the final say when with the goalkeeper out of position he struck the crossbar.

FINAL SCORE: WOLVES 3 CITY 3

Wolves: Gold shirts/black knickers ; Finlayson; Stuart, Harris; Clamp, Wright, Slater; Deeley, Broadbent, Murray, Mason, Mullen
City: Sky blue shirts/white knickers: Trautmann; Leivers, Sear; Barnes, Ewing, Warhurst; Fagan, Barlow, Johnstone, McAdams, Sambrook
Attendance: 34,932 Average: 31,777
Referee: R.H.Chandler (Chester)
Linesmen: J.L.Lockton, London, J.C,Meredith (Shrewsbury)
League position: Stayed 5th
Goals For 89 Against: 90
Reserves: March 19th won at Bolton 1-0

Wolves got the points they needed for the title, winning it with sixty four, five clear of Preston. They won it again in '59, and would have done the double in '60 if we'd not lost to Burnley in the final match of the season. Whilst we almost matched them in 57/58 they gave us an 8-1 drubbing on the opening day of the 62/63 season, as we headed to division 2. Remarkably, despite Blue David Wagstaffe donning the Old Gold, they followed us in '65, and it was especially good to double them in 65/66. They beat us 2-1 in the League cup final of '74 - "following City is watching us lose at Wembley with a forward line of Summerbee, Lee, Law, Bell, Marsh" (City fan Jerry Dowlen) won it again in 1980 with Andy Gray, then sank to the fourth and back, briefly, but have never regained the glory days.

SATURDAY MARCH 22ND 1958
F.A.CUP SEMI-FINAL:
BLACKBURN ROVERS 1 v BOLTON WANDERERS 2

City produced a smart souvenir programme for this prestigious match, the eighth semi-final to be held at Maine Road. The front cover had a good shot of the ground from the Platt Lane End, obviously taken prior to the Kippax stand being in place, as a reverse shot of the main stand had been superimposed over the terrace?! It contained all the usual info and pics of the teams plus articles by various journalists.

Eric Todd gave us the Maine Road semi run down:

> 1928 Huddersfield 1 Sheffield United 0, Huddersfield lost to Blackburn 3-1 in the final.
> 1946 Replay - Derby 4 Birmingham 0. Derby beat Charlton 4-1 in extra time in the final, the only time the M/Rd semi-finalist winners, have gone on to win the cup.
> 1947 Replay - Burnley 1 Liverpool 0. Burnley lost 1-0 to Charlton in the final
> 1950 Liverpool 2 Everton 0. Liverpool lost 2-1 to Arsenal in the final.
> 1953 Bolton 4 Everton 3. Bolton lost 4-3 to Blackpool in the final
> 1954 Preston 2 Sheffield Wednesday 0. Preston lost 3-2 to WBA in the final

Obviously all the games produced entertaining football!

David Jack, who played for Bolton, scoring in their 1923, 1926, 1929 cup finals was hoping that Bolton would do it.

Arthur Walmsley reviewed the careers of the managers Johnny Carey, and Bill Ridding.

Harry Kay leant towards Blackburn, fifteen times semi finalists, cup winners six times, runners up

once and hoped they'd get promotion too, which they actually achieved this season.
City staged further semis:

1960 Sheffield Wed v Blackburn
1973 Leeds v Wolves
1975 Fulham v Birmingham (replay)
1977 Liverpool v Everton
1977 Liverpool v Everton (replay)
1979 Liverpool v Man Utd
1984 Liverpool v Everton
(Milk Cup Final replay)
1985 United v Liverpool (replay)
1990 Oldham v United
1990 Oldham v United (replay)

Today's attendance 74,800. Gubbins 2 for Bolton. Future Blue Dobing for Blackburn

In the other semi United drew with Fulham at Villa Park 2-2, 69,745. Replay at Highbury, United 5 Fulham 3 - "United must win the cup on this form" announced David Meek!

City 0 Barrow 3, in the second round of the Lancashire Senior Cup. City fielded a reserve team with some 'A' teamers and Jack Dyson broke his leg for the second time this season. He may have to quit the game.
City 1 Bolton 0. Kirkman scored a brilliant goal to qualify City to meet Oldham Athletic in the Final of the Manchester Cup.
Ex Blue goalie John Savage was sent off in Walsall's game v Swindon last Saturday. Before John reached the dressing room his stand in, Tony Richards saved a penalty!
Roy Warhurst said he will fly in the USA. United to play Inter Milan in the Euro cup semi final.
Former Blue Eric Westwood is in training for the Jimmy Meadows testimonial game.
March 26: F. Lg 4 Scots Lg 1, Newcastle (38,000)

36) SATURDAY MARCH 29TH 1958: LEEDS UNITED (HOME)

The programme's editorial intended to open the notes with an appreciation of last week's splendid draw at Molineux, but the news of Jack Dyson, who broke his leg for the second time this season in Monday nights game v Barrow at Maine Road, overshadowed all other happenings this week.

Jack will get the very best of specialist treatment during his recovery and on behalf of all at City he was wished a swift and uncomplicated return to full fitness.

Because of City's unusual goal tally this season eighty nine for, ninety against, the deep lying centre forward plan with its attacking wing halves has again come in for criticism but the draw last week once more gave the plan's critics a firm answer.

Announcement was made re tickets being on sale for the Jimmy Meadows testimonial on Monday April 21st.

Maine Road Gossip was hoping for a double against Leeds and thanked everyone for the collection of £121 5s 7d taken on behalf of Henshaw's Institute for the Blind at the home game with Arsenal.

Sportsman's Corner had nothing of too much interest.

Arthur Walmsley on last week's dull semi final said the biggest cheer was from City fans when the 3-2 scoreline went up from the game at Wolves! He reckoned that City had made a fine recovery from the appalling run of injuries and the young forward line, which has hit more goals than any other club bespeaks great scoring potential for seasons to come - and if the defence was tightened, Big Dave playing well last week, an early challenge for honours. Then a good luck message to Jack Dyson, young and keen enough to make it.

David Jack thought that the European cup had obvious disadvantages, despite attendances showing it as the most important competition in football and needed some modification. He suggested one legged ties and more entrants, the F.A Cup winners from each country for example.

Train to Bolton was 2/4d from Victoria and Salford or 2/1d from Pendleton.

Leeds, managed by Raich Carter were sixteenth with twenty eight points, City fifth. with thirty nine points. They'd won nine homes, including 4-0 v Villa, drawn three, lost five, including 4-2 v City. Away they'd only won two, drawn two, lost thirteen including 5-0 at United. In the cup they'd gone out 2-1 at home to Cardiff in the third round.

At City: Pre-war we'd won the last two, 6-2 and 4-0. Post we'd won 4-1 in 50/51 (35,149) and 1-0 last season (34,185). It was the thirty second league meeting plus one cup tie, at City, 1928 third round 1-0 (50,473).

Team News: Unchanged from last week.

From The Guardian's W.R.Taylor: City Win A Game devoid Of Grace Or Distinction - Leeds Frail And Halting Before Goal

Leeds' efforts to score were pathetic and Bert had a comparatively quiet time in City's goal, but it could hardly have been called pleasant because it rained heavily for most of the time, making the pitch muddy and keeping the crowd down.

City's finishing was little better, the forwards opting to pass instead of shooting. After the first twenty minutes the standard of play fell to an almost unbelievable level, sometimes bordering on the almost farcical.

In the second half tempers rose and the referee didn't help awarding many free kicks (sometimes peculiarly) but ignoring even more offences, even though the sufferers complained bitterly about their treatment.

Because of the lack of football it was possible to concentrate on a little publicised aspect of the game - the attitude and histrionics of the players who've had a kick awarded against them.

1) Much the most straight-forward is the quiet, gentlemanly chat about the incident with the referee.

2) Next in order comes the argument with gestulations

3) Then descending the scale of behaviour, comes contempt for the referee followed by open abuse of him with all its attendant perils.

4) Varying the approach there is pained astonishment with the comical opportunities it affords for outraged dignity ("It wasn't me ref. it was two other guys") genuine astonishment, sometimes most justified.

5) Most childish of all petulantly kicking the ball as far as possible which brings us back to the talk with the referee, who earns every penny as a harassed official for whatever he does he is usually wrong in somebody's eyes.

Leeds were weakened by Cush's absence through Injury. Meek was upended heavily just after the start and hobbled about for a long time. It was Leeds who looked most dangerous early on, but they gifted City a goal in the fourteenth minute when a centre from Fagan, easily the best forward on the field, eluded Gibson and **Billy Mac**, who'd hardly touched the ball until then, swept it into the net. City had a similar chance a minute later, Charlton being at fault this time, but Barlow's shot from a narrow angle went straight to the goalkeeper. City then had the better of things until half time with Fagan, Barlow and Johnstone peppering the goal but were kept at bay rather more by good luck than good management.

Jack Charlton

When Leeds did attack they tried to walk the ball into the net, but this was meat and drink to Ewing. At the other end City won corner after corner and just after half time Barnes headed one smartly, the goalkeeper dropped the ball and Barlow rammed it home, but the goal was disallowed for some obscure reason.

Leeds started to show more spirit but lacked punch and the game finished disappointedly.

FINAL SCORE: CITY 1 LEEDS 0.

City: Sky blue/white: Trautmann; Leivers, Sear; Barnes, Ewing, Warhurst; Fagan, Barlow, Johnstone, McAdams, Sambrook.
Leeds: Blue and gold shirts/white knickers: Roy Wood; Dunn, Hair ; Gibson, Charlton, Kerfoot; Crowe, Peyton, Baird, O'Brien, Meek.
Attendance: A surprisingly low 21,962
Average: 33,034
Referee: G.W.Pullin, (Bristol)
Linesmen: A. Lord, L.D.D.Maddock
League Position: Up to Fourth
Goals For 90 Against 90
Reserves: Lost 2-0 at Everton

Leeds took the drop in 1960, despite having future World Cup winning centre half Jack Charlton and Billy Bremner in the team. Rebuilt under Don Revie, they came up in '64 and became a major force in football, winning the league, cups, the Fairs Cup and reached the European cup final twice, but lost or were robbed each time. Hard times again in the 80's but took the title in '92. Overstretched themselves in the Premiership, hit financial meltdown and are striving to escape the Coca-Cola first (old third).

LEAGUE TABLE

	P	W	D	L	F	A	Pts
Wolves	35	24	7	4	91	42	55
Preston	35	22	5	8	88	46	49
WBA	36	16	13	7	81	60	45
Man City	**36**	**18**	**5**	**13**	**90**	**90**	**41**
Luton	36	17	6	13	62	50	40
Spurs	36	16	8	12	81	72	40
Blackpool	35	16	6	13	70	57	38
Man Utd	33	15	7	11	76	59	37
Burnley	35	17	3	15	66	65	37
Notts For	35	15	6	14	65	54	36
Chelsea	36	13	8	15	76	65	34
Arsenal	36	15	4	17	67	75	34
Bolton	35	13	8	14	57	71	34
Everton	35	11	11	13	55	62	33
B'ham	36	11	10	15	61	82	32
Portsmouth	35	11	7	17	64	72	29
Aston Villa	35	12	5	18	61	78	29
Leeds	36	11	6	19	44	59	28
Newcastle	34	11	5	18	59	65	27
Leicester	36	11	5	20	77	97	27
Sunderland	36	8	11	17	44	84	27
Sheff Wed	36	10	6	20	62	82	26

CONCLUSION: Two home wins, one loss, one draw. Away one win, one friendly win, one loss, fourth place with forty one points and ninety goals both for and against! Up from tenth to fourth place. Average home attendance: 33,029 Away 31,777. Debut for Roy Cheetham at Luton and Peter Leigh in the friendly at Derby. Johnny Hart made his come back but Jack Dyson broke his leg again.

APRIL'S FOOTBALL MONTHLY

Charles Buchan's FOOTBALL MONTHLY

Gerry Summers of Sheffield United was on the front cover, and John Watkins of Bristol City on the back cover. CB's editorial opinion reckoned the World Cup could come to Britain. Reported that ex Blue Ivor Broadis became a manager at Carlisle then reverted back to being a player, at City.

Post-War MAINE ROAD Semi-Finals

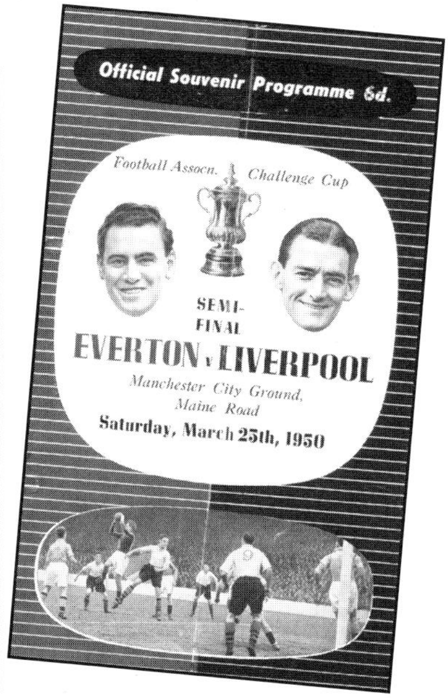

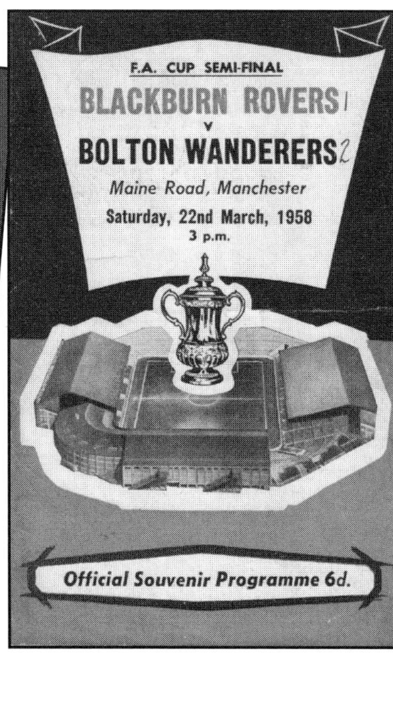

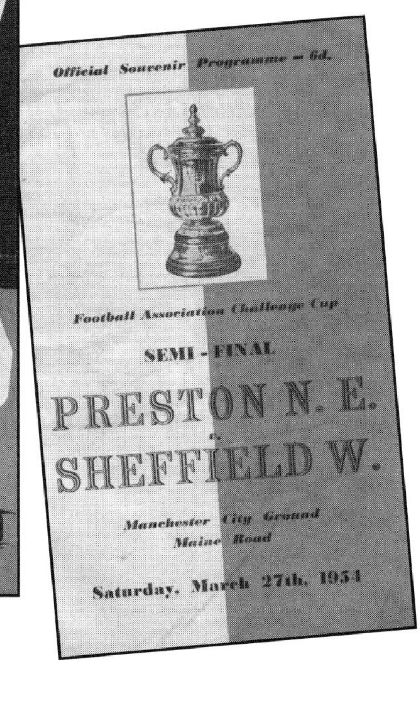

Once A Blue, Always A Blue

PHIL from Marple Bridge's story:

In the beginning, I was the victim of a wicked deception. To an impressionable seven year old results were everything. The pull of the treble triumph over our friends and neighbours - two league (5-0 at OT) and fourth round FA Cup en route to Wembley was all too enticing to resist. How satisfying it was to follow the fortunes of a winning team, attractive and tactically trendy (the Revie plan was all the rage). The honey-trap had been set. Seduced by success!

In matters of football allegiance, sons so often follow their fathers. Dad (a Derby County fan from Burton on Trent who saw Frank Swift make his debut for City at the Baseball Ground on Christmas Day 1933) and I were different. I converted HIM! I apologise to Mum and Dad (who at the ages of eighty five and eighty four respectively continue to renew their season tickets) for the traumas my obsession has visited upon them and on the whole family who are booked for life on the rockiest roller-coaster ride of all time.

In those early days, my (over) protective parents prevented me from travelling to matches alone (four buses on the round trip from Middleton) and mid-week matches were out of the question during term time. All this meant that appearances in the 1950's depended upon coaxing (pestering more like!) Dad to leave Mum and my much younger siblings to their own devices. The 1957/58 season was no exception. We would catch the football special from Aytoun Street (the 76x). We never had a car and always travelled by bus. I recall particularly the long queues after the match near a building which De Lasalle lads in the mid-sixties referred to as "Poyser's Purgatory".

Nothing could match the anticipation as we set off on the second leg of our journey as the overloaded old bus trundled into Cambridge Street (I think we passed the site of the burnt down Pauldens Store). Eventually we would turn into Lloyd Street North and catch a glimpse of the floodlights over the rooftops. There was the sound of supporters rattles echoing around the streets, there were rows and rows of bikes stored in yards off the narrow alleyways. Once inside the ground there was the distinctive smell of tobacco in the stand, the sound of the Beswick Prize Band (on the pitch but huddled together close to the main stand) occasionally accompanied by a "vocalist" called Sylvia Farmer. I remember the sight of the sea of faces out on the open Claremont Road end, the flag-pole beside the scoreboard which was a brick-built distinctive structure and the rows upon rows of wet rooftops beyond and the recently covered Kippax with a small structure on top advertising "Booth Steelwork of Bolton". Above all there was the thrill of the roar of the crowd when the team first emerged from the tunnel in their sky blue shirts, white shorts and hooped socks. The numbers on the shirts were red in those days.

In was a topsy-turvy season '57/58 and, for City, a season for setting records - 100 goals scored and conceded, Ken Barnes's hat-trick of penalties, a match I was particularly miffed to miss. It was a season of bizarre score-lines culminating in the odd sensation of losing at home to Villa on the last day yet feeling quite proud that in conceding two goals a record had been achieved - an eccentricity, quirkiness appealing even to a boy of ten. Those big losses at Preston and West Brom (another tactical plan) fifteen goals conceded in three days. Particularly memorable and propitious was the 5-1 defeat of Tottenham (we trounced them twice by the same score in successive seasons at Maine Road) a match perhaps an augury for three of the greatest performances in the Club's history (the two on snow and ice and the Cup replay come-back miracle). The Autumn '57 Maine Road match against Spurs was one of the many free-scoring encounters of a season which epitomised the eccentricity, the charm and the frustration of our tantalising team and its capacity to delight and irritate in equal measure. It was the embodiment of so many of the characteristics to which we have become accustomed and addicted. The die was truly cast.

Some random reminiscences of the 1957/58 Season:

I was a regular reader of Charles Buchan's Football Monthly and joined the C B Boys' Club that season. The Club motto (from memroy) has served me well:

"Be modest in victory and cheerful in defeat, support your team in good times and in bad. Use your skills to the best of your ability"

I distinctly recall cigarette adverts over the tannoy system - (in particular "never go without a Capstan"). In those days announcements over the public address system were deadpan and businesslike with not the faintest trace of razzmatazz and certainly no prattle from any 'MC'. Teams were never introduced and mention of team news was strictly confined to a formal announcement of changes to the team as printed in the match programme. There was no crowd segregation. It was an era when opposing fans could stand side by side and shout for their respective teams without kicking each others' heads in. It was a simpler and in some ways tougher world in which people were brought up to cope with disappointment and to live with it without throwing dummies out of prams.

As ever, autographs hunters would gather outside the players' entrance. I remember Joe Hayes getting off a bus and signing and the famous Stanley Matthews (put 10,000 on the gate) declining. (I was to catch up with him some forty seasons later at a match at Stoke - Alan Ball's last in charge).

I somehow managed to avoid Asian flu in the widespread epidemic and finished top of the class when everybody else was ill.

There was the disappointment of defeat at West Brom in the FA Cup (F A Cup exits are always agonising moments). It was no consolation that the 5-1 defeat was an improvement defensively at least on the earlier league trip to the Hawthorns.

Notably, only two of the current premier league of 20 finished in the top eight in 1958. All statistics, however, paled into insignificance in the late afternoon of Thursday 6th February with the news from Germany. For me it was the first of the "remember where you were at the time moments" to which the Kennedy assassination, 9/11 and the death of Princess Diana were later to be added (I was playing with a train set at home 53 Crowhill North with a classmate called John Wilson who sadly was to die of cancer before reaching twenty). Reds and Blues alike were stunned. I shed a tear for them that night.

Phil and his family are all still season ticket holders and continue to follow the Blues home and away

CHAPTER TEN

APRIL 1958 - TON UP (AND DOWN)

So to the final month of the season, taking in the Easter period, with away games at Newcastle, Bolton, and Everton, plus home games with Newcastle, Sunderland, and Villa....

The game at Newcastle on Good Friday April 4th was postponed due to poor ground conditions, and the programme for this game is now valued at around £800.

Doncaster Rovers wonder boy Alick Jeffrey was set to join United for £17,000 but broke a leg and later was given a testimonial v City in the early 70's.
Jack Dyson is to have an operation including a bone graft.
Tom Finney wrote an article saying that TV was killing soccer and should be brought under control.
Apprentices Alan Oakes and Mike Pearson signed

37) SATURDAY APRIL 5TH 1958
K.O. 3PM: BOLTON WANDERERS (AWAY)

Programme was 3d for eight pages. The front cover was an improvement on previous issues with a blueish tinge and ground photo on the front. There were plenty of stats and adverts, plus a 'Welcome To our Neighbours' page and a half, with a history of City and 'Personalities' pen pics of the players. For example Bobby Johnstone described as: "brains" of the attack, not very flattering for the rest of 'em?!

There was a brief note re sale of Cup Final tickets, but no big deal was made of their prospective Wembley appearance.

Burnden Park's record attendance was set in the F.A.Cup fifth round of 1933, against City, 69,912 (which we won 4-2). The ground was the subject of the famous Lowry painting 'Going To The Match' where the crowd on the Lever Street terrace looked like they were going to drop onto the pitch at any moment. This was now covered. The main stand was on Manchester Road, which was the standard covered seating and paddock terrace with a kinked bit on the end linked up to the Lever Street stand behind the goal. Opposite was a covered seats and terrace stand, and behind the goal was a huge embankment, part concrete, part cinders and railway sleepers. It was at this end that thirty three people died when fans stormed the gates and overcrowded the terrace causing crushing, in a cup game v Stoke in 1946, (My Dad was at the opposite end). An England v Scotland benefit match was staged at Maine Road for the dependants of the victims. It was also halved in the 70's to make way for a Supermarket, and they moved to the Reebok in the 90's. Most notable feature was the advert on the stands inviting you to 'Dine At The Pack Horse Hotel, in Nelson Square' - we managed to do so once in about 1964. The pitch was raised, so the opposition players could be deposited off it by full-backs Banks and Hartle, Tommy's catchphrase being "If my winger gets past me Roy, chip him back to me" and there was a perimeter fence a bit like United's.

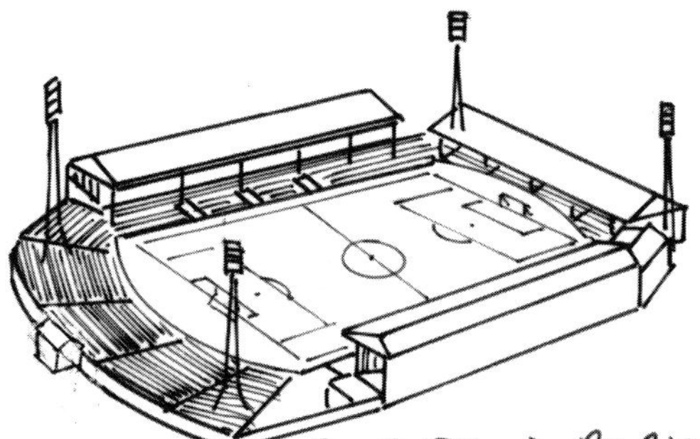

Pitch Size: 113 x 76 yds

Bolton, managed by Bill Ridding were thirteenth with thirty four points and City fourth with forty one points? At home they'd won seven including United 4-0 and Villa 4-0 yesterday, drawn four, and lost five including a 1-5 to Everton. Away they'd won five, drawn three, and lost nine including a 1-5 at Birmingham, 2-7 at United, a 1-6 at Wolves, and 1-2 to us.

At Bolton: Pre-war we'd only managed three wins and hadn't won there for seven games. Post we'd won just the once, the 3-1 in 55/56 (at which I was present, when a City fan reckoned we were going to do what we did in 1936/37, i.e. not lose another game and win the title - but I didn't know that at the time - in the event we finished fourth.), losing seven and drawing one.

Recent attendances ranged from 20,865 (56/57) to 43,706 (55/56). It was the sixty eighth league meeting plus two cup finals and six other cup ties, five at Bolton, 1898 second rd. 0-1 (14,000), 1922 second rd. 3-1 (66,442), 1933 fifth rd. 4-2 (66,912), 1937 second rd. 5-0 (60,979), 1947 fourth rd. 3-3 (41,286).

Team News: Hayes in for McAdams.

From The Guardian's Eric Todd:

It was a grey, cheerless afternoon and City and Bolton provided a mixed feast for a frozen crowd where City won the game 2-0 with the minimum of trouble. There was drama, farce, and even a touch of the supernatural when the goalkeepers vanished from sight amid the smoke from passing railway engines, but not for long. Bert was troubled on only two occasions, once when he underestimated his own strength and threw the ball upfield and Stevens from thirty yards hit it back towards the goal whereupon Bert projected himself sideways and made a one handed save. Near the end he had Birch shaking his head in disbelief as he leapt to flick away his beautiful shot out of harms way. Dean had more work to do especially when Hennin pulled a muscle and retired from active service, but Banks and Hartle covered well. The Bolton keeper faltered only once, in the nineteenth minute, when he fumbled the ball from a fierce cross drive by Hayes and **Barlow** whipped it into the net. He had no chance of saving **Barlow's** second goal on sixty five minutes when Edwards missed his kick and Colin, City's liveliest forward, scored with a hard drive from close range, the ball going in off the post. Bolton never looked like scoring but it was an entertaining game until degenerating from being a 'rich banquet' to 'bubble and squeak' up to the interval. One highlight was the referee being struck amidships by the ball - always good for a laugh. Second half Bolton's ten men tried with commendable enthusiasm but Leivers, Sear,

DOUG HOLDEN

Barnes and Warhurst were on top form and Johnstone was performing midfield magic.

But if all else is forgotten one will long remember the impact on the game - and one or two Bolton players - of Ewing - eighteen hands high, broad in the rump, strong in fetlock and pattern, quite indefatigable and seeking nothing but justice and an occasional kind word. From the moment he collided with Gubbins, the luckless Bolton man must have thought he'd run into a bus - Ewing was damned in the eyes of the spectators. They hooted when he used his weight to bowl over their favourites, they mocked when he appealed to the referee for a throw in and when he telescoped his neck to head from an upright or genuflective position, and they cheered delightedly when he nearly beat Trautmann with the best header of the afternoon. Unorthodox and thoroughly effective.

To his credit Ewing bore it all with a cheerful shrug, for suffrance is the badge of all centre halves especially when they are all so well endowed physically by a generous nature. And let it be remembered that, cumbersome and clumsy though he may be, Ewing has not a shred of malice in his massive frame."

FINAL SCORE: BOLTON 0 CITY 2

Bolton: White shirts/blue shorts:Dean; Hartle, Banks; Stanley, Higgins, Edwards; Birch, Stevens, Hennin, Gubbins, Holden.
City: Sky Blue/white:Trautmann ; Leivers, Sear; Barnes, Ewing, Warhurst ; Fagan, Barlow, Hayes, Johnstone, Sambook
Attendance: 27,733 **Average:** 31,777
Referee: K.Howley (Middlesbrough)
Linesmen: A.Edge (Liverpool), S.Gandy (Chester)
League Position: Stayed Fifth
Goals For: 92 Against: 90
Reserves: Lost 3-1 at home to Barnsley

Bolton finished fifteenth with thirty eight points. They did, of course win the F.A.Cup beating United 2-0. Billy McAdams joined them in September 1960. After that it was downhill all the way, relegation in 1964, transferring Franny Lee to City, then Freddie Hill, down to the third in 1971, promotion in 1973, back to division one in 1978, then down in 1980, eventually to the 4th and back, but now established in the Premiership.

38) EASTER MONDAY APRIL 7TH K.O. 3PM: NEWCASTLE UNITED (HOME)

Newcastle were formed in 1882. They won the league four times, in 1905, 07, 09 and 1927, and the cup six times, in 1910, 1924, 1932, 1951, 1952, and 1955, runners up four times.

Programme editorial thought this could be City's best season since the war, and only once have we been better placed at the start of the Easter programme, in 1956 when third with forty points. We faltered once again then, as we did in previous seasons, over the tough three games in four days period, finally finishing fourth. We were reminded too that fourth this season would be twice as good as fourth in 1956 for the players as talent money was doubled last summer.

Maine Road Gossip reviewed City and Newcastle past encounters, then reminded us that Russia's favourite referee Mr Arthur Ellis of Halifax would be refereeing the Jimmy

Meadows benefit fund game, now rescheduled for April 28th due to United playing Wolves on the 21st (which they lost 4-0).

In Sportsman's Corner G.A.N. Borrowdale was informed that City's first Maine Road floodlit game was v Hearts in October 1953, which we won 6-3. Henry Firth of Wythenshawe was advised that Roy Paul and Roy Clarke had both played for Wales twenty times.

Arthur Walmsley reflected on the City players who have switched positions since joining the Blues, including Meadows, Revie, Hayes, Leivers, Marsden, and now Colin Barlow, he of the wholehearted enthusiasm and thrilling speed. Colin had switched from the wing to inside but Arthur accepted that he may have to return to his wing position, but that he'd already, in his first season, proved his versatility.

David Jack bemoaned the fact that both Newcastle and Sunderland were struggling, and might both take the drop. Newcastle, he thought, were potentially the best supported team in Britain, 60,000 crowds being commonplace in the good old days, and the Geordies' real test of support was shown in away fixtures when thousands used to stream from Tyneside regardless of the distance or discomfort involved. He regretted that Newcastle were no longer a power, having bought, sold, found and even squandered more talented players than any club since the war. Now, David says, they're struggling. Attendances have dropped and interest on soccer crazy Tyneside has decreased, but whilst a gloomy picture it's certainly not the end, and football would be the richer for both Newcastle and Sunderland's revival.

Train to Glasgow for Scotland v England 46/9d.

Newcastle, managed by two Directors were struggling in nineteenth place with twenty seven points, and City were fourth with forty one points? At home they'd won five including a 5-3 v Leicester drawn four, lost nine including a 3-1 defeat at home to Scunthorpe in the fourth round of the Cup, and 4-1 to Forest. Away they'd won seven including 4-1 at Birmingham and 6-1 in the third round of the cup at Plymouth.

At City: Pre-war we had one loss in the last six, and won 5-1 in 1931/32. Post we'd lost the last two, and also the 1957 F.A.Cup third rd. replay 5-4 (46,988). Recent attendances ranged from 22,860 (55/56) to 48,624 48/49). It was the eighty fifth league meeting, plus three cup ties, the 1924 semi-final 0-2 (50,039), 1955 cup final 1-3, and 1957 third rd. replay..

Team News: Unchanged

From The Guardian's Eric Todd: Newcastle Move A Step Nearer Relegation - Splendid Game By Scouler

Newcastle's relegation coffin was taken a step nearer completion at Moss Side when City won a most entertaining match 2-1. Newcastle though looked like being a most reluctant corpse and they may yet be in a position to transfer the aforementioned coffin to one of their neighbours. However there was nothing desperate about their play and they had the hardest worker on view in Scoular who for several years has contrived to reserve his best performances for the approval of City supporters both at home and away and who in spite of a thinning thatch looks like going on for many more years. He played Hayes and Sambrook out of the game, supplied the passes for his forwards and when necessary took over as marksman. At the end of the game he should have been given the ball as a memento as he shook hands with as many City players as he could find and was cheered all the way home. A great character and a fine footballer.

Jimmy Scoular

Hayes put City ahead with a great header in the twenty sixth minute. Sambrook was denied a goal when Simpson pushed the ball against the inside of a post and cleared after an astute piece of juggling, with the crowd claiming it had crossed the line. **Warhurst** scored his first for City in the sixtieth minute. At one point Bert was bundled into the net by three Newcastle players ball and all, and the ref gave a free kick. This was taken quickly, it hit a City player on the back and bounced back into the net for another free kick despite Newcastle protests.

Len White who turned down a chance to join City for £15,000 from Rotherham and joined Newcastle for £12,000 instead, scored a magnificent solo goal beating four City players (Ewing, Warhurst, Sear, Trautmann) in the sixty sixth minute, and City supporters who appreciate genius when they see it gave White a merited ovation. City pressed hard, and Simpson was having a charmed life in Newcastle's goal as the shots rained in. Leivers and Sear (delighted when Scoular singled him out for a commendatory wave) Barlow and Hayes all played well but the latter two missed chances. Johnstone distributed superbly and Ewing distinguished himself as a purveyor of accurate and pre-meditated passes, but his colleagues could only stand and watch in admiration. Finally the referee deserved a fair share of the credit, giving gestures when he awarded free kicks including a wiggle of his posterior to indicate obstruction. City would hope to see Newcastle again next season. Now for Sunderland.

LEN WHITE

FINAL SCORE: CITY 2 NEWCASTLE 1

City: Sky Blue/White: Trautmann; Leivers, Sear; Barnes, Ewing, Warhurst; Fagan, Barlow, Johnstone, Hayes, Sambrook
Newcastle: Black and white striped shirts/black knickers:Simpson; Keith, McMichael; Scouler, Stokoe, Franks; Hughes, Bottom, White, Curry, Mitchell
Attendance: 33,995 **Average:** 33,085
Referee: F.B.Coultas (Hull)
Linesmen: C.S.Wilkinson, J.Tracey
League Position: Fifth
Goals For: 94 Against: 91
Reserves: No game

F.A.Amateur Cup Final: Woking 1 Ilford 0

Keith, McMichael, Stokoe and Simpson can do nothing about this header from Hayes.

39) SATURDAY APRIL 12TH K.O. 3 PM: SUNDERLAND (HOME)

Programme editorial reflected on the Easter games, City picking up full points but playing one game less due to the Newcastle postponement. WBA dropped five out of six points but Spurs are up there too. City, considering Newcastle's poor home record, could do well on Tyneside and a result today could put both North Eastern clubs in big trouble - that would be ironic as the first division would lose some glamour, and affect the "missing millions."

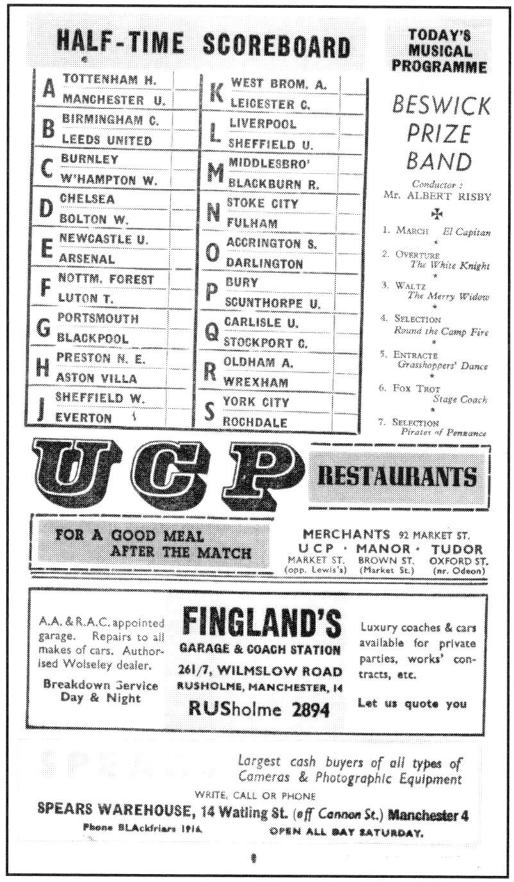

HALF-TIME SCOREBOARD

A	TOTTENHAM H. / MANCHESTER U.	K	WEST BROM. A. / LEICESTER C.
B	BIRMINGHAM C. / LEEDS UNITED	L	LIVERPOOL / SHEFFIELD U.
C	BURNLEY / W'HAMPTON W.	M	MIDDLESBRO' / BLACKBURN R.
D	CHELSEA / BOLTON W.	N	STOKE CITY / FULHAM
E	NEWCASTLE U. / ARSENAL	O	ACCRINGTON S. / DARLINGTON
F	NOTTM. FOREST / LUTON T.	P	BURY / SCUNTHORPE U.
G	PORTSMOUTH / BLACKPOOL	Q	CARLISLE U. / STOCKPORT C.
H	PRESTON N. E. / ASTON VILLA	R	OLDHAM A. / WREXHAM
J	SHEFFIELD W. / EVERTON	S	YORK CITY / ROCHDALE

TODAY'S MUSICAL PROGRAMME

BESWICK PRIZE BAND

Conductor : Mr. ALBERT RISBY

1. MARCH *El Capitan*
2. OVERTURE *The White Knight*
3. WALTZ *The Merry Widow*
4. SELECTION *Round the Camp Fire*
5. ENTRACTE *Grasshoppers' Dance*
6. FOX TROT *Stage Coach*
7. SELECTION *Pirates of Penzance*

Maine Road Gossip reviewed Sunderland's form at Maine Road, and confirmed that Roy Paul and Don Revie should be playing in the Jimmy Meadows' testimonial game.

Season ticket holders were reminded that the form in the back of their books should be retained pending the receipt of the usual notice to be sent out in May re details of 1958/59 season tickets.

In Sportsman's Corner H.Williams of Moss Side asked which teams would Bobby Johnstone be playing against in the World Cup in Sweden. He was advised that Group two included Scotland, France, Paraguay, and Yugoslavia. Details of the other groups were also given.

Arthur Walmsley looked forward to the visit of Sunderland, the only first division team never to be relegated since joining in 1890/1891, but looking dodgy this season. Also for the return of Don Revie (called a traitor by City fans outside the players entrance before the game) and the reminder of our Wembley visits in 1955 and 1956. Our cup winning team had lost five of those players, but turning to the present, Arthur thought that the swift turnover and the team's performances makes this season an extremely satisfying one by any standards and could well have laid the foundations of a most promising future.

Derrick Collier (no David Jack?) reckoned that the third division clubs in the bottom half, particularly those in the southern sections were now not so sure about the prospect of the new third and fourth divisions. He could see clubs going bankrupt and withdrawing from the league.

Train to Liverpool six shillings.

Sunderland were struggling in twentieth place with twenty eight points, whilst City were fifth with forty five points. Away they'd won two (Spurs, Birmingham) drawn four and lost twelve including 0-7 at Blackpool, 1-7 at Luton, 0-6 at Burnley and 0-5 at Wolves. At home they'd won six (including 2-1 v City) drawn six, lost seven including a 1-6 v Birmingham. They went out of the cup in the third rd. to Everton, 1-3 after 2-2 at Roker.

At City: Pre-war we'd drawn one and lost two of the last three. Post we'd lost 5-2 in 52/53, but otherwise won seven and drawn one. Recent attendances ranged from 23,742 (53/54) to 60,611(54/55). It was the eighty second league meeting, plus four cup ties, two at City, 1904 first rd. 3-2 (23,000), 1913 second rd. 0-0 abandoned in ET (41,709) and the 1955 semi-final 1-0 at Villa. (58,498).

Team News: Hart in for Johnstone.

From The Pink/Green (Ray Wergen): Hart-breaker For Sunderland

Sunderland were first on the attack on a firm Maine Road pitch, with shots from Revie, O'Neill and a cross from Grainger which Bert collected, whilst Sear cleared with a flying header. Bollands turned Barlow's cross away, and the winger then hit the post, but City went ahead in the twelfth minute when Hart fed Fagan and when Bollands dropped the winger's shot, **Hart** moved in rapidly and fired it home from a couple of yards range for a great comeback goal.

It was fast, entertaining stuff in the first half-hour as City started to dictate and should have had more goals. City had a penalty appeal turned down for a foul by Elliott on Barlow. Sunderland were pressing and equalised in the forty fourth minute when Ewing leapt high to clear but misjudged his header to let in **Kitchenbrand** who was round him in a flash and slipped the ball confidently round Trautmann into the net.

Don Kichenbrand

Sunderland took heart at the interval with the news that Newcastle were losing 3-1 at Arsenal and City tailing off in the first half but went behind again when Sambrook took the ball to the bye-line before crossing through a crowd of Sunderland players for **Hayes** to shoot past Bollands in the fiftieth minute. City's forwards put further pressure on Sunderland and made it 3-1 when Barlow's shot was blocked by Bollands and **Hayes** was on hand to pick up the loose ball to slam it into the net on seventy two minutes.

FINAL SCORE: CITY 3 SUNDERLAND 1

City: Sky blue/white: Trautmann; Leivers, Sear; Barnes, Ewing, Warhurst; Fagan, Barlow, Hart, Hayes, Sambrook
Sunderland: Red and white stripes/black knickers: Bollands (just signed from Oldham); Hedley, Elliott; Anderson, Hurley, Pearce; Fogarty, Revie, Kitchenbrand, O'Neill,Grainger (the singing winger)
Attendance: 31,166 **Average:** 32,989
League Position: Fifth
Goals For: 97 Against: 92
Reserves: Lost at Sheff U. 5-1 on April 12th

Sunderland did get relegated that year, for the first time in their history. Of the players Billy Elliott (yes) later returned to manage the club. They came back up in '64 down again in 1970. Won the cup in '73 beating us on the way, then selling us Tueart, Horswill and Watson. Ups and downs from then, reached a couple of finals and moved to The Stadium Of Light and are currently back in the Premiership with ex Blue Niall Quinn as Chairman but Keane as manager.

40) MONDAY APRIL 14TH 1958
K.O. 7.30PM: NEWCASTLE UNITED (AWAY)

This was the re-arranged game from April 4th , and a great chance for City to overtake Spurs and West Brom in the table.

Programme was a small size and 3d for sixteen pages, not as good as recent issues, and the front cover had a ground drawing on it from the terrace behind the goal, looking out of proportion to reality.

Gallowgate Gossip thought that Newcastle would survive, even though they lost both Easter games at Blackpool and City. Situation helped by Sunderland and Sheffield Wednesday 'floundering' though "every Geordie will be sad to see the Wearsiders go, and for the North East to lose another 'derby'." (Hmm..... times change)

The rest was just ads and stats, absolutely nothing on City, apart from a pic of Joe's header last week, and the original programme was no different.

The back page gave reasons why fans should join the supporters club and claimed that it was because of the massed voice of the supporters clubs that Parliament amended the laws relating to Small Lottery Schemes, "the revenue from which are so vital to the maintenance of British Football."

St. James' Park's record attendance was 68,386 v Chelsea in Div 1 1930/31 season. I didn't make it here until April 1960, our last away game of that season, when after eleven fruitless journeys I at last managed to see City win an away game, 1-0.
Main Stand was a seated job with a paddock in

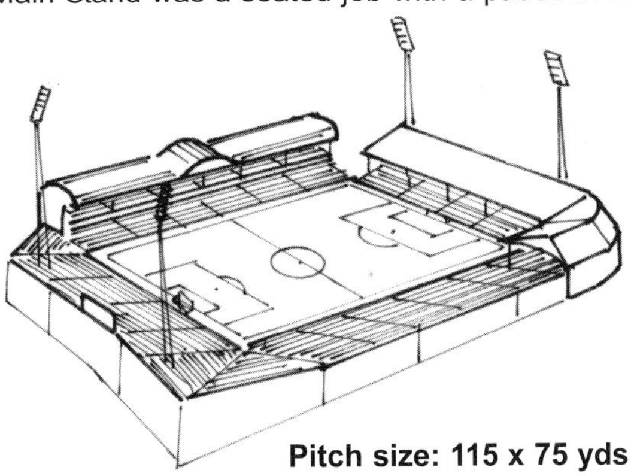

Pitch size: 115 x 75 yds

front, and barrel type roof with a gabled press box. On the rear of this stand were the massive letters NEWCASTLE UNITED. There was an open terrace opposite, and also behind the goal, the Gallowgate end (for those with Gallows humour). Behind the other goal was a ramshackle terrace, with a roof that just turned the corner. This was later demolished for safety reasons and it was years before the ground was eventually upgraded to its present magnificent state.

Newcastle were twentieth with twenty eight points but had three games in hand over their nearest rivals Sunderland. City were fifth with forty seven points. At home Newcastle were poor. They'd won five, drawn three, lost nine.

At Newcastle: Pre-war we'd got a win and a draw in the last two, post, we won 3-0 last season, but lost all seven of the others. It was the eighty sixth league meeting plus three cup ties, one at Newcastle, 1957 third rd. 1-1 (57,890).

Team News: Leivers at five for Ewing, Branagan in at full back.

From The Guardian:
Spirited Rally By Newcastle

The game was played under Newcastle's new £45,000 lights, which City must have found it hard to adjust to, going down 4-1. Newcastle delighted the crowd with a fast skilful display. **Davies** opened the scoring after only five minutes, drawing Trautmann from goal. **Roy Warhurst** equalised after thirty nine mins. with a splendid cross shot. **White**, inevitably, made it two, running through from his own half, then scoring from twelve yards, in the fifty fifth minute, then made it three after seventy one mins with **Franks** finishing it off in the eighty eighth minute.

Ron Simpson

FINAL SCORE: NEWCASTLE 4 CITY 1.

Attendance: 53,326 (Despite David Jack's concern - last home game it was 16,570)
Average: 32,652.
Referee: J.Cook (Pontefact)
Linesmen: G.W.Ward (Selby), W.T.Surtees (Langley Park)
League Position: Stayed Fifth
Goals For: 98 Against: 96
Reserves: Lost 5-1 at Sheff.United on April 12th

Newcastle finished the season in nineteenth place with thirty two points. Of their players, goalie Ronnie Simpson went on to become a Lisbon Lion winning the European Cup with Celtic in 1967, and Bob Stokoe managed Sunderland's F.A.Cup win in 1973. They were relegated in 1961, came up in 1965, won the Fairs cup in 1969, a year after we won the title 4-3 on Tyneside. Lost the '73 Cup final, and the '76 league cup final, to us, 2-1. Took the drop, Keegan came, nearly went down to the third, revived in the 90's with Keegan as manager and are now a force in the Prem., but haven't won a domestic trophy since the '55 cup win.

Jack Dyson was hoping to play cricket in the Lancashire Minor Counties League after his bone graft operation.

City may bid for Bob McMichael from Accrington at £15,000 or Alex Parker from Falkirk for £15,000.
Trautmann and Gregg could be up for Player of the Year, eventually won by Danny Blanchflower.
Frank Swift, who was a Director of a firm of caterers and confectioners left £3,592.
Busby now out of hospital.

Billy Meredith died on 19th April at his daughters home in Withington, at the age of eighty one. Bill won all the honours possible in the game, and took part in more International matches than any other player. He played for Wales regularly from 1895 to 1920. City from 1894 to 1904, scoring the winner in the cup final v Bolton, and for United from 1906 to 1915. He then went back to City until 1925, playing in the F.A.Cup semi-final at 49 years of age.

Home International: Wales 1 N.Ireland 1, Cardiff (38,000).
Joe Hayes named in World Cup 40.
City reserves v England forty minute practice match Kirkman scored two in the fifth and tenth minute.
Home International: Scotland 0 England 4, Hampden Park (127,000).

41) SATURDAY APRIL 19TH 1958
K.O. 3.15 PM: EVERTON (AWAY)

Programme was 3d for twelve pages. Front cover was an impressive dark blue with a nice shot of Goodison Park, before the floodlights went up. Evertonia gave a cordial welcome to City, who were also Everton's last league visitors last season, and thought that but for one or two short periods when nothing went right we could have been challenging Wolves for the title. There was a comprehensive page on City's history, pen pics of our boys, details of season tickets 1958/59 - Ground £2.10s, members stand £6.6s. Stats., ads, full page photo of City (at Blackpool) but the cartoon feature from previous programmes had sadly disappeared.

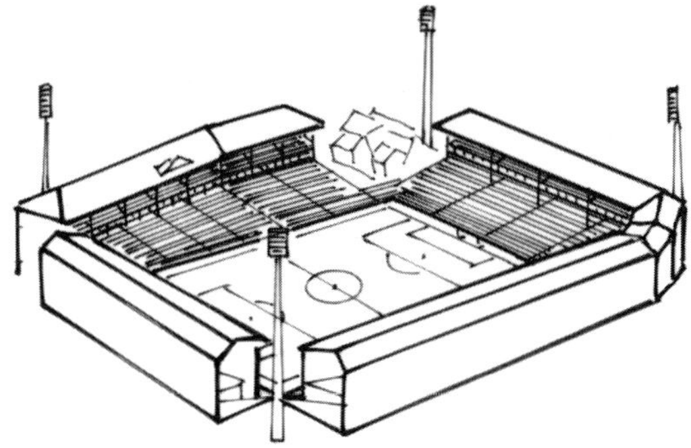

Pitch size: 112 x 78 yds

Goodison Park's record attendance was 78,299 but didn't look that big. There were four impressive double decker stands, the main stand having a decent sized terrace in front and underneath, this petered out to suit the road layout. There was also a Church, similar to that at Maine Road in the corner, still standing. The main stand was replaced in the early 70's and the Park End in the early 90's, but only cosmetic changes made to the other two. So time for a move?

Everton were seventeenth with thirty three points and City fifth with forty seven points. At home they'd won five, drawn nine lost six. Away they'd won six including 5-1 at Bolton, drawn two lost eleven including the 2-6 at Maine Road. They went out of the cup in the fourth rd. 1-2 at home to Blackburn.

At Goodison: Pre-war we'd lost two and drawn one of the last three. Had a 6-2 win in 28/29, and lost 1-9 in 1907 and 1-6 in 23/24. Post, not one win, drawing three losing thrree.

Recent attendances ranged from 20,457 (54/55) to 53,822 (47/48). It was the seventy fourth league meeting plus one cup final and two cup ties, one at Everton 1949 third rd. 0-1 (63,459).

Team News: Unchanged. Johnstone and Ewing (flu) still out so no confrontation with Everton's bustling leader Hickson, much to the dismay of many Evertonians - step in Bill Leivers! Everton had lost five games in a row.

We arrived at Lime Street station and all had a good laugh outside at the nude statues up above. Little things and all that. At he ground we took our places on the Gladwys Street terrace, which quickly became jam-packed.

From The Pink (Ray Wergen)/Green (Harry Hancock):
Two In Two Minutes Rock City - Hundredth City Goal By Hart

Everton kicked off under perfect conditions on a bone hard pitch and straight away went ahead through **Ashworth**, scoring his first league goal after one minute flashing a left foot shot past Bert's right hand into the corner of the net. The crowd were still buzzing when two minutes later **Ashworth** burst through past Leivers and sent a terrific shot that again had Trautmann dizzy. After seven minutes Sear cleared off the line. "At least it gives us time to pull it round" someone said, and we all agreed, disbelievingly.

Then City started to come into the game with Barnes dominating. Warhurst's 'big boot' found Barlow who drew Dunlop and nodded the ball to **Hayes** who was on his own on the left in the twenty fourth minute and he made the most of his chance with a shot that Dunlop hardly saw. City were certainly having their share of the game now and, in fact, they had taken command. Leivers earned some boos for checking Hickson who looked peeved and the referee had a word with Bill.

JOHNNY HART

The game was marred by a series of petty fouls and the light bouncy ball made control difficult. Luck was with City though as they ended the half on level terms. Good work near the half way line by Barnes and Fagan sent the ball up to the City attack. Centre-forward **Hart** gained possession on the edge of the penalty area, moved forward a few steps, beat off a challenge from an Everton defender and then picked his spot before crashing the ball past the dumbfounded Dunlop into the net, for City's one hundredth goal of the season.

Half time and the rivulets of urine splashed down the terrace, though I didn't see anyone peeing into rolled up programmes placed in the bloke in front's pocket (but I knew that was common practice). I thought I was working class until today.

The Blues restarted facing the sun, and after an Everton attack was repelled, showed great fighting spirit after the early set backs, and went ahead as Barlow's header crashed against the crossbar and to Everton's dismay **Hart** latched on to it, whipping through and putting the ball over the line on forty eight minutes

Trautmann made a great save from Hickson then City went further ahead when, after a combined forward effort, **Sambrook** was the man who shot past Dunlop in the fifty second minute. Barlow was in fine form and City got their fifth when he (Hayes in another report) was fouled by Sanders in the area. **Barnes** stepped up to score his fourth spot kick against Dunlop this season in the fifty eighth minute, the ball rocketing into the back of the net where it stuck between the rigging and the support.

The scousers were apoplectic, and were all going to write in to the Echo, then suddenly the packed crowd opened up like Moses and the Red Sea, as an Everton supporter knocked seven bells out of a red headed City fan.

Strangely enough it was Everton who were now doing the pressing but City nearly made it six when Barlow tried to dribble round Dunlop but a desperate dive by the Everton 'keeper saved the day. Trautmann was called upon, twice pushing the ball over the bar, and both teams had chances but failed to increase the score in the final half hour.

The next season at Everton I myself was attacked, subsequently deciding it would be wise not to wear my colours at away games any more.

FINAL SCORE EVERTON 2 CITY 5

Everton: Blue jerseys/white shorts: Dunlop; Sanders, Tansey; King, Donovan, Meagan; Harris, Thomas, Hickson, Ashworth, Williams.
City: Maroon shirts/ white shorts: Trautmann; Banagan, Sear; Barnes, Leivers, Warhurst; Fagan, Barlow, Hart, Hayes, Sambrook
Attendance: 31,433 **Average:** 32,594
Referee: C.H.Sant (Crewe)
Linesmen: H.Burns, F.Carter
League position: Up to 4th place
Goals For:103 Against: 98
Reserves: Drew with Blackpool 1-1 at M/Rd

Everton: Finished in sixteenth place with thirty seven points. They won the league in 1963, again in 1970, and twice in the 80's, '85 and '87, runners up in '86. They won the Cup in '66, again in '84 and '95, and were runners up in '85, '86, and '89, plus being Euro Cup winners Cup winners in '85, and league Cup runners up in '77 and '84. Since then little cheer. Alec Ashworth moved to Luton and scored two against us in the '61 cup tie in the first twenty minutes, so déjà vu nearly as Denis popped in 6. But Alec scored another two in the re-arranged game to finish on the winning team 3-1.

The teams fought out some stirring cup matches in the sixth round of 1966, and City won the Villa Park semi-final 1-0 in 1969, Tommy Booth scoring, and stating later "we had a forward line of Bell, Lee, Young, Summerbee, Colman, and they had to rely on me to score!"

Wed. April 23rd: Wales U-23's 2 England 1 at Wrexham, 20,000 Joe Hayes played.

42) SATURDAY APRIL 26TH 1958 K.O. 3PM: ASTON VILLA (HOME)

So to the last match of the season, with a chance of our seventh double, and the possibility of finishing third if we won; if Spurs lost at home to Blackpool, and West Brom at home to Luton.

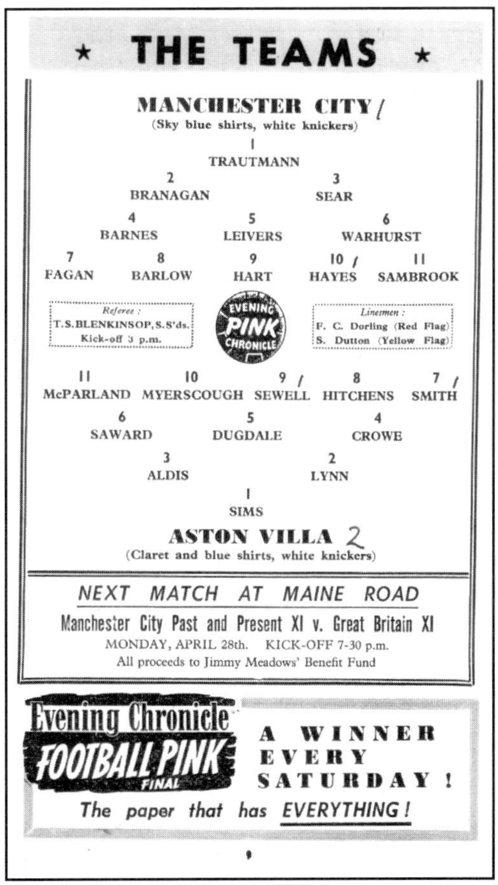

★ THE TEAMS ★

MANCHESTER CITY
(Sky blue shirts, white knickers)

1 TRAUTMANN

2 BRANAGAN — 3 SEAR

4 BARNES — 5 LEIVERS — 6 WARHURST

7 FAGAN — 8 BARLOW — 9 HART — 10 HAYES — 11 SAMBROOK

Referee: T.S.BLENKINSOP, S.S'ds. Kick-off 3 p.m.

EVENING PINK CHRONICLE

Linesmen: F. C. Dorling (Red Flag) S. Dutton (Yellow Flag)

11 McPARLAND — 10 MYERSCOUGH — 9 SEWELL — 8 HITCHENS — 7 SMITH

6 SAWARD — 5 DUGDALE — 4 CROWE

3 ALDIS — 2 LYNN

1 SIMS

ASTON VILLA
(Claret and blue shirts, white knickers)

NEXT MATCH AT MAINE ROAD
Manchester City Past and Present XI v. Great Britain XI
MONDAY, APRIL 28th. KICK-OFF 7-30 p.m.
All proceeds to Jimmy Meadows' Benefit Fund

Evening Chronicle FOOTBALL PINK FINAL
A WINNER EVERY SATURDAY!
The paper that has EVERYTHING!

Programme editorial philosophised on City being "the connoisseur who revels in the unpredictable, as a constant challenge to his imagination. This season we've been such people's delight with our brilliant football, great goals and our inordinate defensive lapses." The season's ups and owns were reviewed and the conclusion was "With such glorious nail biting un-certainty constantly on tap, small wonder that City fans are amongst the most faithful in the country."

Maine Road Gossip reviewed City and Villa's previous encounters, and noted that both clubs were in good form, City gaining eleven points out of the last seven games and Villa nine.

In Sportsman's Corner Ron Filey of Salford asked, "What is the record for gate receipts in any football match". It was Brazil v Uruguay in Rio in 1950, £125,000. Record in this country was £51,716, England v Germany in 1954. Where did the money go?

Arthur Walmsley thought that City had done well this season, in particular recovering from the injuries, which were offset by the emergence of Colin Barlow and Cliff Sear. Joe Hayes had matured, and Ray Sambrook, something of an enigma to City fans - a mixture of devastating brilliance and alarming casualness - could well prove to be the bargain of the season. Finally the return of Johnny Hart had rounded off a season that has had a much happier ending than beginning.

David Jack thought that City's century of goals showed we had the punch up front, but in defence we conceded goals just as easily, and that is why City are interested in Falkirk's Scottish full back Alex Parker. "Whilst City lack the glamour of their publicity conscious neighbours, Maine Road supporters are convinced that we have the potential to equal, or beat, any of the achievements of United - and I don't think manager McDowall and his Directors will disappoint those fans."

Villa, managed by Eric Houghton, were fifteenth with thirty six points and City fourth with forty nine points. They'd won three away from home, including 5-2 at Sheff. Wed., drawn two and lost fourteen including three 4-0s, a 1-6 at Leicester and a 2-6 at Spurs. At home they'd won eleven including a 5-1 v Leicester, drawn three and lost five, including 1-2 to City. They went out of the cup to Stoke in the third rd. 0-2 after 1-1 and 3-3.

At City: Pre-war we'd won the last four including a 5-0 in 1936, Post we'd drawn the last two and lost the previous two. Recent attendances ranged from 24,326 (56/57) to 52,689 (47/48). It was the seventy eighth league meeting plus five cup ties, two at City, 1900 first rd 1-1 (22,000), 1915 second rd. 1-0 (29,661)

Team News: Unchanged

From The Pink (Ray Wergen)/Green: Ahead Then A Blunder Goal Helps Villa - Bert At His Best

City went into the game knowing that only a victory would make certain of a top four place and talent money. A draw would only help City if West Brom and Spurs were beaten. Before the start City and Spurs, with the better goal average, were sharing third place with forty nine points, and West Brom were on forty eight points.

City lost the toss and kicked off on a firm pitch in front of a rather small crowd. The passing was generally short and the tempo fast in the opening stages with City very definitely dictating the play.

Bert was there with nothing to do except face a rare challenge and generally stand between the posts with his hands on his hips. After seventeen minutes City went into the lead they fully deserved. Hart beat one man and slipped the ball to Sambrook who sent in a long curling centre from the left and when the ball came loose **Hayes** made no mistake in turning it back smartly into the far bottom corner of the net from ten yards out.

So it seemed as if City were well on the way to record their seventh 'double' of the season, but it turned out rather differently as within a minute Villa equalised.

From the restart there looked to be little danger but out of the blue came **Smith** with a half-hearted shot which bounced trickily and obviously completely deceived Trautmann on its way to the back of the net. A minute later they could have taken the lead but Bert saved from Hitchens with a smart jump which brought a gasp and cheers from City fans. City went close through Hayes on both occasions, but it was Villa who took the lead in the thirty first minute. Smith took a short corner and pushed a beauty over to **Sewell**, a master of the arts and graces of the game, who without any hesitation whipped the ball into the back of the net from close range. Trautmann didn't have the ghost of a chance to prevent the one hundredth goal City had conceded this season, but it was down to sloppy defensive cover. Myerscough and Leivers clashed heads and needed treatment after slumping to the ground, but both being strong fellows, continued after that magic sponge had been used.

Villa came out with ten men, Myerscough being treated for concussion during the interval. For a time the inside left sat on the trainers bench but resumed on the left.

The half time scoreboard showed both Spurs and West. Brom. losing and City came out with a little more fire, with the forwards trying everything they knew for the equaliser, but their passing was often too loose. With 16 minutes left it looked like City might do it but Sims just managed to grasp the ball at the last second when all seemed lost. Towards the end City had the best of the play and made further late challenges, but without the necessary punch.

FINAL SCORE: CITY 1 VILLA 2

City: Sky blue/white: Trautmann; Branagan, Sear; Barnes, Leivers, Warhurst; Fagan, Barlow, Hart, Hayes, Sambrook.
Villa: Claret and blue shirts/white knickers: Sims; Lynn, Aldis; Crowe, Dugdale, Saward; Smth, Hitchens, Sewell, Myerscough, McParland.

This is the Villa team which lined up for the game, recognised by the Kippax stanchion and drainpipe in the background!

Attendance: 28,278 Average: 32,765
Referee: T.S.Blenkinsop (S. Shields)
Linesmen: F.C.Dorling, S.Dutton
Final league Position: West Brom beat Luton 4-2, and Spurs beat Blackpool 2-1 so City were knocked down into fifth position.
Goals For: 104 Against:100
Reserves: Won 1-0 at Blackburn (Rooney at centre half!)

Aston Villa finished in fourteenth spot. They went down in '59, when Joe Mercer was manager, on the last day of the season Ronnie Allen of WBA scoring a late equaliser, and City were beating Leicester 3-1 on the same night to stay up. They came back up in '60, struggled for a while going down to the third, then came up, won the League cup four times, runners up twice, division one title in 1981, European Cup in 1982, F.A.Cup runners up in 2000, and are now an established Premiership club..

Four up for transfer, Albert Bourne, Rex Grey, David Davidson, Arthur Sadler. Roy Clarke may go on tour, and so might Don Revie. At O/T Dennis Viollet was receiving poison pen letters from United fans re the possibility of him playing at Wembley, as they reckoned he hadn't played in earlier rounds,.

CONCLUSION: Good away wins at Bolton, Everton, losses at Newcastle, home wins v Newcastle, Sunderland, loss v Villa giving us eight points and a final place of fifth with forty nine points. Goals for 104, against 100. Average attendance home 32,760 away 32,594

Full Term Report - Second half of the season

We signed Ray Sambrook from Coventry for £15,000, finished in fifth place, could have been higher, with twenty four points in the second half giving us a total of forty nine, fifteen points behind leaders Wolves.

At home we won a further six games, drew thre lost two. Away we won four, drew one lost five.There were debuts for Roy Cheetham, and Ken Taylor.

Goals continued to pile up, another fifty of them from Hayes 12 - 26, McAdams 5 - 18, Barlow 9 - 17, Barnes 3 - 11, Fagan 2 - 7, Johnstone 3 - 6, Kirkman 4, Sambrook, Hart 3, Warhurst 2, Foulkes (United og), Dudley (WBA og) Kelly H (Blackpool og), Dunne (Luton og), Stuart (Wolves og). And we leaked another forty eight.

Attendances at Maine Road ranged from 21,962 v Leeds to 70,483 v United. Away they ranged from 16,019 at Luton to 53,326 at Newcastle

So, at half term we didn't think we could match the fifty four for and fifty two against but we came very, very close!

FINAL LEAGUE TABLE 1957/58

	P	W	D	L	F	A	Pts
Wolves	42	28	8	6	103	47	64
Preston	42	26	7	9	100	51	59
Spurs	42	21	9	12	93	77	51
WBA	42	18	14	10	92	70	50
Man City	**42**	**22**	**5**	**15**	**104**	**100**	**49**
Burnley	42	21	5	16	80	74	47
Blackpool	42	19	6	17	80	67	44
Luton	42	19	6	17	69	63	44
Man Utd	42	16	11	15	85	75	43
Notts For	42	16	10	16	69	63	42
Chelsea	42	15	12	15	83	79	42
Arsenal	42	16	7	19	73	85	39
B'ham	42	14	11	17	76	89	39
Aston Villa	42	16	7	19	73	86	39
Bolton	42	14	10	18	65	87	38
Everton	42	13	11	18	65	75	37
Leeds	42	14	9	19	51	63	37
Leicester	42	14	5	23	91	112	33
Newcastle	42	12	8	22	73	81	32
Portsmouth	42	12	8	22	73	88	32
Sunderland	42	10	12	20	54	97	32
Sheff Wed	42	12	7	23	69	92	31

With the Reserves in the Central league

Wolves won the title with City ninth with forty points. At home it was: Played 21 won 13 with big wins v Chesterfield, Derby and Leeds 5-1, Villa and Bury 5-0, drawn 3 lost 5. Attendances ranged from 907, to 4,377.

Away it was played 21 won 5 drawn 2 lost 14 with big losses at Preston and Sheff. Utd. 1-5, plus the 6-7 at Wolves. We racked up 98 goals with 84 against, not quite emulating the first team.

Goals coming from Kirkman 25, Clarke 15,

McLelland 14, Fidler 11, Phoenix 8, Bourne 7, Hart 6, Fagan 5, Barlow 2, Murray, McAdams, Johnson, Lister, 1.

Other appearances were by Branagan, Fleet, McTavish, Cheetham, Taylor, Little, Shawcross, Savage, Horridge, Davidson, Meadows, Sear, Murray, Leigh, Faulkner, Mathews, Barnes, Leivers, Stringfellow, Pennington, Rooney, Cooke, Dyson and Warhurst

FINAL CENTRAL LEAGUE TABLE 1957/58

	P	W	D	L	F	A	Pts
Wolves	42	27	8	7	112	64	62
Everton	42	22	9	11	89	56	53
Man Utd	42	22	7	13	117	80	52
Liverpool	42	23	5	14	96	67	51
Huddersfield	42	21	9	12	87	60	51
Barnsley	42	20	7	15	81	78	47
Bury	42	18	10	14	80	75	46
Sheff Wed	42	18	9	15	79	61	45
Man City	**42**	**19**	**4**	**19**	**98**	**84**	**42**
Blackpool	42	15	12	15	58	59	42
Stoke	42	16	10	16	66	71	42
WBA	42	14	11	17	72	80	39
Sheff Utd	42	15	8	19	78	83	38
Aston Villa	42	16	6	20	63	90	38
Newcastle	42	18	1	23	70	89	37
Burnley	42	15	7	20	58	77	37
Derby	42	16	5	21	60	84	37
Preston	42	15	5	22	66	78	35
Chesterfield	42	13	9	20	66	81	35
Bolton	42	12	9	21	63	80	33
Leeds	42	14	4	24	70	95	32
Blackburn	42	13	5	24	61	98	31

42A) MONDAY APRIL 28TH 1958 K.O.7.30: JIMMY MEADOWS TESTIMONIAL MATCH, CITY (past and present) 2 THE ALL STARS X1 4

A souvenir programme was issued for this game, the first Testimonial since the war, priced 6d for sixteen pages. The front cover was a nice shade of sky blue with a good drawing of Jimmy on the front (by Ford).

Inside Jim thanked everyone involved with the game, including all at the club, referee, linesmen and players of the All Star X1. Also to the members of the Testimonial Committee and to the City, United and Liverpool supporters clubs who had worked so hard to make tonight a success. Finally he thanked all the spectators here tonight, "my thanks for your support and for your encouragement in the past."

Walter Winterbottom, the England team manager, gave a one page tribute and Arthur

Walmsley talked of how Jim nearly missed the fateful final with a temperature just twelve hours before the kick off .

Derek Kevan scored for the All Stars after seven minutes. Tom Finney made it two in the twenty second. Joe Hayes pulled one back in the twenty fourth, but Kevan scored again in the thirty third. Billy Liddell made it four just before half time, and Joe Hayes made it 4-2 in the seventy seventh minute for an extremely entertaining evening, and one to remember for Jimmy and his fans.

FINAL SCORE: CITY 2 GREAT BRITAIN X1 4

City: Trautmann; Sear, Westwood (Leivers in the second half);Barnes, Ewing, Paul (captain);Fagan, Barlow, Revie, Hayes, Sambrook
All Star X1: Younger (Liverpool and Scotland); Howe (W.Brom and England), Hopkins (Spurs and Wales) Docherty (Preston and Scotland), Wright (Wolves and England), Flowers (Wolves and England), Deeley (Wolves), Robson (W.Brom and England), Finney (Preston and England), Kevan (W.Brom and England), Liddell (Liverpool and Scotland).
Attendance: 39,948
Referee: J.Clough (Bolton)
Linesmen: G.Gibson, T.Cooper

April 30th: Holland U 23s 2 Scots 1. Amsterdam (13,500).

MAY'S FOOTBALL MONTHLY

Charles Buchan's FOOTBALL MONTHLY

Bolton's Nat Lofthouse was on the front cover and United's Ian Greaves, with two teeth missing on the back cover. CB was looking forward to the World Cup and praised Sweden's English coach George Raynor. *(Ironic as England, and City, eventually had an Swedish manager!)* His tip for the Cup was Bolton. E.Phillips of Wythenshawe is listed in programme swaps - was it Eddie? Journo Clifford Webb remembers when "Football used to be fun" and Peter Morris thought that the fourth division would be a painful soccer death for the likes of Coventry. In Soccer Sideshow, Colin Barlow claims he will never get big ideas about himself. There's a photo of a Reading player called Sylvan (no i!) amongst the Jims, Petes and Toms.

Once A Blue, Always A Blue

JOHN from London's story:

It was during the 1950s that my love affair with the Blues began. Not that I had much choice in the matter. My grandad had been at the first match at Maine Road in 1923, so naturally my Dad brain washed me just as I have made sure our son Nick is an avid fan as well.

To the best of my recollection the first game I ever saw was in 1953. I was seven at the time and we were playing Blackpool who had Stanley Matthews on the wing.

In those days, of course, Blackpool were a force to be reckoned with. That was the year they won the FA Cup in the famous Matthews final against Bolton. And three years after that they were Division One runners up - eleven points behind the team which, even then, I knew not to mention.

When there was a big crowd I, along with other kids, would be sat on the wall of the tunnel through which spectators walked to take up their places. Today's health and safety Stasis would have gone berserk. Then no-one, including my dad, gave it a second thought.

Just getting to the ground was in itself a measure of my father's enthusiasm. He was born and brought up in Denton and as a lad, with my grandfather, he used to cycle to Maine Road leaving their bikes in the back yard of one of the houses close to the ground.

But he and my mum set up home in Saddleworth. We didn't have a car so the journey involved one bus from our home in Diggle to Uppermill, another one from Uppermill to Stevenson's Square and, finally, a trolley bus from Piccadilly to the ground. All up trip time - generally about one and a half hours each way depending on bus timetables. And all that to travel just seventeen miles.

A couple of years later, in 1955, I remember my mum packing dad off to Wembley for the final with Newcastle. He went on the bus and I stayed at home with my mum.

Like thousands of other families we had bought our first television to watch the Coronation and this was the first final I had seen.

Even at that age I was deflated by the result but my disappointment was but nothing compared to that of the old man who, like so many more, had invested so much time and hard earned cash into the trip south only to see poor old Jimmy Meadows carried off and the Blues go down 3-1.

My hero at the time was big Dave Ewing. Why? Because I loved the uncompromising way he dealt with centre forwards. I remember seeing him chase Dave Hickson, Huddersfield's striker, half way up the field for having the temerity to tap the big man's ankle. An hilarious encounter made all the more appetising by the knowledge that Hickson was no slouch himself when it came to dishing it out.

And my admiration for Dave (Ewing that is) became even greater the following year when he played such a pivotal role protecting Bert Trautmann after he had broken his neck in the victorious final against Birmingham.

Fan worship at that age knows no bounds and often involves as much fantasy as reality which is probably why I often stood by the railway line at Diggle convincing myself I had caught a glimpse of my heroes travelling past to a game at Leeds or Newcastle.

And while the fantasies may have evaporated the sense of awe is still with me. I have turned our downstairs loo into a City shrine. Amongst the memorabilia to muse over while otherwise engaged there are three front covers from Charles Buchan's Football Monthly (priced incidentally at one shilling and sixpence).

One, a cup final souvenir issue, features Jimmy Meadows, another the irrepressible Ken Barnes, and the third pictures Dave doing what looks like a handstand to thwart a Wolves attacker.

However pride of place goes to a black and white photograph of the entire l955/56 team. It shows Dave, arms defiantly crossed, as if to say "Thou Shall Not Pass". He is also smiling, reminding us that beneath that tough, gritty Scots facade there was, I suspect, a thoroughly decent man who enjoyed life to the full..

And alongside Dave, in dubbined boots and sky blue collared shirts, Roy Paul, Ken Barnes, Bert Trautmann, Bill Leivers, Roy Little, Billy Spurdle, Joe Hayes, Bobby Johnstone, Jack Dyson and Roy Clarke.

To a lad from Diggle in the 1950's heroes all.

John, exiled in London for proximity to GMTV and other media work, but regular at COMSTAD and most southern away games.

CHAPTER ELEVEN

SUMMER 1958 - AMERICAN TOUR

The Manchester City squad about to depart for the Big Apple, May 1958. Back row, left to right: Ken Branagan, Dave Ewing, Cliff Sear, John McTavish, Don Revie (who had left City in November 1956, but had been asked by the club to accompany the squad as a guest player), John McClelland, Bert Trautmann, Ray Sambrook, Ken Barnes, Johnny Hart, Roy Cheetham, Billy McAdams. Front row, left to right: Joe Hayes, Paddy Fagan, Roy Warhurst, Roy Little, Colin Barlow.

David Meek - "It must be United's cup this year."

It wasn't. Bolton, with their £110 team, won 2-0. Keith Dewhurst in the Chron had predicted 4-1 to United! The MEN print Bolton's route from Manchester back to Bolton and, surprise, surprise, the two Bolton coaches are pelted with clods of earth, stones, and flour bags, on Bolton Rd., Salford. The Bolton players, rising above it, treated it as a joke.

M/C Senior Cup Final : Oldham 1 City 0.
New away strip announced for next season is yellow, with black collar and shorts (and I bought one). United beat Inter 2-1 in the Euro cup semi first leg at Old Trafford. Leeds sack Raich Carter. United were sulking after Wembley. Meek reckoned their spiritless display was because they forgot the practice balls because they'd had too much training with balls. Couldn't have been that Bolton were the better team could it? Oh, and the second goal was a foul. This gave my old fella a quandary - Nat, his hero, shoulder-charging Gregg (the mad Irishman) his fellow countryman! But he didn't make a fuss.
Alex Parker may join City if the club can provide a house (he went to Everton). United were well beaten in the second leg of the Euro Cup semi 4-0 in Milan making it 5-2 on aggregate. They were accused of roughness and of kicking the Italians. United reckoned it was the worst crowd they'd played in front of and according to Meek, the fans and the ref whistled them out of the competition. Is a pattern emerging here?
May 7th Scotland 1 Hungary 1, friendly at Hampden (54,900).
England 2 Portugal 1, friendly at Wembley (72,000).
May 11th Yugoslavia 5 England 0, friendly at Belgrade (60,000).
Poland 2 Eire 2 friendly at Katowice (100,000).
May 14th Austria 3 Eire 1 friendly at Vienna (40,000).
May 18th Russia 1 England 1 friendly at Moscow (104,000).

JUNE'S FOOTBALL MONTHLY

Fulham's Johnny Haynes was on the front cover, and Celtic's Dick Peacock on the back cover. CB's editorial lamented the death of Billy Meredith, and thought out of the four British teams in the World Cup we have a good chance of winning it. Joe Hayes is on the England team group sat next to Brian Clough before the under 23 game with Wales, on April 23rd at Wrexham, lost 2-1. (20,000). On the cup final he concluded that Bolton were the worthy winners and that Nat's second goal, though controversial was a good one. Frank Swift is pictured on page twenty one. Sunderland's singing winger Colin Grainger tells how he was set on at Wrexham by Les McDowall.

Wednesday May 14th - City off to Montreal

After the Jimmy Meadows testimonial game in which Don Revie, then a Sunderland player, starred, Don hinted that he "wouldn't mind going on tour" and as the Wearside club didn't object, he teamed up with his old buddies again.The Blues travelled down to Southampton via London and sailed out on the Mauritania. It took about a week. Roy Warhurst says, "It was a rough trip, some of the players being seasick, the worst hit being Ken Barnes and Cliff Sear. Colin Barlow won the quiz, after swotting up on all the ship's almanacs in the library, earning the nickname 'egghead'. Don Revie was favourite to win the deck tennis but bad weather stopped it! Ken Barnes won the table tennis tournament beating an American in the final.

**1) Sunday May 18th KO 2.30 pm:
City 6 Philadelphia Ukrainians Nationals/ Uhrik Truckers 1, in Edison Field, Philadelphia, Att: 7,000**

In the opening game of the tour, played in a strong cross wind and a temperature of eighty degrees, **Colin Barlow** was the star marksman and scored a hat trick. His first goal came when he raced through on his own, after some neat passing in the tenth minute. In the thirtieth minute Barlow passed to **Hayes** who scored from eighteen yards, and **Paddy Fagan** hooked in the third from a difficult angle in the thirty eighth minute. **Barlow** made it 4-0 in the fiftieth minute after a goalmouth scramble and completed his hat-trick in the sixty seventh minute with a twenty yard drive.

Walter Chyzewych lobbed Bert from ten yards to make it 5-1 in the seventy sixth minute, and **Fagan** finished things off at 6-1 late on with a low shot into the left hand corner of the net..

Team: Trautmann; Sear, Little; Barnes, Ewing, Warhust; Fagan, Barlow, Hart, Hayes, Sambrook.

A twenty page **programme** was produced for this game, priced at twenty five cents, which featured Bert, and lots of adverts.

**2) Wednesday May 21st:
City 7 USA AM Soccer Stars 2, in Fall River. Massachusetts. Att: 2,000**

City outclassed their opponents. **Fagan** dazzled the All Stars, opening the scoring in the fifth minute, and was the star of the match, bewildering the USA defence by his speed and his ball control plus shooting with power and accuracy. **Barlow** made the greatest use of the opportunities provided for him, scored a first half hat-trick, and **Billy Mac** got one before Dan Miller replied to make it 5-1 in the forty fourth minute.

City could have finished with double figures, but for a crop of near misses, several attempts hitting the woodwork, but settled for another two, one each from **McAdams** in the fifty first minute and **Barlow** in the sixty fifth. Lloyd Morsen made it 7-2 in the seventy seventh minute.

Team: Trautmann; Sear, Little; Barnes, Ewing, McTavish; Fagan, Barlow, Hart, McAdams, Sambrook.

No **Programme** available.

Bert Trautmann: "We're on a £2 a day food allowance over here. A cup of coffee is 1s 3d, it's 3s 6d for a hamburger and 13s for an English breakfast - I ask you?! I'm having a wonderful time but I'm eating nothing but hamburgers. I left New York last Friday and we travelled to Philadelphia eighty nine miles away, for the 6-1 win. Then it was back to New York. I stayed back to kick off New York v a German league team, then went on to Fall River two hundred and fifty miles away.

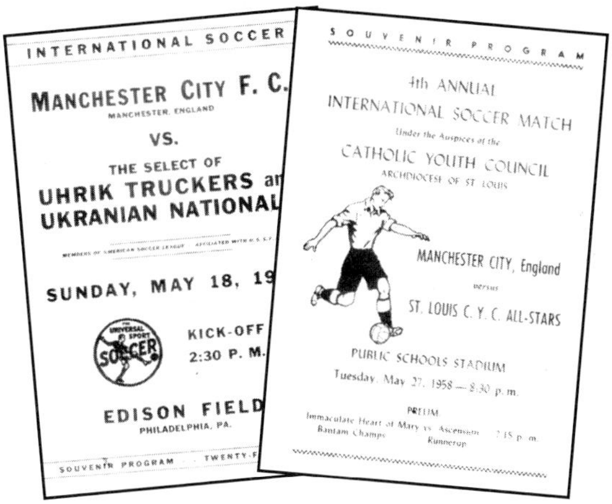

**3) Sunday May 25th KO 3.15pm:
City 5 Hearts 6 in Ebbets Field, Brooklyn, New York Att: 20,000**

This was a thrilling game played in pouring rain which made conditions difficult. Despite the weather, 20,000 spectators turned up in New York. City snatched a 2-0 lead within fifteen minutes, courtesy of **Billy Mac**. after five mins from a goalmouth melee and **Fagan** after fifteen from a Sambrook cross. Hearts attack then got into top gear and they scored four goals in seventeen minutes. **Wardhaugh** cracked home on twenty three mins, then **Young** made it 2-2 in the thirtieth, quickly followed by **Hamilton** a minute later. **Bauld** made it 4-2 in the fortieth minute but a pass from McAdams in the forty first sent **Barlow** through to reduce the arrears to 4-3.

Second half **Wardhaugh** made it 6-3, in the fiftieth and fifty fifth minutes, with headers from Bauld crosses. **Billy Mac** pulled one back in the sixty fifth minute from a goalmouth scramble, and Hearts' **Milne** in the seventy second minute attempted to pass back but only succeeded in lofting the ball over Marshall's head for 6-5. On top of all this both goalies made spectacular saves!!

No **programm**e was issued for this game.

City: Trautmann; Sear, Little; Barnes, Ewing, Warhurst; Fagan, Barlow, Revie, McAdams, Sambrook.
Hearts: Marshall; Kirk, Thomson; Cumming, Milne, Bowman; Hamilton, Young, Bauld, Wardhaugh, Crawford.
Heavy rain postponed this game for a day. Level

4) Wednesday May 28th: K.O. 8.30pm: City 6 St. Louis All Stars 2 at the Public Schools Stadium in St Louis Att: 4,000

at 1-1 at half time City piled on five goals in the next thirty minutes and followed that up by treating the crowd to some exhibition football.

St Louis goalkeeper Bill King helped keep the score down with several spectacular saves and City's only first half goal came in the twelfth minute from a **Revie** penalty. St. Louis equalised in the twentieth minute when Bert collided with Branagan.

A pep talk from manager Les McDowall brought out some City fireworks in the second half. They swept into the St Louis half and in the fifty fourth minute **Hart** headed home Barlow's accurate centre from the wing. **Hayes 2**, **Fagan** and **Hart** again completed the goal rush which took City to a 6-1 lead.

St Louis' second goal came eight minutes from time when Bert was penalised for a foul against a home forward, **Donovan** scoring from the spot kick.

The match, under floodlights was played in good conditions, despite being postponed from the previous night because of rain.

Manager McDowall said afterwards that City had played below their best form "The St Louis goalkeeper made some great saves, but even so we should have done better."

This was the first game in which Barlow failed to score and Fagan has scored in EVERY game.

A thirty two page **programme** was produced for this game (May 27th) It was mainly adverts, for church organisations, and beer, with only a possible line up of the teams.

New wages to be £17 not £20?
Arsenal manager Jack Crayston left the club.
Third and Fourth divisions will be a one season experiment.
City fans helped the Jimmy Meadows benefit fund when they poured through the gates on April 26th by raising £6,063.

5) Saturday May 31st: K.O. 8PM: City 2 Hearts 5 at The Empire Stadium, Vancouver, Att: 20,975

City fell to their second defeat of the tour, both against Hearts, the Scottish League Champions, who were 4-0 up at half time then held a 5-0 lead before City scored their two goals late in the game. Hearts, playing a short passing game took almost every chance that came their way. City had almost as many scoring opportunities but their attacks faded in front of goal.

Willie Bauld the Hearts centre-forward opened the scoring in the early minutes when he turned a pass from right winger John Hamilton into the City net.

Crawford made it 2-0 with a long shot after twenty seven minutes. **Bauld** scored again in the thirty fifth minute, and **Young**, *The Golden Vision*, completed the first half scoring seven minutes before the interval.

Hearts fifth goal came five minutes after the break, **Wardhaugh** netting after a shot by Young had been partially saved by Bert.

Don Revie, leading the City attack, had a long shot brilliantly saved by Marshall, the Hearts goalkeeper, before **Hayes** stepped in with two goals in the last ten minutes. The first came when he took a pass from Revie and drove the ball low past Marshall; the second when he headed in a pass from outside right, Paddy Fagan.

A large A4 type **programme** was produced for this game with a maroon front cover including a Hearts team photo. It was priced at thirty five cents, and also covered the BC All Stars game v Hearts on Monday June 2nd, both kick offs being 8pm. It was a sixteen page effort, and included 'thumb nail' sketches of City, Hearts, B.C. All Stars players, and photos of City (at Blackpool) and B.C. All Stars. There were also team photos of Capilano F.C., Carlings F.C., and - Wallace A.C. *(we get everywhere!)* all paid adverts. There was a page on the World Cup Soccer Championship showing how the teams qualified and plenty of other adverts.

Programme teams:
Hearts: Maroon and white: Marshall; Kirk, Thomson; Cumming, Milne, Bowman; Hamilton, Young, Bauld, Wardhaugh, Crawford.
Reserves were: Higgins, Blackwood, Lindores, Glidden, Conn, Paton.
City: Blue and white: Trautmann; Sear, Little; Barnes, Ewing, Warhurst; Fagan, Barlow; Revie, Sambrook.
Reserves were: Branagan, Hayes, McTavish, McLelland.

6) Wednesday June 4th: City 9 San Francisco All Stars 1, at The Kezar Stadium in San Francisco, Att: 15,000

Colin Barlow opened the scoring after nine minutes from a pass by Fagan. **Sambrook** and **Revie** netted to put City 3-0 up after twenty minutes. **Barnes** then scored from a penalty to make the half time score 4-1. In the second half **Fagan** scored 2, **Barlow** 2 and **Sambrook** got one.

The souvenir programme had a black and white front cover and introduced City as: 'England's Famous Manchester City'. It was an unpriced forty page effort. There were welcomes from the Mayor, George Christopher - "I hope our visitors will enjoy their stay in San Francisco and will return to England with fond memories of our city by the Golden Gate" and Mathew J. Boxer, general chairman, who expressed similar views. There was a programme of events - Miss San Francisco would kick off the game and later in the evening the City players would receive a gold pin. There were pen pictures of the players, (John McTavish was down as McTaege!) of both club's and also photos of both teams. There was a history of soccer in the Bay area, and loads of adverts.

City's team, according to the programme: Trautmann; Leivers, Sear; Barnes, Ewing, Warhurst; Barlow, Hayes, Johnstone *(who didn't even travel)*, McAdams, Sambrook.

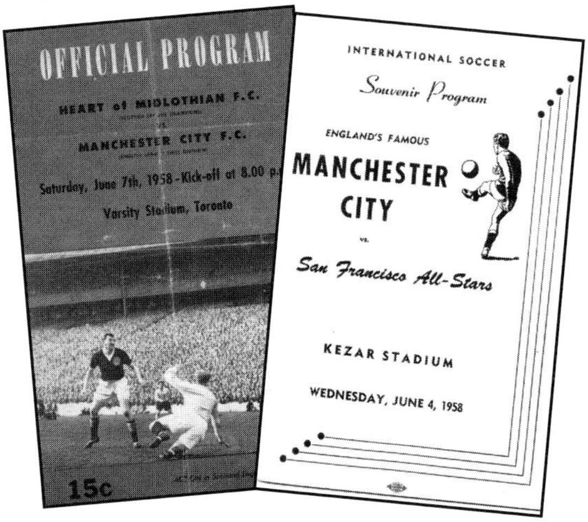

7) Saturday June 7th K.O. 8pm: City 7 Hearts 1 in The Varsity Stadium, Toronto, Att: 24,000

Joe Hayes scored a hat-trick in what was sweet revenge for City over Hearts, who had comfortable victories in the two previous encounters on the North American tour.

City's other scorers were inside left Colin Barlow, and left winger Ray Sambrook with two each. Left winger Johnny Crawford replied for Hearts.

Hearts defence were slow to move when Fagan raced down the wing after a long clearance, and he centred for **Barlow** to blast the ball into the net.

A minute later **Sambrook** tore through to the goal-line before scoring from the narrowest of angles. Again the Scottish defenders looked slow as Sambrook ran through and cut the ball across for **Barlow** to hit his second and City's third two minutes before half time. City went all out in the second half and within five minutes **Hayes** scored his first goal after a great piece of individual play.

He ran on to a pass down the middle raced past two men, dribbled round another, lobbed the ball over a fourth and finished with a shot which beat goalkeeper Marshall all the way. Hearts switched wingers Crawford and Hamilton in a bid to get their attack working, and the move paid a quick dividend when **Crawford** scored from a rebound from the upright in the sixty fifth minute.

But the Scots revival was short lived. Within two minutes **Hayes** made it 5-1 with a crisp shot, and **Sambrook** followed with his second goal.

Hayes wound up the scoring two minutes from time, when he deflected home a free kick by Don Revie.

An eight page souvenir programme was issued for this game with a blue front cover and action shot from a Scotland v England game! It was priced at fifteen cents and included individual photos and pen pics of both clubs plus team photos, and a few adverts.

8) Sunday June 8th KO 3 pm: City 8 Ulster United 2 at the McCabe Field in Detroit, Att: 5,000

After the 7-1 win over Hearts, City went on to beat Ulster United of Toronto 8-2 in an Exhibition match in Detroit. Colin Barlow scored six of City's goals and Don Revie got the other two.

A twelve page twenty five cent programme was issued for this game, which included adverts, team line ups and some basic rules of football.

The all-American gal on the front cover is in fact Terry Bartos, a 26-year old exiled Manc and City fan. Terry, who was presented to the teams before the game, contracted polio in 1953 and spent three years in an iron lung, wheelchair and braces, but after a courageous fight, she fully recovered.

9) Wednesday June 11th KO 6.45pm: City 0 Hearts 6 at the Percival Molson Stadium in Montreal, Att: 7,000

City were one down at half time, took a hammering in the second half and were beaten 6-0. This was the fourth and last meeting of City and Hearts in their North American Exhibition match series, in which Hearts have won three and City one.

Veteran inside left **Jim Wardhaugh** was the scoring star for Hearts with goals all in the second half. Outside left **John Crawford** and centre forward **Willie Bauld** scored the other two goals.

A twenty page programme was issued at twenty five cents. It included a City history, pen pics of the players, all spelt correctly, and similar for Hearts.

City team: Trautmann; Branagan, Sear; Barnes, Ewing, McTavish; Fagan, Barlow, Revie, Hayes, Sambrook.

Hearts (probable): Marshall; Kirk, Thomson; Cumming, Milne, Bowman; Blackwood, Bauld, Young, Wardhaugh, Crawford

So nine games played, with five comfortable wins over the North American teams, with thirty six goals for and eight against. One win and three losses against Hearts, with fourteen goals for and eighteen against. Overall goalscorers being: Barnes (1pen), Fagan (7), Barlow (19), Hart (2), Hayes (8), McAdams (4), Sambrook (4), Revie (4, including 2 pens), own goal (1) - total fifty. Crowds ranged from 2,000 to 24,000. City didn't intend to re-sign Don Revie.

Coming back they had it rough and only Bert Trautmann, who had the constitution of an Ox, having roughed it in the War, enjoyed it. After the week long voyage from Montreal, Ewing, Hayes, Fagan, and McTavish jumped ship at Greenock, rather than continue on to Liverpool, preferring to finish the journey by rail. The first day had been sunny, the next two days it was rough and the final three days were marred by fog with the hooter going every so often. Fagan and Warhurst did not visit the dining room for five days! Revie and Hayes, successful at housey housey (bingo!) on the trip out, did not participate on the way back! Hearts were confirmed as being just as bad sailors.

June 1st: Friendly: Poland 1 Scotland 2, at Warsaw (85,000).

WORLD CUP

Northern Ireland in Group 1 beat Czechoslavakia 1-0 (June 7th, Halmstad, 10,670); lost to Argentina 3-1 (June 11th, Halmstad, 15,000); drew with West Germany 2-2 (June 15th Malmo, 21,990), beat the Czechs again in a play-off 2-1 after extra time (June 17th, Malmo, 6,000) then lost to France 4-0 in the quarter final (June 19th, Norrkoping, 11,800).

Scotland in Group 2 drew with Yugoslavia 1-1(June 7th, Vasteraas, 10,000) lost to Paraguay 2-3 (June 11th, Norrkoping, 8,000) and to France, 2-1 (June 15th Orebro, 13,500)

Wales in Group 3 drew with Hungary 1-1 (June7th, Sandviken, 20,000) and Mexico 1-1 (June 11th, Stockholm,18,000) and Sweden 0-0 (June 15th, Stockholm, 40,000) beat Hungary 2-1 in a play off (June 17th Stockholm, 2,823) but lost to Brazil 1-0 in the quarter final (June 19th, Gothenburg, 25,923)

England in Group 4 drew with Russia 2-2 (June 7th, Gothenburg, 53,000), and Brazil 0-0 (June 11th, Gothenburg, 50,000) and Austria 2-2 (June 15th, Boraas, 20,000) then lost the play off game, 1-0 to Russia (June 17th, Gothenburg, 25,182)

In the other Quarter Finals West Germany beat Yugoslavia 1-0, (20,055, Malmo). Sweden beat Russia 2-0, (31,900 in Stockholm).

In the semi-finals Sweden beat West Germany 3-1, (52,000 Gothenburg). Brazil beat France 5-2, (42,000 Stockholm).

Third place play off was France 6 West Germany 3 (32,000 Gothenburg).

Final was Brazil 5 Sweden 2.

City are after Sandy Wann from Dave Ewing's old club, Luncarty.

Charlie Mitten has taken over at Newcastle.

Marsden and Taylor now 100% fit, Dyson in light training.

Fifteen year olds Alan Oakes, Sandy (Alex) Wann, David Shawcross, Mike Pearson, Bob Stevenson have joined the club.

Ken Barnes is to take over the captaincy from Dave Ewing next season.

So to the start of the next season, (Fixtures came out on May 22nd) and City were tipped in the Soccer Star magazine by Jack Rollin as probable Champions.

Some of the players came back from America with crew cuts and the team started as they left off in the previous season, going 3-0 down at Burnley by half time, but winning 4-3 and finished third from bottom after winning the last game 3-1 at home to Leicester, Villa taking the drop after only drawing 1-1 with WBA, along with Portsmouth.

There is a story that suggests City offered Leicester £30 a man to 'take it easy', but Leicester declined and when asked why at the end of that game, their captain replied that Villa had already offered them £40 a man to win?!

The Blues were then in decline, being relegated in 1963, but came back up in 1966, and won the League in 1968, the Cup in 1969, the League Cup and the European Cup Winners Cup in 1970. There was a league cup loss in 1974, a win in 1976, first division runners up in 1977, a cup final appearance in 1981, and a replay, and then ups and downs, to the (old) third division and back. Never a dull moment and never a repeat of season 57/58 where the big defeats hurt more than the pleasure of the big wins.

MANCHESTER CITY 1958-59

Standing : J. McTavish, C. Sear, B. Trautmann, K. Barnes, D. Ewing, W. Leivers.
Seated : C. Barlow, J. Hayes, R. Johnstone, W. McAdams, R. Sambrook.

JULY'S FOOTBALL MONTHLY

United's Bobby Charlton was on the front cover, and Derek Kevan of WBA on the back cover. CB's editorial opinion complained that England's style had not moved on and he now felt they had little chance of doing well in the World Cup just starting. He also suggests that the old style director had almost died out and was being replaced by the modern business man, who blames the managers when things go wrong. Thirty nine managers having been sacked in the last twelve months. Jimmy McMullen, ex City and Scotland skipper, has an article where his view is that the captain should take charge on the field and not the manager. Tony Macedo, Fulham's goalie, confessed that in the semi-final replay v United, he didn't lose his nerve, no, it was just one of those days when everything went wrong for him - and he was relieved that he had played badly!?

Wimbledon were featured on 'The Amateurs' page. They were now concentrating on youth. Last season they finished half way up the Isthmian league and reached the semis of the London Senior and Sussex Senior cup competitions. Wembley was a long way off then!

Ron Suart has become Blackpool's manager.

Wolves were the first league champs to come from the third division north. Portsmouth previously did it from the third division south.

AUGUST'S FOOTBALL MONTHLY

Blackpool's Bill Perry was on the front cover and 'Boro's Brian Clough on the back cover. Star players of 57/58 didn't include one City player, and John Bond of second division West Ham. was in at full-back. World Cup of 1958 was reviewed.

CHAPTER TWELVE

CLASS OF 57/58 - THE PLAYERS

City fielded three goalkeepers, four full backs, four wing halfs, three centre halfs (though all these switched about a bit), and twelve forwards, to make up a total of twenty six players who turned out in the Sky Blue, maroon/claret, and green goalie's jumpers this season.

GOALKEEPERS

1. BERT TRAUTMANN - 6' 1½", 13st 13½lbs. Born Bremen 22/10/23, so 34 in 1957.

Bert was a POW and signed as an amateur in October 1949, from St Helens Town, turning professional in November, He succeeded Frank Swift and after immense initial hostility (called racism these days), he won over the fans from both City and all other clubs. He was once in trouble for telling the referee he was Stanley Matthews and, after getting plenty of practise in the City net, evoking comments like "what manner of man is this Trautmann fella?" and making us all wonder how we won the war. His finest moments were in the '55 and '56 cup finals, breaking his neck in the latter causing Brummie fans to lament that they couldn't even win the cup against a team whose goalie had a broken neck! He was Player Of The Year that season.

After a slow recovery in 56/57 Bert was back to his best in **1957/58** with remarkable saves and performances, including saving Norman Deeley's penalty at Wolves and Tommy Harmer's at Spurs. But he wasn't totally invincible and let in eight at Leicester! He missed only eight games, due to back and shoulder problems, when he was talked out of quitting the game by Les McDowall. Games missed were mainly early on in the season v Forest, Preston, West Brom., Birmingham away and Preston, Spurs, Sheff Wed and Wolves home when we conceded a total of twenty six goals!

He went on to play for a further few seasons, being selected for the Football League team v The Irish Football League at Blackpool in October 1960. He was sent off v West Ham in '62 for kicking the ball upfield which unfortunately hit the ref!! He retired in the 63/64 season becoming disillusioned with City when new signings were paid more than he was and his testimonial game attracted 47, 901 officially. He went to Wellington Town, moved into management at Stockport, and coached in Germany and all over the world, before finally settling in Valencia. He was awarded the OBE in November 2004 and always receives a tremendous reception when he comes back to Manchester, being one of the all time greats and the reason many City fans, including myself, became Blues.

There have been two biographies published on Bert, *Steppes To Wembley* and *Trautmann, the Biography*.

2) JOHN SAVAGE - 6' 4", 15st 10 lbs.
Born Bromley 14th Dec. 1929, so 28 in 1957.

Big John was signed from Halifax in November '53, and had the thankless task of being understudy to Bert. He made two appearancess in 54/55, two in 55/56 and his big chance came in 56/57 when Bert was recovering from his broken neck. City however went out and bought George Thompson from Preston, but he only lasted a couple of games, so John played until Bert's return in December.

In **1957/58** he managed seven games, away at Forest, Preston, West Brom., Birmingham, all losses, and at home to Preston, Spurs and Sheff. Wed., all wins!

He moved to Walsall in January 1958 for £4,000, and now resides in Lytham St Annes

3) STEVE FLEET - 6' 0½, 13st 7lbs.
Born Salford 2nd July 1937, so 20 in 1957.

Steve was signed as an amateur in '53 and turned professional in '55. He also, like John Savage, had the thankless task of being understudy to Bert, but possessed a wonderful sense of loyalty and, grateful to the club which gave him his break was happy to stay and take his occasional chance and learn from his hero.

In **1957/58** that chance came at last in the November fog when the mighty Wolves of the 50's came back from 3-1 down to win 4-3 in the last twenty minutes of the game.

Steve made only a further five appearances and, after suffering hernia and cartilage problems he moved on to Wrexham, managed by Ken Barnes in June 1963, then Stockport and Altrincham where a broken wrist finished his career.

After a short spell in Zambia he returned as youth coach at Stockport before taking up a similar position at City in 1973. After eight successful seasons, including managing the Youth team in two Cup Final appearances, John Bond arrived and Steve moved on.

He then managed two different Icelandic sides and came back as youth coach at Birmingham, until, ironically, John Bond arrived. He then worked at the Platt Lane complex, and for the council but is now retired and an active member of the Former Players Association (FPA).

Steve: "The City and United players used to mix in those days. We got free passes to help us with our wages, whereas nowadays it's totally different. We used to meet up in town at The Plaza at lunchtimes, the UCP restaurant, picture houses, myself, Billy Haydock, and the United players Eddie Colman, Wilf McGuinness and Bobby Charlton. We weren't allowed to train at all in the afternoon at City, whereas at United they trained on certain afternoons, when I'd go and meet Eddie (Colman), my pal from Ordsall school. The advantage United had was that they had Jimmy Murphy and Bert Whalley, far better coaches than ours, and they'd talk to the players. United's players weren't better than we were but the coaching was. We didn't have anyone to talk to except the senior players.

"In 57/58 I played in the West Brom away reserve game when Keith Marsden broke his leg. He was at centre forward and chased this ball as their keeper Jackman came out and dived over the ball, accidentally connecting with Keith. You just heard this snap, as the ground was almost empty and it echoed round the stands and sickened everyone. As for my first team debut, we'd had some heavy defeats while John Savage was playing, and they decided to play me instead of him in the reserves, then in the first team v Wolves. We were 3-1 up but lost 4-3. Jimmy Mullen was the architect, in that closing phase of the game.

"The players ran things on the pitch, as the manager and coaches didn't say much. Ken Barnes was very supportive, afterwards analysing all the goals re-assuring me that it wasn't all down to me.

"I got nice words from Frank Swift, and Bert who both tipped me as a future England International goalie. Ken and Bert were big friends, very supportive. John Savage was a big fine lad and he was very helpful too even though I'd taken his place. I went back to camp and was square bashing when I got the call from City to travel with the team up to Edinburgh, for the friendly at Hibs, which we lost 5-2. On the flight back I was sick and got my leg pulled.

"I only came out of the RAF at weekends to play, in fact I only found out I was playing v Wolves, from the Press. I lived in Salford, in a 5th floor flat with my parents. I got this knock on the door at nine o'clock in the morning from the Manchester Evening News or Chronicle reporter who said "you're playing against Wolves this afternoon" I'd been told that I might be playing, and to report to the ground at one o'clock as normal.

"I didn't get butterflies or anything. To make your debut for the first team was an achievement, a feeling that you'd finally made it. First milestone, is when you sign professional, to get paid for doing something you love, next is your first team debut. Nobody can take that away from you.

"At the time of Munich I was the one who broke the news of Eddie Colman's death to his family. We'd all congregated in Eddie's house, it was the original Coronation Street, Archie Street next to Ordsall Park. In those days the only phone available was at the local outdoor beer licence and I kept nipping out and phoning Les Olive, United's secretary for news. Then in a late night phone call, he said to me, "Steve, do you think you could tell Mr and Mrs Colman for me that Eddie's gone"? So I had to go back to the house (I remember it as clear as a bell) where all the family, friends, Eddie's girlfriend and everybody were, and I said "I've just spoken to Mr Olive and he said that Eddie has gone". His mother started crying, his dad wouldn't believe me and went to phone Mr Olive himself. So sad.

"I didn't go on the USA trip even though other reserves did. I was out of the RAF by then, and went to see Mr. McDowall. I was playing well at the time, being tipped as a future England goalie, but the Boss wanted Bert to play in every game and if he was to get injured he said that Johnny Hart could go in goal. I thought this was short sighted, I would have loved to have gone and was absolutely gutted. I didn't think it was a good way to treat a young, budding England goalie, but I wouldn't call McDowall too much though, I thought it was mainly his back room staff, Laurie Barnett, and Freddie Tilson."

FULL BACKS

4) BILL LEIVERS - 6' 2¼, 14st.
Born Bolsover, 29/1/32, so 25 in 1957.

Bill was signed from Chesterfield in November 1953. for £8,000, as a tall strapping defender who didn't stand any messing. He became a regular in 55/56, first as a centre half, then right full-back, and is seen in the famous photo

helping Bert off the pitch after the cup final. He also was picked for the FA v The Army in 56/57 In **1957/58** he made thirty six appearances missing the six early games v Forest, Preston, and West Brom away and Portsmouth, Spurs, and Sheff. Wed. home, replaced by Cliff Sear and Ken Branagan. He was then a regular to the end of the season, finishing the last three games at centre half, terrifying centre forwards. In the following seasons he became captain and penalty taker for a while, overcoming a cartilage operation in 1960, playing until February '64, when he was sold for £1,000, to become player manager at Doncaster, then later Workington, and Cambridge United. After a break from football he went to Chelmsford, then Cambridge City, retiring in 1998, and now lives in St. Austell, Cornwall.

5) CLIFF SEAR - 5'11", 10st 1lb (wet through) Born Rhostyllen 22/9/36, so 21 in 1957.

Cliff was signed from Oswestry Town in June '55 and turned professional on 4/1/57. He was a beanpole fullback and all attempts to fatten him up failed. His speciality was the sliding tackle which, on a rainy day was quite something to behold.

He made his debut in the last game of the 56/57 season at Birmingham, the 3-3 draw.

In **1957/58** he made twenty nine appearances, firstly at right back for Bill Leivers and then at left back replacing Roy Little.

He went on to play for City until April 1968 scoring 1 goal, and won one Welsh cap v England in 1962. (Lost 4-0) Cliff always had time for the fans and was one of the nicest people you could wish to meet.

He moved on to Chester who he later managed, famously offering Ian Rush to City, but Mal and Tony "weren't going to rush!" then Wrexham as Youth Development Officer.

He died aged sixty three of a suspected heart attack in July 2000, astounding for someone so slim and fit looking.

6) ROY LITTLE - 5'9", 11st 4lbs. Born Manchester 1st June 1931, so 26 in 1957.

Roy was signed from Greenwood Vic on 6/8/49. He was known as the joker in the City dressing room and was a regular in the fifties, partnering Jimmy Meadows, and Bill Leivers. He played in both cup finals, would have gone in goal in '56 if Bert had come off and caused consternation when he lost his medal, which was later found. He was a firm tackler and accurate passer and made sixteen appearances in **1957/58** as his City career at left-back wound down and Cliff Sear moved in.

He moved to Brighton (he said he thought he was going to New Brighton!) at the start of the next season, then went to Palace, and was player/manager at Dover Athletic F.C.

He came back to Manchester in the Motor Auction business, then at the Manchester University Sports Complex at Wythenshawe, and is a past chairman of the MCFC FPA.

7) KEN BRANAGAN - 5' 7¼, 11st 3lbs. Born Salford 27th July 1930, so 27 in 1957.

Ken was a speedy, reliable full back, signed from North Salford Youth club in 1948. He then did his National Service before playing in the early 50's, scoring a goal each season. An appendix operation in '54 saw first Jimmy Meadows, then Bill Leivers, take his full back spot and he missed the '55 and '56 finals, though he was a reserve in '55, but no substitutes were allowed.

In **1957/58** he played six games at right back replacing Cliff Sear and Bill Leivers at home v Spurs, Villa; and West Brom, Birmingham, Newcastle and Everton away.

He moved to Oldham in October 1960 with Bert Lister and retired with a groin injury in 1966. He returned to Oldham in a coaching capacities, where he was well respected and also had various businesses, but now, sadly, has Alzheimers disease. His son Jim played for Blackburn Rovers.

WING HALFS

8) KEN BARNES - 5'9¼, 10st 10¼ lbs. Born Birmingham on 16th March 1929, so 28 in 1957.

Ken was signed from Stafford Rangers in May 1950, but didn't become a regular until 54/55 season when he was an integral part of the Revie Plan. He was described as 'the best uncapped wing half in the country' and played in the cup finals of '55 and '56, as key to the 'Revie Plan'.

In **1957/58** he played in thirty nine games, all at right half, missing only three, home to Birmingham and Arsenal and away at Luton, being replaced by Roy Warhust and Roy Cheetham.

He was the penalty taker and scored eleven goals, mainly penalties, including three in the home match with Everton, and was captain for a couple of games. He moved to Wrexham in 1961 as player/manager then took up the same position at Witton Albion. He also managed Bangor City before returning to City as Chief Scout, being rewarded with two testimonial games. Now retired he lives in Macclesfield, is a star in Malaysia and is a member of the FPA.

Ken has just had his autobiography, in conjunction with Jimmy Wagg, *'This Simple Game'* published. His son Peter also played for City and was an English International.

9) ROY WARHURST - 5'7" 10st 12lbs. Born Handsworth 18th Sept 1928, so 29 in 1957.

Roy 'The Warhorse' was signed from Birmingham in June 1957 for £15,000. He'd missed the '56 cup final through injury, and it was thought that the Birmingham team suffered as a consequence. After originally signing for Sheff. United he moved to Brum in 1950 making over two hundred appearances for them before replacing Roy Paul at City. He was a fierce, tenacious tackler.

In **1957/58** Roy made thirty six appearances at left half and one at right half missing only five games, at home to Blackpool and Arsenal, and away at West Brom., Portsmouth, and Wolves. He scored two goals both against Newcastle, one home and one away and was made captain for the day at his old club Birmingham, though City lost 4-0! Roy made only three more appearances in '58/59 and left for Crewe then later played for Oldham and Banbury, where he was player manager for two seasons before finishing in 1966 to concentrate on his scrap metal business.

Roy, interviewed in the March '74 programme v Sheff. United, was "glad to leave the place in the end". Nothing to do with the city of Manchester but Roy's unhappiness stemmed from the backroom staff and the lack of spirit. "Things just didn't work out," admitted Roy, "There was too much back-biting and not enough spirit. I love Manchester but I'd have gone anywhere just to get out of Maine Road."

He recalled with affection the times he enjoyed with Bobby Johnstone, Billy McAdams and Ken Barnes: "Johnstone was the greatest footballer I ever played with or against. I was twenty nine when I came to City and I'd seen all Britain's best. But there was no-one to compare with Bobby when he felt like turning it on. Not even Carter, Doherty, Finney, Billy Steel or Matthews. They couldn't touch him. My first game for City was a tour game in Holland. Bobby was brilliant. As the locals cheered him off the park I kept thinking this is some outfit I've joined. It was the greatest display I've seen from any player that night."

10) JOHN R. McTAVISH - 5'10" 11st 4 lbs. Born in 1932, so 25 in 1957.

John was signed from Dalry Thistle in June '52, after completing his National Service in the RAF. He played a few games in each season but was generally a reserve being dropped for Ken Barnes after the 5-0 defeat at Preston in '55.

In **1957/58** he played in six games, all at left half, WBA, Portsmouth, Luton away and Blackpool, Birmingham and Arsenal at home. He was linked with United after Munich, but no bid was made.

John played many more games, generally at centre half for City, taking over from Dave Ewing, notably scoring three own goals in four games in 59/60!.

In November 1960 he moved to St. Mirren as part of the Gerry Baker deal, retiring after five years and establishing his own children's wear manufacturing and wholesale business, from which he later retired in 2000, and he now lives in Glasgow.

11) ROY CHEETHAM - 5' 11", 12st 0lbs. Born Eccles 21st Dec 1939, so 18 in 1957.

Roy was signed as an amateur in June '56 and turned pro in December that year.

In **1957/58** he made his debut, replacing the injured Ken Barnes in the 2-1 win at Luton, the 4-2 home loss to Arsenal, and was a reserve regular..

He was described as a manager's dream, a loyal hard-working club man who did his best at whatever level he performed. He played a record number of games for the reserves, including a spell at centre-half, and was City's first substitute, replacing Mike Summerbee at Wolves in '65. After playing three games in the Championship season of 67/68 he moved to Detroit Cougars (not the Emeralds or the Spinners!) then Charlton and Chester, before returning to the USA with Windsor Stars in Ontario. He then became player/manager with Great Harwood, left football, worked amongst other places at Wythenshawe Hospital and is now treasurer of the Former Players' Association.

Roy: "I was doing OK playing for the reserves, then Ken Barnes was injured, and when the team sheet was pinned up in the first team dressing room on the Wednesday or Thursday my name was on it for the game at Luton. No one said a word, they didn't in those days. We won 2-1 and I got a good write up in the press, so I was kept in for the next game against Arsenal at Maine Road. This brought me down to earth. Their inside left was Jimmy Bloomfield, (every team had good inside forwards then) he scored a hat-trick and I was back in the reserves the next week when Ken was fit.

At the end of the season I was included in the party which went to America on tour, for experience. It was an eye opener, but I was too young to really appreciate it. We sailed out from

Southampton to New York, did a lot of travelling and went sight seeing in San Francisco, Los Angeles and New York. We were representing the club, so the players behaved as such and no-one was sent home for misbehaving! It was a great experience.

Johnny Hart was very helpful to me, and I was so proud to make the first team, after coming up through Manchester Boys, the Colts, and the central league team. We got on well with the United boys, Bobby Charlton, Wilf (McGuinness), Shay Brennan. Bob and Wilf still come to our 'do's', the big rivalry is between the fans.

Training was very competitive, but there were no problems. The senior players liked to put us young 'whippersnappers' in our place though. The club went into decline in the years between probably '58 and '65 until Joe and Malcolm came. There was no drive from the top down, the coaches and trainers didn't talk to us much, there was no spark, the club was stagnating, but Joe and Malcolm changed all that as we went from strength to strength in the late 60's/early 70's"

CENTRE HALFS

12) DAVE EWING - 6' 0¾, 14st. Born Perth 10th May 1929, so 28 in 1957.

Dave was signed from Luncarty Juniors in 1949, became the regular centre half in the early 50's, playing in both cup finals, singing the Brummies' 'keep right on' song to them in the '56 final, and 'protecting' Bert after his injury by charging him to the ground on one occasion! He was what was known as a stopper centre half, tough, craggy, uncompromising. His catch phrase was 'pull up at Dave's' (adapted from that of a north east comedian) but to opposition fans he was known as 'Dirty Dave!' His speciality was to boot the ball onto the main stand roof, or crash it past Bert into his own net (Dave's 10 own goals is the City record), and then stand laughing with his hands on his hips at the German, who'd go berserk at him. He was certainly not the man to promote the M Plan as twin centre half with Keith Marsden.

In **1957/58** Dave played thirty eight times missing Blackpool home, dropped after the Leicester farce, Ken Taylor coming in, and the last three games, Newcastle, Everton away, Villa home, Bill Leivers taking over. He scored one goal, that amazing long distance free kick at home to Pompey.

His appearances then diminished though he was often brought back to assist the annual relegation battle, but in July 1962 he moved to Crewe, then Ashton United. He returned to coach at City, then Sheff. Wed., Bradford City, and Crystal Palace. He also managed Hibs, and became reserve team coach at City when we won the Central league title in 1978. He then worked at the Platt Lane Complex, and moved back to Perth before settling in Heald Green. Dave was often seen at Maine Road and always had a cheery wave for fanzine sellers. Unfortunately he developed Alzheimers disease and died in July 1999.

13) KEN TAYLOR - 5'11", 11st 12½lbs. Born Manchester 18th June 1936, so 21 in 1957.

Ken was signed from Manchester Transport on 26/8/54 (still seen wearing his uniform in the official City photos!) and played in a fairly successful Youth team. He was called up into the Army for National Service and played regularly for the reserves from the end of 55/56 season

In **1957/58** Ken made just the one league appearance at centre half, in the 4-3 home win over Blackpool, his one and only league game, having taken over from Dave Ewing who was dropped after the Leicester 8-4 debacle. .

He developed cartilage problems, had an operation but the knee never recovered and he finished up at Buxton in July 1960.

14) KEITH MARSDEN - 6'1", 12st 8lbs. Born Darley Dale on 10th April 1934, so 23 in 1957.

Keith was signed from Chesterfield in July 1955. He made one appearance that season, against Chelsea at inside left and scored (though Meadows is listed in the original Complete History book) He played nine games at the end of 56/57, eight at centre half and one at left half.

In **1957/58** he played in four games, wearing the number ten shirt, though in fact dropping back as a twin centre half with Dave Ewing. First game was Preston at home a 2-0 win, the birth of the Marsden Plan and Portsmouth also at home and a 2-1 win. Things were looking good until Preston away a few days later, who sussed out 'The Revie Plan' in '55 with a 5-0 win, though we successfully persevered with that one. Unfortunately we lost 6-1, and three days later the 9-2 reversal at West Brom signalled the end of the 'M Plan'. Years later it became commonplace but Keith and Dave weren't the ones to carry it off in that season.

If that wasn't bad enough for Keith he returned to The Hawthorns the following week to play for the reserves, and broke his leg.

Keith later moved to Accrington Stanley but didn't make the side. He went on to own the Poco-Poco club in Stockport, and died tragically in a motor accident in 1986.

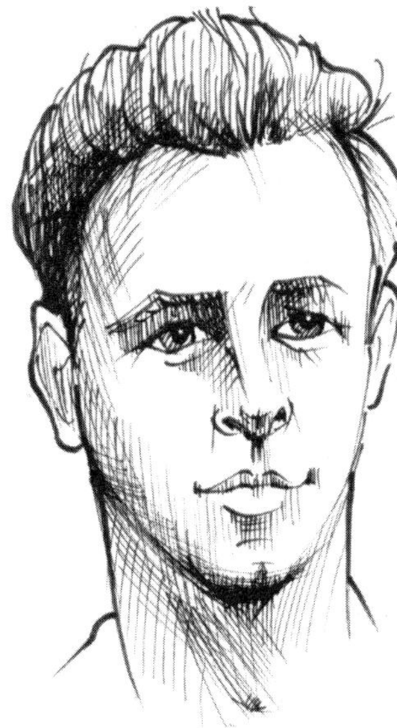

FORWARDS

15) COLIN BARLOW - 5' 6", 10st 13lbs. Born Collyhurst 14th Nov 1935, so 22 in 1957.

Colin was signed as an amateur in December 1956, from Tarporley Boys club after being spotted by ex Blue Billy Walsh

In **1957/58** he made his debut at Chelsea and scored. He played in thirty nine games that season, mainly at outside right, but sometimes at inside left or right. He missed only three games Preston, Portsmouth home and West Brom away, Joe Hayes and Paddy Fagan filling in. He was a speedy winger who could and often did, run faster than the ball. He had his own female fan club of blondes who would squeal with delight whenever he went near them, and when his football ability was questioned they'd come out with things like "yes, but he's got lovely curly hair"

He also scored seventeen goals that season, and went on to be a prolific City goalscorer until he moved on to Oldham in August 1963, then Doncaster to help out Bill Leivers. He was a successful businessman, and became MD of City in February 1994, with the Lee regime. He is now the MD of an engineering firm in Compstall.

Colin, from an interview in *King of the Kippax* No.35: "I remember scoring on my debut at Chelsea in the 3-2 win, and I leapt back to the half way line in 4 strides. It was the proudest day of my life.

"The club used to lie about my age, to make me look a better prospect, and even about my name, calling me Cyril sometimes.

"On the American tour: "It was a long exhausting tour, but I did well and scored lots of goals. We were all ill on the return sea voyage, except for Bert Trautmann who had the constitution of an Ox.

"I learned a lot on that tour, I met so many people and realised that Americans weren't just the movie stars we were led to believe in those days (this was '58 remember, before package holidays abroad) and had the same hopes, fears, and inhibitions as the rest of us. It broadened my outlook enormously.

We had a poor season after the trip, which I put down to this exhausting pre-season tour."

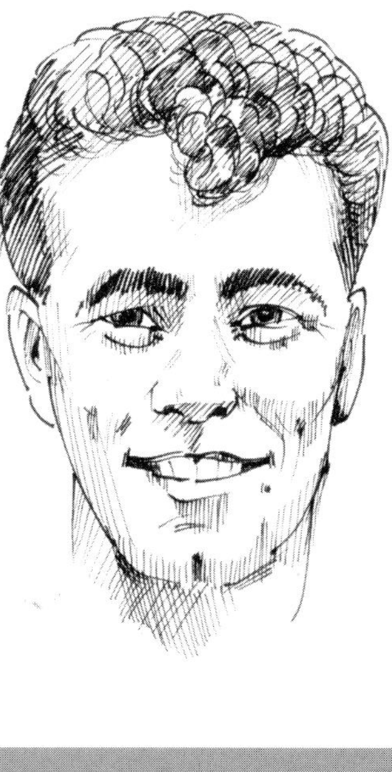

16) JOE HAYES - 5' 7¼, 10st 11½.
Born 20th January 1936, so 21 in 1957.

Joe was signed from Kearsley West YC in August 1953, when he arrived at Maine Road with his boots wrapped in brown paper, scored four goals in the trial and asked for his bus fare home! (Or so the story goes). He became a regular in City's team, played in both cup finals and scored the early goal v Birmingham in '56.

In **1957/58** he was on top form as he made forty League. appearances, scoring twenty five goals, missing just the two games home v Leeds and at Wolves, Colin Barlow taking over. This whilst suffering from poor eyesight. He also played for Young England, an FA X1, and gained two under 23 caps, scoring against Scotland.

He continued in this vein, becoming the first post war City player to score one hundred goals, until suffering a bad knee injury at Bury in September 1963 in a collision with Chris Harker the Bury 'keeper. He moved to Barnsley in 1965, then Wigan Athletic, and finally became player/manager at Lancaster Town. He worked for a finance company, then became a newsagent and grocer, but he died of cancer on Feb 3rd 1999, ironically the same day as our late 60's Scottish full back Arthur Mann.

17) BOBBY JOHNSTONE - 5'5" 11st 2lbs.
Born Selkirk 7th September 1929, so 28 in 1957.

Bobby, a Scottish International, was signed from Hibs on the 2nd March 1955 for £20,700. He was the first player to score in two successive cup finals, was slightly portly, liked a pint and caused fans to observe, "That Bobby Johnstone could pass the ball with his arse". He could, and often did. He was famed, amongst his many other skills, for being able to chip the City goalkeepers in training, even telling them where he would put the ball!

In **1957/58** he made thirty three appearances, a couple at inside right, the rest at centre forward scoring seven goals. He was sent off against Chelsea in the third game of the season, couldn't understand why and threatened to quit the game if he was disciplined, which he was but he didn't quit! In the nine games he missed, Preston, West Brom, Leeds, Luton, Burnley home and the last four at Newcastle and Everton plus Sunderland and Villa at home his place was taken by Joe Hayes, Ron Phoenix and Johnny Hart.

He was struggling to settle in Manchester but played until September 1959 when he moved back to Hibs. for £3,000, briefly, before returning to the area with Oldham. He then went to Witton Albion but a knee problem forced his retirement in 1963. He later worked at various jobs, moved back to Scotland in the mid 90's, then to Manchester again in 1999, but died on the 22nd August 2001 aged seventy one.

His biography, written by City fan John Leigh, has just been published.

18) BILLY McADAMS - 5'9½", 11st 7lbs.
Born Belfast 20th Jan 1934, so 23 in 1957.

Bill was signed from Distillery in December 1953 for £10,000. He played and scored regularly until mid '55 when he suffered back problems, after colliding with the perimeter wall at Millwall in the '55 friendly (we all knew he'd run through brick walls for City!) and returned briefly in 56/57.

In **1957/58** Bill, a Northern Irish International played against Scotland and Italy. He made twenty eight appearances for City and scored nineteen goals, playing at centre forward or inside left. He missed the away game at Birmingham, the home game to Arsenal, six games in Dec/Jan, and the final six games of the season. The Burnley programme informed us that he'd married a lass from Rawtenstall. *The Goal Trail Of Billy McAdams* was featured in the Sheffield Wednesday away programme, highlighting the eleven goals he scored in ten consecutive matches a record only recently

equalled. Stoke reportedly put in a bid for him, but he stayed at City until September 1960 when he went to Bolton for £25,000, then to Leeds, Brentford, QPR, and Barrow - where in 93/94 City sent a team to play a testimonial game.

Bill suffered from M.E. in later years, and died from cancer in October 2002, aged sixty eight.

19) PADDY FAGAN - 5' 6½, 9st 10 lbs. Born in Dublin on 7th June 1930, so 27 in 1957.

Paddy, an Irish International and qualified school teacher, was signed from Hull, where he shared digs with John Savage, in December 1953 for £3,500. He previously played for Shamrock Rovers with his dad, also an Irish International. He became a regular in 54/55, and played in the cup final but missed out in 1956 to Roy Clarke.

In **1957/58** he made twenty nine appearances, scoring seven goals, all before the turn of the year, mainly at outside left, once at inside left and eight at outside right, but was unhappy at the Sambrook signing and reported as being a transfer target by United, though he won back his place for the last nine games.

He was a regular in 58/59, moved to Derby County in March 1960, for £8,000, winning six more International caps; then to Altrincham as player/manager; then Northwich Vics, and finally Ashton United.

He then became a driving instructor and later worked for Trafford Council, and is an active member of the FPA.

20) RAY SAMBROOK - Born Wolverhampton 31st May 1933, so 25 in 1958.

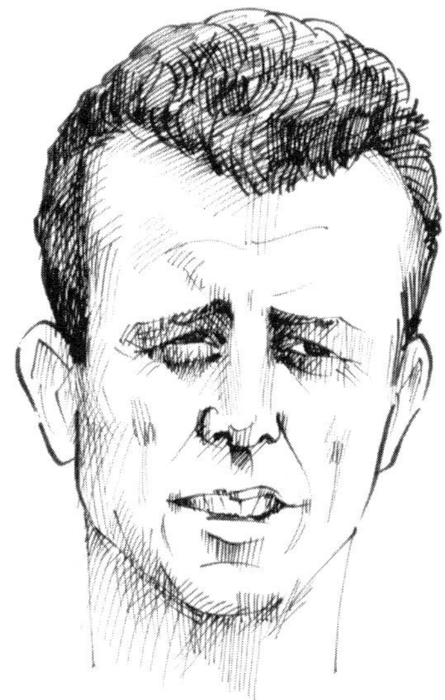

Ray was signed from Coventry in January 1958 for £15,000 after impressing Les McDowall when he scored two in the friendly in November. **In 57/58** he made sixteen appearances at outside left replacing Paddy Fagan. Shuffling Sam was a brilliant ball player but often appeared dosy which infuriated some City fans. He scored three goals, all away, at Portsmouth, Luton and Everton, and they were all wins!

He played regularly in 58/59, having a magnificent game v Newcastle scoring two in the 5-1 win, but tailed off and went to Doncaster in June 1962.

21) ROY CLARKE - 5' 9¾, 10st 12½. Born Newport, Wales, 1st June 1925, so 32 in 1957.

Roy, a Welsh international baseball player, was signed from Cardiff City on 23/5/47 for £12,000 and played in three consecutive games in three different divisions - Cardiff division three south, City division two at the end of the season, and then in division one at the start of the next season. He was a regular on the left wing, scored the goal which led City to Wembley in the semi final of 1955. He missed the final with a knee injury, but made up for it as a winner in 1956.

In **1957/58** he played six games at outside left, scoring just the one goal at West Brom. His other games were all away, at Chelsea, United, Birmingham, Leeds and Sunderland.

After clocking up twenty two Welsh caps, and opening a sports shop, he moved to Stockport in September 1958, later becoming coach, then managed Northwich Vics before returning to City with the Development Association. Then with wife Kath ran the social club. He was also the President of the supporters club for many years. Roy was rewarded with a testimonial game, City v Joe Mercer's Triple Champions in 1976.

Another nice guy with genuine affection for the fans, he contracted Alzheimers disease and died in March 2006.

22) JOHNNY HART - 5' 8½, 11st 2lbs. Born Golbourne 8th June 1928, so 29 in 1957.

John signed from Lowton YC in December 1944, turning professional in June 1945, making him the longest serving member on City's books by 57/58 season. He played fairly regularly in the early fifties, and scored consistently. He broke a leg at Huddersfield just before the 1955 FA cup semi-final, then he suffered cracked ribs and a punctured lung, followed by Achilles problems, and bone grafting in his neck.

In **1957/58**, he came back to make five appearances at centre forward, Luton away, receiving a 'good luck' telegram from Joe Mercer, then Sheffield United's manager, and the last four games against Sunderland, Villa at home, and Newcastle and Everton away, all in place of Bobby Johnstone. He scored at home to Sunderland in an emotional return, and two at Everton including City's one hundredth goal of the season.

He never really recovered from his injuries and served the club as coach, reserves and youth coach, eventually becoming manager in 1973 when Malcolm left, but had health problems and stepped down that November. On recovery John was awarded a testimonial game in 1974, City v Stoke City, then worked in the Building industry. He now lives in Newton-Le-Willows, and is a member of the FPA.

23) ALAN KIRKMAN - 5' 10" 11st 12lbs. born Bolton 21st June 1936, so 21 in 1957.

Alan was signed from Bacup Boro' on 21/02/56 and made his first team debut at Birmingham, scoring two in a 3-3 draw on the last day of the 56/57 season.

In **1957/58** he made four appearances at inside right, coming in for Billy McAdams, away at Sheff Wed., (scoring two but always maintaining he scored a third which was actually awarded to Bobby Johnstone), and Burnley. Then home to Burnley (scoring one) and United.

Despite his goalscoring feats, he made only two more appearances for the Blues, in 58/59, indeed he scored another at Villa, before moving to Rotherham in March 1959 for £3,000 and then played for four other league clubs including Newcastle, Scunthorpe, Torquay, Workington (managed by Bill Leivers). He later managed non-league sides, and settled in Horwich where he managed R.M.I. for sixteen seasons.

24) JOHN McCLELLAND - 5' 8½ - 10st 10lbs. Born Bradford 5th March 1935, so 22 in 1957.

John was the son of City coach Jim who persuaded him to join the Blues and not United, in March '53 as a junior. He made four appearances in 56/57 scoring a goal at Villa.

In **1957/58** he made three appearances at outside right replacing Colin Barlow, at Birmingham, home to Forest and away at Portsmouth - loss, draw, win!. .

After a brief appearance in September '58 and after scoring a goal v Preston, he was transferred to Lincoln in a swap deal with George Hannah. He moved on to QPR for £15,000, then Portsmouth and Newport County. He now lives in Hayling Island, having retired from duties at the local school.

25) RON PHOENIX - 5' 8½, 11st 6lbs. Born Stretford 30th June 1929, so 28 in 1957.

Red haired Ron (Arsenal programme 52/53: "...and like most red heads has any amount of pluck") was one of three footballing brothers and signed from Humphrey Park in March 1950 after completing his two years National Service with the Royal Engineers.

He was kept out of the first team by Ken Barnes, Roy Paul and Bobby Johnstone, though he scored on his debut at Arsenal in '52.

He broke a leg in February '53 at home to Newcastle after scoring and after recovery played just a few games in 55/56 and 56/57, generally at right or left half.

In **1957/58** he made just two appearances, not at half back though, at centre forward, replacing

Bobby Johnstone at Leeds, giving Jack Charlton a hard time, and Burnley at home. Obviously it wasn't the Phoenix plan, but City did win both games!. He was a target for QPR and Crewe, but left City later for Rochdale, then went to Altrincham and Hyde United. He then did some coaching, opened, then sold, a hardware shop and worked at various companies before retiring. He lives in Davyhulme with his wife Pat, whom he met as she cheered him on at Maine Road. Ron goes to Eastlands as often as he can, with one of his sons a season ticket holder.

Ron: "I made my debut at Arsenal in January 1952, and didn't find out until the Friday morning that I was picked. I had to go home and get my gear then catch the bus which was late, back to the station, but was flabbergasted when I found out they'd left at five to twelve, without me! Eric Thornton, the journalist had stayed behind and we caught the 2.30pm train to London. I made my debut in place of Don Revie, and scored *(a goal the Londoners still talked about seasons later)* I spent ten happy years at City, we were one big happy family, there were no big heads. I usually shared a room with Ken Branagan on trips who I got on great with, but we were all big mates. Later I took Alan Oakes under my wing, he followed me everywhere! I played just those two games in the 57/58 season and we won them both, 4-2 at Leeds and 4-1 at home to Burnley, and I was disappointed when I was dropped afterwards, but I couldn't keep Bobby out of the team. I also played in that incredible reserve game at Wolves when we lost 7-6. We gave John Savage some gentle stick about that on the bus coming home, but we were all in good spirits and had a good old sing song about it - it was such an amazing game."

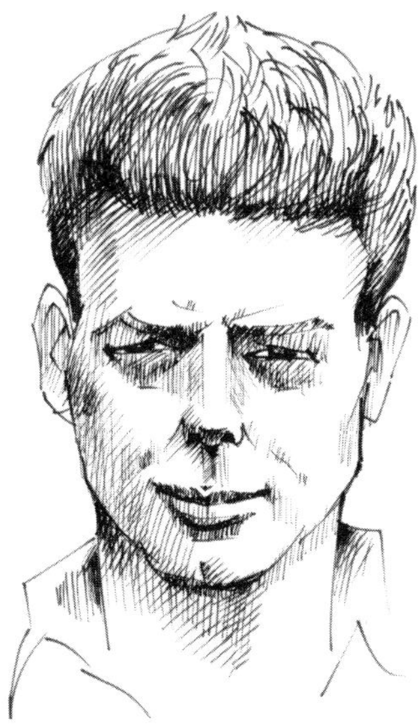

26) DENNIS FIDLER - 5'9½, 11st 2 lbs. Born Stockport 22nd June 1938, so 19 in 1957.

Dennis was an ex United junior who signed as an amateur in '56 and turned professional in January 1957.

In **1957/58** he made his debut at outside left replacing Paddy Fagan in the 2-2 home draw with Luton.

He made a further handful of first team appearances and moved to Port Vale in 1960, then Grimsby, Halifax where he did well, Darlington and finally Macclesfield. He then went into the family fish-and-chip shop business locally, but loved all things Italian and emigrated to Italy in 1990.

JACK DYSON - 5'9", 10st 10 lbs.
Born Oldham on 8th July 1934, so 23 in 1957.

Jack was signed from Nelson in October 1951, turning professional in June 1952, becoming a regular in 55/56, and scoring in the cup final win over Birmingham..

In **1957/58** he had the mis-fortune to break a leg in a collision with Bill Leivers in the second Public Trial Match and suffered the same injury again the following February in a Lancashire Senior Cup game at home to Barrow, then later broke an arm. He won one cap at England under 23 level, was also a Lancashire County cricket player but had disciplinary problems with both codes, particularly when the season's overlapped, and for being disrespectful to the Lancashire captain!

In March 1961 he moved on a free (or £2,000), to Stirling Albion, and played cricket for Forfar. He later returned to play for Oldham and finished at Northwich Vics. He then had a variety of jobs including a spell in City's commercial dept. A testimonial dinner was organised for him in 1991, but Jack died aged 66 in November 2000

JIMMY MEADOWS - 6'-0", 12st 5lbs.
Born Bolton 21st July 1931, so 26 in 1957.

Jimmy signed for City in March 1951, from Southport as a nineteen year old for £8,000, a big fee in those days. He was an outside right, tried at centre forward, then centre-half and finally settled at full-back. On April 2nd 1955 he was capped for England in the 7-2 win v Scotland at Wembley, then in the nineteenth minute of the '55 cup final he keeled over in a tackle with Bobby Mitchell.

He damaged his knee ligaments, made a brave attempt at a come-back in '57 but on October 7th he heard that his playing days were over, and was awarded a testimonial game at the end of the season..

He was appointed City's head trainer-coach, made a brief attempted further come back in 60/61, but moved to Stockport, later managing them. Then it was Bury, Blackpool, Bolton, Southport and Stockport again. Then he went on to Qatar in the Middle East and Sweden. He passed away in 1994.

His picture on the front of Football Monthly, May '55 was the basis in cartoon form for many years as a Carlsberg Advert.

MANAGER - LES McDOWALL - Born India on 25th Oct 1912, so 45 in 1957.

Les, a Scot, was signed from Sunderland in March 1938, for £7,000. He moved to Wrexham as player/manager in 1949, but returned to City the following year when promotion was achieved. He was in charge for the following thirteen seasons taking City to Wembley twice in the 50's and introducing The Revie Plan. In **1957/58**, he also introduced The Marsden Plan, which was scotched after four games, two wins and two heavy away defeats. Les was sacked in 1963 after relegation, going on to manage Oldham Athletic. He died in August 1991.

Of The Remaining players on City's books that year:

DAVID SHAWCROSS,left half, was a junior who made his debut at Arsenal in September 1958, a 4-1 loss. He was an under - 23 International, made 55 appearances for City, but a cruciate knee ligament injury and the form of Alan Oakes caused his eventual transfer to Stockport in June 1965. He then played for Halifax, Macclesfield, Altrincham, Droylsden and Drogheda. Since retiring from the game he has worked in Engineering, but has suffered a number of illnesses and has lived in Hazel Grove for the past forty years.

BERT LISTER, centre forward, was a junior who made his debut in a 2-0 defeat at Wolves in October 1958. He played once more for City, at West. Brom. at Eastertime 1959, but was transferred to Oldham in September 1960, where he was a prolific scorer. He moved on to Rochdale, Stockport and Altrincham. After retiring from the game he worked in various businesses, suffered knee and back problems lived in Northern Ireland, though was regularly seen at Eastlands, and as an active member of the FPA, but died in July 2007.

PETER HORRIDGE, full back, was a junior who made his debut at Blackpool in October 1958 when he performed well against Stanley Matthews. He made only two further appearances before being sold to Crewe, after which he played in the North Wales Coast League. He then became a Chartered Accountant and after retirement took on match day duties at City where he is a member of the FPA.

JIM PENNINGTON, outside right, another junior, who played one game in March 1959 a 2-1 loss at Blackburn Rovers. Moved to Crewe in 1961.

PETER LEIGH, full back, appeared in the friendly game at Derby County in March 1958. He made two further appearances in April 1960 at Bolton 1-3 and home to Preston 2-1 before being transferred to Crewe in 1961. City played a testimonial game for him in May 1967. He retired from Crewe in 1971, and took over the family window cleaning business.

ROBERT MacDONALD, fullback played five times in 1961/62, and moved to Bournemouth in 1963.

ROY FAULKNER, inside left, made seven appearances scoring four goals in season 55/56, but moved to Walsall in 1957.

DAVID DAVIDSON, inside right played once in October 1953 at Bolton, lost 3-2. Moved to Workington in 1958

HUGHIE MURRAY, outside left played one game in April 1956 at home to Sheff. United. Won 3-1. Moved to Altrincham in 1960.

ALAN OAKES, left half signed as an apprentice in April 1958, made his debut in November 1959 against Chelsea (gave away a penalty with a flying handball, which Bert saved) He went on to become a stalwart of the great late sixties/early seventies team making a record number of 676/4 appearances scoring 34 goals, and gave us a glimmer of hope for the future in the dark days of the early sixties.

NONE OF THE REMAINING PLAYERS: Albert Bourne, Ged Johnson, Roy Mathews, Rex Grey. Billy McLardy, Norrie Rucker, and Peter Stringfellow, made it to the first team. Most of the above continue their affection for Manchester City F.C. and are regular attendees at Former Player Association functions.

CHAPTER THIRTEEN
REFLECTIONS

Overall, an interesting and exciting campaign. In the league the early runners were United and Forest, but by October and November it was Wolves and West Brom. At the turn of the year Wolves were pulling away and it was just a question of who the runners up would be. Preston, it turned out, were that team and in the end Spurs came from nowhere, eighth at Christmas, to clinch third place. There were some big, big scores, too, as previously highlighted.

In the F.A.Cup there were plenty of early shocks. In the third round West Ham beat Blackpool 5-1, Leeds lost at home to Cardiff 2-1, Northampton beat Arsenal 3-1, York beat Birmingham 3-0. In the fourth round Spurs lost 3-0 at home to Sheffield United, Everton to Blackburn 2-1, Newcastle to Scunthorpe 3-1 and Chelsea at Darlington 4-1, after 3-3. After the fifth round all the 'minnows' had gone. Rovers won the Bristol tie 4-3 against City, but the semis were contested by two second division teams Fulham and Blackburn, who were knocked out by United and Bolton respectively.

The final, was, of course, won convincingly by Bolton 2-0.

In the World Cup England went out to Russia in a play off game. Northern Ireland went out to France 4-0 in the quarter finals, Scotland went out at group stage and Wales lost 1-0 to Brazil, the eventual Champions in the quarter finals.

Big Issues of the time were the charging of goalkeepers, the possibility of substitutes, the minimum wages, illegal payments in transfer deals at Sunderland, directors being banned and players fined, benefit payments to players for five and ten years' service, players' pay increase from £14 to £17, third and fourth division formation worries, inflated transfer fees, entertainment value, poor standard of play, poor amenities, antiquated transport, 'no personalities in the game' - Finney, Matthews, Bert, Edwards, Docherty were not rated then!

Liverpool fans went on the rampage at Blackburn in the fifth round of the cup where they lost 2-1.

Over The Road things weren't quite as hunky-dory as they would like to have us believe at Old Trafford. Pre-season, Tommy Taylor was set to join Milan in a similar deal to that of John Charles when he went to Juventus, but the deal fell through, owing to a ban on foreign players. There was also a possibility of Matt Busby going to an Italian club for £100,000.

United's league hat-trick was "in the bag" and "as safe as the Bank of England" according to the Manchester Evening News's Tom Jackson, so no point playing the games then? They were then branded as "big heads", as they wanted payment from the BBC for being filmed whilst training.

Peter McParland was sent poison pen letters with Manchester postmarks stating it was "more than his life was worth to appear in the Charity Shield game at O/T with Villa".

Then they were "getting too big for their boots" according to the M.E.N. before they lost five games to bring them crashing down to earth in fifth place with 17 points, the same as City, but six behind Wolves, at the end of October.

Players were becoming unsettled, including Webster and Scanlon. Whitefoot and Doherty were transferred, Goodwin and Colman slapped in transfer requests.

By December the M.E.N. conceded that United's title was slipping away, as they were now fourth on twenty four points and seven behind Wolves. By January Johnny Berry was unhappy and Ray Wood put in a transfer request, owing to the signing of Harry Gregg (which he later rescinded to help United out after Munich). Matt Busby was to be the manager of Scotland.

There is no doubt that the air disaster was a great human tragedy, causing emotional shock waves throughout the country, Europe and particularly at City. Disaster funds were set up, and donations made from supporters clubs.

At this time Wolves were on forty two points, and gained another twenty two to reach sixty four points and the title, including two points against United., who were on thirty six points. With fourteen games left. United would have had to win thirteen games, including beating Wolves, with one draw, then, to clinch the title. Improbable!

David Meek became the new M.E.N. reporter, replacing Tom Jackson, and Keith Dewhurst replaced Alf Clarke at the Evening Chronicle. Despite the tragic losses, United fans were becoming quite excited at the prospects of new signings.

However a ripple of resentment was becoming apparent, as United seemed to expect clubs to sell them their star players, upsetting, in particular, Bob Lord, Chairman of Burnley. This backlash prevailed and the M.E.N. observed in March that "the agony is being prolonged beyond the bounds of genuine sorrow and sympathy" after which journalist John Kay was told to "go and jump in the lake" in the letters page. This feeling probably culminated in United's match at Burnley, where the local paper, noted for its honesty and unbiased reporting was horrified, along with their supporters and neutrals, at United's performance. Bob Lord branded them "a bunch of Teddy boys", an accusation denied by Jimmy Murphy, who promptly made Pancho Pearson shave off his sideboards! Burnley were, of course, just jealous.

After the semi-final replay win v Fulham, where United fans were (wrongly) made to travel mid-week to Highbury, Meek proclaimed that "It must be United's cup". I could go along with this as it was an amazing achievement for them to reach Wembley, under the circumstances, and it appeared that nothing could stop the rollercoaster in full flow.

Dennis Viollet was then subjected to poison pen letters from his own fans, who did not think he should play at Wembley, as he would be taking the place of one of the new United players. In the event Dennis, who DID play in earlier rounds, also appeared at Wembley.

Keith Dewhurst, in the 'Chron', with his cup final prediction, epitomised why everyone ultimately loses patience with United. It is not 'jealousy' or 'bitterness', or arrogance even - every successful club is likely to be a bit arrogant. Remember that Bolton had beaten United 4-0 at Burnden, but lost 7-2 at Old Trafford to the pre-Munich team. Yet, according to Dewhurst, United were going to win the cup, oh yes, not 1-0, 2-1, 3-1, or even 3-2, no, it was going to be a 4-1 'formality'. After the game, and Bolton's 2-0 victory, it wasn't conceded that Bolton were the better team, oh no, the excuses came out, as, according to them and their ungracious supporters, United have NEVER been beaten by the better team.

Then to cap it all, those 'loveable' United fans pelted the cup winner's coaches en route back to Bolton with clods of earth, stones and flour bombs.

In the second leg of the European Cup semi-final in Milan, United were accused by the Italians of roughness and kicking their boys. I have some sympathy here with United, as I always felt that British clubs were generally cheated when playing foreign opposition, particularly in Italy.

Finally, the publicity United got was always annoying. Check out the Football Monthlys from May 1957 to August 1958. Three front covers to City's one. Three back covers to City's none. One centre spread to City's none, three inside colour shots to our one. Bearing in mind that at that time City had recently reached two cup finals and that season were scoring 'for fun', the coverage was unbalanced to say the least.

As for City, early season injuries, chopping and changing, the Marsden Plan etc., saw the Blues drop to fourteenth in September. But with a settled team and formation then climbing up to fifth place by December, where we pretty well stayed until the end of season with just the blip at Spurs and Leicester. It could have been even better with the results against Newcastle and Villa costing us third place. Best run was the four wins in March/April. Worst, none really, just those three big away defeats in September/October, and the two in February.

We managed six doubles Chelsea, Sheffield Wednesday, Blackpool, Bolton, Leeds and Everton, with just the one against - Arsenal.

At home we won fourteen, including the first six, drew four and lost three, scoring in every game totalling fifty eight and conceding thirty three, keeping only three blank sheets .

Home attendances ranged from 20,912 v Everton, to 70,483 v United, 23,000 higher than the previous best 47,285 against Burnley. Average was 32,765, tenth highest. The club must have been disappointed that with the new Kippax stand gates were still poor in the bad weather.

Away we won eight, drew one, lost twelve, failing to score just the once at Birmingham, and keeping a blank sheet only at Bolton.

Away attendances ranged from 16,004 at Luton to 63,103 at United.

In the cup it was an early exit at WBA 5-1. No arguments there then!

As for the players, the forwards and to an extent the half backs did their stuff, but there were obvious deficiencies in defence.

There were debuts for youngsters Steve Fleet, Colin Barlow, Roy Cheetham, Ken Taylor, Dennis Fidler and new signings Roy Warhurst (£15,000) and Ray Sanbrook (£15,000).

John Savage was transferred to Walsall (£4,000), as was Roy Faulkner.

Stars of the team were Bert in goal, Ken Barnes for his penalties and up front the goalscorers, Colin Barlow, Joe Hayes (27 goals, joint fifth top division scorer), Billy McAdams, Paddy Fagan and the ace schemer Bobby Johnstone.

Season ticket sales were up, but gates were down by 6/8,000 by October, reasons being United reserve team gates and their voucher system, lack of quality, paying more for cover and lack of personalities. In March the Evening Chronicle had a 'What's wrong with City feature'. Not too much, really, being the team to watch with the goals ratio and eventually finishing fifth.

City didn't suffer too much with the requirement for substitutes. Only in the Sheffield Wednesday game being down to nine and ten men for a while. Benefit was gained at home to Luton, Dunne being stretchered off and away at Blackpool and Bolton when Ernie Taylor and Derek Hennin were injured respectively. City didn't suffer often from players being away on International duty, just the once when Billy McAdams played for N/Ireland v Italy .

City did go into decline in the following years and it's maybe worth taking a look at the players we came into contact with that season who moved on to other clubs, not that we could have signed them all. Greaves went from Chelsea, Docherty from Preston, Dougan and Crawford from Portsmouth, Quixall from Sheffield Wenesday, Setters from WBA., Taylor from Blackpool, Herd from Arsenal, Jones from Swansea, Bingham from Sunderland. From the Hibernian and Hearts games, Joe Baker, Alex Young and Dave MacKay, all came to England (Baker via Italy). Perhaps we could have signed Banks from Chesterfield to replace Bert as he aged, and a centre half, maybe Mel Nurse from Swansea or Mike England from Blackburn.

Instead we went from paying around £20,000 for Johnstone, Paul and Revie to £15,000 for Warhust, Sambrook then later differing sums for Hannah, Kerr, Colbridge and a record £55,000 for Law (replaced by Kennedy and Dobing), Betts, Plenderleith, Baker, Harley, Gray, Kevan, Bacuzzi, Gratrix, Stobart, Murray. Luckily we had the youngsters coming through, Alan Oakes, Neil Young, (Dave Wagstaffe who we let go to Wolves) Mike Doyle, Harry Dowd, Roy Cheetham, and Glyn Pardoe, so at least McDowall, and the backroom staff encouraged their emergence ready for the Mercer/Allison revolution

So that's it, season 57/58 done and dusted......a Golden Age, maybe, maybe not, but certainly interesting and entertaining.

CHAPTER FOURTEEN

LOOKING DOWN THE LOWER LEAGUES

Division 2:

West Ham, and Blackburn Rovers were promoted in first and second place. Going through the division Charlton made it back in 85/86. Liverpool in 61/62, Fulham in 58/59, Sheffield United in 60/61 along with Ipswich Town. Middlesbrough in 73/74, Huddersfield Town in 69/70.

Bristol Rovers, Grimsby Town, Rotherham United, Lincoln City and Doncaster Rovers never made it.

Stoke City came up in 62/63, Leyton Orient in 61/62 (with Liverpool, then came down with City in 62/63!) Barnsley in 1996/97 Cardiff City in 59/60 Derby County 68/69, Bristol City in 75/76, Swansea Town (as City), and Notts County in 80/81.

FINAL LEAGUE TABLE 1957/58

	P	W	D	L	F	A	Pts
West Ham . .	42	23	11	8	101	54	57
Blackburn . . .	42	22	12	8	93	57	56
Charlton	42	24	7	11	107	69	55
Liverpool . . .	42	22	10	10	79	54	54
Fulham	42	20	12	10	97	59	52
Sheff Utd . . .	42	21	10	11	75	50	52
M'brough . . .	42	19	7	16	83	74	45
Ipswich	42	16	12	14	68	69	44
Huddersfield	42	14	16	12	63	66	44
Bristol R	42	17	8	17	85	80	42
Stoke	42	18	6	18	75	73	42
L Orient	42	18	5	19	77	79	41
Grimsby	42	17	6	19	86	83	40
Barnsley	42	14	12	16	70	74	40
Cardiff	42	14	9	19	63	77	37
Derby	42	14	8	20	60	81	36
Bristol C	42	13	9	20	63	88	35
Rotherham . .	42	14	5	23	65	101	33
Swansea . . .	42	11	9	22	72	99	31
Lincoln	42	11	9	22	55	82	31
Notts C	42	12	6	24	44	80	30
Doncaster . .	42	8	11	23	56	88	27

Division 3 North:

Only four teams made it to the first or Prem - Bradford City in 98/99. Oldham Athletic in 90/91. Carlisle United in 73/74.

Of the rest - Scunthorpe United, Bury, Hull City, Mansfield Town, Chesterfield, Stockport County, Rochdale, Tranmere Rovers, Wrexham, York City, Hartlepools United, Darlington, and Crew Alexandra, never got further than the second.

Accrington Stanley, Halifax Town, York City, Gateshead, Barrow, Workington Town, Chester, Bradford P.A. and Southport all slipped out of the League at some point, as did second division Doncaster Rovers.

FINAL LEAGUE TABLE 1957/58

	P	W	D	L	F	A	Pts
Scunthorpe	46	29	8	9	88	50	66
Accrington . .	46	25	9	12	83	61	59
Bradford C . .	46	21	15	10	73	49	57
Bury	46	23	10	13	94	62	56
Hull	46	19	15	12	78	67	53
Mansfield . . .	46	22	8	16	100	92	52
Halifax	46	20	11	15	83	69	51
Chesterfield	46	18	15	13	71	69	51
Stockport . . .	46	18	11	17	74	67	47
Rochdale . . .	46	19	8	19	79	67	46
Tranmere . . .	46	18	10	18	82	76	46
Wrexham . . .	46	17	12	17	61	63	46
York	46	17	12	17	68	76	46
Gateshead . .	46	15	15	16	68	76	45
Oldham	46	14	17	15	72	84	45
Carlisle	46	19	6	21	80	78	44
Hartlepools . .	46	16	12	18	73	76	44
Barrow	46	13	15	18	66	74	41
Workington . .	46	14	13	19	72	81	41
Darlington . .	46	17	7	22	78	89	41
Chester	46	13	13	20	73	81	39
Bradford PA	46	13	11	22	68	95	37
Southport . . .	46	11	6	29	52	88	28
Crewe	46	8	7	31	47	93	23

Division 3 South

Amazingly eleven teams made it to the first or Prem. - Brighton and Hove Albion in 78/79, Swindon Town in 92/93 Reading in 2005/06, Southampton Town in 65/66 (with City) Norwich City in 71/72, Queens Park Rangers in 67/68, Northampton Town in 64/65, Crystal Palace in 68/69, Watford in 81/82, Coventry City in 66/67, and Millwall (who finished second from bottom!) in 87/88.

Brentford, Plymouth Argyle, Southend United, Bournemouth and Boscombe Athletic, Colchester United, Port Vale, and Shrewsbury Town, never got further than the second.

Newport County, Aldershot, Torquay United and Exeter City all slipped out of the league.

Of the above, City have played them all in the lower leagues and cup competitions with the exception of Aldershot and Exeter City.

FINAL LEAGUE TABLE 1957/58

	P	W	D	L	F	A	Pts
Brighton	46	24	12	10	88	64	60
Brentford	46	24	10	12	82	56	58
Plymouth	46	25	8	13	67	48	58
Swindon	46	21	15	10	79	50	57
Reading	46	21	13	12	79	51	55
S'hampton	46	22	10	14	112	72	54
Southend	46	21	12	13	90	58	54
Norwich	46	19	15	12	75	70	53
Bournemouth	46	21	9	16	81	74	51
QPR	46	18	14	14	64	65	50
Newport	46	17	14	15	73	67	48
Colchester	46	17	13	16	77	79	47
Northampton	46	19	6	21	87	79	44
Crystal P	46	15	13	18	70	72	43
Port Vale	46	16	10	20	67	58	42
Watford	46	13	16	17	59	77	42
Shrewsbury	46	15	10	21	49	71	40
Aldershot	46	12	16	18	59	89	40
Coventry	46	13	13	20	61	81	39
Walsall	46	14	9	23	61	75	37
Torquay	46	11	13	22	49	74	35
Gillingham	46	13	9	24	52	81	35
Millwall	46	11	9	26	63	91	31
Exeter	46	11	9	26	77	99	31

This is the author's very favourite fifties action photograph and epitomises almost everything about that era: Peter Broadbent and Bert Trautmann tussling with each other showing grit, determination, skill, power and aggression with Dave Ewing and Ken Barnes looking on. Traditional colours of Wolves' old Gold, City's Sky Blue and the brown leather boots and ball. In the background is the distinctive Molineux stand, which completes the picture. Peter's magnificent quiff and Bert's spiked up 21st century mantle (OK, it was 50s style, just blowing in the wind, but no trace of peroxide!) are in full flow.

BIBLIOGRAPHY

Barnes, Ken with Wagg, Jimmy - *This Simple Game,*
Empire, Manchester 2005
Brandon, Derek - *A to Z of Manchester Football,*
Boondoggle Ltd, London, 1978
Buchan, Charles - *Football Monthly* magazines
May 1957 to August 1958, Buchan's publications.
Camkin, John and Taylor, Frank - *News Chronicle and Daily Dispatch Football Annual, 1958-59*
Cavanagh, Roy - A Salford Lad, Eddie Colman,
Clayton David - *Everything under the Blue Moon*
Mainstream, Edinburgh, 2002
Clayton, David - *Cult Heroes*
Know The Score Books, Studley, 2007
Doherty, Peter - *Spotlight On Football*
A and E, London, 1948
Eyre, Fred - *Kicked Into Touch*
Senior Publications, 1981
Friend, Dante - *My Blue Heaven, 18 Great Names, 18 Great Games*
Empire, 2004
Goble, Ray - *Manchester City A Complete Record, 1887-1987*
Breedon Books, Derby, 1987
Hall, Stuart - *Heaven and Hell - A Prodigal Life*
BBC Worldwide Ltd 2000
Harding, John, - *Football Wizard, The Story Of Billy Meredith*
Breedon, Derby, 1985
Inglis, Simon - *The Football Grounds Of Great Britain*
Collins Willow, 1996
Inglis, Simon - *Engineering Archie*
English Heritage, London, 2005
James, Gary - *Farewell To Maine Road*
Polar, Leicester, 2002
James, Gary - *Manchester, The Greatest City*
Polar Leicester, 2003
James, Gary - *Manchester City, A Complete Record*
Breedon, Derby, 2006
James, Gary/Cawley, Steve - *The Pride of Manchester*
Polar, Leicester, 1991

Leigh, John - *Bobby Johnstone, The Passing of An Age*
Breedon, Derby, 2007
Oldham, Andrew Loog - *2 Stoned*
Vintage 2002
Paul, Roy - *Red Dragon Of Wales*
Hale, London 1956
Penney, Ian - *Maine Road Favourites - Where Are They Now*
Sutton, 2006
Penney, Ian - *The Essential History Of Manchester City*
Headline, 2000
Pressley, Alison - *The 50's and the 60's, The Best Of Times*
Michael O'Mara Books, London, 2003
Revie, Don - *Soccer's Happy Wanderer*
Museum Press, London, 1955
Robinson, Michael - *Football League Tables, 1888-2005*
Soccer Books Ltd., Cleethorpes, 2001
Rowlands, A - *Trautmann, The Biography*
Breedon, Derby, 1990
Soar, Phil and Tyler, Martin - *Encyclopaedia of British Football*
Willow books, Collins, 1984
Swift, Frank - *Football From The Goalmouth*
London 1948
Tabner, Brian - *Through the Turnstiles*
Yore publications, 1992
Thornton, Eric - *Meredith to Mercer and the F.A. Cup*
Hale, London 1969
Trautmann, Bert - *Steppes To Wembley*
Hale London 1956
Ward, Andrew - *The Manchester City Story*
Breedon, 1984

We are grateful to the following people for subscribing in advance to this book:

1) John Schulman

2) Steve Rigby

3) Wayne Norris

4) Tony Ralls

5) Steven Carter

6) Les McDonald

7) Phil Fallon

8) Mike Baxter

9) Bernard Scanlan

10) Joe Murchan

11) Brian John Topper

12) Kenneth S. Dunkerly

13) Howard Croft

14) Jean Cottle (from Peter Lamb)

15) David Bookbinder

16) Arthur Bookbinder

17) Susan and Zac Bookbinder

18) Steve Pearson

19) Don Lewis

20) David Glyn Hall

21)`Graham Anthony Hall

22) Barbara Moreton

23) Graeme Nicholson
(from Paula Crossfield)

24) Jeff Castle

25) Roland Griffin (from Ross Griffin)

26) David Woodyatt

27) Nigel Goldsmith

28) Don and Sheila Bradley

29) John Davies

30) Roland Foster

31) Kevin Hall

32) Neil Shaw

33) Edwin Humphrys

34) Louise Deeks

35) Ruth Thorne

36) Ben Kelly

37) Chris Barry

38) John Marsden

39) Dave Jones

40) Dave Miller

41) Sue, Ian and Jason Allcroft

42) Colin Savage

43) Kevin Rose

44)`Kevin Parker
45) Sean and Jane Riley

46) Colin Meadows

47) To my granddad Alan Thomas, can't wait until I'm big enough to come to the football with you. Love from Ben. (from Mike Thomas)

48) Bob Haslam

49) Roger Haigh

50) Peter Wilson

51) Richard Burgess

52) Derek Stanfield (from Lee Stanfield)

53) Ian Foster

54) Paul Denny

55) Andrea Griffin

56) Walter Cooke

57) Dennis Reilly

58) Gary and Lisa Millar

59) Mark King

60) Stanley Cannon

61) Steve Parish

62) Jon Mayor

63) Emily Brobyn

64) Ged Isaacs

65) Peter Thornton

66) David and Chris Howl

67) Tom Parish
68) John Burfield

69) Roger and Maureen Hewlett

70) Chris Wallace

71) Pete Roberts

72) Roger Reade

73) Tony Petrie

74) Chris Deary

75) Colin Brinkley

76) Simon Curtis

77) Allan Wilson

78) Frank Fariello

79) Barry Calder

80) Carin Bowman

81) Gary James

82) Mick Thompson

83) Kevin Bell

84) Ron Bellamy (from Phil Bellamy)

85) Ted Knott

86) Albert Gough (from Cath Knott)

87) Lee Walker (from Ann Lundy)

88) Dave and Kay Pugh

89) Stuart Priestley

90)David Addison

91) Mark Freeman

92) Mary Donsworth

93) Ellie Wallace

94) Barbara Chapman

95) Joe Bamford

96) Rodney Bick

97) David Bennion

98) Heather Bamford

99) David Tranmer

100) Roger Shore

101) Chris Williams

102) Mark Bittner

103) John Jackson

104) Raymond Ashton

105) Ollie Williams

106) John Jackson

AUTOGRAPHS

AUTOGRAPHS